D0215489

Matter, Magic, and Spirit

Matter, Magic, and Spirit

Representing Indian and African American Belief

DAVID MURRAY

PENN

University of Pennsylvania Press

Philadelphia

Copyright © 2007 University of Pennsylvania Press
All rights reserved
Printed in the United States of America on acid-free paper

10 9 8 7 6 5 4 3 2 1

Published by
University of Pennsylvania Press
Philadelphia, Pennsylvania 19104–4112

Library of Congress Cataloging-in-Publication Data

Murray, David, 1945–
    Matter, magic, and spirit : representing Indian and African American belief / David Murray.
        p. cm.
    Includes bibliographical references and index.
    ISBN-13: 978-0-8122-3996-6
    ISBN-10: 0-8122-3996-2 (cloth : alk. paper)
    1. United States—Religion. 2. Totemism. 3. Magic. 4. Race relations—Religious aspects. 5. African Americans—Religion. 6. Indians of North America—Religion. I. Title.

BL2525.M87   2006
200.89'96073—dc22

                                                                2006050903

Contents

Introduction   1

1. Hierarchies of Race and Religion:
Fetishism, Totemism, Manitou, and Conjure   9

2. Superstition and Progress   39

3. Primitivism, Modernism, and Magic   71

4. Black Arts: Conjure and Spirit   102

5. The Return of the Fetish   127

Notes   149

Bibliography   189

Index   207

Acknowledgments   215

Introduction

This book is about material objects and the belief in their nonmaterial powers. It is also about race, and the ways in which the discourses and hierarchies of race have intersected with those of magic and religion. In particular, it is concerned with those distinctive conjunctions of racial and religious categories that have linked and divided Native Americans, African Americans, and whites in America.[1] In the first part of the book I trace in some detail the ways in which certain forms of belief were ascribed to particular races prior to the twentieth century, and what this reflected about the changing beliefs of white Americans. In the second half, I move into the twentieth century and focus on the ways in which some African American and Native American writers and artists have dealt with traditional beliefs in the context of these prevailing discourses, and the implicit hierarchies of matter and spirit that come with them. So the book is addressing several large and rather separate bodies of scholarship on Native Americans and African Americans, but with two distinctive and unusual angles of approach, which are closely related throughout the book. The first angle is an attempt to deal comparatively with Indians and African Americans, and specifically their beliefs, and the second challenges the very common invocation of spirituality as an unexamined and privileged concept in relation to these groups.

While there is a huge range of materials on Native American and African American beliefs, there are remarkably few attempts to deal with them together or comparatively. Their very different histories and cultures do militate against this, and there are real methodological difficulties in trying to do so. One difficulty is knowing how far we are comparing like with like in dealing with religious or magical practices, given not only the different contexts but also the different methodological and ideological lenses through which the practices have been seen and represented. Another is trying to locate examples of the interaction and mixing of practices and beliefs when racial terminologies obscure the degree of actual mixing and blending of the races. There are also political implications in assuming a position from which to make the comparison at all. Recent postcolonial critical accounts of the comparativist method in general have sometimes viewed it as a totalizing gesture that organizes similarities and differences within an overall framework or overview that is available only to the supposedly objective outsider. To the degree that this overview relies on knowledge gained, for instance, by colonial structures of power, it replicates that political situation of inequality. The claims that are implicit within many comparativist enterprises for the existence of universal or underlying values could then also be seen as suspect, in the same ways that some larger Enlightenment claims for universality may be suspect—namely that they may incorporate ethnocentric Western values, which are simply assumed to be universal. According to this critique, the comparativist impulse, rather than decentering the West, always comes back to reconfirming a center, or an overall intellectual structure established by that center.

I hope what follows avoids this pitfall, if only because one fundamental theme of the book is the way that the dominant American culture has used other groups to understand and justify its own place and changing beliefs. My aim is to show a triangulation of beliefs, or rather of representations of those beliefs, that undermines the position of privileged observer claimed by whites, even while my own skeptical approach could perhaps be said ultimately to reinscribe an overall Enlightenment authority—a point to which I shall inevitably return. My argument is that at key points in the past the assumption that different races had very different capacities and qualities has meant that they have been conceptualized and treated differently, in what might be called a differential racism in America, and that this remains a real issue. The different political and legal status of Indians and African Americans was often reflected, or paralleled, in the assertion of a clear distinction between the mental and spiritual capacities of the two races. This distinction was not always explicit but operated differentially, and I want to argue that, for instance, much of the theorization of the so-called primitive, which tends to concentrate on Indians in the later nineteenth and early twentieth centuries, needs to be seen in relation to African Americans, even when—and perhaps especially when—they are absent from the discussion.

It is instructive, though, to look at the way earlier theorizations and representations of the spiritual capacities of different races developed in the particular circumstances of America. The existence in America of successive generations of newly arrived Africans and a wide range of Native American societies presented white observers with the opportunity for comparative observation of both racial difference *and* the processes of cultural change and adaptation, but what is noticeable is how little of this we find recorded. Thus, while we have masses of contemporary accounts of Indian religions (and considerably fewer of African American practices and beliefs), we have very few that either bring them together for discussion or record any cultural interchange or borrowing. This lack of contemporary observations is perhaps one of the reasons for a corresponding shortage of later critical commentary that brings together Indian and African Americans comparatively or deals with the mixing of cultures and races. For a long time, where it was to be found at all, academic interest in the mixing of races was more likely to be in folklore studies, or in work on African Americans, as in the *Journal of Negro History*, than in works on Native Americans, though this has certainly begun to change quite radically.[2]

Jon Butler, who has traced the stages in the development of African American Christianity, has noted the scarcity of comment on slave religion from colonists, in contrast to the interest shown in Indian religion. Writing of Jefferson he points out that "the philosopher who otherwise took an interest in 'natural' religion and mined both the classics and the New Testament to uncover universal religious precepts wrote nothing about slave religion."[3] One reason for this, which I will be developing in the first chapter, is the early characterization of Africans as a sort of zero point in the development of religion, so that there seemed to be simply nothing to write about, whereas Indians were seen as having recognizable and distinct beliefs that corresponded in varying degrees with what was recognized by Europeans as religion.

One of the very few early instances where Indian and African spiritual capacities are explicitly dealt with together is from William Knox, in his advice to the Society for the Propagation of the Gospel in 1768. This is a plea for more action in America to convert both groups, but Knox is unusually explicit about how the Christian teaching should be tailored to match the capacities and situations of the target group. He characterizes the Indians as "vagrant in their manner of life, without social intercourse," and stresses their individualist and war-like character. One of the obstacles to their conversion is that they already have well-defined beliefs. "[W]ere they only ignorant of our religion, their natural good sense would give hopes of their imbibing its doctrines, so soon as they were properly explained and set before them; but the misfortune is, that they are not only ignorant of it, but what they do know, and are taught, is diametrically opposite to the doctrines of christianity."[4]

With unusual clarity, Knox distinguishes between the Protestant missionaries who confronted the Indians head-on, ridiculing their "talismans, and at once exhort[ing] them to cease to be Indians," and the Roman Catholics, who used their medical knowledge and would "soon get the Indians to trust more in their talismans for their cure, than in their own." Thus the Catholic missionary "becomes the Indian conjurer, before he discloses his purpose," which is to show "Christ Jesus the great conjurer." Knox is in fact unimpressed by this tactic, because he sees it as producing people who see Christ as just a benefactor to mankind, rather than as "their redeemer."[5] In other words, he sees this as catering to a pragmatic belief in magic and its efficacy, rather than in religion. Indians, in his view, have a set of beliefs, and the question is how to supplant them. By contrast, the Africans are for him simply a blank, a tabula rasa.

The quick sagacity of the Indian keeps him aloof from every effort to convert him. The dull stupidity of the Negroe [*sic*] leaves him without any desire for instruction. Whether the creator originally formed these black people a little lower than other men, or that they have lost their intellectual powers through disuse I will not assume the province of determining; but certain it is, that a new Negroe [i.e., newly imported] is a complete definition of indolent stupidity, nor could a more forcible means be employed for the conversion of a deist, than setting one of these creatures before him as an example of a man in a state of nature unbiassed by revelation or education.[6]

For Knox this does not justify giving up on missionary work, but it does reflect the wider refusal to see anything that took place in Africa as falling within the category of religion. In general, commentators on African Americans, unless they comment on their Christianity, either assume a complete spiritual absence, as we find in Knox, or more commonly give a disgusted recital of the elements of what they call fetish worship, a topic I deal with extensively in the first chapter. We can also find this pattern expressed in popular fiction by the nineteenth century. For example, in Joseph Holt Ingraham's *Lafitte, the Pirate of the Gulf*, which is set in the Caribbean and in New Orleans, we find in successive chapters differing characterizations of primitive religion along racial lines. A party of white sailors encounters an Indian mound locally known as "The Temple," and they are moved to speculate on the sun worship that they believe the Indians of the past practiced. "Next to the invisible God—whom they knew not—in their child-like ignorance, and with the touching poetry, which seems to have been the soul of the Indian's nature, they sought out that, alone of all His works, which most gloriously manifested Himself to his created intelligences. . . . How infinitely is this pure emblem above the stocks and stones of the civilized idolaters of old Greece and Rome."[7]

The Indians worship something beyond the earthly, and their nature worship here seems closer to Christianity than to much other idol worship and fetishism. In contrast are the Africans in the book. The captain has a slave, Cudjoe, who has a pocket, or bag, that is a sort of "Pandora's box" containing "a heterogeneous display of broken pipes, chicken breast-bones, beads, ebony hearts, broken dirk-knobs, charmed relicks, and spells against obeahs, fetahs, and melay men."[8] We also hear of an old African woman practicing Obeah using the beak of a parrot that had been "taught to speak the three magic names of Fetish" and "a little red bag filled with grave dirt, and tied up with the hair of a murdered woman."[9] The Indians, in addition to being firmly in the past, are presented as well on their way to religion, whereas the Africans and African Americans are strictly limited to superstition and magic—and are also, of course, very much still present.[10]

Clearly these are isolated instances, which can offer only a snapshot of attitudes, but my point is that we are in fact restricted to such glimpses if we want to find comparisons actually being made. White missionaries and preachers, who might be counted on to be interested in the beliefs that they are contesting, offer very little help, since the missionaries are largely focused on Indians, and in general preachers and missionaries have little to say on African American beliefs, beyond dismissing them as superstition. One intriguing area of potential interest is the few instances of cross-racial encounters between Indians and African American preachers. John Stewart of Virginia, for instance, was the child of free blacks who were Baptists. Having met Delaware and Wyandott Indians, he preached to them via another African American, Jonathan Pointer, who had been taken prisoner by them and spoke the language. He encountered problems from whites, who thought he was a runaway slave, and from Indians, who rejected his message, saying they had their system of religion given by their own God, or "Great Spirit." One of his opponents, Mononcue, or Two Logs, "would sometimes tell the people that it was really derogatory to their character, to have it said, that they had a Negro for their preacher, as that race of people was always considered inferior to Indians. 'The Great Spirit,' said he, 'never created Negroes, they were created by the Evil Spirit.'"[11] Stewart's response is that there is only one God, who created all races, and there is only one true religion for them all. His response reflects the hope that religion would supersede race, and in fact being Christian does seem to have been seen by some African American converts as an identity that enabled mobility and transcended race—though whether their white fellow Christians or the Indians shared their view is less clear.[12]

Certainly many Indian converts remained intensely aware that Christianity in practice hardly disturbed racial categories, but there is little evidence about how the different groups viewed each others' beliefs or made common cause. The Pequot William Apess does represent a particularly complex but rare instance. Married to a woman of African as well as Native American descent whom he describes simply as "a woman of nearly the same colour as myself," he performs a brilliant extended play upon the idea of whiteness and color in his writings.[13] Though recent research such as that on Apess has continued to suggest the many forms of creative adaptation by and between Indians and African Americans that were actually taking place, these changes were rendered pretty much invisible to contemporary white observers, because of the restricted and reductive categories available to them. They recognized only religion or paganism and superstition, and while Indian practices might have been visible as something comparable to religion—and by the end of the nineteenth century even Africans could be seen as having a spiritual system underlying and informing their material practices—there could be no question of extending this to African American beliefs other than Christianity.

The case of Apess and his political activism does point, though, to a developing theme in this book, which is the relation between spiritual/magical belief and political consciousness and action. Here again there are marked imbalances in the material available to us. The importance of Christian spiritual beliefs in inhibiting or empowering black liberation movements has been extensively discussed, and more recently attention has been paid to the role of conjure and voodoo in slave rebellions. On the Indian side there has been extensive work on the Ghost Dance and revitalization movements, and more recently on the political resonances of the various adaptations of Christianity. I will be dealing with all these elements, but what is much more difficult is to find ways of talking about these often-contemporaneous phenomena in any meaningful relation to each other. What would happen, for instance, if we tried to adapt the language of anthropology and talked of African American beliefs and actions in terms of revitalization movements, or Ghost Dances? Or if we tried to compare or assess just what sort of claims for practical as opposed to symbolic efficacy are being made for conjure bags or medicine bundles? The general dangers of a comparative approach outlined above are compounded by the inevitable Native American suspicion that such an approach would seem to deny their unique legal and political position, which makes their politics incommensurable with that of other groups, and a more widespread suspicion that such an approach might trivialize the specificities of each group's historical situation. As the book develops, these themes gradually develop, to come to some sort of focus in the final chapter.

If one distinctive point of focus in the book is on the conjunction of races, another is on objects and their power. What would it mean to believe that an object had nonmaterial power? I begin the book by focusing on this issue in Chapter 1 because in many ways it has long been at the uncomfortable intersection between magic and religion. According to James G. Frazer's eventual codification of what was becoming an accepted, if implicit, narrative of human progress by the end of the nineteenth century, human beings began with magic and progressed to religion and science, as they developed their ability to explain the world. Different races and their beliefs were charted across this schema, in which worshipping an object was seen as the lowest form of ignorance and superstition and was diametrically opposed both to the "higher" religions, like Christianity, and to scientific reason. Whereas a magical view confused material and nonmaterial causes, religion and science in their different ways gradually divided the realms of matter and spirit and found a modus vivendi. This was the theory, but the problem, as I will show, was that Frazer's convenient categories persistently failed to hold, and what was being dismissed as magic simply refused to go away.

The idea that "primitive" people believed in magic and superstition, as opposed to either the more elevated belief in spiritual power represented by Christianity or the scientific belief in strictly material causality, played an important part in maintaining the hierarchies of race, and one key idea in early theorizations of what came to be called primitive belief was that of fetishism. In Chapter 1 I begin by tracing the complex history and changing uses of this term before focusing on North America and the nature and treatment of Indian and African American beliefs. What were seen as irrational or superstitious beliefs (in fetishes, charms, medicine bundles, ghosts, and the occult) were systematically disowned and consigned to the primitive, and usually racially categorized, mind—and yet such neat categories were consistently breaking down, as the persistence of the idea of the fetish, and its changing associations suggests. Not only did irrational beliefs continue to haunt the white society that had supposedly moved beyond them, but such beliefs often involved an intimate and ambivalent or unresolved relation to Indians and African Americans, those racial groups to whom these practices were dismissively consigned. In Chapter 2, therefore, I focus on the importance of superstition and magic, even as it was being disowned and identified with "lower" races, in the writings of late nineteenth-century America.

The fascination with primitivism in the early twentieth century provided ways in which a whole range of exotic objects and beliefs could become grist to white artists' mills. In Chapter 3 I outline some Modernist treatments of African American and Indian belief, and Modernism's relation to anthropology, before moving on to a detailed account of Zora Neale Hurston's work on conjure and Voodoo, as a key instance of the conjunction of many different discourses of magic, aesthetics, and ethnography.

In the final two chapters I continue with this emphasis, exploring how some contemporary Native American and African American writers and artists have dealt with questions of magic, spiritual power, and belief. This involves looking both at what they are drawing upon from their own cultures and histories and at the wider discursive fields of literature and art in which their work also inevitably circulates and takes on meaning. The degree of reevaluation and celebration of previously discredited and ignored traditional practices is striking, and it provides a rich vein for contemporary artists and writers. But any use of conjure or traditional ceremonies and spiritual practices also operates in a complex and potentially uncomfortable area, which overlaps with the widespread and popular discourses of spirituality often lumped together as New Age. The universalizing assumptions implicit in New Age appeals to a common and translatable spirituality sit uncomfortably, for instance, with Native American writers' and artists' sense of cultural and spiritual property, so that the various invocations of spirituality need to be disentangled.

Those Enlightenment thinkers who looked forward to an era of rational thought and secular values and saw irrational beliefs as something to be outgrown would no doubt be surprised and disappointed at the strong persistence of belief in magic and religion in America. They would perhaps be even more disappointed at the popularity not just of organized religions but of a whole range of objects claiming to have magical or spiritual power, such as New Age crystals and charms, which they might call fetishes. Furthermore, their hope that what they saw as the superstitious and backward beliefs of the African American and Indian peoples of the time would give way to more rational ones as they became more like the civilized whites would be dashed by the widespread and positive use made of traditional religious and spiritual beliefs in much of the most ambitious and powerful African American and Indian literature and art.

With hindsight it is perhaps easy enough to see the limitations of the Enlightenment trust in reason, and the ways in which the universal values that it asserted were underpinned by ethnocentric and Eurocentric assumptions. Similarly, we can now see the pitfalls of categorizing other races and their mental and moral capacities according to European standards and values, which were falsely assumed to be universal. As a result, any questioning of belief, or any skepticism about the claims made for magico-religious practices, can run up against the charge of using inappropriate Western models of causality or efficacy. Nevertheless, in what follows I want to take the risk of approaching contemporary as well as past discourses of spirituality with something of this skepticism. My approach throughout the book is to question the oppositions of matter and spirit and in particular to challenge the hierarchies of value that accompany these ideas. This entails maintaining a skeptical approach to many of the terms, regardless of who is using them. It means, for instance, exploring whether the word "spiritual" could in many instances be replaced with a different term from another register altogether, such as the psychological or aesthetic. To put it another way, I have tried to maintain a materialist approach to claims for supernatural or spiritual power, and I use the complex reevaluations of such ideas by writers like Nathaniel Mackey and Leslie Silko to help me to do so. In the later sections, where I deal with Native American and African American writers and artists, such a radically skeptical approach may be seen as an act of dismissal coming from a position of implicit (white) critical superiority—the return of an Enlightenment superiority, with all its Eurocentric limitations. My assumption, though, is that in order to take a fresh look at what is too often taken on trust under the protected category of the spiritual, this is a risk worth taking.

Chapter 1

Hierarchies of Race and Religion: Fetishism, Totemism, Manitou, and Conjure

This chapter explores the ways in which ideas of what came to be called primitive religion were informed by underlying assumptions about established hierarchies of religion and race. The increasing systematization of race and of religion through the eighteenth and nineteenth centuries meant that the ability to describe and understand not just what but *how* other races believed became an important concern. This was important not only to the larger classificatory enterprises of anthropology and comparative religion but also to the more widespread fixing of inferior races on a political and religious scale, which reflected the existing social and racial hierarchies. One way of exploring these hierarchies is to look closely at a number of key terms used to describe forms of belief and trace their changing uses. I begin with the most generally influential term, "fetish," and then relate this to other terms more specific to America, particularly "totem," "Manitou," "conjure," and "hoodoo," tracing their careers as concepts, and their relation to the particular racial configurations in America involving Indians and African Americans.

The concepts of fetishism and totemism in particular emerged as products of multiple cultural and linguistic conversions of value, rather than as descriptions of any actual system of indigenous primitive practice or belief, and then became crucial instruments in the development of ideas about primitive religion. In this chapter, after outlining the origins of the idea of fetishism in the eighteenth century, and moving through its employment in the discourses of anthropology and religion in the nineteenth, I focus on its use in the different characterization of Indians and African Americans in America. The development of the idea of totemism, though less documented, has a parallel and to some extent complementary career to that of fetishism in the way that it is adapted and extended by a whole set of discourses beyond anthropology, while becoming most associated in the United States with Native American cultures far distant from its Ojibwa origins. Although linked from the beginning with African fetishism, Native American beliefs were nevertheless progressively distanced in later accounts from what was seen as the base materiality of African practices. I argue that the particular "spirituality" that became associated with

Indians and is still evident in New Age versions needs to be seen in relation both to a persistent hierarchy of religious beliefs and to assumptions about the differential mental and spiritual capacities of Indians and African Americans. These combined forces were enough to place African American folk practices, like conjure, below what came to be presented as Indian religion.

The word "fetish" developed out of a term used on the Guinea coast by Portuguese traders and Africans and was applied to a wide range of objects of economic as well as religious value or importance before it was elevated into the concept of fetish*ism* by Charles de Brosses in the eighteenth century. It was then employed through the nineteenth century as a key concept in formulating ideas of a primitive or original form of religious belief that could be contrasted with that of the West. Before this, the false ascription of magical or religious power to objects had been conceptualized in Christian writings through the idea of idolatry, but fetishism reflected a new configuration, which was about civilization and progress as well as Christianity. Enlightenment interests in primitive beliefs began to focus not on questions of true or false worship but on the progression from polytheism to monotheism. The idea of fetishism played an important role here in focusing attention on states of mind rather than on the question of religious validity, which was always implicit in the term "idolatry."

Though by the late nineteenth century the term was already becoming superseded or rejected in anthropology, the idea of fetishism has continued to have a curious half-life. Its general use to describe a false ascription of special value to some undeserving material thing has made it a useful term in the skeptical questioning of all sorts of objects and systems of value. It is in this role that it was taken up in the discourses of Marxism and psychoanalysis, where, as well as in the area of art criticism, it is mainly found today.[1] In the context of religion it represents the importance of a stubborn materiality and that materiality's relation to the spiritual or transcendent categories claimed by the "higher" religions. Fetishism was to be found in folk belief as well as in the belief of those groups who were the targets of conversion, but as it became systematized in the eighteenth and nineteenth centuries, it took its place as the lowest point in a hierarchy of beliefs, which were, of course, racialized. Contemporary "primitive" people of certain races were lumped with "our" ancestors as examples of a mentality that was mired in materiality and was without the capacity for abstraction and spiritual awareness to be found in advanced peoples.

What this account leaves out, though, and what William Pietz's genuinely groundbreaking work on the development of the term itself draws attention to is the way that the fetish and fetishism are products of a situation of cross-cultural economic, cultural, and religious exchanges. Fetishism is an idea about materiality that has its own material base, and to understand its persistent role as a point of misrecognition and disavowal, we need therefore to see its full historical dimensions. Pietz insists on the etiology of the term as itself a product of exchange and hybridity.[2] The term crosses over from the use of the term *feitico* (stemming from the Latin *facticius*) by Portuguese sailors to describe their own culture's witchcraft or magic, to a pidgin form, *fetisso*, which seems to have become used to describe something of value, both religious and commercial. The term is then reused by the Portuguese, and then everyone else, to apply to what is falsely described as the particular form of worship of objects found on the Guinea coast, as if it were an African word.

Pietz argues that it is in this space where several different systems of value meet—Christian feudal, African lineage and merchant capital—that the fetish emerges to point to "the capacity of the material object to embody—simultaneously and sequentially—religious, commercial, aesthetic, and sexual values."[3] Pietz's detailed treatment of the West African origins is invaluable, as are his later accounts of the operation of the term in other colonial contexts and in later Marxist discourse. Nevertheless, his account of the development of the term gives little sense of the more complex racial categories, which involved America as well as Africa, and I want therefore in this chapter to open up the question of the differential and comparative use of races and cultures and show how this affects the use of the idea of fetishism in America. This involves a set of distinctions between the religious practices of Indians and African Americans, which reflected a larger set of key oppositions that includes purity versus pollution or mixedness, and spiritual versus material, which will be explored in the course of the book.

When in 1760 Charles de Brosses published his *Du Culte des dieux fétiches, ou parallèle de l'ancienne religion de l'Égypte avec la religion actuelle de Nigritie* in Paris, he drew upon a wide range of scholarly and travel writings from Africa and the Americas, as well as from antiquity. As the title suggests, his book was part of a larger comparativist impulse of the time,[4] but what was new was the creation of a whole new category and its application across time and across cultures. The word "fetish" in different forms had been present in travel accounts and descriptions since the sixteenth century, when it was used as a description of a number of different objects and practices developing, like the pidgin *fetisso*, out of the interchanges between Portuguese traders and Africans on the coast of West Africa. The Dutch traveler William Bosman, for instance, describes the Africans, when about to "make offerings to their Idols," crying out "Let us make *Fetiche*; by which they express as much, as let us perform our Religious Worship." These offerings, he says, are made to bring good fortune or inflict evil on others.[5]

Bosman and other commentators actually acknowledge in their accounts a *range* of practices and beliefs among the Africans, including a belief in more abstract or overarching deities, but the assumption of the Africans' limited mental capacities means that the more abstract ideas are often put down to Christian influence, and the Africans are made to represent just the early stages of mental development. John Atkins, in 1734, anticipating de Brosses, describes the first stages of belief, in which, unable to reach above a "material God," people worshipped the equivalent of "the *Fetishes* of the *Negroes*," namely "*Stocks, Stones, Serpents, Calves, Onions, Garlick, &c.*"[6] This sense of the random and worthless nature of the things that are worshipped is also found in Bosman's description. "They have a great Wooden Pipe filled with Earth, Oil, Blood, the Bones of dead Men and Beasts, Feathers, Hair; and to be short, all sorts of Excrementitious and filthy Trash, which they do not endeavour to mould into any Shape, but lay it in a confused heap in the Pipe."[7]

De Brosses extends this idea of the fetish as the most basic form of belief to other places and peoples and thereby creates the category of fetish*ism*. At first sight, the term as de Brosses uses it might not seem so different from the traditional usage of idolatry to describe the polytheistic worship of false gods. In David Hume's *Natural History of Religion* of 1757, for instance, a work from which de Brosses borrowed extensively, Hume rejects the standard Christian view of idolatry as a falling away from an original revelation. In this view, humanity degenerated from an original monotheist belief in the true God to polytheism and worship of heathen gods, animals, and idols. In accounting for this degeneration, Christians saw polytheism, in Frank Manuel's words, as "a bad habit which had slowly crept up on mankind."[8] Hume, on the other hand, begins with the idea of primitive human beings as locked in the physical and immediate and rejects the idea that we regressed from an original monotheism or original knowledge of the true God. This would be to believe of ancient people that "while they were ignorant and barbarous, they discovered truth, but fell into error as soon as they acquired learning and politeness. . . . We may as reasonably imagine, that men inhabited palaces before huts and cottages, or studied geometry before agriculture; as assert that the Deity appeared to them as a pure spirit, omniscient, omnipotent and omnipresent, before he was apprehended to be a powerful, though limited being with human passions and appetites, limbs and organs."[9] Underlying Hume's thinking is the idea that even when humankind *has* progressed to monotheism, it is still driven by the same needs and fears, rather than by reason. He sees a fluctuation between idolatry and monotheism, between worshipping gods and a single god, rather than a steady progression—what he calls the "flux and reflux of polytheism and theism."[10]

Hume's cool treatment of religious sentiment not as a primary and fundamental part of humanity but as just a stage in humanity's fitful struggle to overcome fear and to aspire to something more rational is ultimately corrosive of religion's claim to centrality. As Moshe Halbertal and Avishai Margalit say more generally of Enlightenment critiques, "what the elite religion has done to the folk religions now revenges itself against the elite religion itself. The entire project of religion is now placed under suspicion of being idolatry, or false worship."[11] The fundamental concern with origins during this period carries through into the nineteenth century formulations of what comes to be called the primitive mind. The nature of Christian belief could be interrogated under the cover of an exploration of pagan or primitive belief, while the *relation* of that discredited conception of religion to Christianity itself could be left deliberately unarticulated.

But if de Brosses' new formulation of fetishism was just an extension of Hume, what was the added dimension that the term offered that enabled it to be taken up so widely in the next century, and to have led such a strange career thereafter? William Pietz points to what he calls "the untranscended materiality of the fetish."[12] Building on this, my argument is that fetishism, as a theory *about* misrecognition and the false ascription of value or divinity to worthless things, itself embodies a process of misrecognition and disavowal. In the discourse of fetishism in the nineteenth century and even into the twentieth, there is first an insistence that there *could* be a primitive mental condition in which objects were worshipped as having power within themselves. Then, as soon as it is asserted, this idea of a belief in material power without spirit is seen as problematic and is replaced by the idea of a spirit behind or within matter, and a consequent denial that pure fetishism could ever have existed. Yet the term and the idea persist, only to be regularly denied. This pattern of disavowal is similar to the mechanism of the fetish in the psychoanalytic tradition, which follows the pattern "I know it isn't (the woman's body, the phallus, etc.) but even so. . . ." More relevantly here, perhaps, it is also similar to the operation of religious symbols, which, as Henry Krips puts it, "signal the presence of the divine by the paradoxical device of admitting their own poverty of representation."[13] In other words, it transposes the tensions about representation and materiality that were previously played out within the idea of idolatry.

The *Oxford English Dictionary* tries to draw a clear distinction as follows: "A fetish differs from an idol in that it is worshipped in its own character, not as the image, symbol or occasional residence of a deity." The trouble with this distinction is that the definition of "idol" is much more limited than that found in earlier discussions of idolatry, and in fact it is only with the invention of "fetishism" as an end term that "idol" can be restricted like this to describe representations of something else. Within the Christian discourse on idolatry there are two connected but distinct elements. Worship of a false god is wrong, but so is worshipping the image—or what one takes to be the image—of the true God, because the true God is impossible to represent.

We can find a detailed discussion of this in Joseph de Acosta's early seventeenth-century account of Indian worship. In spite of the original light offered by knowledge of the true God, he tells us, these people have been led astray by false worship, and he is at pains to distinguish between different forms of idolatry, "the one grounded uppon naturall things, the other upon things imagined and made by man's invention." The first form, the worship of natural features, such as hills and stones, marked out by singular features is found particularly in Peru, whereas the second is found among the Aztecs and is "more pernicious and hurtfull then that of the Yncas, . . . for that the greatest part their adoration and idolatrie was employed to Idols, and not to naturall things."[14]

The distinction here is between what is made by God and what is made by men, and clearly in this Christian view something made by man cannot be worthy of worship. The worst idolators, then, are "those that worship Images and figures made by the hand of men, which have nothing else in them but to be of wood, stone, or metall, and of such forme as God hath given them." Acosta's gradations of idolatry here are explicitly based on scripture (Wisdom 13:10–19; Romans 1:25; Hosea 8), and the two disparate aspects of idolatry are in fact present in the Commandments, where the first and second commandments have a curiously overlapping relation to each other. The effect is that the different strands within the term "idolatry" create an instability in its meaning and application. To this extent it is never, like fetishism, just a practice "out there" or "back then" performed by pagans, but is always potentially inside Christianity as well.

Contained within the idea of the idol and idolatry and their Greek etymology (*eidolon*, image, form) is the idea of appearance, image, and representation, but what is added in the English usage is the idea of the falseness of what is being represented, the idea of a false God. (As the *OED* points out, the English word has a sequence of meanings, which is the reverse of the Greek, in that the earliest usages in English are about false gods rather than about representation.) With the creation of fetishism, the worship of objects that was previously contained within the accusation of idolatry became separated off as the ultimate contrast to monotheism, and idolatry became more of a middle position, in that it was not entirely restricted to the objects themselves and suggested a capacity for representation and therefore figuration, if not abstraction. The invention of fetishism gave the possibility of moving attention from the question of true or false gods to the mentality and psychology of the worshipper or fetishist—to consciousness rather than behavior. To this end de Brosses isolated a rudimentary human behavior that could be found in the ancient world as well as in present-day primitive people. The evidence is clear, he says, that "What is now the religion of black African and other savage tribes was formerly the religion of ancient peoples; and down through the ages and whichever part of the world you choose you will find established there this direct worship, rendered without figures to animal and vegetable objects."[15]

Here we have the central element that is to distinguish the idea of fetishism from idolatry—the lack of any mediation or representation (*sans figure*). There is no attempt on de Brosses' part to explain the logic of this. In fact, "common sense makes it difficult to claim any plausible reasons for such a senseless doctrine."[16] He asserts that people worship "the first material thing which it pleases each nation or individual to choose," and he then produces a list that goes from mountains and trees to a lion's tail, a pebble, a scallop shell, and salt. This idea of the random fixing on the first object that people happen upon is recycled with great frequency in early accounts and is meant to underline the sheer contingency and materiality that forms the contrast with proper religion, but de Brosses also points to an operation of mind, a sort of mechanical connection or associationism. "Man is so constituted that, left in his raw and savage natural state, not yet shaped by any reflexive idea or by any imitation, he is the same in his primitive customs and his way of doing things in Egypt as in the West Indies, in Persia as in Gaul; everywhere it is the same mechanism of ideas from which their actions spring."[17]

One of the key elements in the book is the parallel of ancients and primitives as animal worshippers, but the really significant factor is his identification of a category of people who operated in this way because of their mental limitations rather than, as with idolatry, because they had slipped backward because of sloth or evil. Thus the idea of fetishism became useful as a baseline position from which a series of different arguments about progress and ways of thinking could be developed. By positing an original materialist conception of the world, it allowed philosophers and rationalists to sidestep the terms of idolatry versus true faith, as well as the other materialism of magic. In the many accounts of fetishism that followed de Brosses, there was a constant recourse to a narrative of origin and development, in line with the developmental and later evolutionary climate. This narrative functioned as a way of both explaining and dismissing fetishism, as it was seen to be transcended by later forms. In this sense it has always been the lowest or most basic form of consciousness, against which abstract thinking, whether in the form of religion or philosophy, could be distinguished.

In August Comte's elaborate scheme, for instance, the theological phase, which preceded the metaphysical and positive phases, "could begin no otherwise than by a complete and usually very durable state of pure Fetichism, which allowed free exercise to that tendency of our nature by which Man conceives of all external bodies as animated by a life analogous to his own, with differences of mere intensity." Even with the progression toward the dominance of reason rather than emotions, modern rational men "are not preserved even by high intellectual culture from being plunged by some passion of hope or fear, into the radical fetishism—personifying, and then deifying, even the most inert objects that can interest their roused sensibilities."[18] In such an original state, language would be metaphorical, not because it lacked enough terms to go around or was incapable of abstraction, but because it saw the world as animated. The "excessive abundance of figures belonged naturally to the prevalent philosophy, which, likening all phenomena to human acts, must introduce as faithful description expressions which must seem metaphorical when that state had passed away in which [they] were literal."[19]

De Brosses drew heavily on a wide range of travel accounts, as well as classical texts, to show the widespread nature of fetishism. For the Americas, he referred to Oviedo, Le Clercq, Lafitau, Léry, Harriott, and Marquette, among others, and it is instructive to follow up one particular source in some detail. Father Joseph-François Lafitau's *Mœurs des sauvages ameriquains, comparées aux mœurs des premiers temps* of 1724 drew on firsthand observations from his work as missionary to the Mohawk Indians in New France, but as its title indicates, his book has a larger sweep, which in some ways anticipates de Brosses. Where he differs, though, is in his concern not just to show the similarities between ancient and contemporary American beliefs and customs, but to demonstrate that they are all a falling away from an initial unity of revelation. There is a tension in Lafitau, as a Jesuit, between condemnation of Indian practices as evil and an interest in them as ethnography, which reveals his affinity with some Enlightenment ideas. We see this in a telling vignette in which Lafitau examines, with an older priest, some of the objects that have been surrendered by the Indians when they renounced their religion for Christianity. "Father Garnier had in his hands several of these charms which the Indians whom he had converted had given him. One day I begged him to examine them with me, arousing his curiosity for the first time."

The older man had dismissed these objects as superstition and the work of the devil, and we can find other instances in which missionaries examine the contents of medicine bundles or pouches with mixed feelings, but little intellectual curiosity. Chrétien Le Clercq, for instance, some thirty years earlier had given a detailed inventory of what he found in a medicine pouch, but only to dismiss it as "this little bag of the Devil."[20] In this instance, though, Lafitau speculates about their use. "There was a great quantity of them; they were little bundles of twisted hair, bones of serpents or extraordinary animals, pieces of iron or bronze, figures of dough or corn husks and other similar objects which could not, in themselves, have any connection with what they were supposed to effect but could operate only by supernatural power in consequence of some formal or tacit agreement."[21]

He refers to bags in which the shaman (*jongleur*) carries, together with tobacco and pipe, "what I have called his *Oiaron* and his *Manitou* which may be regarded as his talismans in which all his virtue resides."[22] And elsewhere he comments that "each has his own personal God which they call their Manitou. It is a serpent, bird, stone, or other similar thing, of which they have dreamed while sleeping, and in which they put all their confidence for the success of their war, hunting, or fishing."[23]

Lafitau uses the word "Manitou" here to describe a specific god or spirit rather than the overgeneralized concept of a Great Spirit, which developed in the nineteenth century, as I show later, and it is in this context that he makes a brief but significant comparison of American Indian and African religion. In a footnote to a quotation about African women, where the word *fetisso* appears,

Lafitau explains, "The fetish is a kind of talisman or something which corresponds to the *Manitou* of the American [Indians]. These idolatrous negroes of Africa have, especially in things pertaining to religion, customs very like those which are seen widespread in America."[24] This is the single use of the term by Lafitau in the French original,[25] and it is used as a synonym for "idol," but whereas Lafitau is content to leave it merely as a passing comparison de Brosses elevates it into a fundamental approach, and it is this change that reflects the larger shift from Lafitau's Christian view to de Brosses' more Enlightenment-based comparativism. "Although, in its specific meaning it particularly relates to the African Negro's beliefs, I inform you from the outset that I also intend to use it in speaking about any other nation whatsoever where animals or inanimate entities are deified as cult objects."[26]

In spite of this general application of the term, though, what is significant for my later chapters is that the term "fetishism" tends to stick to Africa, as if it were the name of an actual religion there. This is in spite of the fact that, as Pietz has shown, the term is not a native one and does not refer to anything specifically African at all. In the nineteenth century it is used to characterize Africa as uniquely primitive, as in Hegel's sweeping dismissal of it as standing outside the realm of history. His view of Africans as fetishists worshipping "the first thing that comes their way" allows him to see them as lacking "the principle which naturally accompanies all *our* ideas—the category of Universality."[27] The reduction of people to this level conceptually has clear relevance in justifying the economic and political actions that were enslaving them, and this will also be relevant in the context of African American slavery and its aftermath. What I am particularly interested in here, though, are some of the ways this differentiation of races and capacities is reflected in the theorizing about the primitive mind and religion. During the nineteenth century, fetishism becomes incorporated into animism (or perhaps I should say sublimated, as it loses its emphasis on materiality), and I want to look briefly at some of the most prominent expositions of these ideas before moving to specifically American adaptations.

The anthropologists of the nineteenth century, who tried to formulate a concept of primitive thought and religion within their presentation of a linear progression to monotheism, constantly came up against the problem of conceptualizing the supposed base materiality of fetishism and its relation to religion and to magic. Perhaps the most important formulation was Edward Tylor's animism. The two large volumes of his *Primitive Culture* are in fact prefaced by a quotation from de Brosses about the need to see humankind for what it is rather than what it might become, and Tylor begins by trying to establish a lowest common denominator for religion, namely "the belief in Spiritual Beings,"[28] which he calls animism. One of the most fundamental elements is reverence for natural objects, and the belief that a spiritual power resides in them. This, as he says, has been identified by de Brosses and later by August Comte as fetishism, but he wants to confine this to "that subordinate department which it properly belongs to, namely, the doctrine of spirits embodied in, or attached to, or conveying influence through, certain material objects. Fetishism will be taken as including the worship of 'stocks and stones,' and thence it passes by an imperceptible gradation into Idolatry."[29]

Once he has established fetishism as the lowest condition, idolatry's place is seen as "intermediate" between it and the "higher" spiritual activities found in advanced civilizations. As soon as the stone or other natural object is made to resemble something else, it can be seen as an idol. "A few chips or scratches or daubs of paint suffice to convert the rude post or stone into an idol."[30] This can also point toward a change in the mental process. Instead of seeing the object as powerful in itself, the worshipper sees it as a material representation of a spiritual power. But this change from what is effectively a metonymic to a metaphoric approach is a slippery one, as Protestant critics of Roman Catholic "idolatry" have always pointed out, and as he acknowledges.[31]

The old and greatest difficulty in investigating the general subject is this, that an image may be, even to two votaries kneeling side by side before it, two utterly different things; to the one it may be only a symbol, a portrait, a memento; while to the other it is an intelligent and active being, by virtue of a life or spirit dwelling in it or acting through it. In both cases Image-worship is connected with the belief in spiritual beings, and is in fact a subordinate development of animism. But it is only so far as the image approximates to the nature of a material body provided for a spirit that Idolatry comes properly into connection with Fetishism.[32]

One of the major problems Tylor has in wanting to expand religious belief into a larger area of belief in spirit and nature is that there are some aspects he cannot include as religion. One of these is magic, or occult science, which "belongs to a lower level of civilization" but has persisted as a "survival." As "one of the most persistent delusions that ever vexed mankind" it is contrasted not with religion but with science.[33] Magic is the point of resistance and represents the fault lines of the religion/science distinction. In this respect, though Tylor has apparently included the fetish within the history of religion, he has only done so by stressing its kinship with forms of belief in an underlying spirit *beneath* the material, and downplaying its claims to material efficacy, which would take it into the realm of magic.[34] As Peter Pels puts it, fetishism is "animism with a vengeance. Its matter strikes back." For Pels, if animism was spirit *in* matter, fetishism was the spirit *of* matter.[35] In other words, animism sidesteps the real challenge implicit in the idea of fetishism—that there could be a nonmaterial power in objects, which is not the same as an indwelling spiritual power. Fetishism suggests matter having force and effect that it is not supposed to have, a scandal of categories, which is marginalized as magic or superstition.

Animism attempts to solve the problem by an overarching idea of spiritual presence, but this presence is not one that acts specifically and materially, and so Tylor is still left with the problem of magic. In discussing the inhabiting of objects by the souls of the dead, he quotes an instance from Charles Darwin's journal, where two Malay women "held a wooden spoon dressed in clothes like a doll; this spoon had been carried to the grave of a dead man, and becoming inspired at full moon, in fact lunatic, it danced about convulsively like a table or a hat at a modern spirit-séance."[36] The reference to nineteenth-century spiritualism here is in fact very relevant. Tylor did say that if the word had not already been in use for the controversial modern movement, "spiritualism" would have been his preferred word for what he calls animism, and he himself had firsthand, if extremely skeptical, experience of séances.[37] Most relevantly, spiritualism was grappling with precisely the problems that animism was failing to address in magic, for while spiritualism stressed the realm of the spirit, it was precisely by the most crude material effects that it was judged. Thus it presented a curious and often bathetic scenario of the clash of the highest idealism and the lowest material trickery—as another student of religion's relation to the material world, Karl Marx, was keenly aware.

In his famous passage about commodity fetishism Marx also uses the idea of the animated table, which, "as soon as it steps forth as a commodity . . . is changed into something transcendent. It not only stands with its feet on the ground, but, in relation to all other commodities, it stands on its head and evolves out of its wooden brain grotesque ideas, far more wonderful than 'table-turning' ever was." To find an analogy with the "mystical character" of commodities, Marx directs us to "the mist-enveloped regions of the religious world," where "the productions of the human brain appear as independent beings endowed with life. So it is in the world of commodities with the products of men's hands. This I call the Fetishism which attaches itself to the products of labour, so soon as they are produced as commodities."[38]

His use of the idea of the fetish here, based directly on his own reading of a German translation of de Brosses, is designed both to show the "magical" nature of the ascription of inherent value to commodities, and of course to demystify the process, so he is using fetishism in Enlightenment fashion to critique modern society's retention of the primitive or irrational practices that they pride themselves on having outgrown. Nevertheless, his concern with ghosts here is more substantial than just a rhetorical device to be used against the proponents of modern capitalism, as recent critical work has shown, and I will return to the ways in which Marx can be used to open up for scrutiny the Enlightenment move to disenchant the world in the final chapter.

Freud's later use of the term "fetish" takes us in an entirely different direction, but one that is relevant. His use of anthropological terms that were already being discredited in their own field and his general view of primitive mentality were in themselves conventional, but the way in which he developed and extended what he wrongly believed to be the practice of fetishism in other cultures, in order to apply it to modern societies has proved to be revolutionary.

His development of the idea of fetishism as an ambivalent process of simultaneous assertion and denial to be found at the heart of personal as well as social behavior in modern civilized societies has proved to be useful not just in dealing with sexual compulsions. It has also proved a powerful tool in looking at the ways in which racial difference and its conceptualization operates in a quite bewildering oscillation of mystification and demystification, assertion, and denial. This is ironic, perhaps, given the limitations of his own racial categories.

While the term "fetish" was being taken up in these influential directions, it was continuing its strange pattern of use in the description of African practices. As presented in a steady stream of accounts produced as a result of increased commercial and missionary activities, African religion retained its character as fetishist, even if only in the titles of books where, in a typical act of assertion and disavowal, it was then disowned in the actual text. In *Fetichism and Fetich Worshippers*, for instance, produced for the French Society of African Missions, there is plenty of sensational presentation, including a title page with a beheaded man hanging upside down from a tree near a fetish in its own small fetish house. The initial impression in the preface, too, is of a place of total depravity, where "human nature is degraded . . . by a singular mixture of materialism and spiritualism."[39] As usual, what is emphasized is the dirt and grotesque jumble of elements. "Grotesque statues and other symbols of the god, with dishes and earthen pots to receive the libations and offerings, all horribly smeared with palm-oil, blood and chicken-feathers, form a mixture anything but agreeable to the sight, and still less so to the sense of smell, but worthy in every aspect of the ceremonies of worship of the ragged fetichpriests and of the ignoble fetiches."[40]

As is also usual, though, there is then a qualification. When we "read through this veil" and beneath this "coarse and repellant exterior" we find "a complete religious system of which spiritualism forms the greatest part." The author does note the Portuguese derivation of fetish and tells us that such objects are actually called "in the Nago dialect *oricha,* a word which signifies custom, religious ceremony, usage," but nevertheless he continues to use the term "fetich", even while undercutting its basic associations.[41] He sees "an odd mixture of monotheism, polytheism and idolatry," and a people in "decadence." The idea of the true god remains in the figure of Olorun, but he is ignored in favor of the fetishes and of Legba, whom Baudin sees not as trickster but as the "evil genius."[42] Baudin is at pains to distinguish the Catholic use of saints as mediators, from fetishism. Catholics do not worship the material object, whereas the Africans adore not only the "physical objects which they are supposed to inhabit and animate . . . but they adore them also in the statues and symbols which represent them."[43] There is a characteristic slippage, though, when he stresses that they worship the spirit *in* the object and tells us that they throw away all the objects when the fetish priest dies and the spirit leaves them.

Here we have the classic paradox—that the case against fetishism rests on the idea of a base materiality, and yet it dissolves as soon as we look at it. Baudin accepts that there is a spiritual dimension to be rescued, and his final indictment is that fetichism "presents the most clearly defined spiritualism and the most repugnant materialism."[44]

One of the clearest early rejections of the idea of African fetishism is to be found in a brief journal article by the philologist and missionary Heli Chatelain, who sees the term as the source of "lamentable confusion." All those proficient in an African language know that "the African negro believes in a Creator, who is invisible, and is therefore not represented by an idol." This figure is not formally worshipped, but there are spirits who must be propitiated, and it is here that the various intermediaries like priests or material objects come into the picture. Ultimately, Chatelain insists, there is a fundamental unity in the religious conceptions of all races, including the African, but they all actually pay less attention to this Supreme Being than they do to "amulets, talismans, incantations, quacks, priests, soothsayers, spiritists," and other paraphernalia representing "the one universal disposition of mankind, known as superstition."[45] As we go further into the twentieth century the word "fetish" disappears from scholarly works on Africa, together with the characterization of African religion as deficient in spirit, but it maintains its strange career in other discourses.

As fetishism was superceded in anthropology, other terms were emerging to be used to grapple with similar issues. Along with Tylor's animism, which I have already discussed, another crucial term, and one in which many of the same arguments around primitive religion and thought were rehearsed, was "totemism." Like "fetishism" it is a term that is misapplied almost from the beginning. The word "totem" itself has a complex history and is a classic instance of a native term (another would be "mana") carrying a massively extended burden of signification. It was first introduced into English in 1791 by the trader and interpreter John Long, who not only described the belief in the "totam" but, like de Brosses, made it into a system, coining the term "totamism." "One part of the religious superstition of the Savages consists in each of them having his *totam* or favourite spirit, which he believes watches over him. This *totam* they conceive assumes the shape of some beast or other, and therefore they never kill, hunt or eat the animal whose form they think this *totam* bears."[46]

He describes a particular instance during an encounter with a "band of Chippeways" of a man who mistakenly shot a bear, which was his own totam, and felt that he had incurred the displeasure of the "Master of Life" and had blighted his future hunting prospects. Long extrapolates from this by claiming that "This idea of destiny, or, if I may be allowed the phrase, '*totamism*,' however strange, is not confined to the Savages." (In support he cites a rather strange instance of a prominent French banker's superstitious attachment to a hen!)[47] In fact it seems that Long misleadingly combined two separate ideas. The Ojibwa did indeed use the term, or something like it, but as a clan name based on an animal or object in nature. They also had a practice, which was widespread in North America, in which a guardian spirit would be identified, for instance through a vision quest, in the form of a particular animal. It was in this second practice that the animal would be seen as having special powers, sometimes necessitating avoidance, and such powers were more usually described by other words, including "Manitou."

The exact career of the term after Long is hard to trace until it surfaces in surprising forms. Though the Ojibwa Indian William Whipple Warren did devote a chapter in his book *History of the Ojibwa Nation* to "Totemic Division of the O-jib-ways," the book was not published until 1885, though written some thirty years earlier.[48] This means that Long's coinage was not really taken up in print for three-quarters of a century, until J. F. McLennan wrote a two-part article for the *Fortnightly Review* on the worship of animals and plants in which he argued that totemism prevailed among at least two groups, American Indians and Australian aborigines. Adopting the then-familiar developmental model, he describes the "mental condition of men in the Totem stage" as in effect like fetishism, in that they attributed "a life and personality resembling our own, not only to animals and plants, but to rocks, mountains, streams winds." Totemism, then, is fetishism, but "fetichism *plus* certain *peculiarities*. These peculiarities are, (1) the appropriation of a special Fetich to the tribe, (2) its hereditary transmission through mothers, and (3) the connection with *jus connubii*."[49]

McLennan's extension of the idea to Australia, and in particular the extension of it to a system of classification that linked kinship systems to animal ancestors, was extremely influential but goes beyond my concerns here. Nor need we pursue the most dramatic (and absurd) implication of his work, taken up in studies of Australian peoples, that primitive people were so ignorant of the processes of procreation and paternity that they assumed a literal descent from animal spirits, not a human father.[50] Though the full-blown theory of totemism was eventually comprehensively dismissed by anthropologists,[51] the word retains a presence among the arsenal of terms that seem to have a power granted by their association with the primitive, such as "taboo" and "mana", and, like "fetish," it was used by psychologists, sociologists, and others with varying degrees of precision. Emile Durkheim devotes almost half of *The Elementary Forms of Religious Life* to totemism,[52] and Freud's *Totem and Taboo* accepts this characterization of primitive thought as his foundation for seeing such processes in civilized behavior. I will return to some recent uses of these terms in the last chapter, but one other intriguing twist in the career of the term needs to be noted, and that is the migration of the word from its Chippewa origins to its almost exclusive association with the beliefs and particularly the wood carvings of the Northwest coast, where the elements of totemism supposedly found in the Chippewa, including a developed and dramatic public display of family crests and a linked belief in guardian spirits, can be also be found.[53]

So far I have been demonstrating how both fetishism and totemism have been taken up and used as part of the larger comparativist approach, which accompanied the partial decentering of the Christian assumption that all religions were to be judged by its own single yardstick. "Fetish" and "totem" are among a number of native terms used to describe more general concepts or categories of what came to be called the "primitive mind." But such words also become freighted with layers of exoticism, as well as their original meanings, and if we look more specifically at the American dimensions of the debates over primitive religion, we find them affected by the particular American configurations of races and the power relations between them.

American contributions to the theorizing over the development of religion followed Tylor in finding at the heart of all religion a fundamental belief in a spirit that animates matter, rather than the brute worship of objects, and when American Indian materials were used, it was to support this idea of animism and nature worship. Daniel Brinton's wide-ranging *Religions of Primitive Peoples* of 1899 insisted that what is called "fetishism, polytheism and idolatry, the worship of stocks and stones" is not in fact a worship of objects. "Every fetish, be it a rag-baby or a pebble from the roadside, is adored, not as itself, but as possessing some mysterious transcendental power, by which it can influence the future."[54] He relates this directly to the role of totemic animals of North American tribes, which, far from being the fearful animal worship of de Brosses, is a worship of higher forces. "The totemic animals or 'eponymous ancestors' of the clans or gentes among the American Indian are not to be taken literally. They were not understood as animals of the sort we see today, but as mythical, ancient beings, of supernatural attributes, who clothed themselves in those forms for their own purposes."[55]

This movement, from materiality to a mythical or ideal level, becomes an increasingly common one for commentators dealing with Indians. Whereas de Brosses, for instance, noted that the manitou of Algonquian tribes could refer to material objects, which he identified as fetishes, as well as to a wider spiritual entity, the word "manitou" became increasingly used only to describe the wider, more abstract concept. Accordingly, while the possession of charms and medicine bundles was regularly noted, these were not usually described as fetishes, and increasingly by the end of the nineteenth century, what was being stressed was the harmony of Indians with a nature that was immanent in such objects.[56]

It is worth going back in time and showing in some detail the ways in which this common term "manitou" was treated, to show this movement toward spirit and away from matter, before extending this to the move to nature worship in general. One difficulty with the term manitou is its range of meanings, and determining how much of this may be due to failures of understanding and translation. Certainly it was used regularly in early accounts to describe the power of very specific objects—in fact what would have been called fetishes in accounts of African practices—so that it is not clear whether the more generalized meaning of God or Supreme Being was an extension by Europeans, or whether it really corresponded to native usage or thinking. Sébastien Rasles, for instance, implied several levels of meaning. As the Indians knew "hardly anything but the animals with which they live in the forests, they imagine that there is in these animals—or rather in their skins, or in their plumage—a sort of spirit who rules all things, and who is the master of life and of death." Some of these were held in common, and some only by individuals, and the following sounds very like what Long later mistakenly identified as a totem.

Besides these common Manitous each person has his own special one, which is a bear, a beaver, a bustard, or some similar animal. They carry the skin of this animal to war, to the hunt, and on their journeys,—fully persuaded that it will preserve them from every danger, and that it will cause them to succeed in all their undertakings.[57]

Louis Hennepin also noted the localized use. He described both Algonquians and Iroquois as using a wide range of objects that are considered to have power. Speaking of the Algonquins, he tells us that "every one has his peculiar God, whom they call *Manitoa*. It is sometime a Stone, a Bird, a Serpent, or any thing else that they dream of in their Sleep; for they think this *Manitoa* will supply their Wants."[58] Elsewhere he tells us that "These people admit some sort of Genius in every thing; they all believe one Master of Life, but they make divers applications of it. Some have a lean Crow, which they carry always about with them, and which they call their Master of Life. Others have an Owl, others a Bone, some the Shell of a Fish, and such like things."[59]

On his journeys he is pleased to see a cross "adorn'd with several White Skins, Red Girdles, Bows and Arrows, which that good People had offered to the Great *Manitou*, to return him their Thanks for the care he had taken of them during the Winter," and comments that "*Manitou* is the Name they give in general to all Spirits whom they think to be above the Nature of Man."[60] His use of the term "Great Manitou" suggests an acceptance that they are worshipping the true God via the cross and using their own term to do so, but he has earlier referred to "the *Manitou*, that is, in the language of the *Algonquins* and *Accadians*, an evil Spirit, which the Iroquese call *Otkon*; but the name is the only thing they know of him."[61]

This sort of vacillation reflects the difficulty earlier Christians had in knowing how to categorize the beliefs of others. In his various passing accounts of the seventeenth-century Narragansetts' beliefs, for instance, Roger Williams translates their term "Manittoo" as God, or a god, but his examples of its use might lead us to use a different term.

> There is a generall Custome amongst them, at the apprehension of any Excellency in Men, Women, Birds, Beasts, Fish &c. to cry out *Manittoo*, that is, it is a God, as thus if they see one man excell others in Valour, strength, Activity &c. they cry out *Manittoo* A God; and therefore when they talk amongst themselves of the *English* ships, and great buildings, of the plowing of their fields, and especially of Books and Letters, they will end thus: *Manittowick* they are Gods: *Cummanittoo* You are a God &c.[62]

Elsewhere he points toward a broader definition: "*Manittooes*, that is, Gods, Spirits or Divine powers, as they say of every thing which they cannot comprehend."[63] This is echoed by a comment from a minister from New Netherlands in a letter of 1628, referring to "Menetto; under which title they comprehend everything that is subtle and crafty and beyond human skill and power."[64] The fact that the same term was regularly applied to objects of trade and new technology as well as traditional areas of spiritual power points to its flexibility, and also to the impossibility of separating it out as referring to purely spiritual or intangible matters. As with the origins of the term "fetish" we have a complex set of material and cultural exchanges. Bruce White has pointed out, for instance, that the French most often translated it as *esprit* but that its association with trade objects was also remarked upon.[65]

Paul LeJeune noted that the Montagnais "gave the name Manitou to all Nature superior to man, good or bad. This is why, when we speak of God, they sometimes call him the good Manitou; and when we speak of the Devil they call him the bad Manitou."[66] This may indicate not so much that they used the word to describe both good and bad power as that they did not make the good/bad distinction at all in relation to such power—in which case their usage here is just an obliging translation back to the Jesuits of their own dualistic distinctions. The missionaries, having used a religious term to translate what seems to have been the Indians' word to describe a range of expressions of mysterious or supernatural power, were then confronted with the problem of whether this term could be used the other way round to translate the Christian God. This was a problem, since there could be no guarantee that all sorts of other associations would not also be implied, or that He would be seen in the same way as all the other more mechanistic or magical properties covered by the term.[67]

Similar difficulties were encountered by missionaries working with other Indian tribes. Gabriel Sagard, writing in 1632, noted that the Mi'kmaq worshipped one God, as did the Hurons, though the latter also respected "those spirits which they call Oki; but this word Oki means a great devil just as much as a great angel." Later, he says the Christians were called this because they taught them things "above their intelligence." That this is at least similar to the large general concept of manitou described by Roger Williams is confirmed when Sagard comments that "Our Canadians and Montagnais call theirs Piro-tois and Manitous, which meant the same thing as Oki in the Huron tongue."[68] For Jean de Brebeuf, an impressive linguist attempting to translate Christian thought into the Hurons' own terms, the danger of using such flexible terms was that God could be translated into a term, *aki*, which could also mean "devil." John Steckley has demonstrated in detail the lengths to which Brebeuf went to control the meanings of Christian terms. The problem was the missionaries' perception of what Steckley describes as "an essentially asymmetric relationship between the Christian God (and his cohorts) and the 'Indian gods.' God may partake of the essence of an *aki* in that he is powerful, but a Huron spirit cannot partake of the essence of God."[69]

Dismissing native belief as idolatry and superstition still left open the question of whether the Indians were completely deluded in worshipping simple objects, or whether the objects did have a power, albeit one that came from the devil. The other important possibility for Christians was that this belief had a vestigial connection with an initial revelation. Chrétien Le Clercq, as part of his description of "this blind people who have lived in the shades of Christianity" in his *New Relation of Gaspesia* in 1691, gives an account of the activities of a particular Indian woman, whom he describes as a "pretended *religieuse*." As well as beads taken from a rosary she holds in "singular veneration a King of Hearts, the foot of a glass, and a kind of medal," before which she prostrates herself "as before her divinities." She also has a cross decorated with "beadwork, wampum, painting and porcupine quills. The pleasing mixture thereof represented several and separate figures of everything which was in her devotions. She placed it usually between her and the French, obliging them to make their prayers before her cross, whilst from her side she made her own prayers, according to her custom, before her King of Hearts and her other Divinities."[70]

This is an intriguing glimpse of native practices, and it has been sensitively explored by Laura Donaldson in a wider discussion that sees what has often been categorized as syncretism in terms of postcolonial discourses of hybridity and *mestizaje*.[71] I will return to these issues in later chapters but for now my concern is more with the contemporary white approaches. Le Clercq's response to the woman is revealing. Clearly at one level he needs to insist on an absolute distinction between Christian objects of devotion and other objects that are just rubbish. He describes these as "trifles," and with this word we are connected with larger tropes of value and non-value in early encounters, as well as with the "excrementitious" nature of the fetish discussed earlier. But the distinctions between value and rubbish, between unredeemed materiality and spirit, are always unraveling. In this particular case what puzzles Le Clercq is the presence of the cross.

The woman is referred to as "of the Cross-bearer [Porte-Croix] nation," and he spends a chapter trying to account for the fact that this particular group of the Gaspesians (the usual and preferred term is now "Mi'kmaq," with the adjective "Mi'kmaw") venerates crosses, wears the design of the cross on their clothes, and seems to have done so for a long time. There is enough evidence, he says, "to make us conjecture, and even to believe, that these people have not been wholly deaf to the voice of the apostles, of which the sound has reverberated through all the earth."[72] He tentatively offers their own explanation— that a beautiful man appeared in dreams to their elders at a time of crisis to the nation, telling them to construct crosses, which saved them from disaster. Having presented evidence of the vigor of this belief, he then mentions that, because of the depredations of the Iroquois, they have "gradually relapsed from this first devotion of their ancestors," so that many now preserve "only the shadow" of their customs.[73] Some later commentators have identified this as evidence that what he is describing are vestiges simply of earlier missionary influences, rather than independent revelation, while others have pointed to evidence of the pre-contact use of the symbol, perhaps as a conventionalized depiction of a totemic animal.[74] For Le Clercq, though, the presence of a cross without Christ is enough to summon up the memory of Paul in Athens. "This great Apostle, having viewed that famous inscription which the Athenians had caused to be graven in letters of gold on the front of the temple which they had dedicated to the Unknown God, *Ignoto Deo*, took advantage of the opportunity to make them understand that this Unknown God . . . was the very same who had made Heaven and Earth; who was made man in the womb of a Virgin."[75]

In many ways Le Clercq's concerns here reflect a larger problem for the Christian missionaries in general. Do they insist on the absolute distinctions of magic versus religion, spell versus prayer, and belief in the devil versus belief in the true God, which would be one psychological reaction to their own sense of beleaguered isolation? Or do they play creatively across these lines, as they see the Indians doing all the time? Consider, for instance, what is happening in the following episode. Le Clercq has developed a written pictographic system, probably based on existing practices, to teach the Gospel, and he comments that the Indians hold the writings themselves in such veneration that "they scruple to throw them into the fire. When they are torn or spoiled, they bring the fragments to me. They are more religious, a hundred-fold, than the Iconoclasts, who, through a sacrilegious impurity, broke the most sacred images."[76] When a young woman throws the letters into the fire, Le Clercq uses the opportunity to reinforce the Indians' beliefs. He rescues some ashes from the fire, pretends to be upset, and says she has offended Jesus. In other words, he plays upon their belief that there is "some enchantment or jugglery" in the letters themselves, rather than drawing any clear line between magic and worship.

The issue of the cross is taken up by Father Joseph-François Lafitau, whom we have already encountered as a source for de Brosses, in his *Mœurs des sauvages ameriquains, comparées aux mœurs des premiers temps*. Like Le Clercq, Lafitau worked as missionary to Indians in New France, specifically the Mohawk at Kahnawake, and drew upon firsthand observations. As the title of his book indicates, though, he has a much larger agenda than Le Clercq, and his book needs to be seen in the context of a number of other works that were drawing a comparative net across ancient and modern practices and beliefs.[77] The Mi'kmaq cross would fit in with his book's larger scheme of showing common elements in ancient and modern American societies, but on quite careful scholarly grounds he finally rejects Le Clercq's claim that in this particular case it preceded Christian preaching and he sees it as more likely the vestigial result of earlier missionary contact. The early existence of the cross elsewhere cannot entirely be accounted for in this way, though, and he invokes a range of authorities, including the Inca Garcilaso, to show the presence of the symbol of the cross in the Americas, Egypt, Greece, and elsewhere in the ancient world.[78] It existed there, and he follows Le Clercq's parallel of "the rainbow, which God in olden times displayed across the face of all the universe,"[79] as a sign of the presence of God, if it could only be interpreted as such.

This matters because Lafitau's main concern is not only to show the similarities between ancient and contemporary American beliefs and customs beneath the surface differences, but to demonstrate that they are all a falling away from an initial unity of revelation. If the connections are not always so clear, this is because the Indians have been losing their original beliefs under European influences. So, whereas the comparativists of the later nineteenth century were finding similarities based on underlying patterns, Lafitau and others were seeing these similarities as themselves only remnants of an initial common revelation. To them this was the evidence that the Christian God preceded all others and that all men and women originally had the opportunity to embrace the faith but had fallen away from it.

These different alternatives all have implications for the translatability of the Christian faith and its key concepts. In one instance Louis Hennepin does get closer to exploring just what it would mean to worship or ascribe power to objects. " 'Tis a lamentable thing to consider what wild Chimaera's [sic] the Devil puts in these People's heads. Tho' they believe that the Soul is Corporeal (for they understand nothing else by their *Otkon, Atahanta*, or *Manitou*, but some material principal Being, that gives life and motion to all things) nevertheless they profess their Belief of the Immortality of the Soul, and a Life to come, in which they shall enjoy all sorts of pleasure."[80]

It is hard to see how his description of manitou here is of a being that is any more material than the Christian God. Both could be said to have material efficacy in giving "life and motion" to material things, but he insists that manitou is only material. What perhaps fundamentally worries him is not that it is material but that if we accept it is also spiritual, then all sorts of trivial and ordinary things might also be seen as having a magical or spiritual dimension. The Indians "think all sensible things have Souls, therefore they reckon that after Death men hunt the Souls of Beavers, Elks."[81] Later commentators might well describe this as a world imbued with spirit, but Hennepin's fundamental assumption is that the Christian view of the relation of spirit to matter is the only valid one, which means that he has to categorize the Indian view as reducing everything to the material, leading to the idolatrous worship of objects. (This is presumably why the editors of the 1906 English translation of Hennepin's book group such practices in their index under the anachronistic and rather surprising category of "fetichism.")

In trying to compare Christian worship to the various Native American expressions of reciprocal relations among animals, spirits and humans, the terms available to Christian missionaries were not helpful. Idolatry was the only alternative to true worship, but it was already too complex and confusing a category to be useful. Was it worshipping false gods that was wrong, or was it the use of objects and images—in other words the material rather than spiritual? In this second definition there is a concern about the use of images and objects, more absolutely condemned among the Protestants but equally of concern to the Catholics, who used religious objects and images as aids and intermediaries, but needed to prevent the actual worship of them. Bishop Baraga's *Dictionary of the Otchipwe Language*, of 1878 translates *manito* as spirit or ghost, and *manitoke* as "I practice idolatry" and "I worship idols,"[82] but already by the time of this entry the use of idolatry as a catch-all category had largely given way, in religious and anthropological academic circles, to interest in the exact nature of other beliefs and the psychology of them. If there is no clear distinction between the world of matter and spirit, with each object having a way of being that is similar to that of people (possessing an identity that is not exhausted by its physical appearance and properties), then it is not so much a question of worship, which implies a subjection and a hierarchical relation, as a reciprocal relationship between two beings of the same sort. Mary Black has usefully identified and described the Ojibwa category of "living things," which includes not only humans, animals, and plants, but also spirits, and in this definition the category of spirit extended to winds, shells, and stones as well as culture heroes and forest spirits. This is what was being described as *manito*, for which she coins the term "power-control," which she argues is preferable to "spirit" in avoiding a misleading relegation of the material world.[83]

The debate in anthropological circles over terms to describe magical or spiritual power also shaded off into the popular periodical literature, as I will show in the next chapter, and some figures happily straddled both camps. Frank Cushing's adventures and his initiation into Zuni society and religious societies were dramatically recounted in the pages of *Century* magazine, and his privileged role as mediator between the Zuni and American society was enacted not only in his own writings, but in his well-publicized trip to New York and other Eastern cities with members of the tribe.[84] While his main ethnographic contribution was perhaps the huge range of objects he acquired for museums, he is also notable in the context of this chapter for a short piece, *Zuni Fetiches*, which appeared in the second *Annual Report of the Bureau of Ethnology* of 1880–81, published in 1883.

His text is a sober and quite detailed account of the small stone figures and their significance, which includes illustrations, translations of relevant myths, and a section on "Zuni philosophy." Cushing places Zuni belief in the animal images in the context of animistic beliefs, and he follows Tylor's formulations, in which normal Western divisions between animate and inanimate, and objective and subjective, are broken down. In a letter of the time he makes the point explicitly: "It is characteristic of savage or Primeval thought that it reversed the Nature we conceive. It insisted on *Subjectivizing* every object, and objectivizing every Subject, and on always personifying [im]personalities."[85] Animals, and especially those at the higher end who, like men, are prey animals, have a special importance and kinship with us, and Cushing associates the Zuni term for these fetishes with the name for "prey gods." His concern to present fetishism as a meaningful system with intellectual credibility is combined uneasily with sensationalism, a mixture characteristic of Cushing, whose respect for Zuni culture went hand in hand with an emphasis on the primitive and on exotic difference, often to enhance his own exotic glamour as privileged and sole interpreter of the Zuni. He ends his account, for instance, by asserting "'As with the Hunter, so with the Warrior, the fetich is fed on the life-blood of the slain." Cushing was never averse to this sort of melodramatic flourish, which also underlined the drama of his insider status as a member of the Bow clan, but he is also drawing on the widespread associations at the time of fetishism with blood and savagery.

Apart from these sensational flourishes, Cushing's use of the term "fetish," or "fetich" as he spells it, is positive, and quite consonant with the other terms more commonly preferred at the time. A rare parallel use of the term in an Indian context, perhaps influenced by Cushing's use of the term, is to be found in Charles Lummis's reference to war gods as "tiny fetiches which were rather *worn* than carved to shape, and a few larger but very crude fetiches of softer rock." He contrasts these with some life-size relief carvings, which are "the homotypes of the chase-gods of wandering Cochiti," and constitute "a life-size fetich."[86] Elsewhere by this date the word was consistently being used more negatively, and later ethnographic accounts of Zuni religion have shifted away from the term because of its discredited associations,[87] though as I shall show in Chapter 5 the term survives in one significant context in connection with the Zuni.

By the end of the nineteenth century, then, there was a growing agreement that there existed a belief in an underlying spirit that was common to Indian religions and that elevated them above others, but there was no consensus about a term to describe this common entity. One quite explicit but ultimately unsuccessful attempt to establish a term was made by the Tuscarora anthropologist J. N. B. Hewitt. In an article in 1902 he makes the case for the concept *orenda* to be adopted as a common denominator of all religions. What he calls the "inchoate mentation of primitive man" recognized a "mystic potence" which underlay all phenomena. He argues that the English language has no word to express this (magic being too restricted to mechanical efficacy rather than immanent power), and, having listed a range of other possibilities like *wakan* and *manitowi*, he proposes the Iroquoian *orenda*. The use of the term "precipitates, so to speak, what before has been held in solution" and defines it as "a hypothetic potence or potentiality to do or effect results mystically."[88] He refers to the long journey from "the monody of savagery to the multitoned oratorio of enlightenment" and seems to be arguing that *orenda* is the essence of religion itself, which the higher religions had then distilled.

In his entry on *orenda* in the authoritative *Handbook of American Indians North of Mexico* in 1910, Hewitt defines it as "the fictive force, principle or magic power which was assumed by the inchoate reasoning of primitive man to be inherent in every being and body of nature."[89] Comparing it with other terms like *manito* (to which he gives an entry only one quarter of the length), he reinforces his bid to see *orenda* as the master term. He rejects other simpler translations, arguing that those who use such terms as "mystery," "magic," "sorcery," or "wonderful" "fail to appreciate the true nature and functions of the assumed power denoted by these terms." This could be seen as a rebuttal of Boas's entry under "Religion" in the same volume, where Boas identifies "belief in the existence of magic power" as the fundamental element. In his view, terms like *orenda* express the idea of "a power inherent in the objects of nature," but this idea already "seems adequately expressed by our term 'wonderful'; and it is hardly necessary to introduce an Indian term, as has often been attempted."[90]

Apart from Hewitt, though, the focus for discussions of the transcendence of Indian religion increasingly switched to the Plains Indians, and particularly to the Sioux.[91] The preeminence of Plains Indian religion as a model of Indian spirituality was and remains partly a byproduct of their general adoption as a pan-Indian symbol by whites, but it has been supplemented in the twentieth century by Black Elk's account of traditional religion as found in the versions by John Neihardt and Joseph Epes Brown, and the many responses to it.[92] This will be taken up in the final chapter, where I deal with the contemporary ramifications of this elevation of spirituality, but it is time now to return to the question of the larger racial context for this elevating of Native American spirituality and in particular to relate it to the complementary representation of African American beliefs.

While a great deal of effort was expended to explain the connections between Indian and Christian beliefs, even extending eventually to seeing them both as religions, no such attention was paid to African or African American beliefs.

The dismissal of African beliefs ensured that what African Americans believed would be seen in the same way, if it was noticed at all. As a documentary record of the actual practices and beliefs of Africans and African Americans, the early Christian missionary accounts are not nearly as useful as, for instance, the *Jesuit Relations* are as evidence of Indian practices. This is perhaps because of the idea that Africans were blanks to be written on, or because anything other than full Christianity was dismissed as wholly meretricious and not worth discussion. It is as if the textual form (self-advertising accounts of success and conversion) and the requirements of Christian orthodoxy together bleach out the details of what is actually being encountered, so that the only thing that can be registered is paganism or full Christianity, and the same characterization of African religion came from abolitionists, who otherwise looked favorably on the capacities for development of the Negro in America. For instance, in *The Octoroon*, an antislavery novel that has scenes in Liberia, some American visitors are introduced to an example of a newly Christianized African. When he is asked what he worshiped before he was converted, he gives a stock response. "Ballasada then fear devil, no care for God, hab fetish, leetle grasshopper on pole, beat tom tom, scare away devil, feed sassawood, eat enemy, make beads and spike for nose and ears, from bones."[93] Here, then, in what we might expect to be a pro-Negro account, we have all the ingredients of savagery rehearsed in almost cartoon form in order to underline the need for the colonization program, which was seen as an answer both to the need for conversion in Africa and the problem of what to do with freed slaves in America. It is interesting, in fact, to see in the American Colonization Society writings themselves how completely the firm lines of Christianity seem to insulate the African American missionaries from making any more connection with the indigenous beliefs than their white colleagues do. This is in sharp contrast to the sort of racial connections and kinship celebrated in the work of the later African American novelists and artists, whom I discuss in later chapters.

In his *A Lecture on African Civilization, Including a Brief Outline of the Social and Moral Condition of Africa and the Relation of American Slaves to African Civilization*, David Christy gives long accounts of fetishism, the use of gris-gris, and human sacrifice, and these are designed to underline the need for missionaries, a role for which, he argues, educated American Negroes are particularly suited.[94] Christy was an agent of the American Colonization Society, and the phrase 'African civilization' in his title refers, of course, to a task still to be achieved, rather than a description of the past or present. There is no mention of any sort of positive cultural continuity carrying over from Africa to the Americas. Where such links can be seen, as in the West Indies, they are cited as examples of what sort of backsliding can happen without full missionary vigilance. To this extent, the African American churches also subscribed to the idea of Africans as the spiritual tabula rasa on which the Christian civilization was to be written. As well as being sent to Africa, missionaries were also used to spread the word at home, but there are few instances of these on-message Christians ever noting any syncretic practices among slaves.[95]

The prevailing view was that what had traveled to America was not a religion so much as a set of superstitious practices, which, in their indiscriminate use of whatever was at hand, seemed to exemplify the concern for the impure and the low. The only time African Americans were recognized specifically as having spiritual capacities was when associated with Christianity, as in the so-called Negro spirituals, a topic I deal with in the next chapter. What was categorically not spiritual or acceptable were the folk practices of conjure, hoodoo, or root-work, and it is the persistence of these practices, and their significance to practi-tioners and to observers both white and black, that will be my point of focus in the rest of this chapter. Having been dismissed or overlooked, they have now be-come regularly invoked and used by contemporary artists as well as historians. This is related to a renewed concern to fully recognize African continuities, as well as a methodological openness to questions of syncretism and hybridity, and a wider conception from theologians of what actually constitutes religion.

In early accounts, though, African American magico-religious practices were associated with African rites and superstitions and were dismissed as re-grettable survivals if they were noticed at all. African elements were normally seen as "backward," and even as proof of the inability of African Americans to develop or progress, and one of the effects of this was that little attention was paid to them, or to any changes or American adaptations that might have been taking place. Early observers, influenced by the sorts of assumptions out-lined above, could misinterpret what they saw. Mechal Sobel has pointed out, for instance, that early writers mention Indian knowledge of snakes, and the use of them in folk practices, but ignore African uses. She argues that "Whites were not willing to give any 'credit' to blacks in terms of ideas or values, but they were sharing them nevertheless."[96] Much of the early collection of folk-lore can be seen in this racist context, as I will show in the next chapter, and this sort of attitude prevented serious consideration of these beliefs as a valu-able religious or cultural resource, but recent scholarship on hoodoo and con-jure has allowed a fuller sense of what was actually involved.

The most detailed actual analysis of hoodoo or conjure materials is to be found in Michael Edward Bell's 1980 Ph.D. thesis, "Pattern, Structure, and Logic in Afro-American Hoodoo Performance," which is based largely on Harry Middleton Hyatt's five volumes of material, collected during the second half of the 1930s but not published until the 1970s.[97] Bell's concern is to demonstrate the patterns, structure, and logic underlying the many apparently random conjunctions of materials, actions and beliefs in hoodoo. This involves seeing it synchronically and structurally as a full-fledged African American tra-ditional practice, rather than as fragmentary survivals from Africa. He uses the term "performance assemblage" to describe an aggregation of components that includes not just objects but actions, locations, and times, which will constitute hoodoo performance. This allows for initiative and choice within certain implicit, but understood, patterns. Bell does not mention the close parallels between the magical practices as he describes them here and artistic practices, but the term "assemblage" prompts comparisons with a whole range of artistic as well as magical compositional and performance practices by African American artists, which I will develop in Chapter 4.

Following Bell's focus on system, David Brown has argued that conjure should be seen "as an idiom, an explicit, culturally specific way of thinking and talking about cause, effect, power, and agency, and as a practical, creative process of mobilizing spiritual and material resources to address problems and to effect change."[98] Indeed, he wants to avoid the idea that demonstrating the social issues involved, or presenting them as "social practice" will reveal something more "real" than the conjure as experienced by its practitioners or will productively demystify it. Brown's approach to conjure as a "black discourse" involves him treating the stories of conjure events as "a sub-genre of African American literature,"[99] and recognizing that many accounts of conjure are as significant as retellings and reshapings as they are as empirical evidence. This is not, he would argue, simply to turn everything into textuality or to sidestep the question of whether conjure "works." Indeed, in seeing conjure as an idiom, Brown is at pains not to seem to be reducing conjure entirely to the level of symbolic practices and performances, which have a social function without having to work in any other way. Rather, it is to reconstruct or give full weight to all the elements of the culture in which it is accepted as working. This is partly a question of understanding modes of thinking that operate through metonymic and metaphoric connections (usually known as sympathetic magic), rather than downplaying these or relegating them to those areas of the imagination that have supposedly given way to the linear causality and empiricism of science. In this respect Brown's approach chimes with a wider concern in the social sciences to question the investment in the models of causality and rationality on which they have been based.[100]

The idea that objects and events are given meaning by different forms of assemblage, including retelling, can be related to Grey Gundaker's work on vernacular signs, which traces a tradition of "reading" that is distinct from conventional ideas of literacy but possesses huge cultural significance. Gundaker argues that the wide range of African American signs she has noted can be and are meant to be "read" in complex ways, and she talks about "double vision" (being "four-eyed") and the ability to see "across the boundary between material and spiritual worlds."[101] In the Eurocentric narrative of the development toward literacy, there is an assumption that the movement is towards transparency and away from ambiguity, but Gundaker raises the idea that there is a vernacular tradition of prizing the doubleness, so that someone who assembles objects sees them as signs that can be read, but not unambiguously. Like hieroglyphs, they can be read "through."[102]

All these approaches provide ways of counteracting the older dismissive treatments by taking hoodoo and conjure seriously as interpretive and creative acts within a complex tradition of such acts. Another aspect of this rehabilitation has been the undermining of the clear distinctions between the spirituality recognized and celebrated in black Christianity (most iconically in the Negro spirituals), and the supposed magic and materialism of conjure, seen as a continuation of fetishism. Writing from a Christian point of view, Theophus Smith is concerned, in his significantly named *Conjuring Culture*, to give full weight to a distinctively African American orientation in the uses and adaptations of the Bible and Christianity. His stress on the idea of conjure is designed to deny any simple oppositions of Christian and pagan, or religious and magical, or even sacred and secular. Related to this is a rejection of other distinctions often made between different aspects of African American culture, which he sees as exemplified by the common distinction between blues as secular and spirituals as religious. Instead he follows Lerone Bennett in seeing them as "contradictory, and yet complementary strains" that need to be held together in the mind in order to understand African American traditions, as well as the relation between blues and spirituals.[103] Increasingly, the inclusiveness of an African view of spirituality is stressed, together with the syncretic nature of African American religion, so that the secular or magical elements such as conjure are now seen as being, in David Brown's words, in a relation of "horizontal complementarity" to Christianity within "the plural Afro-American religious experience."[104]

Yvonne Chireau, in her important full-length study of conjure, argues that the African cosmologies, even as they became eroded, "still provided the philosophical basis by which new beliefs could be assimilated." The continuity that was established included "an emphasis on ritual efficacy, the appropriation of invisible powers, and ceremonial spirituality."[105] She identifies as an African characteristic the idea that power can be focused and localized in an object but only briefly makes the connection with the way these African beliefs led to the false characterization of fetishism—as worship of objects themselves. She does usefully point to "the emphasis on materiality," though, and she sees this carrying over into black American supernatural traditions.[106] I want to hold on to this materiality by keeping the focus on the objects of conjure and their material efficacy, rather than having them prematurely subsumed as spiritual within a larger Christian orientation, or read as symbolic rather than material practice. Like the fetish, and like magic in the older taxonomies, conjure and hoodoo keep materiality uncomfortably to the fore.

If, as I have been arguing, the terms of difference that marked off Africans and African Americans and their beliefs revolved around an unredeemed materiality, it is, of course, also true that around their physical material bodies revolved the whole edifice of slavery, and the way that the black body remained a fetishized site of white desire and denial has increasingly been discussed. As

Rachel Harding argues, it was after all the American experience that made the African body a contested site, and to that extent slaves could be said to stress the material as the only thing they had.[107] This approach puts the emphasis not on yearning and transcendence, which was the comforting image created by hearing the Negro spirituals as the definitive expression of black subjectivity, but on the physical realm that was the ultimate resource available for slaves to help themselves. Conjure's concern with efficacy and materiality could then be seen as representing an important pragmatic strand that was complementary to the transcendent and utopian dimensions of religion. My intention, though, is to work with the instability and undecidability of this relation of religion and magic, or transcendence and pragmatism, rather than see them as in opposition, or as seamlessly blended. This idea of a complex and shifting mixture seems closer to the orientation of African American cultural expression, whether found in the blues or in the very different works of Zora Neale Hurston, Renée Stout, and Nathaniel Mackey, explored in later chapters.

One particular aspect of conjure's role in early African American life is its relation, whether physical or psychological, to slave resistance. Did the "superstition" and belief in magic operate as a source of resistance, or as a distraction from the real struggle? Its main importance has often been seen as located within the slave community itself, where the power of the conjure practitioners was accepted, and where it operated within a coherent set of beliefs that ensured psychological and cultural survival. Eugene Genovese interpreted this as "a tactical withdrawal into a black world that offered joys, fears, and a sense of existence as a people apart; but it presented no direct threat to the regime for its survival rested precisely on acceptance of the existing relationship of forces." Ultimately Genovese did not regard the conjure practitioners as matching the Christian preachers as "a force for cohesion, moral guidance, and cultural growth."[108] Another way of putting this would be that conjure's misplaced stress on efficacy prevented it from having the larger utopian or oppositional dimension that black Christianity in its many forms achieved, but there seems also in Genovese's accounts to be an implicit assumption that conjure, as a lower religious form, is inferior to Christianity. In any case, Genovese seems to assume a sort of separation of realms, in which charms and spells were only thought to work on African Americans, whereas the belief in their efficacy may in fact have been more widespread and more ambiguous.

Probably the most discussed instance of conjure's role in resistance is to be found in Frederick Douglass's various versions of his autobiography. He recounts how, at the crucial moment when he was able to summon up the power and sense of self to confront the slave breaker Covey, he had in his possession a root given to him by another slave for protection. The way in which Douglass describes the root and its effect seems ambivalent, and the changes in the different versions of his autobiographies are instructive. In the first version, he tells us that when offered the root by his friend Sandy, "I at first rejected the idea, that the simple carrying of a root in my pocket would have any such effect [protection from whipping]" and he only takes it "to please him." He then meets Covey, who does not ill-treat him, but Douglass assumes this is because it is Sunday, and Covey is on his best behavior. On Monday, though, "the virtue of the *root* was fully tested." Beaten to the ground by Covey, Douglass turns. "At this moment—from whence came the spirit I don't know—I resolved to fight."[109] There is no further reference to the root, or judgment on its "virtue."

In the later version there is a slight expansion. Sandy is described as "an old adviser. He was not only a religious man, but he professed to believe in a system for which I have no name. He was a genuine African, and had inherited some of the so-called magical powers, said to be possessed by African and eastern nations."[110] There is also in this account more of a sense of Douglass's initial skepticism. Talk of the root was "to me, very absurd and ridiculous, if not positively sinful. . . . I had a positive aversion to all pretenders to '*divination*.' It was beneath my intelligence to countenance such dealings with the devil." Persuaded by Sandy, he accepts, with the thought "how did I know but that the hand of the Lord was in it?" The language in this second version has a more Christian inflection in setting up an opposition between black magic and Christianity, but he then inverts the terms. Sunday is again referred to as the time when Christian codes rule over Covey, but on Monday Covey attacks Douglass, and Douglass ponders in the text "whether the root had lost its virtue, or whether the tormenter had gone deeper into the black art than myself (as was sometimes said of him)."[111]

Douglass is clearer in this version about his rejection of "the slave's religious creed," which enjoined obedience to the master, following his own illtreatment, and it is perhaps this rejection that lies behind the rather strange phrase he uses at the point when he stands up to Covey. "I now forgot my *roots*, and remembered my pledge to *stand up in my own defense*." Roots may here refer here to the magical object, or since Alex Haley we might even be tempted to see this as a reference to African religious practices as a resource, but it may also carry some sense of his past Christian indoctrination of servility. What it clearly does emphasize is the free act of will, the existential moment at which he defines himself as a man and not an object created by his past.[112]

Ultimately, Douglass may be ambivalent about the root's power, but in a narrative notably short on expressions of religious sentiment, its inclusion in itself is telling and can be related to other evidence of the use of magical power as a slave resource scattered throughout contemporary accounts. Renewed attention to these has been an aspect of the increased valuation of African continuities. The insurrections of Gabriel Prosser, Denmark Vesey, and Nat Turner all involved supernatural inspiration or help at some points, though this is quite varied. Walter Rucker, for instance, in his detailed study of African enclaves in America and their importance in shaping black resistance, argues that the role of blacksmiths in Prosser's rebellion needs to be seen in the context of "technospiritual" forces associated with Ogun.[113] Turner's visionary impulses are well known, as is the key role in Denmark Vesey's conspiracy of Gullah Jack. He was identified in contemporary reports as a sorcerer, necromancer, and Voodoo, though, as Chireau points out, never as an African Christian, even though he was practicing a syncretic blend of African and Christian religion.[114]

Such use of magic or superstition as a site of possible resistance to white authority was the antithesis of the elevated and unthreatening spirituality of the African American Christianity expressed in spirituals. It was also distinguished, though, from Indian religious practices, even though the actual use and meaning of material objects like medicine bundles may have been comparable in many ways to conjure bags. This reflects my general argument in this chapter that while African American practices were only recognized as superstition and magic, Indian practices were progressively elevated above this into the realms of spirituality. In this way the particular racial configurations of power, and the very different economic and material roles of Indians and African Americans, shaped the larger debates taking place over belief and religion around terms like fetishism. Ensuing chapters will develop these ideas and their implications, first amplifying the materials of this introductory chapter through an examination of late nineteenth-century approaches to belief and superstition and their relation to race, and then moving on to twentieth-century expressions and explorations of the relations of the material and spiritual in literature, music, and visual arts.

Chapter 2
Superstition and Progress

In Chapter 1 I outlined how questions about materiality and spirit were re-hearsed in racialized terms in debates over fetishism, and various forms of an-imist belief. By the last decades of the nineteenth century different ways of categorizing these beliefs were emerging, with James Frazer's tripartite division of magic, religion, and science reflecting a diverse but widespread set of evo-lutionary and hierarchical assumptions. One of the most interesting things about these debates is the way in which there was a constant return, as a point of reference, to the state of mind that "we" (the educated white writers) were supposed to have moved beyond. Though dismissed as a relic or remnant, this state of primitive belief or superstition was seen to persist and to haunt the new systems of thought as a ghost or revenant. As a result we find a pattern of alternating recognition and denial of these irrational areas. In this chapter I want to trace this pattern as I explore some of the ways in which race inflected the representation of forms of belief in the later nineteenth century. I will do this by first looking at the intersections of ideas about science and the occult, and then moving to the discussions of superstition and magic found in a range of scientific and popular publications. Finally I will relate this to the emerging discipline of folklore, and the activities of white collectors, including Joel Chandler Harris, before moving to the work of African American writers Pauline Hopkins and Charles Chesnutt.

One strong current in American thought in the nineteenth century was a developing confidence in science and in rational thought. These were regarded as mainstays of the civilized society that white America saw as its contribution to the world, as well as the justification for its authority over its subject popu-lations of Indians and African Americans. During the century the potentially conflicting claims of Christianity and scientific rationality were uneasily recon-ciled, and the massive potential for conflict between reason and faith, between science and organized religion, was eventually held at bay by means of a po-lite separation of powers. Organized religion had always been concerned to dissociate itself from magic and to distinguish prayer from magic spells. Prayer's role was not to demonstrate its everyday efficacy or to challenge or af-fect the mechanical laws of cause and effect, but to direct attention to the un-derlying or transcendent realm of spirit, which could coexist with science. But this left a whole range of practices and beliefs—the areas dismissed as magic, or superstition, which did not simply disappear. Here such a division between spirit and matter was not so clear, and spirit seemed to be acting upon or within matter.

One problem for the church has always been that the actual practices and beliefs of common people, inside as well as outside the official Christian belief, have included magic and superstition. As well as just folk practices, though, which could be dismissed as vestigial, the new "sciences" of mesmerism, spiritualism, and related occult pursuits threw into question again the relation between spirit and matter. Science based its arguments on causal links that could be physically demonstrated. The idea of connections that could not be physically shown through a model of material cause and effect (for instance, with sympathetic magic, which operates through relations of similarity or contiguity) was inimical to it. Yet if we look more closely at the way material causality was described, we are often returned to some rather mystical thinking, and it can be argued that many of the scientific beliefs were in fact close to occult in that they found it necessary to posit a cause that they could not show to be material. Peter Pels has shown, for instance, how the idea of race as a determinant of behavior operated in the same way as an occult force. Race and the occult, as what now would be seen as pseudoscience, were both apparent causes that could not actually be physically pinned down. The unsubstantiated belief in the role of the Aryan race in the "spiritual determination of historical evolution" was similar to occultism, and Pels sees them as inalienable parts of anthropology's development and its contribution to modernity, even if they are now consigned to the area of the popular.[1]

The idea of race as an essence, as opposed to a set of different characteristics spread among human beings on various spectra of biological markers, was nowhere more ideologically significant than in America, where fixed racial traits were insisted on as determining causes without evidence. In other words, race was operating as an occult cause in that it could not be causally demonstrated, and as the claims became more "scientific," they also paradoxically became more dependent on an occult (because not materially demonstrable) cause. John Kerkering quotes a doctor writing in a medical journal in 1886, trying to understand the particular immunities and weaknesses that he finds in Negroes, and that he describes as the "medical mystery of the negro race." After dismissing environmental causes, he looks for "an undiscovered something still behind all this silently working."[2] Disease is claimed to come from a predisposition to believe in voodoo and occult causes, but if whites assume this is a racially inherent characteristic, then they are themselves ironically subscribing to an occult cause and are implicated in the process they dismiss as primitive. Kerkering argues that the idea of voodoo and possession offered doctors a "general logic, explaining how anyone, whether white or black, could have a racial inheritance. . . . In effect, if one's racial past asserts itself as a remote agency producing local bodily effects, effects ranging from disease immunity to an inclination to practice certain religious rites, then the influence to which one is subject is the race to which one belongs. Much as one may resist, this agency will have its way, and such a condition of subjection to a remote force amounts to a form of possession, something voodoo readily explains."[3]

Kerkering deals mainly with white beliefs, and I will be looking later at other aspects of these, but the idea of the occult and its relation to race, and an "undiscovered something" was also used for more positive purposes by some African American writers. This was sometimes linked to ideas of African origins, but the idea of race as a hidden and mysterious force could also be used to powerful effect to deal with areas of miscegenation and the denial of fixed racial identity, as I will show later in the chapter. What I want to outline here first, though, are some of the ways in which other problematic areas where spirit and matter interact were also implicated in issues of race. Susan Gillman has written of "the persistent entangling of familiar US racial discourses with another, more shadowy zone, less well-known but equally disreputable, defined by a range of transnational cultural phenomena that we might colloquially, and loosely, call *occultist*."[4]

The American interest in mesmerism and spirit rapping often went along with assumptions about Indian spirituality and sometimes also coincided with abolitionist interests. Not only were the spirits or mediums often identified as Indians,[5] but the concern for a transcendent freedom from material limits was often fairly glibly associated with the slaves' desire for freedom in what Russ Castronovo has described as a "depoliticizing overlap between abolition and the occult, between liberal concern for black bodies and popular interest in white souls."[6] An example of this can be found in the work of Nathan Francis White, who was a spirit rapper, and whose book *Voices from Spirit-land* tells us that "In so far as he has been made aware, he was first impressed by the spirit of an Indian chief—Powhattan." Under the Indian's influence, White is able "to speak in the presence of and with living 'Red Men' in the Indian tongue, and to manifest all the peculiarities of the Indian in a surprising manner."[7] The book is dedicated to friends of truth and spiritual freedom, "without which all other freedom is as a shadow," and in a long celebratory poem called "American Freedom," he ends with an indictment of slavery, linking together different forms of freedom, notably freedom from physical bondage, with the mind's freedom from the limits of the body.

Ye who have felt
Its biting chain rust deep into your hearts
Shake off your lethargy! Take Freedom's part,
And boldly strike against the tyrant might
Which would deprive you of your manly right.
Leave not one hateful damning link to bind
The Body or its rightful monarch, Mind.[8]

The invocation of Indian spirituality can also be found in the work of the African American Paschal Beverley Randolph. Best known as a prophet of a sort of sexual mysticism, and later associated with Madam Blavatsky, he also wrote some quite revealing fiction. Though he is identified on the title page of one of his books as "The American Dumas," in his fiction itself, African racial origins are rather played down in favor of others. In his introduction to *The Wonderful Story of Ravalette*, he is scathing about most spiritualist claims, but he insists that even if the majority of practitioners are charlatans, "spiritualism is yet the great *non sequitur* of the age, so far as the vast majority of mankind is concerned," and points to something crucial.[9] The main character's mother seems to be "a Mississippi octoroon," but he has a vision that links him to a mystical or ancient past that seems to be located in the East. He himself is described as having a complexion that is "tawny, resembling that of the Arab children of Beyroot and Damascus." Wide cheekbones and lack of facial hair betray his "aboriginal ancestry." Elsewhere, we are told that "his complexion told that he was a *sang melée*—not a direct cross—but one in which at least seven distinct strains of blood intermingled, if they did not perfectly blend."[10] His mother "claimed immediate kindred with the red-skinned sons of the northern wilderness, but that blood in her veins mingled with the finer current derived from her ancestor, the Cid—a strain of royal blood." Unhappy in marriage she aspires to spiritual things, becomes "a seeress, a dreamer," and finds comfort in "that mysterious balm of healing, which the red man in his religion—or superstition, if you will—believes can only thus and there be had." She tries to connect her heart and feelings with what she takes as "the low whisperings of the aerial dwellers of the viewless kingdom of MANATOU."[11] Race seems to be an operative factor here, in that Ravalette's racial heritage seems to make him open to visions of his own spiritual identity, but the African element, which is presumably part of the "*sang melée*," and which under American convention and law would be the definitive element, is elided and made generally Eastern.

As the nineteenth century went on, theories of race, interlocking with the political realities of slavery and its aftermath, created new ways in which Indians and African Americans were separately categorized, but they remained in implicit relation to each other, even if this was not always evident. The hierarchy of races affirmed by scientific racism was accompanied by the belief that the products of the mixing of races, both human and cultural, were undesirable and degenerate.

The intersections of ideas of race with the larger exploration of the place of belief in what was seen as an increasingly materialist and rational society can be found in explicit discussions, but also in various absences and displacements. One of the set pieces in which American society celebrated its achievements and placed itself in relation both to the past and to the rest of the world was the World's Columbian Exposition of 1893 in Chicago. While the contrast between the high idealism represented by the White City and the popular and promiscuous mingling of cultures and peoples of the Midway has been widely examined and discussed ever since the event itself, what is still worth looking at is the role of religion and folklore, especially in some of the ancillary activities generated by the exposition. A novel of the time is remarkably explicit about this. One character in *Sweet Clover: A Romance of the White City* describes the Midway as "just a representation of matter" and the white City as "an emblem of mind." "In the Midway it's some dirty and all barbaric. . . . and when you come out o' that mile-long babel where you've been elbowed and cheated, you pass under a bridge—and all of a sudden you are in a great beautiful silence. The angels on the Women's Buildin' smile down and bless you, and you know that in what seemed like one step, you've passed out o' darkness into light."[12]

Another novel also saw the exhibits through a "folk" lens, and its view of the religious exhibits is interesting. The fictional narrator of *Samantha at the World's Fair*, a woman visiting from the country, describes the ethnographic collections merely as ugly idols, but comments that "If the secret things that folk worship today could be materialized, they would look enough sight worse than this. . . . What would the mammon of greed look carved in stun [stone], or the beast of Intemperance?"[13] Marx would presumably say that they were indeed materialized as commodities in the consumer objects of the American city as well as the Midway.

At the 1893 World's Parliament of Religions, held in Chicago to complement the inclusive and celebratory impulses of the exposition, the representation of different races was revealing. Though it proclaimed its worldwide scope and inclusiveness, the parliament's idea of what constituted a religion effectively limited the participants to representatives of the "higher" religions, and there was a pervasive assumption that human evolution was about what Julia Howe called "an evolving of a God out of the material man."[14] Judaism, Islam, Buddhism, and Hinduism had their own representatives, while African religions were completely ignored, and those African Americans who were present were representing Christian churches. Native Americans did not apparently merit a full presence, but there was an account of Indian religion in a presentation by the ethnographer Alice Fletcher, which perhaps suggests their intermediate status at that time in the scale of religions. Here, and in her writings on Omaha Indian music, Fletcher was concerned to stress the common spiritual yearnings, which could take different expressive forms. This expression of a common comparativist viewpoint justified and validated what was different by demonstrating what it had in common with the ruling culture, and this also corresponded to the assimilationist defense of Indians, which argued that they were savable only insofar as they could be made to fit into white society. Fletcher's concern to validate and preserve the *cultural* forms went together with a firm conviction that the Indian way of life was doomed and that assimilation was the only humane way forward. Her support for the allotment of Indian land thus went hand in hand with her acquisition of ceremonial objects for museums, though she did come to have doubts about the reform movement and its assumptions.[15]

The almost total exclusion of African Americans from any of the exhibits, and the protests of Frederick Douglass and others, is well documented, but what is perhaps less well known are the actions of the Potawatomi Indian Simon Pokagan in trying to organize an Indian congress, and distributing to visitors to the fair a birch-bark scroll version of a letter explaining the grievances of contemporary Indians, as a response to the exclusion of such problems in the Indian exhibits organized by museum curators. Partly as a response, Pokagan was later invited back by the mayor of Chicago to attend a ceremony.

It is significant that it is only at the International Folklore Congress of the World's Columbian Exposition in 1893 that those elements excluded from consideration as religion were more fully represented, with talks on voodoo, comparative Afro-American folklore, and Indian mythology. The contribution of Charles Eastman, though titled "Sioux Mythology," could well have been meant for a conference on religion in that it is a serious attempt to defend Indian religion as a "higher" religion. "The tendency of the uncivilised and untutored mind is to recognize the Deity through some definite *medium*," but he argued that this should not obscure the fact that the Sioux did worship one Great Spirit, in their case Wakan Tanka.[16] Even in the case of an object like the medicine man's pouch, which might be considered as an idol it was only as an intermediary of the Great Spirit that it was seen as having power.

While Eastman was concerned here only to present the most sympathetic view of Indians, Simon Pokagan also made links to the beliefs of white Americans, while defending Potawatomi beliefs against charges of idolatry. In an article of the same year, titled "Indian Superstitions and Legends," he made the same defense as Eastman and stressed the worship of nature, arguing that "their 'religion' taught them that each mountain, stream, and lake had its spirit." He also deliberately titled a section describing the tent-shaking ceremony "Indian Spiritualism" in order to underline its similarities to the spirit rapping and séances of white society. More explicitly, he compared Indian and white superstition. He had earlier thought that belief in superstition was a sign of inferiority, he tells us, but after seeing the pervasiveness of superstition among "the dominant race," he realizes that such simple belief, far from undermining higher beliefs can be seen as part of a continuum, in that it "most emphatically declares that man is spiritual and immortal."[17] Just as a little girl's love of her doll is a sign of her capacity for a larger maternal instinct, so superstitions indicate our larger religious capacities. In his conclusion he rather strangely moves into a third-person form of address ("permit Pokagan to say. . . ." "Pokagan does not wish"), perhaps as an act of formal politeness, or to take on the mantle of wise Indian, as he makes a remarkable move. Skillfully putting the dominant society on the back foot, he argues that to persist in thinking that other people believe in objects is itself an irrational belief. "As reasonable beings, without prejudice, we cannot for a moment believe that heathens who bow down to idols, or savages who trust in totums [*sic*], or the civilized who have faith in mascots, believe that there is any power in the object itself, but simply that there is somehow or other, a spiritual intelligence connected with it." Here the "we" includes himself as a rational being, and in insisting not only on a continuum of belief and on the similarity of Indians and whites, but on the perverseness of insisting otherwise against the evidence, Pokagan is in fact identifying what I have been arguing is a persistent pattern in which the idea of object worship has to be raised and ascribed to others, even if it is then discarded. This is surely a fetishistic act in the Freudian sense, in which fetishism in its older anthropological sense is both asserted and denied.

Pokagan is here highlighting a problem. Any attempt to make forms of belief correspond to a linear temporal framework of progress, which also corresponds conveniently to a hierarchy of race, is immediately undercut by the presence of "lower" beliefs persisting alongside the higher, even in white society. Even Frazer, whose grand scheme of the progress from pattern through religion to reason was so influential, recognized the persistence of the irrational. "The smooth surface of cultured society is capped and mined by superstition. Only those whose studies have led them to investigate the subject are aware of the depth to which the ground beneath our feet is thus, as it were, honeycombed by unseen forces. We appear to be standing on a volcano which may at any moment break out in smoke and fire to spread ruin and devastation among the gardens and places of ancient culture."[18] While commentators often suggested that the problem was in the lower or uneducated classes, or just a remnant to be swept away,[19] Frazer's description does not allow this sort of separation and thus presents a much more dynamic model of the individual and communal mind, and the parallels with a Freudian model of the psyche are only too clear.

Interest in popular beliefs and the related topics of psychology, folklore, and religion crops up in a wide range of journals and popular fiction of the late nineteenth century. Most significant may have been the new folklore publications, notably the *Journal of American Folklore*, which was introduced following the foundation of the American Folklore Society in 1888. Weekly and monthly journals including *Popular Science Monthly*, *Atlantic Monthly*, and *Harper's* offered popular science as well as fiction and commentary. Brad Evans, in tracing the changes in concepts of culture, folk and the exotic, points to the importance of the circulation of such ideas in the periodicals, such that "the circulation of something like 'cultures' became a sign of 'Culture' in the late nineteenth century."[20]

Situating herself very cannily within the debate over superstition, and revealing a clear sense of the white journal readers' interest in exotic peoples and beliefs, the Sioux writer Zitkala Ša wrote several pieces in *Atlantic Monthly* and *Harper's Monthly* around the turn of the century that echoed Pokagan's strategies in expressing an Indian identity at odds with white Christian expectations. This is particularly marked in "Why I Am a Pagan," where, in the name of a rather amorphous nature religion, she criticizes a Christianized Indian who tries to convert her. She sees him as "hoodooed" because he has been made to believe in evil spirits and hell, and she takes on in contrast a stance of child-like simplicity. "Still I would not forget that the pale-faced missionary and the hoodooed aborigine are both God's creatures, though small indeed their own conceptions of Infinite Love. A wee child toddling in a wonder world, I prefer to their dogma my excursions into the natural gardens where the voice of the Great Spirit is heard in the twittering of birds, the rippling of mighty waters, and the sweet breathing of flowers."[21] She seems determined in this piece to move beyond any racial specificity, as the effects of universal fellow feeling with nature make racial lines seem no more than the marking out of "a living mosaic of human beings." She then rather strangely uses the metaphor of a keyboard where "men of the same color are like the ivory keys of one instrument where each resembles all the rest, yet varies from them in pitch and quality of voice."[22] What is missing altogether here, of course, are the black notes, and, implicitly, therefore, African Americans, which suggests that like other invocations of melting pots and mosaics this is not a fully inclusive vision. We might be reminded of James Weldon Johnson's use of the two colors of the piano keys in his novel *Autobiography of an Ex-Colored Man*, as well as many later (and clichéd) uses of this metaphor to suggest racial harmony.

The concluding flourish of her essay, "If this is Paganism, then at present, at least, I am a Pagan," is significantly dropped from the version of the piece printed later, in 1921 in her *American Indian Stories*, under the anodyne title "The Great Spirit." Zitkala Ša also adds a sentence expressing her awareness of the "fluttering robe of the Great Spirit," and the phenomenal universe as "a royal mantle, vibrating with His divine breath," apparently reflecting her later Christianity (to which I will return in Chapter 3).[23] Even without these later revisions, it is difficult to know how much such an appeal was a real step toward imagining not just pan-Indian but universal spiritual values, and how much a rather easier sentimental appeal. (The issue will recur in my discussions of Leslie Silko's *Gardens in the Dunes* in Chapter 5.)

In another *Atlantic* essay about her schooling, Zitkala Ša does describe something more specific, but here again her attitude is difficult to pin down.

In the second journey to the East I had not come without some precautions. I had a secret interview with one of our best medicine men, and when I left his wigwam I carried securely in my sleeve a tiny bunch of magic roots. This possession assured me of friends wherever I should go. So absolutely did I believe in its charms that I wore it through all the school routine for more than a year. Then, before I lost my faith in the dead roots, I lost the little buckskin bag containing all my good luck.[24]

The passage creates and sustains a disjunction between her loss of faith in the power of roots and her actual loss of them, so that she never quite denies their power, in a maneuver reminiscent of Frederick Douglass's account, described in the previous chapter.

The concern with other peoples' beliefs and superstitions in magazines and journals also involved some reflexivity. We find, for instance, in an issue of *Harper's Weekly* a conventional short story entitled "The Obi Man," which uses the idea of primitive superstition for sensational effect,[25] but then just a few months later there is a short piece, asking "Is Everybody Superstitious?" This argues that superstition does still persist, even though, if we do throw salt over our shoulder, we now apologize for it. "The act itself was prima facie evidence of a deep-seated superstitious belief, which however the intellect repudiates." The author chooses to insist that "the repudiation is of more significance than the reminiscent act" and can therefore assert our progress toward a rational conviction that "law, not chance, rules the world."[26] In the characteristic pattern I described in the previous chapter, fetishism as a belief in the power of objects is invoked and almost immediately denied, something which is close to the pattern of Freud's fetishism—a pattern of simultaneous belief and denial.

The institutionalization of folklore studies in the later nineteenth century was part of a larger movement to find a distinct cultural space for "lesser races" and their culture in an evolutionary hierarchy, but it also betrayed an ambivalence about the status and value of what was collected in relation to modernity. Jon Cruz has identified a shift in approach from the earlier Transcendentalist and abolitionist sympathy for Negroes and Indians to what he calls an institutionalized ethnosympathy in which "professional folklore . . . aided capitalist modernity by providing a partial map of its own sense of cultural superiority." The mission was to record and preserve, but there were many reasons given for doing this. These ranged from the salvage of apparently disappearing cultures and a scientific desire for taxonomic completeness to a more sympathetic and universalist impulse, which is often expressed through what Cruz describes as "a neoromantic and sentimentalized framework."[27]

He calls this "a new *cultural-interpretive* reservation," and while aware of the Indian resonances of the word reservation, he does not develop them. This is because his own concern is with the Negro spirituals, which I will be dealing with later in this chapter, but it also reflects the difficulties in keeping both Indian and African American materials in the frame at the same time—as if the exclusions of the past continue to dictate the shape of later studies. He exploits the range of meanings within the word ("a form of hesitation" as well as "an enclosing tactic"[28]) to explore the ways in which a concern for certain sorts of approved African American culture, notably the spiritual, closed it off from its social and political dimensions, and he contrasts this with what he sees as different form of partial and exclusionary treatment of Indian materials. The description of aims in the first issue of the *Journal of American Folklore* in 1888 by the editor, William Wells Newell, does identify both Indian and black folklore as appropriate subjects but sounds altogether less comfortable with its African American than with its Indian materials. Whereas American Indian lore is to be "the most promising and important part of the work," that of the American Negroes is important because they "for good or ill" are to form an indissoluble part of the body politic.[29]

Cruz suggests that the main concern was to salvage Indian languages before they disappeared, but this rather underestimates the persistent interest in Indian stories and music. In fact it could be argued, contrary to Cruz, that the main interest in folklore, as opposed to anthropological research, was in myths and beliefs rather than language, and it is here that the importance of the idea of superstition comes into play. True, there was a scientistic and institutionalizing impulse in folklore that overlapped with the methodology of anthropology, but it retained an amateurism in the personnel and methods of its collecting and in its (sometimes rather fey, sometimes powerfully imaginative) indulgence of the world of folklore and fairy tales. What interested so many whites about the world of black folklore seems to be, in varying degrees, an arm's length fascination with the exoticism of magic, the satisfaction of rehearsing the simple and reliable qualities of black people fixed in a premodern stance of protective subservience, and the pleasures of a vernacular form that reassuringly underlined and fixed difference and inferiority. In some of the instances in the later nineteenth century, at points of maximum uneasiness about the status of African Americans post-Reconstruction, it often seems that the recording of an item of Negro superstition or folklore acted not only as a service to science and knowledge but as a rehearsal of its inferiority, a reassuring act of placement.[30] The ways in which Negro "superstition" and "folklore" were described combined, in an uneasy mixture, a genuine interest and sometimes even a respect for the material, with a language that contained and fixed it. By language I mean both the terminology used to describe it ("superstition," "quaint," "fetishism," for instance) and the insistent way in which the stories are told in a dialect that acts as a clear marker of blackness. The persistent adoption of a limiting vernacular is the equivalent of blackface performance and indeed, because this material is nostalgically recreating slave times, Eric Lott's description of the earlier development of the minstrel show fits very well. "While it was organized around the quite explicit 'borrowing' of black cultural materials for white dissemination, a borrowing that ultimately depended on the material relations of slavery, the minstrel show obscured these relations by pretending that slavery was amusing, right, and natural."[31]

The extra ingredient to be added for this later period is the force of nostalgia, and the mediation with modernity, in which superstition plays a curious role. In a manner parallel to the projections and borrowings of minstrelsy, the persistent interest in folk magic and remedies that often moved between the herbal and the occult was often given an exotic legitimacy through association with African Americans or Indians. Thus we find a credulous public using Negroes and Indians as exotic locations or points of reference for their own superstitious beliefs—while at the same time these same groups were being "othered" in restricting and damaging ways on the basis of these very characteristics.[32]

If the lurking threat of insurrection under slavery fuelled the need to control and fix African Americans in place, Reconstruction brought the threat of change and loss and a renewed impulse to fix African Americans in a world of superstition. In other words, it was important for whites to believe that the African Americans believed, and I want to show how this compulsion operates more broadly in the treatment of African American superstition. One particular instance in which an insistence on the superstitious credulity of Negroes is directly linked to anxiety about keeping them "in their place" is the persistence of the idea that African Americans actually believed that the night riders of the Ku Klux Klan were ghosts. Such a belief on the part of whites managed to combine the exercise of real terror (the threat of violence) with a demeaning view of the victim of that threat, which made him fair game and in fact softened the whole thing almost to the dimensions of a Tom Sawyer-like game.

A bizarre example where we can see this disjunction very clearly comes in a strange volume, James Melville Beard's *K.K.K. Sketches, Humorous and Didactic.* The title itself indicates some of the weird disparities of the book, which claims to be a dispassionate account and is at pains to present the Klan as a logical and reasonable response to carpetbaggers. What is most interesting for my purposes, though, is the conjunction of several stock elements of caricature. In the middle of an entirely sober book, we have two "stump speeches." A regular ingredient of early minstrel shows, these involved the pretentious use of language by characters speaking in what passed for black vernacular. One of these scenes depicts two Negroes' frightened reaction to a train, and the other (a full ten pages in dialect) a supposed political meeting of the freedmen. These caricature roles are the only ones given to African Americans, other than criminals being justifiably hunted by the Klan. Beard also provides a lengthy discussion of what he sees as the Negro proclivity to superstition, in the context of explaining the way that the first appearances of the ceremonially robed armed men are remembered and exaggerated by the local people, who saw them as "sperrits." "That the negro is by nature grossly superstitious, no one who has had even tolerable means of information will deny. . . . Left to himself, with all the appliances of civilization and the encouragement of its examples about him, his superstition will subject him . . . to heathenish lapses." Beard sees "Voudooism" as the worst of these, and he insists that "the world of shadows is to the imagination of the black man a thing of gloom."[33]

He gives a full description of the relish for ghost stories told in a communal setting and shared and enjoyed by young white children as well as slaves, and it is this shared knowledge that the Klan later exploits. Its members, as grown men, are able to deceive the freedmen because "trained up in this school" they know "the precise extent to which the plantation darkey was controlled by the superstitious notions which he disseminated." They understand that "the superstition of the negro was not a weakness, but a ruling characteristic; and at this central idea of his being the Ku-Klux movement was directed."[34] This is an interesting reflection of how superstition was seen. In whites it was a remnant that could eventually be erased, and those who viewed African Americans positively saw it as erasable for them too. For racists like Beard, though, it was an *essential* part of African Americans, and one that allowed whites to constitute the Negro in such a way as to maintain *their* belief in *his* belief.

To reject Beard's claims is not to say that the African American response to the Klan figures was necessarily just disbelief. As William Piersen has shown, the forms of dress and performance may have chimed with African traditions sufficiently for them to be recognized within a set of beliefs quite different from the idea of European ghosts in white. Indeed, the early outfits were more often red than white, and Piersen argues that the Klan regalia may, ironically, owe a great deal to African and African American masking traditions, whether as conscious adaptations in order to frighten the slaves, or as a less conscious influence. He even draws atttention to what seems to be a mojo "hand" or conjure bag displayed in an early costume.[35]

Another more positive way of seeing these supposedly superstitious beliefs is to see the general belief in "hants" and ghosts as keeping alive the idea that there was more than just the material world. Elliot Gorn has argued, for instance, that the insistence that "Men ain't all" was a way of denying that blacks "could ever become pure property, cut off from blood dependencies."[36] This is certainly a far cry from the demeaning characterizations of Beard, but one element in Beard's account is worth pursuing a little further. His invocations of a nostalgic storytelling situation shared by white children and African Americans came only three years before Joel Chandler Harris influentially used the same scene in his account of Uncle Remus's tales. But whereas in Beard the power relations quickly became explicit as boys turned to men, a great part of the appeal and power of Harris's writings lay in the indefinite suspension of any recognition of power relations or historical change. Keeping the focus on the close relation between the boy and Remus made it possible to provide a sentimental image of rapport as well as to deny the African American any mature manhood. This was not new. An earlier book, Edward E. Pollard's *Black Diamonds Gathered in the Darkey Homes of the South*, quotes an approving review from the *New Orleans Delta*, which affirms that the author knows the Negro nature "not by intellection merely, but also by heart; knows it, not through the cold light of ethnological science only, but most of all through the warm, enkindling recollections of boyhood and youth. The negro, who in his true nature is always a boy, let him be ever so old, is better understood by a boy than a whole academy of philosophers."[37]

Joel Chandler Harris built on this idea, but, as I hope to show, his work goes interestingly beyond this framework. Based on stories first published in the *Atlanta Constitution*, his *Uncle Remus, His Songs and Sayings: The Folklore of the Old Plantation* of 1880 was hugely influential, and produced a series of imitations and responses, which I will deal with later. The popularity of the central figures of Brer Rabbit, Brer Fox, and the other animals, and the comforting situation of the unthreatening family retainer telling the stories to the young white boy, and overheard by his mother, can tend to obscure the fact that this is in many ways a deliberately ethnographic collection, which includes a collection of songs and proverbs, as well as stories and sketches. Harris's introduction is at pains to stress its "perfectly serious" intentions, and to distinguish it from the "intolerable misrepresentations of the minstrel stage." Elsewhere, too, he is scathing about the current stage versions of the Negro. He dismisses a minstrel show "which is supposed to present to us the negro as he was and is and hopes to be" and in which there is an entire scene devoted to "the happy-go-lucky darkey with his banjo." In fact, he strongly contests the automatic association of Negroes with the banjo and rejects the reduction of the Negro to a figure of burlesque, "for his life, though abounding in humor, was concerned with all that the imagination of man has made pathetic."[38] This is not to say that Harris in his own work rescues African Americans from demeaning stereotypes, of course, and though most of the work is set in postbellum times, much of its appeal seems to lie in the ways in which Remus harks back to an idealized plantation life complete with obedient slaves. On the few occasions he refers to the present, Remus expresses views unthreatening to white Southerners. He is scathing about Negroes going North, for instance, and one story refers back to an occasion when Remus defended his master against a Yankee soldier.

By 1883 in *Nights with Uncle Remus: Myths and Legends of the Old Plantation* Harris has explicitly moved the setting back, instructing the reader in a prefatory note that the stories are meant to be told "to a little boy on a Southern plantation, before the war, by an old family servant."[39] In this way the myth can be more insulated, while at the same time, the retention of the word "servant" rather than "slave" manages to soften the transition. His introduction to this collection insists not only on the authenticity but the community context of the stories. He recounts an evening encounter with Negro railway workers in 1882 when he is able to be party to their storytelling by himself contributing a story, to which they respond enthusiastically. The situation he describes is a classic ethnographic one in which the outsider is allowed into the inner circle and gains knowledge through rapport. The darkness makes it impossible to take notes, but it is also enabling, since "but for this friendly curtain, it is doubtful if the conditions would have been favorable to story-telling."[40]

It is interesting to compare this scene with the well-known description by Thomas Wentworth Higginson of collecting songs from his Negro soldiers during the Civil War. He approaches their campfire in the darkness while they are performing a "shout." "Writing down in the darkness, as I best could,—perhaps with my hand in the safe covert of my pocket,—the words of the song, I have afterwards carried it to my tent, like some captured bird or insect, and then, after examination, put it by."[41] As Cruz puts it of abolitionist collectors in general, "By capturing and classifying black culture, and by refining their discovery of the Negro spiritual, they were casting an interpretive net that *caught* what had (presumably) been *taught* by the hegemonic culture—the performative, singing, and spiritualized subject."[42]

Where Higginson's is a sort of collecting raid, in which he uses the darkness to maintain distance and stealth, for Harris the "curtain" of darkness seems here to include him within the group by obliterating differences and distinctions in a sort of timeless storytelling folk community. Harris's second collection as a whole is created much more consciously than the first to seal off this timeless world, and it ends with a story in which the family gathers on the night before Christmas "with swelling hearts and tears in their eyes"[43] to hear Remus lead the other slaves in songs, As the little boy falls asleep, the last words of the book are Remus's "Good Night." As Juniper Ellis points out, Harris's closing off of the plantation society is the equivalent of what Fabian has called the "denial of coevalness" created by use of the ethnographic present.[44]

The reassuring frame created by Remus's protective relation to the boy is very clearly used to contain any elements that might be disruptive. In the first volume, *Uncle Remus, His Songs and Sayings*, the only reference to conjure is in the story "A Plantation Witch," in which Remus explains to the boy that "Dey comes en dey conjus fokes"[45] and can change skins. He describes a rabbit that could not be caught and was seen "caperin' 'roun on a toomstone," at which point the white master finds an excuse to leave. "Mars Jeems say he sorter feel like de time done come w'en yo' gran'ma was 'specktin' an him home." When the boy says that his father doesn't believe in witches, Remus says merely "Mars John ain't live long ez I is."[46] The potentially unsettling material is emphatically closed off at the end of the story when the boy, from his bed, going to sleep, is "soothed" by the voice of Remus singing a spiritual—although we may want to see this particular spiritual as itself containing the unsettling idea of the slaves' longing for something beyond their present condition, which might not be confined just to a spiritual release.

Hit's eighteen hunder'd, forty en eight
Christ done made dat crooked way straight—
En I don't wanter stay here no longer;
Hit's eighteen hunder'd, forty-en-nine,
Christ done turn dat water inter wine
En I don't wanter stay here no longer.[47]

In *Nights with Uncle Remus* we have the interesting figure of African Jack, an elderly Gullah from the Georgia Sea Islands, who is given a different dialect by Harris. He is "a wizard, a conjurer and a snake-charmer,"[48] and his meeting with the child is presented in such a way as to emphasize his atavistic qualities. Remus acts as a sort of mediator between them, reassuring the boy when the other slaves start telling ghost stories, and then, in "Brother Rabbit and His Famous Foot," moving the area of spirit and conjuring back to the familiar animal stories. In general there is no sense that conjure is more than a superstitious belief in spirits—certainly no sense of its curing or culturally sustaining properties.

In general, then, we can say that while Harris's work makes African American folk belief accessible, it also tends to infantilize it by ignoring the complexity of its meanings. In the area of conjure and religion in general, this is certainly true, but there are ways in which Harris's own compulsions are revealed. In the later novel of 1905, *Told By Uncle Remus*, we find an older Remus telling stories to the original little boy's son, who is a sickly child. The implication is that he is too cosseted by his mother, and a product of the emasculated New South. Uncle Remus, if given the chance, can make him more robust—as if the past can redeem the weaknesses of the present, and this attitude toward the past is most intriguingly developed in Harris's 1909 novel, *The Bishop and the Boogerman*, which shows Harris struggling to reconcile past and present. The tone is playful, even whimsical, and the novel exemplifies even while it explores the compulsion to escape into fantasy away from a less pleasant reality. The central figure, Jonas, is a crusty individual and guardian to a little girl, Adelaide. He has a friend named Sanders, who is often referred to as the Bishop. Vegetables are being stolen from the garden, and they decide for the amusement of the little girl that it is the work of a "boogerman." They subsequently discover it is actually Randall, the son of their African American cook, Lucindy, who escaped before the Civil War to avoid punishment at the hands of an overseer, whom he struck. He has returned and is now set to become a preacher, and he is referred to ironically by his white superiors as a bishop. He is thus described playfully as both the boogerman and bishop of the title. Adelaide grows up to have a suitor who is a progressive thinker committed to the putting through of a railroad, which will bring modernity to the community. The comic resolution of the novel involves the acceptance of this change, but only after Adelaide's suitor is brought to believe in the existence of an imaginary figure, who has run through the book and constitutes, for my purposes, the most important part of it. As a child Adelaide has had an invisible friend, whom she calls Cally-Lou, and she is humored by the adults in her belief. In this way Cally-Lou can be seen to represent the soft-focus romance and legend of the South, which the suitor has to be able to believe in before the modern and the traditional can be combined.

A contemporary review in the *New York Times Saturday Review of Books* praised the handling of the figure of Cally-Lou, who comes to be "a name for—a sort of intangible embodiment of—all sorts of evasive, immaterial influence and motives that the people of the household might feel."[49] What the review does not pick up here, though, is that the little girl, when explaining Cally-Lou's supposed shyness and refusal to appear to others, describes her as "not right-white" and on another occasion as "not quite white."[50] In a strange scene, old Jonas recalls that his grandmother had a mulatto called Cally-Lou and begins to speculate, only to be cut off immediately by Sanders with "No, Jonas: you don't wonder, an' you needn't pertend to. Neither here nor here-arter will that sort of thing work."[51] The direct context suggests that he is dismissing belief in spirits, but it also resonates with the taboo about miscegenation, and in another scene involving Cally-Lou, old Jonas and the black servant Lucindy are sitting over the bed of the child Adelaide. She is breathing so lightly that each of them stretches out a hand to see if she is all right. "Old Jonas was feeling, and Lucindy was feeling, and their hands met; the cold hand of old Jonas touched Lucindy's hand. This was enough!" The scene is intended to explain how Lucindy, as the conventionally superstitious Negro, comes to believe in Cally-Lou's existence, as she assumes that she is encountering the ghostly figure when she touches Old Jonas's cold hand, but the theme of interracial contact seems also to be forcing itself to the surface here in the linked "feeling" hands, one white and one black, which are mistaken for the "not quite white" phantom figure.

It seems that once he has moved from the frame of the Remus stories, where black people are clearly in their right places, Harris simply does not know what to do with them.[52] Not only do we have Cally-Lou, but the figure of the returned slave Randall also seems about to burst the bounds of his allowed role at points. Referred to as both bishop and boogerman, he is at one level a good Negro who in the course of the novel becomes "a pattern, a model, for the men of his race." He obligingly rolls around and plays dead when Adelaide pretends to shoot him and is ingratiating to the white characters, but some of his comments are problematic. Refusing a tip for blacking shoes, he says he is just grateful to be around whites who don't want to kill him. Harris comments that "To any one who knew little of the negro race, Randall's remarks would have sounded tremendously like a sly joke, with a little irony thrown in for good measure; but though the negro's voice was soft and deliberate, he was terribly in earnest, and those who heard him understood and appreciated his simple recital of a harrowing experience."[53]

As an explanation, this both defuses the danger of the remark and draws attention to it. In a later scene where the white men are arguing over Randall's fate, Sanders asks, "What in the confounded nation does this mean?" Randall replies laconically, "It means lots mo' to me, than what it do to anybody else, suh,"[54] and it is difficult not to see irony, or at least a hint of a quite distinct voice here that is different from the stock representations of African Americans. In fact, when put alongside the unsatisfying role allowed to Jim in the later parts of *Huckleberry Finn*, we could say this is a hint of the voice that is so lamentably absent there. The parallels with Twain's novel go further. The compulsion to reenact the slave South as a way of denying the realities and difficulties of Reconstruction, which many have found in Twain's novel, or at least in Tom Sawyer's deceptions, can be seen as part of a wider pattern expressed in Harris's text as a retreat into a protective whimsy and make-believe, and a defense of the South and its culture in these terms. The brutal ways in which reality impinges are held at bay (reflected in the wonderful phrase Huck comes up with when trying to explain Tom's gunshot wound, "he had a dream and it shot him"). Harris's odd novel is revealing about the unmanaged compulsions and the way they crop up in the form of the supernatural. While the folk stories of Remus are notably thin on the supernatural, this novel does connect up in surprising ways with larger Gothic themes of haunting and repression that have been much discussed in relation to Southern writing and race. As Avery Gordon puts it,

If haunting describes how that which appears to be not there is often a seething presence, acting on and often meddling with taken-for-granted realities, the ghost is just the sign, or the empirical evidence, if you like that a haunting is taking place. The ghost is not simply a dead or a missing person, but a social figure, and investigating it can lead to that dense site where history and subjectivity make social life. The ghost or the apparition is one form by which something lost, or barely visible, or seemingly not there to our supposedly well-trained eye, makes itself known or apparent to us, in its own way, of course.[55]

The relation of this to more recent African American fiction, which uses haunting as a way of talking about the presence of the past and of something otherwise impossible to acknowledge, is clear, but it seems that Harris himself was at least intermittently aware of the way that the underlying fear of disorder meant that whites inhabited a world of Gothic proportions. In a short story, "Free Joe and the Rest of the World," Harris describes Joe, a free Negro living on the edge of slave society, as "a black atom, drifting hither and thither without an owner, blown about by the winds of circumstance, and given over to shiftlessness." He is, quite literally, matter out of place, and while Harris, in his paternalistic way, is at pains to suggest how unsatisfactory this is for him, in comparison with the other slaves who "belong" somewhere, he also describes his effect on the whites. Joe is "the embodiment of that vague and mysterious danger that seemed to be forever lurking on the outskirts of slavery, ready to sound a shrill and ghostly signal in the impenetrable swamps, and steal forth under the midnight stars to murder, rapine and pillage—a danger always threatening and yet never assuming shape; intangible, and yet real; impossible, and yet not improbable.[56]

In these admittedly few instances, Harris links up powerfully with an altogether less comfortable tradition of the Gothic, which has long operated in America, especially the South, alongside the celebrations of rural harmony, hospitality, and gentility. The elements of the Gothic and the uncanny have been valuable tools for artists wanting to explore the social contradictions, which it is the role of the prevailing ideology to contain and manage, and to portray the psychological tensions and torsions that ensue. Writers from Poe through Faulkner to Morrison and Naylor have used the occult and the Gothic to probe what has been kept hidden—to show the fictions supporting accepted social conventions and the realities expressed indirectly in what has been dismissed as a phantom realm. This can also apply to the persisting identity and claims of Native Americans, whose often brutal displacement was masked under claims of benevolence and the need for progress, as well as the repressed history of African American slavery. Often the real anxieties which fuel the sense of haunting—the social and historical realities that it reflects—have been obscured by a celebratory and commodified version of the South stressing its romantic and otherworldly qualities, and folkloristic interest has sometimes reflected this.[57]

Harris's Uncle Remus stories stimulated the production of several similar collections, as well as numerous articles. Charles Colcock Jones's *Negro Myths from the Georgia Coast*, a selection of animal stories in a fairly impenetrable vernacular transcription, gives more information than does Harris about the role of conjure, and he departs from storytelling at the end of the book into a more documentary account. In a chapter called "Sperits" he asserts that "Memories of Fetichism, of Totemism, and of Anthropomorphism were strangely mingled with the teachings of Christianity, and in their religious exercises the emotional predominated over the intellectual," and he records that the making and sale of "fetiches" was widespread. Typically they consisted of "a bunch of rusty nails, bits of red flannel, and pieces of briar-root tied together with a cotton string. A toad's foot, a snake's tooth, a rabbit's tail, or a snail's shell was sometimes added," and he notes that "In the conduct of plantations, difficulty and annoyance were not infrequently experienced from the interference of these old negro women,—conjurers,—who, in plying their secret trade, gave rise to disturbances and promoted strife and disquietude."[58] Just what sort of strife is not clear, but here we have the context for Charles Chesnutt's conjure woman, to be dealt with later in this chapter. As in Harris, though, the material on conjure is ultimately closed off by a Christian resolution, and the book ends with a chapter called "Daddy Jupiter"'s Vision," in which the old Negro man of the title finally dreams of a Christian heaven. In a review of Jones's book in the *Journal of American Folklore* William Wells Newell comments thoughtfully about the relative absence of African elements. "Where is the mythologic furniture which belongs to the native mind? Where is the cruelty, the cannibalism?" He is struck by the distinctive patterns of what is retained and adapted. "We doubt if the history of the world presents such another example of complete obliteration of ancestral faith; while at the same time the ancestral fables which had nothing to do with faith, and these only, survived in an altered form, compounded with the nursery lore of the governing race."[59] Newell seems unaware, though, of the extent to which this apparent peculiarity actually reflected the limitations of what white observers were able or allowed to see. In re-presenting them only as children's stories, they demonstrated their own and their audience's inability to recognize the extent to which trickster stories were fulfilling more complex functions.

The exploitation of Caribbean Obeah and voodoo and African fetishism to provide a frisson of fear is not uncommon in stories of the period, and this fearful fascination extends to various African American practices, which, with the exception of the privileged area of the Christian spirituals, are denigrated as superstitious and even evil. Even so, there are still some accounts that stray from the norm. A piece in the *Atlantic Monthly* on "Voodooism in Tennessee," written by someone only identified as the wife of a Colonel Park, is a good example. In this reminiscence of the activities of a "Voodoo woman" who cures someone apparently bewitched, the whole incident is very positively presented. The suspicion of bewitching first falls on an old woman, presented as a stock figure ("the wretched old centenarian, a mere bundle of bones and clothes, began to mumble and chatter"), but when the voodoo woman appears she discerns that the illness is caused by grief and by a loss that has not been accepted, so her "cure" is psychological. Furthermore, her appearance is notably different from what might be expected. Unlike her male companion, who is fully African, she is "a delicate light mulattress, of reddish tinge," and when she speaks it is in standard English ("It is this that ails you").[60] The generally positive tone of this piece may just be a case of sentimentalization of the past ("Did the sun really shine more brilliantly upon the old plantation home in those ante-bellum days?") but it is at least arguable that it is the "reddish" aspect that is the most important factor in allowing such a benign portrait, as it triggers a particular set of idealized and Romantic associations with Indian spirituality.[61]

This distinction between Indians and African Americans can be found in the work of Mary Alicia Owen. Her 1893 collection of stories, *Old Rabbit, the Voodoo and the Sorcerers*, is a clear response to Harris, but she broadens the origins of the stories, as well as stressing the role of conjure.[62] Based on her experience of her mixed-blood neighbors in Missouri, the book has a little white girl, known simply as "Tow Head," being told stories by a group of old women, whose mixed racial origins, ranging from full Indian to full African, Owen records in some detail. Their beliefs are similarly eclectic. One of them, of Indian and French blood, has a faith "of as many hues as Joseph's coat, as was evinced by her keeping her medicine-pipe and eagle-bone whistle along with her missal and 'Key to Heaven'; by carrying a rabbit's-foot and rosary in the same pocket, by wearing a saint's toe dangling on her bosom and the fetich known as a 'luck-ball' under her right arm."[63]

Other characters are part Indian and part African American, and the tales are similarly mixed. In his introduction to her book, the English folklorist Charles Leland acknowledges that "we find the African Voodoo ideas very strangely mixed with the Indian," but he carefully separates out the Indian beliefs, which he associates with Aryan civilization, from the African. Whereas the former are based on fasting, contemplation, and prayer, the African cures are "fouler and far more revolting" than the Indian "medicine."[64] Though in this book of stories Owen seems quite content to revel in the promiscuous mingling of cultures, in a later novel she makes a more traditional distinction, and the Indian-white heroine, when offered the chance to use magical charms by an African-white woman, draws the conventional lines. "I am not a Voodoo. I have no belief in your tricken-bags, your luck-balls, your mysterious revelation from the snake, and spells from conjure-stones. Frighten the poor Negroes out of all they can earn and steal, but let me alone."[65]

Owen reflects the generally more sympathetic attitude of folklorists toward magic in her lectures at the International Folklore Congresses of 1891 and 1892, where she plays upon her own experience of what she calls voodoo to dramatic—even melodramatic—effect. In *Old Rabbit* she has a section devoted to the making of a luck ball and the instructions of the conjure doctor. Here she calls him the Voodoo, and identifies him only as "A," but in her lectures he is called "Alexander" or "King Alexander" and she refers to him as "this ancient, ill-smelling, half-naked black sinner."[66] There is also a caricatured drawing of him in *Old Rabbit*, with a whiskey bottle, titled ironically "The King of the Voodoos." Even though she does mention that he is "half Guinea and half Cherokee Indian,"[67] he is represented visually as a stock Negro, as are all the other figures mentioned, in spite of her descriptions in the text of the various racial mixtures. It is as if the illustrator is unable to cope with racial mixtures because it would mean moving from the template of "Negro," to looking at what was actually before his eyes, and the use of the vernacular often seems to fulfill the same reassuring function. In one of her lectures Owen begins to relate a folk story by insisting "I really must give it in dialect; it loses its character in grammar-school English."[68] This is not the same urge to maintain authenticity as that of later ethnopoetics. Rather, it allows a very specific form of audience enjoyment based on knowing exactly what to expect. Owen plays up her personal knowledge, but her insistence on understanding "the Negro" in all of his contradictions is a typical rhetorical move.

How *could* I describe to the man who knows him not the cunning, simple, cruel, kindly, untruthful, suspicious yet credulous, superstitious negro, who sees a ghost or devil in every black stump and swaying bush, yet prowls about two-thirds of the night and sleeps three-fourths of the day. The old-fashioned negro, who is destined to have no son like him, who conjures in the name of his African devil on Saturday and goes to a Christian church, sings, prays, and exhorts, and after "meetin'" invites the minister to a dinner of stolen poultry.[69]

Owen's work reflects the impulses of much of the folklore world in its combination of genuinely useful information about conjure practices, particularly the fusion of Indian and African American materials, with racist pigeonholing.[70] In her unpublished letters to Charles Leland, we can see the different elements brought together most transparently. She sends Leland carefully transcribed minstrel songs and talks of knowing a famous minstrel well (though she doesn't mention his race). In the same letter she talks about getting information on "all the sacred Apache chants" and says she has acquired "a beautiful specimen of Moqui weaving." Not long before, though, she complains of living in "Niggerland." Her African American servants have disappeared overnight, and she phones the jail "to learn if our domestics had been 'run in' for some trifle such as using a razor on a fellow-man, or stealing somebody's chickens. The latter was the offence. We lock them out of the house at night, you know, so we don't know what goes on from dark till dawn."[71]

So far I have been concentrating on white commentators and the often contradictory or conflicting intellectual frameworks within which they dealt with a whole range of religious/superstitious beliefs and practices, but of course these same frameworks and discourses were also what African American writers had initially to work with. It is worth noting that the chapter of W. E. B. DuBois's *The Souls of Black Folk* titled "Of the Faith of the Fathers" originally appeared in *The New World: A Quarterly Review of Religion, Ethics and Theology* in 1900 without the framing poem and music from the spirituals. It is to be found alongside essays by other contributors on primitive religion, and it is useful to see DuBois's historical account of African American religion in this context.[72] Recognizing the crucial importance of the church and the preacher in Negro life, he wants to trace the "successive steps of the social history." The African religion of "nature-worship, with profound belief in invisible surroundings, good and bad" and "worship through incantation and sacrifice" was destroyed, but the "Priest or Medicine-man" retained a role. He became healer, interpreter of the unknown, and "supernatural avenger of wrong," and was consequently the figure who "rudely but picturesquely expressed the longing, disappointment, and resentment of a stolen and oppressed people."[73]

DuBois sees this role crystallizing under slavery. The African's "deep emotional nature which turns instinctively towards the supernatural" reacted to the situation by calling up "all the resources of heathenism to aid,—exorcism and witchcraft, the mysterious Obi worship . . . the witch-woman and the voodoo-priest." But where later African American writers have valued the persistence of these beliefs and have regarded them as a cultural source and resource, DuBois rather dismisses their current relevance, referring to "that vein of vague superstition which characterizes the unlettered Negro even today." For him, the present mood of African Americans is split between useless defiance and servility, both created by the baffling of black expectations and aspirations.

He ends, as he began, with the idea of the "deep religious feeling of the real Negro heart" fuelling an awakening that which will sweep Negroes toward claiming for themselves the "Liberty, Justice, and Right" reserved for whites.[74] By the time the essay reappears in *Souls of Black Folk*, DuBois has give it a more Christian dimension with the addition of the music and lyrics of a spiritual. By bringing together the spirituals and an emphasis on worldly liberties like this, DuBois also marks a departure from the way whites had presented spirituals. He sees the religious feeling not as an end in itself, or as a simple solace, but as a reservoir of feelings, that are capable of being turned to social and political ends.

In his novel *The Quest of the Silver Fleece*, published in 1911, DuBois dramatized some of these issues of religious belief and development, but with a different emphasis. As the title implies, he draws upon classical mythology, rather than African American tradition or myth, for his framework. The relation between the fertility of the swamp and the pure white cotton that is grown out of it is part of a larger opposition of base matter and spirit—an opposition complicated and undercut by the hard materialism involved in turning the fleece into money in an exploitative and racist Southern economy. It is further complicated by the idea expressed by one of the characters that white folk "just got things,—heavy, dead things. We black folks is got the *spirit*."[75] This black spirit, though, seems uncomfortably related to remnants of African belief, which are represented in base and earthy terms. Zora's mother is referred to by one character as a "voodoo woman," and by DuBois as a "hag," and she is associated with inchoate power and the formlessness of the swamp. What Zora has inherited from her is dismissed by the narrative voice as "mummery" and "mystic remnants of a half-forgotten heathen cult."[76] But even if the old woman herself seems to be explicitly rejected, her power is manifested at key moments, like the planting of the cotton, which she says she has "sowed wid the three spells of Obi," so that the fundamental action seems at variance with the more rational progressive stance of the book.[77] At a key point in the narrative, a confrontation occurs between a Christian preacher who dismisses self-advancement for the African American farmers and urges acceptance of their lot, and a rather mysterious man who insists that "Faith without works is dead" and unites the people in action. This man's appearance is signalled by "a rhythmical chanting, wilder and more primitive than song," and he seems to be the same mysterious figure who appears at the conjure woman's death.[78] One critic describes him as a conjure man, but DuBois does not use the term in the novel, and in fact his language is consonant with that of a Christian preacher.[79] In this way the novel presents a less clear-cut sense of a one-way progression from superstition to reason than in DuBois'earlier essay.

For DuBois the spiritual aspiration and the material goals are fused in *Souls of Black Folk* in what has been seen as Hegelian language. In one chapter, "The Coming of John," the fictional protagonist John attends a performance of

Wagner's *Lohengrin*, where he recognizes the music's transcendent possibilities in a revealing metaphor. At the sound of the orchestra "a deep longing swelled in all his heart to rise with that clear music out of the dirt and dust of that low life that held him prisoned and befouled."[80] What is notable here is the idea that the material world is imprisoning and limiting, and the realm of the spirit is one of elevation and possibility, embodied in music. It is interesting that in the same year as the publication of *Souls of Black Folk* we find a strangely parallel use of Wagner in the pages of the *Journal of American Folklore*. Charles Peabody, from the Peabody Museum, describes a chance encounter with African American music during the excavation of Indian mounds in Mississippi. Having employed a group of African American workers to dig a trench, Peabody hears them singing. "Busy archaeologically, we had not very much time left for folk-lore, in itself of not easy excavation, but willy-nilly our ears were beset with an abundance of ethnological material in song."[81] As the workers dig deeper, the sound is changed. At first the woods would "echo their yelling with faithfulness. The next day or two these artists being, like the Bayreuth orchestra, sunk out of sight, there would arise from behind the dump a not unwholesome muymos [moaning] as of the quiescent Furies." The parallel is presumably suggested here for Peabody by the fact that Wagner positioned the orchestra below the stage at Bayreuth to create a distinct aesthetic effect, but the suggestion is also of a sort of folk expression that could be made transcendent, as in Wagner's operas.

The tone of this short piece is uneven, an uneasy reflection of the mixed attitudes toward the music as well as the mixture of music itself,[82] but what is interesting is the conjunction of two sorts of folk collecting, and their relation to a spiritualization. As the Negro workers go deeper into the ground, Indian relics are unearthed, and African American folk culture becomes acceptable ("not unwholesome" is as far as Peabody can go). The Indian objects will go to Harvard, and categorized as antiquities and ethnographic objects. The songs are also collected, but only as objects of curiosity, like Higginson's furtively collected specimens gathered from his Civil War troops. In his description, though, they are etherealized, made mythic and Wagnerian, but only by being aesthetically screened or distanced. The conjunction, in Peabody's essay, of Indian absence and antiquity with the more disturbing modern presence of African Americans is reminiscent of the scene among the Indian mounds in Ingraham's *Lafitte: Pirate of the Gulf* discussed in my introduction. Whereas Ingraham stressed the differences between earthy blacks and spiritual Indians, though, Peabody's tone flirts with the ironic similarities.

His ability to use his playful Wagnerian analogy (the highest Western art music with the lowest Negro noise) depends on a secure sense of these hierarchies. His comparison invokes Wagner but it relies on the strength of our sense of a cultural scale of value (as civilized people who know Wagner) to know that it is only a joke. It relies on bathos, the figure of speech that depends on the fall from high to low, similar to the idea of African Americans going deeper into the dirt to become more ethereal. The connection is thereby asserted and simultaneously denied. It may sound too heavy handed to call it a fetishistic pattern, but this does have the same structure of simultaneous connection and separation, of assertion and denial. In this respect DuBois's adoption of the same hierarchies in his use of Wagner and spiritual elevation is markedly different in refusing any idea of bathos. An even more striking instance of an African American writer taking over and reversing the racialized hierarchy of body and spirit can be found in James Weldon Johnson. After describing a lynching, he reports the explosive realization that "in large measure the race question involves the saving of black America's body and white America's soul."[83] Here the power of the statement comes precisely from the insistence on the interconnectedness of what had been assumed to be separate, and the consequent overturning of the hierarchy. If the white soul was so connected to the black body—and in fact could only be saved by acknowledging its links to it—how could the polarity and hierarchy of body and soul, and black and white, be sustained?

In *Souls*, DuBois uses the spirituals to represent an enduring cultural resource and an expression of spiritual aspiration. This is a development out of the white accounts, from Higginson and Allen onward, as well as from Frederick Douglass, and the ways in which the spiritual comes to be a privileged site of African American religious expression and aspiration have been extensively discussed. Ronald Radano, for instance, has argued that white commentators, "by conceptualizing difference as a realm beyond white access," could invest "a re-invented slave music with formidable 'spiritual' power. Figured as transcendent and otherworldly, black musical difference became the key to the recovery of a forgotten past, to the re-membering of a realm of American sound, constituted by, while existing beyond and even prior to, the containments of writing."[84] I will return to the notion of this investment in the realm of sound as somehow more expressive of a cultural essence, or of an African American subjectivity in Chapter 4, but for now I want just to note the ways in which it fits in with broader negotiations over spirit, matter and race.

An interesting example of the essentialist use of the spiritual can be found in Pauline Hopkins's novel *Of One Blood*, published the same year as DuBois's book. Reuel Briggs, the novel's central figure, is fascinated by spiritualism, animal magnetism, and similar phenomena, which Hopkins says are too often dismissed as "effects of the imagination."[85] Immediately after a discussion about the idea of the hidden self and the "unclassified residuum,"[86] the characters go to see the Fisk Jubilee singers perform songs that are described in strongly essentialist terms. Later, Briggs rescues one of the singers, Dianthe, from a state of suspended animation, but she does not remember who she is. Only he knows she is black, and therefore, as she is light-skinned, he allows her and everyone else to assume she is white. When Dianthe later sings in Boston society as a white woman, she seems impelled by something mysterious to sing "Go Down Moses," and another voice, "a weird contralto, veiled as it were," appears.[87] Thus the music reveals an essential and racialized self.

This idea of a latent identity is crucial to the larger plot, in that Briggs's ancestral African identity is eventually revealed. He is Ergamenes, prince of a lost kingdom in the ancient city of Telassar, Ethiopia. This city is discovered in the course of an imperial-style scientific collecting expedition and with the help of a spirit figure, Mira, who appears to various characters. Thus real identity (blood) ultimately reveals itself. This has negative repercussions for whites, who have hidden the effects of miscegenation and the crimes of the fathers, but positive effects for the African Americans, who discover their African and noble ancestry, and Hopkins invokes a biblical phrase from Luke: "For there is nothing covered that shall not be revealed."[88] The use of the occult here is entirely devoid of any ideas of black or satanic magic. The journey into Africa, in fact, is explicitly one to civilization, in contrast with the idea of the white fantasy of Africa as the heart of darkness. "Reuel noticed that this was at variance with the European idea respecting Central Africa, which brands these regions as howling wildernesses or an uninhabitable country."[89] The description of the Africans' science and religion (which are really one) stresses the idea of one God and the development of higher spiritual faculties, but Reuel finds that they all lack knowledge of Christ, which, as their new ruler, he duly gives them. Thus there is the suggestion of a common religion, which can be improved on by the advance into Christianity, but this African religion sounds more like the spiritualized versions of Indian religion described in the first chapter than contemporary accounts of any actual African religion. Hopkins describes no culturally specific practices or beliefs at all, and the whole account is very generalized. The death of Dianthe merely makes way for her avatar, and her actual moment of death is described quite fully, because, as in Poe, it marks the border of matter and spirit. We have classic Gothic and Romantic concerns here, but they are racialized not only around a reversal of black and white as terms, but around material and spiritual as well, so that Africa becomes the realm of the spiritual, in forms not just limited to music.[90] This emphasis on African spirituality runs alongside references in the text to African American conjure, or at least clairvoyance, in the figure of Aunt Hannah. She is referred to as "the most noted 'voodoo' doctor or witch in the country," and Jennie Kassanoff has pointed to the importance of the conjure woman in offering "the healing antidote of narrative—of decoded genealogies."

Psychic phenomena are treated positively here and elsewhere in Hopkins,[91] but in *Contending Forces*, an earlier novel about miscegenation that is notable for an uneasy and unstable positioning of the narrative voice towards "the Negro," her treatment of magical practices is fairly dismissive. Discussing a "spiritualistic soothsayer" who appears at a fair, she comments that "Superstition is supposed to be part of the Negro's heritage. They have brought much of it from their native Africa. . . . Claiming kinship with the Egyptians and other black races of the Eastern continent, the Negro is thought to possess wonderful powers of necromancy." She seems to grant that some races "like families," have particular gifts, but when transplanted abroad, "much of their power vanishes." While we hear of charms being effective against neighbors, she says, "these wonderful and terrorizing acts were never perpetrated against the inhuman master or mistress . . . never upon enemies wearing a white skin." But then Hopkins turns the tables by pointing out that "the Negro no longer holds the distinction of being the only race" that believes in such superstitions. "In these days of palmistry, phrenology, card-reading, mind-reading, lucky pigs, rabbit's feet worn on the watch-chain for luck, and four-leafed clover encased in crystal and silver for the same reason, who shall say that the Negro has not lost his monopoly of one great racial characteristic."[92]

The syntax here reflects quite a complex point of view. The disapproval of superstition is compounded by the suggestion of extravagance on the part of those who should know better (they have crystal and silver). It could therefore be seen as a general lament about the spread of superstition, but the theme of the book is the persistent but unacknowledged mixing of races, and the slipperiness of the syntax ("who shall say the Negro has not lost"—meaning that he *has* lost the monopoly over superstition) suggests a sort of ironic revenge. It is as if the power of magic itself has not traveled, but the belief in magic has, and it has infected whites as well. As I have shown, this concern over the persistence of superstition is often encountered in white commentators, but here it is given an extra ironic twist that corresponds to the rhetorical move of Pokagan described earlier. Like many others, Hopkins uses the possibilities apparently opened up by new science to make a bridge to beliefs in the occult, which the material orientation of science had been undermining. Where she differs from others is in the way she also connects this with a more positive view of African civilization. Even so, her genteel stance (and that of *The Colored American*, for which she wrote) allowed for spirituals, but no lower expressions of African American culture, and she does not connect the positive aspects of the occult with homegrown magical practices like conjure.

In Charles Chesnutt's 1888 collection *The Conjure Woman* we have the first serious engagement with this "lower" aspect of African American life, and it is framed very much as a continuation of, and response to, Harris's work. Uncle Remus and the rabbit were still sufficiently popular for Chesnutt or his publishers to have on the cover a picture of the central figure, the old man Julius, and two rabbits, as a direct echo of its predecessor.[93] The actual collection was the result of an editor's initiative as much as Chesnutt's, and it only used a sample of his stories. Richard Brodhead's later and fuller collection, which brings together all the related stories, allows us to see that conjure as such plays a relatively small part, and it is not exoticized in the manner of Mary Owen. In this sense, Chesnutt remains, perhaps surprisingly, very close to the limits of Harris and the terms of the folklore debate. A couple of years after *The Conjure Woman*, he published a brief account of conjure beliefs and practices in which he praised Harris's "fine literary discrimination," but his own attitude is interestingly ambivalent. The language he uses seems to reflect an intellectual superiority to such superstitions and their primitive origins. The belief in conjuration, or "goopher," probably grew, he tells us, "out of African fetichism which was brought over from the dark continent along with the dark people, and which had affinities with Voodooism, or snake worship," which he associates with tropical America. In a diluted form it became mixed with European witchcraft and "the tricks and the delusions of the Indian conjurer."[94] The scorn of educators and ministers has driven such beliefs to "the remote chimney corners of black aunties," from where he has gathered them. But while most of his article, even while detailing the practices, sees them as the product of a "lack of enlightenment," he does mention that he has himself acquired a conjure bag, or charm, together with a rabbit's foot. His tone seems to be ironic when he says that "considering its potency, the small sum of silver it cost me was no extravagant outlay," and that together with the rabbit foot he has acquired, "I would seem to be reasonably well-protected against casual misfortune." Overall, though, the framing of the short vernacular account from Old Aunt Harriet, which is immediately labelled and contained as "vagrant imaginings," is reminiscent of the work of an amateur folklorist rather than the complexities of his short stories.

One of the key differences between these stories and those of Harris and his white imitators is that the supernatural level of the story is always shown to be entangled in the power relationships between black and white. Like the original Remus volume, this is set in the post-Reconstruction present, and though the themes hark back to times of slavery, there is no comfortable nostalgia. In a later essay looking back to the literary context out of which he arose Chesnutt refers to Thomas Nelson Page as "disguising the harshness of slavery under the mask of sentiment."[95] In contrast, Uncle Julius's telling of the stories is not just for entertainment or ingratiation. We are not looking at black people through white eyes, but at a white person through the eyes of the black author—but also, as we glean Julius's agenda, through his eyes as he manipulates his white neighbors by telling them his stories. The Uncle Remus pattern of an old African American man's vernacular tale framed implicitly by an educated white narrator, is given an extra level of irony since the author is African American, thus demonstrating the mastery of the master's voice. As Brodhead puts it, "in their telling his tales perform a conjure of a second order."[96]

What is noticeable about Chesnutt is that he does not use conjure itself as a resource to be used in the present. It is an archaism, which the pragmatic Julius uses as an ingredient in his stories rather than in practice, thus transforming the idea of conjure into a means of power and manipulation. In this way he is different from some of the modern celebrations of women's spiritual power, such as that in Gloria Naylor's *Mama Day*, for instance, which I discuss in Chapter 4. Chesnutt's approach to conjure is always complex and ambivalent. In "Po' Sandy," for instance, we have a particularly interesting use of conjure in relation to the material body of the slave. There are several twists to the story, which is told by the old ex-slave Julius to the skeptical narrator and his more sympathetic wife. In it Sandy, a slave whose master has overused him by continually sending him out on loan to work elsewhere, expresses the wish to be able to stay put, near his new wife, Tenie. This wife turns out to be a "cunjuh woman," and grants this wish by turning him into a tree. He will have no ears or mouth, she says, but she will bring him back to life periodically so that they can be together. One day, though, she returns from nursing a sick white woman to find that the tree has been cut down. Her distress is interpreted as madness by the whites, and she is tied to a post at the sawmill. Thus restrained, she has to witness her husband, in the form of the tree, being sawn into pieces.

Any awareness of the way that slavery itself was a system of objectification and commodification of the slave's body makes the ironies here clear and poignant. Sandy has been turned into an object to save him from being used as one, but the stratagem only results in his destruction. The other aspect I am interested in here, though, is the way that conjure, the investing of objects with nonmaterial occult/spiritual powers, is the obverse of this process of objectification. In the story, Tenie might seem to have been tragically trapped in that process while trying to subvert it, since her husband is turned permanently into a thing and dismembered before her eyes. Instead, the larger narrative provides another twist, when the wood, after it is used to make the mistress's new kitchen produces sounds, "a-hollerin' and sweeekin' lack it wuz in great pain and sufferin'."[97] Unable to get any slave women to work in the kitchen, the master eventually gives up, demolishes the kitchen, and uses the wood to build a schoolhouse, which, according to Julius, is still inhabited by "hants." This schoolhouse returns us to the present, because it is now disused, and it is the narrator's plan to use its timber to build his wife a new kitchen that has triggered the whole story from Uncle Julius. The wife is put off by Julius's story from wanting a new kitchen made from this wood, and the schoolhouse is left untouched. We realize that this has been Julius's intention all along when a few days later he persuades the mistress to allow it to be used for a colored Baptist church. When she asks about the ghost, she is told by him that ghosts don't stray into worship, but that if Sandy's spirit did, the preaching would no doubt do him good. So the story uses a tale of conjure to demonstrate the inhumanity of slavery in reducing men to things—something the mistress recognizes and the master doesn't.

"What a system it was," she exclaimed, when Julius had finished, "under which such things were possible."

"What things?" I asked, in amazement. "Are you seriously considering the possibility of a man's being turned into a tree?"[98]

In its final twist, though, it also shows how Julius has used this tale of magic and materiality. The power of the conjure woman's "goopher mixtry,"[99] as is suggested in the wonderful coinage "mixtry," lies in the combining of otherwise trivial and meaningless material objects into a form that has efficacy. In this way there is a transformation equivalent to that performed by Julius to acquire a space for spiritual activities, in this case his own church.[100]

In "Dave's Neckliss," which was not included in the original collection, the African American body and its abuse are central. Though in this case there is no transformation by conjure, Dave's punishment (having to carry around his neck a ham, which he is falsely accused of stealing) drives him into the delusion that he is himself a ham. As Sundquist and others have pointed out, the minstrel clichés of Negro appetite (also played upon in "A Victim of Heredity" with its explanation of why Negroes like chicken) are made real and tragic here. Dave's final actions of smoking and hanging himself like a ham have gruesome overtones of another iconic treatment of the black body, that of lynching and burning.[101]

Dave's reduction of himself to a ham is, as Brodhead points out, equivalent to seeing himself as an object, a commodity, in other words like a slave. The body as merely meat is in fact the literal rendition of what would happen without the complex stratagems and resources of spirit and will by which slaves and their descendants managed *not* to accept this valuation of themselves. Chesnutt's stories balance the brutal realities, which are there for those who want to see them, with the humor and guile of Julius. This is not just to sweeten the pill for white readers, but because Julius represents a resource much more powerful than outrage, which is the intelligence and creativity to get what he wants by indirect means—to "hit a straight lick with a crooked stick." At the same time that he is telling the story to his white neighbors Julius is helping himself to large portions of their ham. "I nebber kin eat mo' d'n two or th'ee poun's befo' I gits ter studyin' 'bout Dave," he tells his hosts,[102] and by the end of the story he has acquired the whole ham from the wife, who has been put off it by his story. Chesnutt's whole enterprise in these tales is an example of how not to reject an aspect of African American life just because it has been caricatured or used to demean. Rather, the trick is to use it and not be used or limited by it, and we can see both Chesnutt and Julius doing this and claiming with relish what might be thought of as too tainted by earlier associations. (A later example, which almost seems to echo Dave's ham, is the protagonist of Ralph Ellison's *Invisible Man*, who, in learning to accept without shame the bodily enjoyment of food for which his race has been reductively caricatured, eats a yam on the street and pronounces "I yam what I yam.")

One characteristic device in these stories is the literalization of a metaphor, as in "The Marked Tree" where the curse brought down on the white family because of the heartless action of selling off a young slave, who then dies, is expressed by marking a tree, which has come to represent the family lineage.

From that time the "family tree" in both senses is blighted. In this story, like so many others, we find a connection between white and black that is so close as to demand intimacy but is destroyed by the divisions of race and slavery. The black boy and the white boy are born on the same day, but in order to pay for the wedding of the white boy (and the furtherance of the lineage), the black boy is sold away from the home, with disastrous results leading to his death. Through Phillis's curse, the misfortunes which affect one branch of the family tree also affect the other, recalling the central theme of Twain's *Pudd'nhead Wilson*. The use of a connection through sympathetic magic and the marked tree here, like the association of the growth of the vine with the hair of the slave Henry in "The Goophered Grapevine" is a way of actualizing in the narrative, through the device of conjure, what is already a metaphoric or metonymic connection.[103] The narrative techniques common to folk stories, and tales of magic may depend on that crucial ingredient of magical thought that has been called sympathetic magic, namely the idea of a homologous relation based either on resemblance or proximity, already dealt with in earlier chapters in my discussion of fetishism and primitive religion, but the same processes are operating in a symbolic novel through literary devices.

Julius's particular relation to the elements of conjure is caught in John's description of him in a story, "Tobe's Tribulations," not included in the original collection, but published in *Southern Workman*. "There clung to his mind, like the barnacles of a ship, all sorts of extravagant beliefs. . . . But from his own imagination, I take it . . . he gave to the raw material of folklore and superstition a fancifulness of touch that truly made of it, to borrow a homely phrase, a silk purse out of a sow's ear."[104] The language here is interesting, reflecting the collector's interest in survivals and the power of tradition as well as acknowledging Julius's creativity and ingenuity. The transformation from the abjected and very physical sow's ear to the elegance of silk is achieved by imagination (so that John's appreciation is aesthetic) but what we also see is Julius achieving material ends by his ability to "charm" (in several senses) John with his stories. In "Dave's Neckliss" John's assessment of Julius is of someone calculating and emotionally stunted by the experience of slavery. "He would speak of a cruel deed, not with the indignation of one accustomed to quick feeling and spontaneous expression, but with a furtive disapproval which suggested to us a doubt in his own mind as to whether he had a right to think or feel, and presented to us the curious psychological spectacle of a mind enslaved long after the shackles had been struck off the limbs of its possessor."[105]

This is of course what happens to Dave, whose mind retains the burden of the ham even after his body has been freed from it, but the passage is also laden with other ironies. We might say that in a period of lynchings and fear it is not a question of what to feel, but of how much to express of those feelings, and it is John's blindness to the present situation that allows him not to see this.[106] William Andrews quotes John's doubts as to whether Julius had "more than the most elementary ideas of love, friendship, patriotism, religion," or whether he "even realized, except in a vague uncertain way, his own degradation." Andrews argues that in this way "Chesnutt revealed the crucial deficiencies of Julius as a developable literary character," and responds to those who idealized the old-time slave by showing the damage done to Julius.[107] But this does assume that Chesnutt accepts John's view here. If we see what is described as an emptiness or lack in Julius as a place that John cannot reach (and a place that could not then be represented, even by an African American author), then rather than assuming a vacuum we can appreciate the slipperiness of Chesnutt's positioning of the reader. John's description is certainly very relevant, in that Chesnutt does rigorously avoid giving much insight into Julius's thinking, and he avoids any heartwarming moments of shared understanding or humanity, which would allow Julius to approach the role of Uncle Remus. Furthermore, the comic balance of the tales between John's modernity and a past world that Julius has learned to invoke for his own purposes is not one achieved elsewhere in Chesnutt.

In *The Colonel's Dream* of 1905, the town of Clarendon finally thwarts the returning colonel's plans to bring Northern efficiency and industry, as well as philanthropy to his hometown. Not that tradition triumphs either, since what remains is a corrupt New South that has replaced slavery with exploited black convict labor, a scheme run by the aptly named Fetters. The idea of the violated body is still here, in a reworking of an earlier story, "Dumb Witness," in which a woman has been punished so brutally that she appears to have lost the ability to speak. In the original story, she is the only one who knows the whereabouts of the family money, as she has been entrusted with this information by her master before his untimely death. Only at the end does she speak, and then it is to express her outrage at the punishment. In the short story she speaks in the vernacular, but here she talks "strangely, slowly, thickly, but passionately and distinctly"—and intriguingly, in standard English. In the later versions of the story Chesnutt is also exploring the idea of miscegenation, and in the novel he describes the woman, Viney, as part Cherokee, but it is notable that here he underlines the idea of a person being treated as thing, and then becoming mute like a thing. The voice "from the wrinkled old mulattress seemed as strange and weird to Ben as though a stone image had waked to speech."[108]

This may seem far from the idea of the conjure woman, but in fact the basic story of the buried treasure is an old one, and appears in a much earlier book, claiming to be a *Complete Fortune Teller and Dream Book*, by "Chloe Russell, a Woman of Colour of the State of Massachusetts, commonly termed the Old Witch or Black Interpreter."[109] Chloe Russell describes helping a white planter whose uncle had buried treasure on his estate to locate it, and she is rewarded with cash, with which she buys her freedom. Chesnutt seems to be drawing on a common or traditional theme here, and there are numerous references from the eighteenth century onward deploring the common people's enthusiasm for divining and conjuring to locate treasure,[110] but he has transformed it from fairytale to realism. Whereas magic, in Chloe Russell's account, could work for both sides in revealing the money and reinforcing a shared heritage of the South, in Chesnutt's various versions it does not. There is no money, and the violence that makes the witness dumb is not to be erased or forgiven, by magic or anything else.

The African American writers I have dealt with so far took up the available discourses of race and belief and used them for their own ends, but in very different ways. Where Hopkins stressed the spiritual dimensions and the intersections with the new occult sciences, Chesnutt followed up the folk dimension, but neither writer directly exploited or even positively approached the world of African American magico-religious practice and belief. In the next chapter, I try to show how in the twentieth century new currents of thought such as primitivism brought new elements and configurations into view and allowed for a more positive view of elements that had previously been ignored or dismissed, even while they perpetuated many of the same racial distinctions.

Chapter 3

Primitivism, Modernism, and Magic

In the last chapter, I looked at the ways in which calls for a rational progression beyond superstition and toward a clearer division between material and spiritual powers were racially nuanced. I argued that there was an attempt to consign irrational beliefs to primitive people, and to assume that these superstitions would evaporate, but that such optimistic claims to progress were consistently belied by various returns and persisting traces in American society of what had supposedly been left behind. In the early part of the twentieth century, the Modernist engagement with primitivism represented a different approach, which was partly a reaction against the earlier celebration of a world desacralized by a reductive rationality, and the technological progress associated with its apparent mastery of the natural world.

Working counter to the accepted narrative of progress developed by early anthropologists and comparative religionists, in which there was a movement from magic to religion to science, Modernist artists insisted that art took us back to the beginning in connecting us with a world that had not been disenchanted. The ways of thinking dismissed as primitive—for instance, sympathetic magic, based on metonymic and metaphorical connections rather than linear causality—were seen as the core of creativity, and the new methods of composition like imagism, collage, and montage were often theorized in these terms. T. S. Eliot wrote a review of Levy-Bruhl's work on primitive mentality before his better-known use of Jesse L. Weston's book on comparative mythology. Sergei Eisenstein read Levy-Bruhl on Native thought as a precursor to developing his own ideas about prelogical or "sensual thinking," which he saw as an expression of continuing and deep-rooted animistic beliefs that could not just be ignored. In different degrees Modernist art was an expression of a fascination with "prelogical" and animist thought, but, as with Eisenstein, it was combined with other elements, including political orientations. These could either celebrate a return to the irrational and religious, like Fascism, or seek to critique and explain such an attraction, as in Marxism. Thus a double and often divided impulse—whether to give full weight to the irrational or to demystify it—runs through a great deal of modernist art and anthropology.

A particularly suggestive exploration of these concerns is Walter Benjamin's discussion of the ways in which the object in cinema, as in modern capitalism, gains its power not by being endowed with life, as it was in primitive thought, but by being made into an object, a commodity. Once separated from its production context, this can then be endowed with mysterious significance. In Benjamin's account, cinema creates the illusion of a reality and seems to endow objects with life by modern and technological means that are themselves entirely effaced and obscured and he sees this as the equivalent of the magical processes that Marx identified in commodity fetishism. For Benjamin "the true, creative overcoming of religious illumination . . . resides in *profane illumination*, a materialistic, anthropological inspiration."[1] The way in which the cinema presented an enchanted world and gave objects themselves a phantasmagoric power was also powerfully expressed by the filmmaker Jean Epstein in a lecture of 1923.

I would even go so far as to say that the cinema is polytheuristic and theogonic. Those lives it creates, by summoning objects out of shadows of indifference into the light of dramatic concern, have little in common with human life. These lives are like the life in charms and amulets, the ominous tabooed objects of certain primitive religions. If we wish to understand how an animal, a plant or a stone inspire respect, fear and horror, those three most sacred sentiments, I think we must watch them on the screen, living their mysterious silent lives, alien to the human sensibility.[2]

The place where primitive objects themselves were most easily to be encountered, and where the primitive was contained within a modern framework in a very different fashion from the cinema, was the museum, where all the elements and ingredients of primitive thought could be found in provocative conjunctions. The work of James Clifford and others has served to remind us of the importance to Modernism of ethnographic material. Not only was there the stimulus of disparate objects in new conjunctions, which the new orientations of Dada and surrealism brought into positive view, but some ethnographic objects in themselves embodied principles of assemblage.[3] As objects were incorporated into a collection, their meanings were changed. Christian Feest has described collecting as "a process by which samples of a complex whole are removed from their meaningful and functional context in order to be preserved under artificial conditions and within a new frame of reference."[4] Losing their original context, where they supposedly had meaning and power, objects collected from "primitive" cultures became exotic remnants or fragments standing for whole cultures, or specimens for objective research. Objects did, though, retain some of their original qualities. Mary Helms describes the precursors of the modern collections, the wonder cabinets of the Renaissance, in ways that underline the fundamental similarities still to be found. "The emperor's zoo and botanical garden, like the shaman's pouch, contained bits and pieces of the animate cosmos, power-filled natural wonders, examples of the rare, the curious, the strange and the precious—all expressions of the unusual and the different attesting to the forces of the dynamic universe that by definition lies outside the (again by definition) controlled, socialized, civilized heartland."[5]

The nature and purpose of Western collections may have radically changed over the years, from the early cabinets of wonders to the modern museum. Even so, Helms's stress on the metonymic effect that is created by separation and fragmentation as objects move from one culture and context to another, and come to stand for the whole context from which they have been torn, offers an important way to see some persisting similarities. In spite of the modern emphasis on reason and objectivity, the associational and metonymic connections still operate at a more "primitive" level of association. This may mean that exotic objects are never quite denatured for study and contemplation but continue to exert their power.[6] James Clifford reverses the primitivist implications of the term "fetish" when he describes the compulsions and reductiveness of the Western collectors. "If the notion of the African 'fetish' had any meaning in the twenties, it described not a mode of African belief but rather the way in which exotic artifacts were consumed by European aficionados. A mask or statue or any shred of black culture could effectively summon a complete world of dreams and possibilities—passionate, rhythmic, concrete, mystical, unchained: an 'Africa.'" As he has shown, for a short but heady period, the conjunctions created in such collections crossed over disciplinary and aesthetic boundaries, even if all too soon they were contained. "With the emergence of twentieth-century modernism and anthropology figures formerly called 'fetishes' (to take just one class of object) became works either of 'sculpture' or of 'material culture.'"[7]

While this may be generally true, it is interesting that Picasso's own description of the iconic moment of his encounter in the Trocadéro with African masks actually emphasizes magic, not art.

We all of us loved fetishes. Van Gogh once said, "Japanese art—we all had that in common." For us it's the Negroes. . . . When I went to the old Trocadéro, it was disgusting. The Flea Market. The smell. I was alone. I wanted to get away. But I didn't leave. I stayed. I stayed. I understood that it was very important: something was happening to me, right? The masks weren't just like any other pieces of sculpture. Not at all. They were magic things. But why weren't the Egyptian pieces or the Chaldean? We hadn't realized it. They were primitives, not magic things. The Negro pieces were intercesseurs, mediators. . . . They were against everything—against unknown, threatening spirits. . . . All the fetishes were used for the same thing. They were weapons. To help people avoid coming under the influence of spirits again, to help them become independent. . . . Spirits, the unconscious (people still weren't talking about that very much), emotion—they're all the same thing. I understood why I was a painter. All alone in that awful museum, with masks, dolls made by the redskins, dusty manikins. *Les Demoiselles d'Avignon* must have come to me that very day, but not at all because of the forms; because it was my first exorcism painting.[8]

In another account, Picasso also stresses his realization of art's relation to magic: "I realized what painting was all about. Painting isn't an aesthetic operation; it's a form of magic designated as a mediator between this strange hostile world and us."[9] It's worth noting here the extent to which such fears went beyond the circles of supposedly impressionable artists. Collectors and curators could also be influenced. One collector is recorded as showed an uneasy recognition of the power of the fetishes he was collecting, which he believed could cause "the offender to shuffle off this mortal coil, with the aid of a lingering throat disease power." He even thought of attaching a warning label addressed to his English contact. Another collector warned that "Great care should be taken in handling these fetishes as cases have been known of the above diseases [dropsy and syphilis, among others] attacking persons merely through placing their hands on them. I supply gloves, owing to the medicine with which they are covered."[10]

I will return in Chapter 4 to the ways in which the iconic nature of Picasso's use of primitive masks, particularly in *Les Desmoiselles*, has been used by a later generation of African American painters for their own purposes, but I want now to focus on another aspect of this incident. It is significant, though seldom remarked on, that Picasso specifically mentions Indian and not just African objects here. There were substantial collections of Indian materials in European collections, including the Trocadéro and the Berlin Ethnographical Museum, and these items, which included bead and leather work from the Great Plains, pottery from the Southwest, and wood carvings from the Northwest coast, were presumably being exhibited as ethnographic rather than art objects. In any case, they formed part of the exciting conjunction of exotic and discontinuous elements that so excited the surrealists in their responses to collections.[11] In fact it is interesting that unlike African sculpture, Indian materials were not exhibited specifically as art until the late 1930s.[12] As well as such collections, though, there were traveling exhibitions and shows with Indian dances and music of varying authenticity. The Penobscot Indian Molly Spotted Elk performed her Indian dances in Europe but also played the tom-tom in the United States Jazz Band at the 1931 International Colonial Exhibition in Paris.[13] Under the same broad primitivist umbrella, the European celebration of black exoticism did not necessarily make much distinction between African American and African. The enthusiasm for Florence Mills, who sang and danced in a series of shows in London and Paris, including The Plantation Revue, and Blackbirds, and for Josephine Baker, with her semi-naked *la danse sauvage* in the Revue Négre, as well as for a series of touring jazz bands, tended to be for their atavistic and primitive qualities, even if the language of appreciation ranged from the aesthetic to the racially reductive.[14]

Europeans may not always have distinguished between Indian and African American objects and performances, which they could bracket off in another realm and time in what Johannes Fabian has called a "denial of coevalness,"[15] but white Americans were in a more immediate relation, at least to African Americans. Thus, while American visitors to Europe had their interest sparked by the same exhibits as the Europeans, and they saw them within the same

Modernist framework, their use of racial primitivism as it related to a specifically American identity was significantly different and is worth pursuing.

The painter Marsden Hartley visited the Indian exhibitions in Paris and Berlin[16] and while in Europe painted a series of works, beginning in 1914, with names such as *Indian Compositions* and *Indian Fantasy*, and incorporating traditional Indian images into a modernist assemblage of designs and abstract forms. He referred to this series as his *Amerika* paintings.[17] The effect of the spelling here suggests perhaps a German view of America, in which America itself is seen as primitive, and therefore representable by its primitives in European eyes. It is interesting that much later, the substitution of K for C in Black Power writings and slogans signified a move from American to African orientation, a strategic political invocation of a primitive bogeyman of white America (and perhaps with echoes of the use of the letter by the Klan as well). Here, though, Hartley's titles reflect the curious way in which the Indian was seen as exotic within America but also potentially representative of America itself. A conceptual framework already existed in which the Indian was both a symbol of America, representing the original and natural, as opposed to Europe, but was at the same time that which, according to America's manifest destiny, had to be effaced and removed in order for America to exist as a historical modern nation. This awkwardness could be accommodated in an ideological maneuver by which white artists took over the spirit of the "vanishing American," and both Marsden Hartley and his fellow painter Max Weber wrote articles calling for a new American aesthetic based on Indian artistic values. During his trips back to America at this time, Hartley visited the Southwest and, like countless other artists and writers of the time, found what were apparently simple, natural cultures imbued with aesthetic values, which contrasted sharply with the materialism and shallowness of modern life. This view was reflected in his poem "The Festival of the Corn." This was the original and essential America, which could be reclaimed through art, not the modern America of cities, commerce, and mechanization. Primitivist modernism, then, sets itself against the threat of mass society. As Leah Dilworth points out, "What these arguments about the Southwest's superior aesthetic value were also speaking about was class. . . . As much as artists were 'othering' themselves in their alliance with the region or with native Americans, they occupied an elite realm. They maintained strict boundaries between art and mass culture."[18]

The artist was in a position to recognize this and therefore to take over from the tragically but inevitably vanishing Indians. In one of several articles he wrote on the subject, Hartley insists that "We are not nearly as original as we fool ourselves into thinking." Nevertheless, "We have the excellent encouragement of redman aesthetics to establish ourselves firmly with an aesthetic of our own."[19] But what does Hartley mean here by "original"? Innovative, in the modern sense, or "existing from the beginning," as in the primitivist sense? And is the move from "redman" to "our own" one of continuity or replacement? One of the conceits used in both essays is of the Indian as aristocratic guest, and the whites as the inhospitable hosts. "Inasmuch as we have the evidence of a fine aristocracy among us still, it would seem as if it behooved us as a respectable host to let the redman entertain himself as he will."[20] This rather breathtaking flight of fancy (in that it is, of course, diametrically opposed to the historical reality in which whites are the less-than-welcome intruders or guests) allows Hartley to present the Indian as temporary, and the whites as permanent owners and inhabitants. Thus his idealized view of these timeless and noble people is, as so often, only the flip side of an imperialist assumption of the manifest destiny of the whites to replace them, and the aesthetic aura is produced by the idea of their transience. At points he seems to argue for their preservation, but it is really their aesthetic which interests him. "It would seem to me to be a sign of modernism in us to preserve the living esthetic splendors in our midst."[21]

Hartley contributed poems to Harriet Monroe's magazine *Poetry*, which in 1917 had a special issue on American Indian or "Aboriginal" poetry, offering "not translations but interpretations." The collection is a strange mixture reflecting the same uneasiness as Hartley's about authenticity and originality, but one of the contributors, Mary Austin, develops some of these same ideas in her later volume of Indian poetry, *The American Rhythm*. Here she offers "re-expressions" of American Indian song in which she finds a rhythm, "the very pulse of emerging American consciousness" that is formed from an engagement with the land of America itself and can therefore be shared by all later Americans.[22] In an earlier essay, she had rejoiced that "Probably never before has it occurred that the intimate thought of a whole people should be made known through its most personal medium to another people whose unavoidable destiny it is to carry that thought to fulfilment and make of that medium a characteristic literary vehicle."[23] This gives the poetry a universal, transhistorical quality, which would be "the means by which men and their occasions are rewoven from time to time with their allness; and who is there to tell me that this, in art, is not the essence of modernity?"[24] This introduction of modernity manages to cancel out historical differences, revealing in a usefully simplified and overt form the ideological work being done by the word "original" in the quotation from Hartley referred to above. This reweaving and unifying is crucial, as is the stress on the communal in invoking an idea and an ideal of the original and primal America, but what is also intriguing is what needs to be carefully excluded.

Hartley points out that up to now the only recognizable Native expression was one that Americans had not taken to their heart. "Other nations of the world have long since recognized Congo originality," but for white Americans it would be much more comfortable to claim kinship with the red rather than the black native. "It is singular enough that the as yet remote black man contributes the only native representation of rhythm and melody we possess. As an intelligent race, we are not even sure we want to welcome him as completely as we might, if his color were just a shade warmer, a shade nearer our own."[25]

Why African Americans should be "as yet remote" in comparison with Indians need not detain us, but we find in Mary Austin the same determination to privilege the Indian and exclude the African American. She defines the positive effects of rhythm in such a way as almost entirely to exclude what to most people of the time would be the most obvious instance of American rhythm, namely jazz. "The Amerind," she says, "admits none of the bond-loosening, soul-disintegrating, jazz-born movements of Mr Sandburg's Man Hunt," which would lead to "spiritual disintegration." She is obviously bothered about how to cope with jazz and returns to it later in a long footnote. As jazz is "a reversion" to our earliest responses, it could create disintegration, which would make "an excessive exclusive indulgence in jazz as dangerous as the moralists think it," whereas an intelligent use of it "might play an important part in that unharnessing of traditional inhibitions of response indispensable to the formation of a democratic society." So, for Austin here, this sort of rhythm must not be regressive or atavistic, and I think it is clear here that she is really skirting around issues of race. The implication seems to be that jazz is acceptable when used intelligently (by whites of a certain class and education, presumably), but when "indulged in," as by blacks, it is dangerous, whereas there are no such reservations expressed about Indian rhythms. In this she reflects the curious way in which jazz was criticized as both mechanical and primitive, and used to raise the specter of an inhuman and disintegrating modernity as well as a bestial savagery.

It is interesting to see the influence of such thinking on Martha Graham's description of American dance some years later in 1932. "Our two forms of indigenous dance, the Negro and the Indian, are as dramatically contrasted rhythmically as the land in which they root. The Negro dance is a dance toward freedom, a dance to forgetfulness, often Dionysiac in its abandon and the raw splendor of its rhythm—a rhythm of disintegration. The Indian dance, however, is not for freedom, or forgetfulness, or escape, but for awareness of life, complete relationship with that world in which he finds himself; it is a dance for power, a rhythm of integration."[26]

For Mary Austin, then, the rhythm found in Indian poetry was both the expression of a national identity and a connection to something transcendent and universal. In her reworkings of Indian songs, the idea of Native spirituality, separated out from its material and specific base, was turned into an occasion for aesthetic rather than religious appreciation, and she enthused over locating "the earliest suffusing flush of human consciousness under a sense of its relation to the Allness."[27] Dilworth argues that "Modernist primitivism was never about practicing Native American belief systems. It was, rather, about an aesthetic practice that would lead to spiritual experience,"[28] and we might go further and question whether this "spiritual" end result could be distinguished from an aesthetic one in any case. Both represented a transcendence of materiality, which meant a privileging of those aspects of Indian culture that seemed to allow themselves to be etherialized, and a consequent downplaying of any others. The rather flippant discussion by William Brandon, the editor of a later anthology of translations of Indian poetry, of his treatment of Plains Indian buffalo songs is revealing in this respect. He stripped down the repetitions, which were part of their original ritual, he tells us, as it would not only be "wearisome" to follow all the magic numbers, but "we might also, who knows, materialize a buffalo. We don't really want the buffalo. We only want the feeling of the earnest repetition, the feeling of the hypnosis, of the marvelous emerging, the feeling of the magic. All that we want from any of it is the feeling of its poetry."[29]

I would suggest that the idea of "poetry" here is fulfilling a similar function to the idea of "spirituality" in the 1970s and beyond, so that the realms of the aesthetic and religious, or at least religiose, come together. Brandon's remark looks less innocent, of course, if we see it against the real anguish at the destruction of the buffalo and the livelihood and cultures associated with them, expressed in the Ghost Dance, and the ritual singing and dancing designed to invoke a world in which the buffalo might indeed return. Some of the earliest recordings of Indian songs were collected by James Mooney as early as 1893 in his work on the Ghost Dance, and they include songs about the return of the buffalo.[30] In its flippant reduction of the whole tragic experience, which gave rise to the prophetic movement now known as the Ghost Dance, to an occasion for fleeting aesthetic contemplation, Brandon's comments are likely now to make uncomfortable reading, but I will return to the Ghost Dance in the larger context of the relation of spiritual, material, and aesthetic powers in the final chapter.

Such uses of Indian material as Brandon's stem from a larger pattern from the late nineteenth century by which the specificity of Indian religions was obscured within Romantic ideas of a harmony with a transcendent nature, and a celebration and sharing of universal values through an aesthetic experience that can transcend language. Discussing Indian music, the anthropologist Alice Fletcher in 1894 saw it as a common ground on which universal communication could take place without need for translation. "If a more universal common structure prevails in vocal folk-music, may not the reason be that the emotions of the heart of man are more in common the world over than his intellectual ideas? These separate, while the former unite the human race."[31]

So far in this chapter I have been concentrating on primitivism in terms of white Romantic and Modernist appropriations, but of course Native Americans and African Americans made their own particular negotiations between the prevailing aesthetic movements and their own political and cultural agendas. Progressive Indian artists and spokespeople, most notably represented by the members of the Society of American Indians, used tableaux and musical entertainment as well as lectures and writing to perform a version of Indian identity that in fact was not far removed in conception and tone from the work of white artists like Austin and Hartley. In 1913 Zitkala Ša (whose early work "Why I Am a Pagan" I dealt with in the last chapter) wrote and produced, together with a white musician, *The Sun Dance Opera*. This was a conventional love story, set against a very thinly sketched ceremony, though in performance it may well apparently have incorporated more authentic and interesting performances from the local Ute community.[32]

Zitkala Ša is an interesting example of the changing and diverse Indian positions of the Society of American Indians.[33] She did continue to celebrate Indian heritage, but she also became a Christian, and a firm opponent of the use of peyote in what came to be the Native American Church, testifying against it in congressional hearings in 1918. In her suspicion of such newer syncretic developments, she reflected the views of many members of the Society of American Indians, who, though committed to the advancement of Indians, were ambivalent about just what aspects of Indianness to value. James Mooney criticized her rather spurious use of traditional dress for her appearance at the hearings. He suggested that her Sioux Indian identity as presented was "pretty much made up," and that by dressing up in this way she was making claims for a sort of Indian identity that made her and her associates vulnerable to such criticism.[34] Though Christian, they also subscribed to the idea of what sounds, from the outside anyway, to be a rather bland pan-Indian spirituality, as expressed for instance by Charles Eastman, another opponent of peyote, in his *The Soul of the Indian*. The book draws on Eastman's own Sioux background, but he talks throughout as if there were one "Indian" religion. Eastman wants to present the original beliefs as a counter to practices that are "without value," because "modern and hybrid, inextricably mixed with Biblical legend and Caucasian philosophy."[35] Yet he is at pains in the introduction to insist that there is only one God, whom all religions worship, and his invocation of St. Peter at the end suggests that Christianity is at least some sort of privileged point of development.[36]

The stance of the Society of American Indians as a whole does raise the complex issue of the degree to which native religion could be viewed as a cultural and religious resource in a time of change. Both the Ghost Dance and the Peyote Cult have been seen as revitalization movements, but there was little sense among the society's members, or other Indian artists of the time, of any recognition of such potential. It is as if there were two quite separate and incommensurable spheres—traditional and spiritual on the one side, and progressive, Christian and political on the other—and any syncretism or adaptation that might offer a renewal of the spiritual past that would have real political efficacy, as opposed to aesthetic appeal, was suspect or unthinkable. In this sense it could be argued that Indian artists and intellectuals at that point in history were less attuned or disposed to take up the more radical possibilities of Modernism than their African American equivalents.

Educated African Americans were cut off from any unmediated relation to a generally admired traditional past to a much greater degree than the Native Americans. In the last chapter I showed how Chesnutt and others used what African American legacy was available, but with the emergence of Modernism and its uses of Africa, another whole area of resources became freshly visible. Initially this was often mediated through the same European Modernism that had influenced Marsden Hartley. For instance, in a passage that seems to echo Picasso's fears before the African masks and Indian "manikins," the African American painter Aaron Douglas describes his fears when encouraged to take an interest in African art by another painter. "I clearly recall his impatience as he sought to urge me beyond my doubts and fears that seemed to loom so large in the presence of the terrifying specters moving beneath the surface of every African masque and fetish." He then takes cautious steps to "the unknown," but it is not Africa or even an African American art tradition that he focuses on. Rather, he tries to "objectify with paint and brush what I thought to be the visual emanations or expressions that came into view with the sounds produced by the old black song makers of the antebellum days, when they first began to put together snatches and bits from Protestant hymns, along with half remembered tribal chants, lullabies and work songs."[37]

The artist urging him on was in fact the European Winold Reiss. His first interest when he came to America was actually Indians, of whom he painted many portraits, but his main significance here is as a mediator for Douglas and others of European cubism and primitivism. The way in which Africa as a cultural resource is largely mediated in this period through Europe creates many ironies. A little later, in 1938, when Lois Mailou Jones painted *Les Fétiches* in Paris under the influence of African art that she saw there, she had to defend her painting's angularity and boldness by citing Picasso and Modigliani as precursors who used "the inspiration of Africa," and by insisting that "if anyone had the right to use it, I did. It was my heritage, so they had to give in."[38]

The way in which Douglas invokes music, rather than art, as the route to the deepest folk or racial feelings in the quotation above reflects a more general use of African American music in writers and artists of the Harlem Renaissance, but this itself reflects the fundamental debates taking place over Negro identity in the Harlem Renaissance. Concerned to draw on continuities and roots from which the New Negro could go forward, artists and intellectuals variously combined the folk materials of the South and the more distant and mediated materials of Africa. But for most African American artists, Africa was an idea more than an experienced reality and was thus subject to the same exoticisms as it was for the dominant white culture. When Countee Cullen, in his poem "Heritage," asks "What is Africa to me?" his initial answer is a series of exotic clichés. This is not to deny, of course, that the idea of Africa sometimes has very real cultural and political resonances. I have shown some of these in Chapter 1 in relation to the debate over African survivals and their relation to conjure, but my purpose in this chapter is to see how artists in the twenties and thirties operated out of a particular nexus of ideas of religion, magic, and folk and racial identity. In this respect, Locke's *The New Negro* of 1925 is a classic text, juxtaposing illustrations from Reiss and Douglas with poems celebrating the energies and modernity of Negro life, essays on music, and a wide range of cultural and sociological analysis.

There was an ambivalence in the period of the Harlem Renaissance not only about Africa but also about the popular and folk forms that had developed in America. This is related to an ambivalence about primitivism itself, and the degree to which the use of folk, vernacular, or African materials was an expression of continuity and strength or a reinforcement of damaging stereotypes. Alain Locke's view of African art stressed the hieratic and "classic" qualities, which could be combined with the "higher" art of the West, and when it came to music, Locke tended to see folk forms as having value for what they might become, rather than what they were. "Negro folk music, properly maturing, has the capacity to produce new musical forms as well as new musical idioms; that is indeed the task of the trained musician who has the sense and devotion to study seriously the folk music at its purest and deepest sources."[39] Interestingly, though, the trained musicians who will help it to "mature" will succeed by going back to its "purest and deepest sources" so there is a circularity reflective of much of the feelings about originality and the primitive in the period.

Shirley Graham's opera *Tom Tom*, which was first fully produced in 1932 (though there was an early version in 1929), is interesting because it presents in its three acts a panoramic sweep of African American history. It needs to be seen in the context of Harlem Renaissance debates over the cultural and political relevance of Africa to black Americans, which extended to the political programs of Marcus Garvey. Earlier works like *In Dahomey* had offered a reductive view of African continuities, but pageants like *The Star of Ethiopia*, developed by DuBois (whom Graham would later marry), offered a historical sweep in which African continuities and the progress of African Americans could be presented more positively.[40]

In each act of Graham's play, we see decisive changes taking place, and some sharply opposed positions, but also continuities, most notably symbolized in the survival of the tom-tom. In the first act, which takes place in Africa, the drum is connected with the power of the voodoo man, and the caricature of African religion, which focuses mainly on human sacrifice, seems to be recycling the crudest sort of primitivism. The tom-tom is also shown to have a communicative function, though, and is used at the end to warn others of the threat of slave traders. In the second act, set on a Southern plantation, the tom-tom is again connected with the voodoo man who is in open conflict with the Christianized slaves. He dismisses their spirituals and camp meetings.

Shake yo' chains.

Oh! Da music's sweet

An da crackin' ob da whip

Will make yo leap!

This is just

Dancin for slaves!

But if you'd be free

To da swamps we'll go

Dan we can plan

While do sun is low.[41]

After the South's defeat, when the rest of the characters go hopefully to freedom in the North he remains

Bound in the shackles I myself have forged,

Sunk in a grave that I myself have dug!

Drums! Jungles![42]

African survivals here seem to be totally negative, and the positive presentation of spirituals and Christianity would suggest the sort of celebration of the ultimate superiority of Christianity that can be found in a range of Ethiopianist writings. (It also echoes the theme of Scott Joplin's opera *Treemonisha*, written in the early years of the century but not performed until 1972.) But this is not the whole story. For one thing, Graham did have considerable musical knowledge. Like other Harlem Renaissance artists, she had acquired her vision of Africa partly via Paris, where she had thoughts of making a living as a jazz pianist, but she had also worked as music librarian at Howard University.[43] In the play she used at least some African musicians, and according to a report in *Crisis*, she had also imported "a native voodoo man" from Africa.[44] The voodoo man survives because, as he says,

The gods of Africa will help me

. . . .

For they know all the secrets of ages

And they've seen all the mysteries of time.[45]

In act 3 the voodoo man appears as a back-to-Africa visionary. The action of the play dooms this vision in that the boat his followers build to take them there is overloaded and sinks, partly because his original vision has been taken over by commercialism in the shape of a real estate man. When he is killed by an angry mob, his vision is defended, and the tom-tom is saved by characters who had earlier represented Christian values. As one of them says, "This man saw a vision—he saw a race of people black and strong." Another takes the tom-tom, which the voodoo man fears will be silenced for ever. Striking it with "a mighty blow" he appeals:

Who will go with me

Not to distant lands,

But here, beating the tom-tom

We'll find kingdoms unknown.

The opera ends with a scene in a cabaret, where the music seems to be jazz along the lines of Ellington's so-called jungle music, but in the course of the play there are also spirituals and of course the tom-tom, together with the tramp of feet "seeking for a Kingdom." The synthesis here is thus intellectual, political, and musical, and the play is unique in the explicitness with which it carries this out. The central importance of music also makes an interesting parallel with Duke Ellington's "Black, Brown and Beige," which also traces a larger narrative of African American development in which the drum and music are central. The more atavistic uses of the tom-tom also suggest O'Neill's *Emperor Jones*, and in fact Graham would later adapt O'Neill's *The Hairy Ape* for an all-black version.[46]

A great deal of critical attention has been paid to the cultural flowering of the Harlem Renaissance, but the period saw a series of interlocking debates that involved not only Modernist interest in primitivism, and a changing role for folklore studies, but also changes in anthropology under the influence of Franz Boas, against which the negotiation of African American and Indian identities were being worked out. It is the relation of the Harlem Renaissance to this developing anthropology, in which African Americans, like Native Americans, were both contributors and subjects, that I want now to explore in order to set a context for Zora Neale Hurston, who will eventually be my main focus in the rest of the chapter.

This question of folklore and other cultural survivals was particularly important in the debates over the extent of the retention of African elements in North America. The debate itself need not be rehearsed again here, but it is worth stressing the way that, at different points in the argument, different things have been seen to be at stake.[47] To assume that all cultural continuity had been destroyed could be seen as characterizing African Americans as (re-)created by and from white culture—and therefore without resources to resist this power. This would seem to risk reinforcing the demeaning view of Africans as passive, as a tabula rasa on which a new identity was written. On the other hand, if one accepted that there were African survivals, one's view of them depended on how one saw Africa itself. As long as Africa was seen as the nadir of human achievements, survivals were only evidence of backwardness and the inability to progress. There were, though, many more positive ways of viewing such remnants. The development of more neutral and inclusive concepts of culture under the influence of Boasian anthropology meant that surviving African elements could be valued as part of an African American culture that could be seen synchronically, as whole and coherent in its own right.

Lee Baker describes "an auspicious convergence"[48] between New Negro writers, who wanted to celebrate and collect their folk culture and the white folklore collectors of the *Journal of American Folklore* that resulted in the collection of impressive bodies of African American folklore, but there were limits to their shared goals. The effect of academic folk collectors, with their insistence on survivals and the idea of an undifferentiated anonymous folk, had been to reduce the sense of folk culture as a changing and adapting resource. Although Boas's work was crucial in giving validity to cultures in their own right, and in countering the racist dismissals of other cultures, he did not give any particular importance to the role of folklore as an area of creative resistance. William S. Willis has argued that Boas gave insufficient weight to the sociocultural environment, in this case the role of whites and the context of oppression. He was actually more used to dealing with isolated groups, like Indians, and was completely resistant to the interpretation of folklore and to attempts to foster racial solidarity through it, perhaps as a personal reaction against the nationalist and racist uses of it in Europe at the time.[49]

African Americans, though, were more likely to combine the new validation of cultures with a more positive view of African continuities and to find a spiritual continuity. DuBois, for instance, in his use of the "sorrow songs" could claim that precisely those spiritual capacities whose existence had been denied in earlier accounts were what held African American people together. As Jon Cruz puts it, "With W. E. B. DuBois the meaning of 'survivals' was reversed and resignified. Neither 'cultural lag' nor 'cultural residuals,' folk practices represented a crucial retention of solidarity in the face of dehumanization and marginalization."[50]

Melville Herskovits's attention to the ways in which African elements could survive, not so much in discrete enclaves or as separate unchanging elements but, as Albert Raboteau puts it, "as aspects hidden under or blended with similar European forms," was important in encouraging a new awareness of the fluidity and dynamism of religious practices.[51] It also seemed to imply a greater predisposition to religion on the part of African Americans, and in the arguments over this, the question of the survivals themselves became less important than whether the predisposition toward religiosity (or credulousness, as it was pejoratively seen in the nineteenth century) was an inherited and even an immutable racial attribute. This claim for a greater spiritual capacity on the part of African Americans, whether cultural or biological in origin, is one that has continued to be made, as I show in later chapters.[52]

We see many of these conflicting and changing views reflected in *The New Negro*, which includes (rather uncharacteristic) contributions by Melville Herskovits and Arthur Huff Fauset.[53] There is an irony in the fact that Herskovits, who would become so influential in arguing for the importance of African continuities and survivals, appears not in the section "The Negro Digs Up His Past" but in a section on Americanisms, where he argues that what is distinctive in Harlem is "a remnant from the peasant days in the South. Of the African culture, not a trace."[54] Both Fauset and Herskovits were to change or refine the positions they took in *The New Negro*, and in fact Fauset is a useful illustration of the intellectual and artistic crosscurrents of the time. Like Hurston, he contributed to *The New Negro*, wrote some short fiction, and conducted fieldwork for white anthropologists, notably Frank Speck and Elsie Clews Parsons, both of whom worked on Indian as well as African cultures. Fauset's major work, *Black Gods of the Metropolis*, argued for the importance of religious cults as an important locus for various forms of positive creative and community expression, which to some extent challenged Herskovits's view of an African American predisposition to religiosity as a remnant of their African heritage, and his consequent tendency to see contemporary cults as just survivals. Fauset's early work was on mixed-race peoples of Nova Scotia, and later on urban religious groups, and though he was committed throughout his life to political activities to better African American life, he never particularly identified with the objects of his field studies. This may well have been because of his own marginality, coming from a middle-class mixed-race family, but in any case he never claimed the sort of community with a folk culture that Hurston and others did.[55]

It is in this context of anthropology, folklore collecting, and religion that Zora Neale Hurston needs to be seen. While there are other writers who deal with magic and folk traditions, and others, like Fauset, involved with anthropology, no other African American writer describes such extended firsthand experiences or is more creative in finding forms to combine her interests. Hurston's position has always been problematic. Ignored for a long time, and then critically and popularly rehabilitated by Alice Walker, she is now the subject of a huge critical output. She remains controversial, though, not only because of her conservative positions late in her life over civil rights, but because this was only a late reflection of a deeper and more fundamental belief that the essence of African American identity was in folk communities. For her this was too valuable to be swept away by progress, including forced integration policies that would destroy what was distinctive in black communities. Hazel Carby has pointed out some of the dangers in overemphasizing this folk identity. Against a backdrop of migration to cities and the impact of modernity even in the South, the insistent representation of the "folk" as the real or quintessential black "people" in Hurston needs to be seen not as inevitable but as a choice, and one not taken by all writers.[56] Running through Hurston's work is a belief in the existence and the profound value of a distinctive set of attitudes and beliefs—what she doesn't, but we could, call a "culture" in Boasian terms—one found in African American communities, and particularly in those least affected by modern changes. While her views need to seen in the context of the work of Herskovits on African retentions, her emphasis is on the actual American communities in the present.[57] It is the exact nature of the continuities and cultures, and the way in which she explores them, that makes her work worth exploring further in terms of the operation and representation of magic and spirituality.

The actual effect of Hurston's formal training in anthropology has perhaps been overstated, as it was brief and problematic. It could be argued in fact that she was at least as influenced and helped by Alain Locke, Herskovits, and Ruth Benedict as by Boas,[58] but it is certainly true that she made full dramatic use of her position as outsider-cum-native informant in several of her works. This role was common for Indians but unheard of for African Americans, and by playing it to the hilt in *Mules and Men*, she was able to accentuate both the strangeness and the completeness of the folk culture of Eatonville and thereby make her liminal role more dramatic. It is useful, therefore, to see her not only alongside other writers, and other African American anthropologists like Fauset, but also alongside Indian intellectuals and writers who were under the patronage of whites. Her mentor, Boas had a number of native informants, including George Hunt and William Beynon, but Ella Cara Deloria may be the closest parallel with Hurston. Both women offered an insider view and experimented with different forms, including fiction, to do so but perhaps were never taken quite as seriously as they deserved. This was especially so in later life, when Hurston was employed by the Works Progress Administration in a lowly position not reflecting her expertise and experience, and Deloria's important and extensive work on Dakota texts was long neglected.[59]

For Indians who were educated enough to be able to act as mediators or spokespersons, the tension was between the imperatives of change and assimilation on the one side and the preservation and continuity of cultural identity on the other. Anthropology allowed them to use their expertise to preserve and record their culture, but only in scholarly texts or in museums, as most anthropology of the time was uninterested in contemporary problems and often implicitly accepted the destructive changes taking place. (Even Boas opposed the appointment of John Collier, who as commissioner signaled a change in the direction away from inevitable assimilation and toward the recognition of tribal continuity and integrity.) A range of writers, though, did take on the role of explaining Indian life in forms ranging from ethnography and children's stories to polemic and full-blown fiction. These included Arthur Parker, whose work as an anthropologist was at an oblique angle to Boasian anthropology, Francis La Flesche, Charles Eastman, and John Joseph Mathews.

Hurston's relation to anthropology may have been uneasy in her awareness of the power structures and of the restrictions of the objective text to be produced, but anthropology's assumption of a bounded culture that needed to be preserved was something she worked with more comfortably than others, including many Indians. In one letter she notes that many people are forgetting what they once knew and even laments that "the Negro is not living his lore to the extent of the Indian. He is not on a reservation being kept pure. His negroness is being rubbed off by close contact with white culture."[60] Here the problem of her antimodernist stance becomes evident, as she follows its logic to the ultimate by suggesting the need for protected cultural enclaves. Native Americans suffering the deprivations of reservation life at the time could certainly have shown her the limitations of such policies. She also ignores here the evidence of the racial and cultural mixing in the South, which might have led her to question this idea of Indian purity. In this respect the work of her Indian contemporary Ella Deloria with the Lumbee of North Carolina is particularly interesting, as is her clearheaded recognition of cultural changes and losses, even while she is attempting to fulfill the requests of her anthropological superiors.[61]

What her mentors Boas and Herskovits both shared was an interest in what was obscured and perhaps disappearing with change and modernity, whether African survivals or African American folk patterns developed in isolation from modern America, and it is useful to situate Hurston's work and perhaps a surprisingly large amount of her activities within this context of collecting and preservation. This ranged from so-called salvage ethnography to the collecting of folk material she carried out in the New Deal era, which has tended until recently to be downplayed in favor of her Boas connections. As well as collecting for Mrs. Osgood Mason, who also had a previous interest in collecting Indian materials, she collected objects for Boas. Immediately following the passage quoted above invoking Indian reservations and lamenting the loss of "negroness" she writes to Boas about acquiring "a 'hand,' a powerful piece of conjure for the museum, and I have bargained for two more pieces, from a still more powerful 'doctor.'"[62] Here she is fully involved in the academic denaturing of items of folk culture into objects of study, while elsewhere she is immersed in, and fully respectful of the "power" of the materials.

Her own description of her approach in a letter to Alain Locke was of "using the vacuum cleaner method, grabbing everything I see,"[63] but she was also acutely aware of the other more analytic elements. In *Mules and Men* she refers to using "the spyglass of anthropology," and the phrase nicely captures the combination of analysis and intrusion into the subject culture. Her use of fictional techniques, variously combined with the standard forms of objective ethnography, has been seen as anticipating the "reflexive" anthropology of later years,[64] with its concern to undermine any firm opposition between scientific and fictional prose, and demonstrate that all ethnographic work is rhetorically and narratively patterned to some degree. When we look at the larger narrative shape that Hurston gives to her ethnographic encounters, we can detect an attempt to give them what we could call a comic rather than tragic overarching shape. It is possible to see two different narrative lines in many ethnographies. One, often implicit, is what happens to the community. The other is what happens to the ethnographer in his or her quest for knowledge and penetration into that community. In many Indian ethnographies, for instance, the first narrative, dealing with the community, is one of tragic decline, even if the second, portraying the individual's quest for insider understanding, can sometimes be one of success. These narrative lines also correspond to the shape of much early Indian fiction, where the conflicted protagonist also often reflects the problems of the community and its threatened identity, and parallels could be drawn with the work of Zitkala Ša and Darcy McNickle as well as Ella Deloria. Occasionally Hurston suggests ways of seeing African American folk communities in the same way, as requiring salvage, but in general her work celebrates the positive and enduring values of the culture as well as of her own ability to succeed in capturing it. As I will show, though, when we come to the issue of hoodoo and conjure, this pattern becomes more complicated.

Magic in anthropological terms can be seen within a larger comic narrative as a positive survival of a valuable cultural resource and a resistance to modernity and reductive rationality, or as a regrettable survival, a refusal to join the larger comic narrative of modernity and progress and enlightenment. Many of the works of the Harlem Renaissance contain both positions, and it is important to see, therefore, that the issue is not just confined to the creative shaping of fiction versus the objective facts of science. All the discursive realms are involved in similar rhetorical and larger shaping patterns, and what is most interesting is the way Hurston moves between them. Her work may not have been designed to reflect back critically on the dominant American culture, as Ruth Benedict's and Margaret Mead's often did, but in her letters we do find some interesting instances of her turning anthropological tools back on Christianity, not just on "primitive" religions. She questions Boas, for instance, about how far she may apply the terms of anthropology to Christian ritual and belief. The tentative form of the questions ("Is it safe for me to say baptism is an extension of water worship? . . . Is not . . . ? May I say that . . . ?") suggests a nervousness about the acceptability of treating Christianity in the same way as conjure and magic, but it is notable that in a letter to Langston Hughes, another African American and one fully aware of the power imbalances of patronage, she is much more outspoken. She firmly categorizes Christianity as "an attenuated form of nature-worship," and after describing its key rituals, comments caustically, "Sympathetic magic, pure and simple. They have a nerve to laugh at conjure."[65] The stance here is typically elusive, though, in that it is not clear whether she is dismissing *both* forms from a rationalist standpoint as "only" sympathetic magic or merely pointing out less critically the similarities as a way of defending conjure. Anthropology has tended to deal with native belief in magic, witchcraft, and the like from outside rather than phenomenologically, and one of the significant ways in which Hurston anticipates later ethnographies is her direct involvement in hoodoo and voodoo practices.

Hurston's first main period of collecting and fieldwork was between 1926 and 1930, when she amassed extensive notes on conjure in the United States. During the early 1930s she drew on this material in a variety of textual and dramatic forms. Later periods of collecting were in 1935–1936 in the West Indies, resulting in *Tell My Horse*, and during the later 1930s and early 1940s. Her work for the Federal Writers' Project and Alan Lomax, intended to become "The Florida Negro," was not published until 1993.[66] Apart from some quite impersonal and detached sketches appearing as "The Eatonville Anthology" in *The Messenger* in 1926, her first nonfiction folklore accounts were for the *Journal of American Folklore* in 1930 and 1931, and these were tuned to the journal's particular disciplinary requirements. She did sometimes use first-person narrative and refer to personal experience, most notably in the account of her own initiation into hoodoo practices, but in general the intention was to frame the materials and present them as information for scientific analysis. She was then approached to contribute to Nancy Cunard's *Negro* and produced six short but important pieces, which were published in 1934, a year before *Mules and Men*. The pieces in *Negro* are much more personally engaged, either discursively as in "Spirituals and Neo Spirituals" or in developing the distinctive stance of insider and outsider which would be more fully developed in *Mules and Men*, where she dramatizes her position as an outsider who gains entrance to the storytelling circles. Her unique position as a member of the community who returns with the spyglass of anthropology is only briefly presented as a problem when she asks the wrong questions in the wrong linguistic register (asking for "folklore," for instance, which she comes to realize is not how the tellers would describe their own stories). After this, the narrative in *Mules and Men* is one of a gradual inclusion that allows her to be both within and without in a way that is celebratory of the folk culture she is representing.[67] In the area of magic and religion, though, there is a rather different pattern. We still have the idea of entry and initiation, but I want to argue that there is in fact a significant limit to her involvement.

The final section of *Mules and Men* is devoted to hoodoo. A reworking of an earlier *Journal of American Folklore* article, it was apparently added to the book at the request of the publisher,[68] but the changes Hurston makes are worth looking at, especially in relation to magic. Both pieces move between the impersonal—"they believe"—and the personal—"I met"—and they include much of the same material, with some changes of names. The element that is much more present in *Mules and Men*, though, is the folk "we" that is invoked as a continuation of the tone set in the first part of the book. The scholarly article begins with a description and definition of hoodoo that places it in relation not only to other practices in Africa and the Caribbean, but to spiritualism as well, with which it often merges, and Hurston shows a detached awareness of pragmatic and institutional considerations. Discussing the association with spiritualism, for instance, she notes the advantages for a hoodoo doctor. "A spiritualistic name protects the congregation, and is a useful devise of protective coloration."[69] She refers to the work of Mother Leafy Anderson and her original "Eternal Life Spiritualist Church," the only one not associated in some degree with hoodoo, and attends the service of one of Anderson's followers, where she notes that Jesus as a separate figure gives way to "a nameless 'Spirit,'" by which name the deity is always addressed.[70] What she does not explore, though is the distinctive use made by groups influenced by Leafy Anderson of the Indian leader Black Hawk.

The improbable adoption of this nineteenth-century Indian leader by some African American Spiritual churches has been explained by his widespread fame in the nineteenth century. The object of great interest and even lionization in the East, and the subject of one of the first Indian autobiographies, he remained, we might say, a name to conjure with. According to Jason Berry he "surfaced slowly, deep in Louisiana, through the prism of a syncretistic religion that took his rebellion to its heart and soul." This perhaps overemphasizes the element of rebellion, and I think it is easier to see him in the larger context of Indians invoked as guides to a general, amorphous, and apolitical spirituality.[71] Berry sees the churches as "an extension of African cultural memory—celebrating those long dead as dynamic presences in the life of the flock, like ancestral shades in an animist tribe. Black Hawk was one spirit in a pantheon that was borrowed from Catholicism, Voodoo, Protestantism, and the churches' own deceased ministers." He quotes a present day practitioner's view. "I feel that Black Hawk has always been a part of the black spirit. We was took from Africa and that left us—we didn't hear any of those drums. It was the Indians that brought us back to the drums and the music."[72] While Black Hawk's followers are distinct from the celebrated and secular Mardi Gras Indians, the two groups clearly share common element of performance and syncretism and reflect a wider and underdocumented set of mutual influences.[73]

Though she does not discuss Black Hawk, Hurston is in general quick to note and enjoy syncretisms and borrowings, seemingly as part of a folk creativity as well as religious feeling. In an earlier piece published in *Negro*, she described Mother Catherine Seals, a disciple of Mother Leafy Anderson. Mother Seals used dramatizations involving Indian spirit guides and a "spirit cantata" called "a White Man's Sin and a Squaw's Revenge,"[74] and she is presented very positively by Hurston as practicing a totally syncretic religion. In her account, Hurston notes the freedom of animals to wander in during the service "without seeming out of place," epitomizing the inclusiveness at all levels, which also ensures that everyone is fed. She celebrates an eclectic and syncretic matriarchal religion in which, contrary to Christianity, there is no sinful birth. Unlike most religious dictators, Seals "does not crush the individual."[75] Hurston's stance here is sympathetic but still concerned to report, and there is an occasional recourse to scientific categorizing. Describing the providing of certain foods she comments, "All sympathetic magic. Chicken beef, lamb are animals of pleasing blood."[76] In general, though, the care with which Hurston blends sympathy with detail in her description is notable. Catherine of Russia, she tells us, could not have been more impressive than this Catherine as she presides over her followers, but she also tells us that Seals has a "box of shaker salt in her hand like a rod of office. I know this reads incongruous but it did not look so."[77] She is acknowledging here that to the outside reader the possibility of bathos is present but for the participant (as seen through her eyes at the time), "it seemed perfectly natural for me to go to my knees upon the gravel floor."

This sort of balance is also something Hurston is aiming at in the final hoodoo section of *Mules and Men*. On the first page she not only invokes the authority of the insider (the use of "we") but stakes a claim for hoodoo as the founding religion at the heart of the Christian creation story. "The way we tell it, hoodoo started way back there before everything. Six days of magic spells and mighty words and the world with its elements above and below was made." Here God's act of creation is like conjure. It is a spell, and the description of Moses as "the first man who ever learned God's power-compelling words" puts God in the tradition of Moses as the first conjurer or hoodoo man and squares the circle of Christianity and magic.[78] At the same time, there is a recognition of the limitations of this insider knowledge. "Nobody knows for sure how many thousands in America are warmed by the fires of hoodoo, because the worship is bound in secrecy." This becomes more marked when she goes to New Orleans and has to recognize the difference between the folklore of Eatonville, which could be accessed once she was recognized as part of the community, and the hidden nature of hoodoo. This is because believers conceal their faith. "Mouths don't empty themselves unless the ears are sympathetic and knowing. That is why these voodoo ritualistic orgies of Broadway and popular fiction are so laughable. The profound silence of the initiated remains what it is. Hoodoo is not drum beating and dancing."[79]

This reticence perhaps explains the detached tone in the account of her own initiation. During the lengthy process, which involves lying naked on a snakeskin for sixty-nine hours, followed by the ritual slaughter of a sheep, we are given little sense of her frame of mind. She tells us that "For sixty nine hours I lay there. I had five psychic experiences," but not what these experiences were or whether they produced a believer. Interestingly, although much of the account is considerably changed from the *Journal of American Folklore* article, this bald statement remains unchanged and undeveloped. Elsewhere in *Mules and Men*, she does add a passage elaborating upon the experience of being crowned, for which this is the preparation, but really only to lead us away from its core. Her hoodoo doctor, Turner (he is named Samuel Thompson in the original article), crowns her with a consecrated snakeskin, but the crown in essence is "Nothing definite in material. . . . I have been crowned in other places with flowers, with ornamental paper, with cloth, with sycamore bark, with eggshells. It is the meaning, not the material that counts. The crown without the preparation means no more than a college diploma without the four years' work."[80] This idea is supported by her statement in the section of the appendix titled "Paraphernalia of Conjure." "Anything may be conjure and nothing may be conjure, according to the doctor, the time and the use of the article."[81]

Part of the dramatization of her role in *Mules and Men* involves an emphasis on the depth of her involvement and commitment, but with conjure there is a countervailing aesthetic of reticence. We are told that Turner offers her a chance to be a partner. She does not accept, telling us only that "it has been a great sorrow to me that I could not say yes."[82] This certainly suggests a real commitment, but we are not told why she cannot, and the tone as a whole is rather reticent. Hurston as a detached individual perhaps questioning the claims made for hoodoo is simply not present. It could be argued that her style reflects a very artful positioning whereby she achieved both ethnographic detachment and a warm empathy with the world she describes, in which testing the strict truth of all claims would be intrusive and inappropriate. In the context of later, more celebratory writings on black spirituality, though, her reluctance to claim or dramatize magical powers is noticeable. One way of seeing this is as the silence that indicates knowledge. Robert Hemenway, for instance, argues that "What lies behind that reticent paragraph is Hurston's awareness of the spiritual possibilities in the hoodoo experience, and what informs the paragraph is her belief in the magic."[83]

Brian Carr and Tova Cooper also see deliberate reticence here and make a similar distinction between Hurston's treatment of voodoo and of spirituals. Although she says there can be no adequate or final representation of spirituals, as they are newly made each time, and although she criticizes their commodification as what she calls neospirituals, she does offer her own account—implicitly as a version that continues their process of making rather than restrictively defining them.[84] With hoodoo, however, she ultimately does not offer an account, either in the journal essay or in the later books, and for

Carr and Cooper this is a sign of what they see as modernism's critical limits. Another approach, though, is to see it as part of a larger reticence about magic, as opposed to spirituality or religion. Is there a silent place here created as a rhetorical effect—the equivalent of the invocation of the Romantic sublime? In support of this we can point to the prevalence of phrases like "we will never know" and "no-one can tell" as not so much the adoption of an insider folk attitude toward mystery, as a rhetorical trope to suggest something that is beyond expression. It may also be worth pointing out parenthetically that her degree of commitment went against the prevailing views at the time, so there may have been other reasons for reticence. A contemporary review of *Mules and Men* in the *Journal of Negro History* ends with a clear rejection of conjure. "Certainly the writer if she has not convinced all readers of the powers of Voodooism has offered new evidence of widespread ignorance and superstition."[85]

Most accounts of *Mules and Men* tend to concentrate much more on the folk stories and the position of the narrator than on conjure, and in general, discussions of Hurston have focused more on issues of narrative, race, and gender than on magic. This is a theme that runs right through her work, though, and one in which she remained interested to the end of her life,[86] and it is worth pursuing. Her 1938 book *Tell My Horse* gets little attention, but it is important to look at what she does with what is in many ways her most testing material. *Tell My Horse* is often thought to be a disappointing work, and certainly not the "proper voodoo book," that Hurston felt was "crying for me to do it."[87] Quite a lot of the book consists of rather flat general accounts of Jamaica and Haiti, and though there is a keen awareness of class and of the role that religion can play in power relations, this is not really integrated into her accounts of voodoo as a whole. There is an uneven mixture of participant observation and generalized guidebook account, and one reason may be the lack of a clear sense of audience or purpose. It is not clearly directed ethnographic research, and in fact the publishers thought that the book could be aimed at a wider audience already created by Charles Seabrook's sensationalized *The Magic Island* of 1929. Hurston's book needs to be placed alongside this sort of work and contemporary titles like *Cannibal Cousins*, but also the works of Haitian intellectuals who reflected the Negritude movement's values in stressing African continuities while being suspicious of the exoticized portrayals of voodoo and zombies by outsiders.[88]

Hurston wanted to engage with voodoo and with Haitian culture at the same level as she had with Eatonville, but in the end it defeated her. This may well be simply because of her lack of linguistic and background knowledge, about which Herskovits had warned her, as much as the impenetrable supernatural mysteries of voodoo. Her failure could be compared with another ambitious project, Maya Deren's later unfinished film project,[89] but a surprisingly neglected comparison is with the anthropologist and dancer Katherine Dunham, who also went to Haiti as a recipient of a Rosenwald scholarship and met many of the same figures as Hurston. Unlike Hurston, though, this was for Dunham the beginning of a long association with Haiti and a whole series of initiations, and her account, though written later, offers some interesting parallels. She writes, for instance, of the oscillation of roles and of attitudes on her part and of remaining for years on "a fringe border of belief and nonbelief." "A thing happens, you experience it often without seeing it and it is true. From then on the bitter battle with society begins, whether the thing that happened was acceptable in the society judging it." In retrospect she thinks drugs were involved to create trance sensations and the feeling of being possessed by the god. "Then the sensation would leave me, and instead of feeling the god in possession of me, the calculating scientist would take over." Overall, she feels uncomfortable about "the feeling of being outsider within, or vice versa, as the occasion dictates."[90]

This is a fine description of Hurston's position, too, but in *Tell My Horse* she herself is less articulate about it and less successful in finding ways to dramatize it. The English edition, published a year later in 1939 as *Voodoo Gods: An Inquiry into Native Myths and Magic in Jamaica and Haiti*, is more clearly aimed at a general audience, with a more accessible title, revised openings, and some changes and cropping of the photographs (and perhaps most intriguingly, a striking photograph of Hurston herself drumming, which does not seem to appear elsewhere). It is not clear whether either of these titles was Hurston's own choice, but it is tempting to see the opaqueness and reticence of the American title as reflective of what Wendy Dutton has referred to as "the choked language" of the book, which comes from what Dutton sees as "a heightened awareness of what it means to tell."[91] The title refers to the metaphoric description of possession by the spirit, or *loa*, as being ridden by a horse and would thus seem to suggest an emphasis on the secondariness of the medium or intermediary, so that perhaps the book is the "horse" through which the voice can be indirectly heard.

It is hard to characterize the approach of the book as a whole, or even the section on Haiti, on which I concentrate here at the expense of the more straightforward travelogue sections on Jamaica. In some places we find the stance of scholarly and scientific detachment towards "the Haitian peasant" and his or her beliefs. There is a tendency to look for a core of folk belief and practice rather than to differentiate practices and beliefs or explore their larger social functions. Hurston comments on the widespread fear of grave dirt and gives a rational and scientific explanation related to disease, which justifies the folk belief while destroying its magical rationale. Dealing with Haitian mythology, she regrets the absence of any systematized account of the huge range of gods that would be comparable to Frazer's *Golden Bough*.[92] Elsewhere, though, she shows an awareness of the ways in which religion can be used for social control (in the case of some of the secret societies) and for the expression of a range of social views. "Gods always behave like the people who make them" is the arresting opening to a chapter on the figure of Guede, the *loa* most identified with the sort of possession that forces or allows the "horse" to behave transgressively. Hurston suggests that the popularity of this "entirely Haitian" divinity with the lower and blacker parts of society is not accidental and acknowledges that while many are actually possessed, others are "feigning possession in order to express their resentment general and particular."[93] Her skepticism is, I think, related to her uneasiness with the particular use of cultural/religious heritage for political ends in Haiti. Commentators have been uncomfortable with some rather imperialist passages in the book exhibiting an impatience with Haiti backwardness and implying the need for American-style progress, but this can be seen as an aspect of Hurston's reaction against the political implications of the racial nationalism she saw there.[94]

In general her stance is that of the anthropologist, intent on making sense of an alien culture, but sometimes her stress on complexity and multiplicity can also have the opposite effect in suggesting the impossibility of capturing such richness because of the endless creation of new myths and beliefs. This in effect sets up the folk world as a totality to be lived rather than understood and goes beyond an emic approach, as it does not assume that one can come out again at the other end with the information to be processed. As in *Mules and Men*, we do have a shifting position, but this is much less assured and less comic in its overall shape. When it does move away from the impersonal scientific or personal travelogue, the book is less adventurous and less celebratory of the advantages of what Gwendolyn Mikell calls Hurston's "double vision."[95] One chapter begins, "Everybody knows that La Gonave is a whale that lingered so long in Haitian waters that he became an island."[96] The use of "everyone" here might remind us of the assured sequence in *Mules and Men* discussed above, where the community view was invoked through the phrase "the way we tell it" and held in tension with the outsider's view, but this tension between insider and outside status is not maintained beyond the opening paragraph.

The large final section on voodoo begins with an informant's voice and slides into a broader definition. "Doctor Holly says that in the beginning God and His woman went into the bedroom together to commence creation. That was the beginning of everything and Voodoo is as old as that. It is the old, old mysticism of the world in African terms. Voodoo is a religion of creation and life. It is the worship of the sun, the water and other natural forces, but the symbolism is no better understood than that of other religions and consequently is taken too literally."[97] There is an etic attempt here to put the material magical practices on the same level as religion, with objects having symbolic significance, and her enterprise is to explain the logic and meaning of voodoo practices. But there is also the emic countermovement in the book, which obscures or fails to disclose, reflecting the silence of the initiate and the danger of disclosure. Sometimes her expression of the limits of knowledge ("no-one knows") can suggest the pleasure of being the first to discover, but sometimes it can also be insisting on the final unknowability and impenetrability of voodoo. Part of the tension is created by Hurston's remarkable style, which is characterized by a sort of restless directness that moves on before we have time to ask any questions. In this instance, immediately after insisting on the need to see things symbolically, she presents us very directly with an unusually graphic and concrete image—an unveiling and disclosure of the most fundamental sort. According to Dr Holly, when asked what the truth is, the richly clad priestess at a voodoo ceremony "replies by throwing back her veil and revealing her sex organs. The ceremony means that this is the infinite, the ultimate truth. There is no mystery beyond the mysterious source of life." The moment of truth for initiates, then, is to come face-to-face with the truth in kissing "her organ of creation."[98] This is both the ultimate materiality, and the absolute revelation—and yet it reveals nothing about voodoo, unless it is that the ultimate secret is materiality itself.

Crucially, in her account of her own initiation, the moment of spiritual truth is never directly presented, and the climactic moment, which comes almost at the end of her account, is actually all at one remove. Describing the state of possession experienced by Dr. Reser, the white doctor who also practices voodoo, Hurston pulls out all the stops. As he speaks, he moves further and further "into the territory of myths and mists. Before our very eyes he walked out of his Nordic body and changed. . . . You could see the snake god of Dahomey hovering about him. Africa was in his tones. . . . He was dancing before his gods and the fire of Shango played about him. Then I knew how Moses felt when he beheld the burning bush. Moses had seen fires and he had seen bushes but he had never seen a bush with a fiery ego and had never seen a man who dwelt in flame, who was coldly afire in the pores."[99] This is an oddly oblique comparison. Moses' vision was of God's presence, whereas hers is of a man possessed, not a vision in itself, and in general her own experiences are not dealt with to the extent that they are in *Mules and Men*. We are told she is being prepared for the second stage of initiation, but not whether she makes it through. We know from other sources that Hurston left Haiti because of an illness, which she attributed to malign influences—whether poisoning or voodoo is not clear—but this is not even mentioned in the book itself. In other words, the most tangible evidence or experience she could have used is left out of the book, which is typical of the "choked" and indirect nature of the account. One way of describing this is to say that in *Mules and Men* the conflicts are reconciled within an overall comic plot of inclusion, whereas *Tell My Horse* has the potentially tragic ingredients of exclusion, or of being swallowed up altogether and losing identity, something only avoided at the cost of incoherence and silence.

The photographs in the book are mainly documentary, showing aspects of ritual, but there is one striking exception, which is titled *The Loa "Mounts" the*

Houngan. This has clear echoes of African masks and the uses made of them in Modernism.[100] In its lack of context and background and its dramatic sense of confronting something impenetrable, it perhaps sums up an underlying impulse in Hurston's overall approach. It runs counter to the plainer documentary approach of the other photographs (though the striking frontispiece photograph, *Ascending the Sacred Waterfalls at Saint d'Eau*, is a dramatically lit and almost Gothic presentation) and also points back in style to Miguel Covarrubias's illustrations to the first edition of *Mules and Men*. One of the most striking of his illustrations there accompanies Hurston's account of her initiation and shows her lying naked, facedown, on a snakeskin laid on a bed. It is heavily stylized and, like his other work in the book, presents a separate but linked aesthetic enterprise to Hurston's, rather than a straightforward illustration of events. Martha Jane Nadell usefully points out that his technique here draws attention to Hurston's body rather than the ritual in which she is involved, and the fact that we cannot see her face also means that she is the one being observed. In this way, the illustration "raises the questions that Hurston herself has and that she does not answer. Should the reader/viewer think of Hurston as anthropologist or as hoodoo initiate?"[101]

One other picture in *Tell My Horse*, apparently taken by Hurston of what she claims is a zombie, is significant because of the claims she makes for it. She devotes a whole chapter to the subject of zombies, beginning in dramatic manner. "What is the whole truth and nothing else but the truth about Zombies? I do not know, but I know that I saw the broken remnant, relic, or refuse of Felicia Felix-Mentor in a hospital yard."[102] Here the photograph is clearly meant to act as evidence, but of course we have only an image of a disturbed-looking woman, and we need to see Hurston's claims here as part of a more widespread argument over the existence of zombies. In fact, the case she cites as evidence was later shown to be false, but a later researcher, Wade Davis, does credit Hurston with identifying the real cause of the zombie state as the administering of a poison, which creates the appearance of death. As he points out, this is, of course, only effective as part of a network of actions and supporting beliefs, including the operation of the secret societies which Hurston investigated but eventually drew back from.[103]

The overall drama of the voodoo theme of the book is that of getting closer to an inner realm or ultimate truth, but, as in many accounts of the quest for religious truth, there is also an inherent contradiction at the end between the sort of knowledge acquired and its representability. It may be that the point of success in the quest is also the point at which representation gives out, as revelation cuts the participant off from also being an observer. It is here that the idea of possession is crucial. Viewed negatively, the term suggests a loss of self, and the idea of the zombie is an extreme example. As Joan Dayan puts it, "The phantasm of the zombi—a soulless husk deprived of freedom—is the ultimate sign of loss and dispossession."[104] This is the negation of the state of possession as experienced by voodoo practitioners, who experience it as being filled with the *loa*, or god, or being mastered and ridden like a horse. This is a positive experience because, as Dayan argues, it is not simply becoming an object, or another form of slavery. She quotes a modern informant who insists that "instead of being turned into a thing, you become a god." In Dayan's view,

> Whereas the zombi is the husk of the human emptied of substance—nothing more than a thing—the human "possessed" can satisfy needs and impulses, can open up to a plenitude possible only because of the ultimate nonidentity of the spirit and the spirit-possessed. To conceive the *image* of the god in oneself is to be possessed. It is a deed of the most serious conception. Thought realizes itself in the imaging of the gods. . . . The experience of possession localizes and materializes what, for the uninitiated, might remain abstract or vague.[105]

According to Dayan, "the lwa most often invoked by today's vodou practitioners do not go back to Africa; rather, they were responses to the institution of slavery, to its peculiar brand of sensuous domination. A historical streak in these spirits, entirely this side of metaphysics, reconstitutes the shadowy and powerful magical gods of Africa as everyday responses to the white master's arbitrary power."[106] She argues that this sort of possession challenges "the imperial dichotomy of master and slave." "Submission to the god thrives on the enhancement of ambiguity, which could be described as follows: you let yourself be taken over by something outside of you, a force you want and don't want, control and don't control, and you get a sense of yourself that you did not have before. . . . In this exchange of spirit and matter, sacred and profane, the alleged disjunction is suspended."[107] This "exchange of spirit and matter, sacred and profane" is, of course, what I have been tracing in debates over the fetish in America and elsewhere, and in the assemblages of objects in conjure, and Dayan does refer to such mixtures after independence in the nineteenth century. "African and European materials converged: bags with fetishes, human bones, and snakes were employed in Catholic rituals, while vodou practitioners, called 'frères,' carried out priestly functions and recited Catholic liturgy."[108]

I have quoted Dayan at some length here because her careful balancing of the historical and political functions of voodoo with a sense of the realness and validity of the beliefs themselves is something notably lacking in most accounts of voodoo or hoodoo, including Hurston's. While it contains many of the necessary ingredients, *Tell My Horse* never becomes the work Hurston originally envisaged. Nevertheless the theme of magic, of conjure and its relation to African American identity, remained crucial in her work, as is evident in her novel of the following year, *Moses, Man of the Mountain*. Moses had long been a key figure in African American Christianity as a model of leadership, but Hurston chose also to stress his relation to magic and to Africa. Published the same year as Freud's *Moses and Monotheism*, the book can be seen in the context of a larger discussion of the role of African religions, which involved claims for Egypt and

Ethiopia as specifically African centers of civilization. These claims, though, sat uneasily with the widespread use of Moses and the Exodus story in spirituals and folklore as a metaphor for the experience of slavery and liberation, since this involved casting the Egyptians—the Africans—in the role of villains,[109] and Hurston's book moves, not always coherently, to deal with this contradiction.

In the Bible, the case for Moses' Jewish origins depends on the story of his discovery and adoption by the Pharoah's daughter. Hurston sidesteps this by making Moses an Egyptian but having the myth of his Israelite origins, which is kept alive among the oppressed Israelites, play a crucial part in making him act out his eventual prophetic role. The identification of American slaves with the Israelites is drawn on, not least through the use of vernacular speech by Moses and the Israelites, but the book presents a far from heroic picture of the mass of Israelites (and, by extension, African Americans) who fail to rise to the challenge of freedom and are full of backbiting and petty resentments, as seen in the characters of Aaron and Miriam. Moses gains much of his power from his association with Jethro, who is clairvoyant and is described as "Midian." His daughter, whom Moses marries, is presented as dark and exotic. In this way the customary allegorical uses of the Moses story are undermined, and this dissonance of levels is a characteristic of the book, nowhere more so than in the role of Moses himself.

Robert Hemenway comments that the two roles of Moses, of divine leader and conjure man, are simply juxtaposed in the novel, rather than integrated,[110] and this perhaps reflects a larger sense in which the potentially conflicting claims of religion and magic are held in suspension in Hurston's own work and in the larger community. The many levels of the novel (exploration of slave psychology and the impact of liberation, study of leadership, historical reconstruction) are perhaps not finally sustained in relation to each other. Part magician, part leader, Moses' speech moves rather uneasily between black vernacular and a more formal English as he mediates between God and the Egyptians and the Israelites. He learns magic from the Egyptians and becomes, according to Jethro, "the finest hoodoo man in the world."[111] In *Tell My Horse*, Hurston argued that the popularity of stories about Moses and his magic powers among Negroes suggested an African origin and a "tradition of Moses as the great father of magic scattered over Africa and Asia." There she described the common theme of the staff turned into a serpent and suggested that witch doctors were known to be able to hypnotize a snake so that it became rigid and could be carried like a stick.[112] In the novel this power over snakes and his ability to turn his staff into a serpent are emphasized, and there is the suggestion that Moses knew of the tradition and could turn it to his advantage.

In his spiritual quest, Moses has to fight the snake that is guarding the book of Thoth, where he gets the magic with which he can contact God, so the novel is far from a celebration of Israelite—or by extension Christian—

uniqueness or purity. In fact it is through his syncretic adaptations that Moses has access to the power latent in him. Once he has the word from God, though, in the form of the graven commandments, he destroys the idols being celebrated by Aaron when he returns, literally smashing the golden calf with the tablets.[113] In this respect his relation to his supposed sister Miriam is interesting in that she is described as "a two-headed woman with power" and also as having "a certain little bundle that she makes, that ain't no bigger than a man's thumb. You put that around your neck and wear it, and nothing can't do you no harm." Moses is rather dismissive of these powers in comparison with the need for change-inspiring oratory and vision. According to him, she "is called to prophesy to Israel and I am called to save it."[114] It would be wrong, though, to put too much emphasis on the move toward the "higher" powers of the Judeo-Christian God, and the renunciation of magic. There is in fact rather an uneasy grinding of gears in the book when we come to monotheism in that while Hurston seems to accept the idea of the supreme God, she also stresses the supplementary and even necessary role of magic and conjure.

Hurston's concern with hoodoo and voodoo runs though much of her work, and she presents it as a fundamental and distinctive aspect of African American culture, which relates back to Africa, but she is also capable in other pieces of playing down this aspect or at least stressing the American and more universal aspects. In "High John de Conquer," written for *American Mercury* in 1943 for a general American audience, she uses the well-known mythological figure to suggest that at a time of national challenge, with America at war, the Negro has something to offer. She describes High John as a trickster figure "playing his tricks of making a way out of no-way. Hitting a straight lick with a crooked stick. Winning the jackpot with no other stake but a laugh. Fighting a mighty battle without outside-showing force and winning his battle from within."

She suggests that he was of particular importance in times of slavery, and seems to imply rather a rosy picture of what has happened since. He offered solace, rather than anything more confrontational, and in her account of how he showed the slaves the comfort of music there is no sense of the spirituals as doing more than interiorizing a realm of freedom unreachable by the white master. Significantly, perhaps, she makes very little of the well-known root named after him. When he returned to Africa, he "left his power here, and placed his American dwelling in the root of a certain plant. Only possess that root, and he can be summoned at any time." There is little sense here of something prized for its magical efficacy. It is something people may keep on their person in order to "help them overcome things they could not beat otherwise," but this seems to be only psychological. It will "bring them the laugh of the day." He will help the weak, and convey a message of hope, and she even extends this into a patriotic gesture in a time of war. "Things are bound to come out right tomorrow. That is the secret of Negro song and laughter. So the brother in black offers to these United States the source of courage that endures."[115]

Hurston describes John the Conquer surviving in people's wishes. "First off he was a whisper, a will to hope, a wish to find something worthy of laughter and song. Then the whisper put on flesh. His footsteps sounded across the world in a low but musical rhythm as if the world he walked on was a singing-drum." He came from Africa "walking on the waves of sound."[116] Referring particularly to this passage, Eric Sundquist has argued that the essay "rewrites the drum passage of *Jonah's Gourd Vine* into an allegory of retentions (and physical survival) and it does so by locating the origin of African-American song-making and storytelling, especially trickster tales and Master-John stories in *spirit* itself."[117] This directs us usefully to the ways in which Hurston's use of the drum and the voice reflects her views of African retentions and survivals. In *Jonah's Gourd Vine* she describes the way that Africans, divested of everything and made "nameless and thingless," continued the memories and functions of the drum within their own bodies. In this novel, though, the African elements are stressed in primitivist terms. She describes "the great drum that is made by priests and sits in majesty in the juju house" in human terms, as "the drum with the man skin that is dressed with human blood, that is beaten with a human shin-bone and speaks to gods as a man and to men as a God."[118] So we have a thing becoming human, or a human becoming thing, as in her description of a Jamaican dance in *Tell My Horse*, where "the drums become people and the people become drums. The pulse of the drum is their shoulders and belly. Truly the drum is inside their bodies."[119]

Sundquist links this to Hurston's view of vernacular and the rhythm of voice as spirit. "High John, in this configuration, *is* spirit or soul, the rhythm of black life in the voice that links body to drum, mediating between humans and gods, as between language and sound." But what is the meaning of "spirit" here? Is rhythm or sound in itself spirit or a material expression of spirit? Sundquist remarks that "what is most notable about Hurston's theory of survivals is that it often dwells especially in the world of the phenomenal rather than the concrete."[120] The root itself (not mentioned by Sundquist), like the drum, is concrete and material enough, but it is the continuity and memory which they represent—a sort of larger vernacular rhythm or process—that prompt talk of spirit.[121]

The idea of spirit and how the term is used in relation or in opposition to other key terms like matter and magic is of course a recurring concern in this study, and I have concentrated on Hurston because of her prolonged engagement with folk practices of hoodoo and voodoo. Her personal involvement, combined with her keen awareness of the requirements of literary and ethnographic production, results in rich and fascinating works, but as I have tried to show there are also intriguing absences and ambiguities in her work. In any case, her positive and serious treatment of conjure and related practices points forward to the increasing use of these materials by later writers and artists, to whom I turn in the next chapters.

Chapter 4

Black Arts: Conjure and Spirit

In moving from the 1920s and 1930s up to recent times, we find a much wider range of representations of Indian and African American magic and religion. Native American and African American artists themselves have reformulated the terms in which they are represented, and anthropological approaches have become more reflexive and dialogical. But even if the power to define "others" and the terms in which their beliefs and practices are represented may have partly moved away from white anthropologists and collectors, to be replaced by greater self-representation and a greater openness to cultural and racial hybridities and impurities, the increased interest in spirituality has also brought with it new forms of commodification. As a result, we need to see recent reformulations by artists and writers not just in terms of the earlier hierarchies outlined in my earlier chapters, but also in relation to the circulation and commodification of objects and ideas in contemporary commercial and New Age as well as artistic and ethnographic spheres.

Within this context claims for "power" increasingly often move between the aesthetic and the spiritual/magical and efface, or at least blur, any clear distinction between the two realms. In these final two chapters, I will be examining a number of such claims and looking at the confluence of art and conjure in the case of African American works, and of art and ceremony in the case of Native American works. Beginning with recent revisions of the Modernist primitivist aesthetic and the idea of assemblage, I look at the ways in which African American artists (particularly Betye Saar and Renée Stout) have used techniques of assemblage to incorporate abjected and discarded material into their work. I explore in detail the claims being made by them and their commentators for spiritual power and the relation of this to the claims made for music and spirit as African American cultural resources in Ishmael Reed and Houston Baker. I then use the work of Nathaniel Mackey to further explore claims made for music as a privileged site of African American culture and spirituality.

In the last chapter, I touched on the conjunction of Modernist aesthetics and ethnography, focusing on Picasso's encounter with the "fetish" objects of the Trocadéro and some of those moments when the projects of ethnographic collecting and Modernist assemblage richly coalesced, only to diverge again into different realms. This Modernist engagement with the primitive has been extensively retheorized and discussed as part of a larger postcolonial critique of Western conceptions of the Other. Of particular relevance for my inquiry, though, is the revisionism expressed in the responses to a number of exhibitions, most notably the Museum of Modern Art exhibition *"Primitivism" in 20th Century Art: Affinity of the Tribal and the Modern*, which triggered a stream of critical discussion, much of which accused it in effect of repeating the Modernist assumptions. The idea that, as Hal Foster puts it, "the primitivist appropriation of the other is another form of conquest" has been widely elaborated and explored.[1] Creating a similar if more circumscribed controversy was the *Sacred Circles* exhibition, which sparked a hostile reaction from Native American artists, who complained about the exclusion of contemporary work. This omission served to reinforce assumptions that "real" Indians or Indian art were only in the past, and the protestors also questioned the assumptions in the exhibition that ritual and ceremonial objects, and even objects of practical use could be presented unproblematically under the category of art.[2] The work of a whole range of contemporary artists has since productively explored the issues ignored by such an approach, as in the work of Jimmie Durham, whose writings also offer a useful commentary on the issues.[3]

There have also been continuing disputes over the legitimacy of exhibiting ritual or ceremonial objects at all, whether as art or ethnography.[4] These various debates centre on issues of the ownership and use of objects and the power to control their display and reception, but I want to concentrate on only one aspect of this, which is the sort of power claimed for objects, alone or in combination, and the relation between artistic and magico-religious techniques and approaches. We can begin by revisiting Picasso's encounter with masks discussed in the last chapter via the contemporary artist Fred Wilson, who is of mixed African American and Carib Indian descent. Wilson's *Picasso/Whose Rules?* consists of a full-size photoreproduction of Picasso's *Les Desmoiselles d'Avignon*, but over one of the painted faces he has fixed a wooden Kifebwe mask, and when the viewer goes close and looks through the vacant eyes of the mask, he or she is confronted, by means of a video installation, with the face and voice of a person of color.[5] Originally part of a 1991 exhibition, *Primitivism: High and Low*, which was designed as a response to the implicit hierarchies of earlier exhibitions such as that by MOMA described above, *Picasso/Whose Rules* was accompanied by a group of full-size models of four headless figures in the uniforms of various New York museum guards titled *Guarded View*.[6] The fact that the figures' skins are brown draws attention to the disparity between the attention paid to the objects of "otherness" and the anonymity and invisibility of actual people of color.

Wilson's exhibitions represent a sustained and fascinating engagement with the objects and the underlying ideologies of museum collections in which the colonized and objectified other is represented. In his display *The Other Museum,* the levels of ambiguity in the title prepare us for his different perspective, which partly involves restoring to the decontextualized objects their full emotional context and provenance. He displays a collection of African masks that are blindfolded or gagged with the flags of the colonial powers, Britain and France, and the title, *Spoils*, points both to appropriation and destruction, rather than preservation and custodianship. Wilson also points to the way that museum collections and exhibitions stress the visual and aesthetic at the expense of other dimensions. "You are encouraged to turn off any spiritual connections that result in ritual acts when looking at a religious object, as ocular veneration is all that is allowed."[7] Veneration is an interesting term here in that it might apply to aesthetic or scholarly/ethnographic contemplation, which has displaced the original context-specific conception of the object.

Not only have associations and context been regularly stripped off in the act of collecting, but in some cases what seemed to the collector to be extraneous physical elements were also removed. A striking example of this process, by which religious and ritual aspects were removed so as not to interfere with the supposed aesthetic dimension can be seen in what has happened to some West African sculptures, or *nkisi*. Wyatt MacGaffey points out that "The bits of rag, chicken feathers, pieces of raffia and other 'mixed media' which some collectors in search of pure form used to clean off before varnishing the piece were part of the visual effect originally intended."[8] This echoes a larger process in which what seems to be extraneous or incidental rather than essential is excluded in the name of formal integrity, but of course this formal integrity is an externally imposed criterion. Furthermore, what might look like a random collection of separate objects, or even a collection of rubbish, may have significance precisely as an ensemble. Frank Hamilton Cushing, for instance, stole objects from shrines, often unaware that part of the significance of the object was its place in the ensemble, which looked to the collectors like a disorganized pile of abandoned objects.[9]

Wilson's work is a powerful exploration of the interfaces of modernist art and colonial collecting and control. His use of juxtapositions and assemblages carries a strong critical and even educative charge, but there are many other ways of assembling that raise other issues closer to my concerns with claims for spiritual and magical power. William Seitz's book *The Art of Assemblage* was perhaps the first study explicitly to draw together a range of procedures under the term. His focus was on artists whose work consists of "preformed natural or manufactured objects or fragments not intended as art materials."[10] Under this general idea of assemblage, though, William Rubin has made an interesting distinction between a Western modernist approach to assemblage and an African one. Whereas, he says, quoting Seitz, the former's orientation is "ironic, perverse, anti-rational and even destructive," African assemblages "emphasize consensus, and consolidation, and the affirmation and reinforcement of social values and cultural continuity."[11] Whether this is entirely true of

African practices or not, it does, I think, open up a way of looking at African American approaches to assemblage without necessarily assuming direct African continuities.[12]

Critics have noted this approach in a range of work. David Driskell describes how Barbara Chase-Riboud, for instance, "uses the modernist medium of assemblage to create works that are reminiscent of slave-craft and fetish," and Driskell sees other artists employing bricolage "to invert the appropriation of 'primitive' art by Western modernist artists, which not coincidentally occurred during the expansion of European colonialism. This is achieved by reclaiming the aesthetic of African art: the use of assemblage, 'found' materials, improvisation, accumulation of materials, formal contradictions and tensions."[13]

The extension of Western aesthetic frameworks by the inclusion of African conceptions means that all sorts of elements and practices are given new meanings. Thus, neglected practices such as yard art, bottle trees, and cemetery practices can be seen as processes designed to order and control by symbolic and metonymic actions. Whether this is called art or religion or magic is thrown into question by the inclusion of an African or African American aesthetic frame—if indeed aesthetic is even the word. In my earlier discussion of conjure in Chapter 1 I outlined some approaches that saw it as, in Michael Bell's term, "performance assemblage," and the overlapping of aesthetic with what we can broadly call magical compositional activities needs to be carefully considered. To pursue this idea of assemblage I intend to concentrate on the work of a couple of artists, Betye Saar and Renée Stout, who both use collections of objects and explore the complex emotions and associations they provoke. Like Wilson, they are aware of the nexus of modernist and ethnographic interests and indeed play off them, and both are influenced by the boxes of the surrealist Joseph Cornell. Though both Saar and Stout are of mixed descent, and acknowledge their Native American ancestry in their work as well as in interviews, their most characteristic quality is the use they make of African American artistic and religious traditions. Their engagement draws on and often interrelates with the rich body of scholarship that has developed on African art and its African American continuations, as in the work of Robert Farris Thompson and Wyatt MacGaffey.[14]

Influenced by early memories of Simon Rodia's Watts Towers, Betye Saar (like her daughter Alison) regularly uses and combines discarded and abandoned objects to create assemblages. Her use of stereotypes and objects with negative connotations, as in her Aunt Jemima pieces, in which the iconic figure of accommodation is transformed into an armed freedom fighter, and her use of elements from the minstrel tradition carry a powerful political and satirical charge and echo Fred Wilson's use of mammy figures. The title of one of her most Rodia-like works, *Spirit Catcher*, though, also points toward a dimension beyond the political. In a series of boxes, she has assembled objects with religious, magical, and racial associations, and it is worth focusing on what sort of claims are made by her or by critics. Jane Carpenter sees a development from an early collection like *Africa* of 1968 to a more "nuanced and spiritual understanding of African art and ritual." This may coincide with what Carpenter calls "an accumulative aesthetic,"[15] which Saar first recognized in an African cloak that she and David Hammons saw displayed in Chicago's Field Museum, and which she felt gave an extra dimension of cultural memory to the aesthetic of collecting that she had taken from Cornell's boxes. Her ensuing works brought together ancestral objects, which operate like "mojos," a term that she has defined as originally "referring to a magical amulet or charm that either works magic or heals or does something like that."

She applied the term to her pieces because these pieces were "emulating African art," and this emulation involved following one compositional practice in particular, which was to incorporate a hidden element into ritual objects. "Many of the pieces have secret information, just like ritual pieces of other cultures. There is always a secret part, especially in fetishes from Africa. There is a mirror piece, and behind that there's something, but you don't really want to know what it is. It may be a pouch containing an animal part or a human part in there. To me, those secrets radiate something that makes you uneasy."[16] This hidden element has often been noted. Wyatt MacGaffey, for instance, quotes a missionary account from 1902. "A fetich may be an image decorated with strips of cloth and feathers, often with a bit of mirror set into the belly, behind which is the bit of rubbish containing the potent power. It is often a small sack, made of pineapple fiber, containing bits of stone, bird-claw and feathers, powder, pepper, bits of snakeskin, etc."[17]

The borders between magical practice and art are not clear here, and it seems to be precisely the liminal area between spiritual and aesthetic (assuming for the moment that these are separate fields) that interests Saar and other artists. Her reference above to "something that makes you uneasy" is to a state of mind that seems some way short of religious feeling, but I want to pursue some of the larger religious and spiritual claims made by critics and commentators. Mary Schmidt Campbell describes Saar's *Nine Mojo Secrets* as "an assemblage combining seeds, fiber and beads," and sees it as "a totemic piece with magical powers that increase self-knowledge and communal belief in an ancestral heritage. A five-step ritual produces the spiritually endowed artifact."[18] We might ask what her authority or evidence is for the claim that it has magical powers, and the claim that it is "totemic" also raises questions. It is true that in similar boxes like *Mojo Secrets* and *Gris Gris Box* of 1972, or more altar-like structures like *Mti* of 1973, Saar does draw heavily on the physical paraphernalia of African and African American religion and magic, but she makes less specific claims than Schmidt Campbell. She refers to what she does as "power-gathering," and the suggestion seems to be that the gathering and the assembling in new contexts creates power in addition to what the objects may already have. "There's power in changing uses of a material, another kind of energy is released. I am attracted to things because they have multiple meanings."[19] The nature of this power, though, is not necessarily clear. Are we talking about something similar to Bell's description of the processes of conjure or about the aesthetics of assemblage?

In an interview with M. J. Hewitt, Saar uses terms like "magic" quite freely, but here again it is difficult to know quite how much weight to put on the terms. Hewitt begins by talking about Saar collecting materials "to make her own particular magic,'" and Saar talks of the process of assembling objects for the work *Mojotech* as "my intuition, my particular magic."[20] Later she says of the same process, "You just get your own personal mojo working, your own intuition. Your spirit guides have to be there to lead you." But then she mentions her background in design, which means that "the intuition is not just going all over the place. It is reeled in by the design thing."[21] Her titles (*Spirit Chair* and *The Ritual Journey*, for instance) regularly invoke a generalized religious tradition, but one of her installations is based on a play about Zora Neale Hurston, *Sanctified*, and it is notable that she and the playwright focus on similar aspects of Hurston's life. She has references to the voodoo goddess Erzulie "because those things were part of her culture."[22]Actually, Hurston encountered this material as an outsider, as I have shown, but Saar's concern is less to be historically or even culturally specific than to find resonant images. In another piece, *Fragments of Fate*, she uses "things that suggest rituals in many cultures, not just African. That's what I'm trying to find: universal themes but something that appeals to me at the same time."[23]

In another interview with Saar, Ishmael Reed raises directly the question of how this collecting and assembling is to be seen. "Do you practice religion or is this art? How important is religion in your work?" Her response is really to the second question rather than the first. "Well, I don't consider myself religious. But I consider myself spiritual. So spirituality is an important aspect in my work. And also I consider myself a Christian." She relies on the "creative spirit, which I don't disconnect from the higher being."[24] In a comment in an accompanying essay, Reed perhaps answers his own question. Commenting on the way that folklore, so often rejected as artistically inferior, forms perfect material for Saar because of her interest in the discarded, he remarks that "The highest form of folk art is the paraphernalia of religion; the objects become art in themselves, apart from the doctrine."[25] This would correspond to the change of use described by Saar above, but it also implies that the power gained is not religious. It also might suggest a *parallel* process to the way that conjure operates, according to Bell's account, quoted in Chapter 1. As elements become loosed from the metaphysical system of "higher" or organized religions, they become available for the bricoleurs of conjure, as they select and combine disparate elements in improvisatory ways—though Bell insists that conjure is not without its own system and sets of rules within which conjure performance takes place.

Reed is at pains to categorize Saar's particular form of collecting and assembling as African. "Her Blackness is the authentic West African Blackness that, like its permanent symbol, the python, assimilates everything it devours. Everything."[26] This claim leaves open the question of how much the disparate elements are also digested and thereby lose their specificity. The idea of assimilating all it devours would, if taken in isolation, make Saar sound very similar to the unjustifiably appropriative and homogenizing tendencies for which Western culture is now criticized. I think, though, that we have to see Reed's description alongside his celebrations elsewhere of what he calls the "NeoHoodoo Aesthetic," which is like a gumbo, in which the ingredients are varied every time,[27] and of a voodoo aesthetic that is 'eclectic. It picks up whatever ideas are around. It's always contemporary."[28] Reed does not really explore the extent to which what happens as a result of the conjunction and assemblage of different objects depends on the actual method of composition or on the assumptions and ways of viewing of the creator and viewer, but it might well correspond to Rubin's description of different forms of assemblage discussed earlier in this chapter.

Saar herself regularly acknowledges the many other elements in her work. She is of Native American as well as African American and European descent[29] and has used elements from Native American culture as well as from Africa, Mexico, and Asia. One of her most striking paintings, *Redbone and Black: Crossings of 2001*, reproduced on the cover of this book, includes old photographs of Native American and African American life. In one of them two Indian women sit with babies, one of whom is clearly African American. Iconic images are blended (a slave ship is combined with a canoe, for instance), and the power seems to come from the surprising melding rather than the disjunction of the images, given the larger context of specifically African and African American materials in her work. Her own comments suggest a concern for continuity across the material. "I use Egyptian and Oceanic and American Indian and African, any kind of culture." Her method evolves from "putting materials and symbols together so that in one piece you may find materials or symbols or signs or designs from several cultures, but it all works together as a tribal thing."[30] The last phrase here, though, hardly answers questions about the degree to which elements are honored in their cultural or aesthetic specificity, as it seems to imply an indiscriminate thematic melding of the sort that is problematic in New Age appropriations.

The same concerns and many of the same ingredients are found in Renée Stout's work, where there is a more direct engagement with African art and religion. This is demonstrated most markedly in the volume *Astonishment and Power*, which combines a study of African *minkisi* by Wyatt MacGaffey with one of the most sustained studies of Stout's work. The striking visual effect of the beautifully reproduced museum objects in conjunction with Stout's work not only demonstrates the continuities but serves to throw into question any clear distinctions between aesthetic and religious categories for the reader and viewer. One noticeable difference between the African and American sections (we might also say between the ethnographic and arts sections, if that didn't prejudge the relation) is in terminology. While MacGaffey's work, like all modern studies, uses the term *nkisi* to describe a range of objects that were earlier described in the West as fetishes,[31] Stout's deliberate use of the discredited term "fetish" as the title for several of her most celebrated works serves to frame the objects ironically within the reductive and negative conception of African worship evoked by the word. We are made to think about and reevaluate this frame itself, in the same way as with Wilson's reframing of museum exhibits.

This is particularly striking when we compare some of her *Fetish* works. Many of them combine the ingredients expected in a Congo *nkisi*, but *Fetish 2* consists of a model of Stout's own body in plaster, naked, painted in black, and adorned with a variety of religiously and culturally resonant objects, including cowrie shells, human and monkey hair, conjure bags, a photograph, and an African postage stamp. In her title she is clearly referring to the fetishization, in quite other than religious senses, of the black body, a topic that has been extensively discussed.[32] Harris argues that she has "transformed her own body into a figure of power that is like a Kongo *nkisi*, or perhaps the work is one of the first African American power figures." Here again, though, we might ask how similar is this "power" to that claimed for the *nkisi*? Is it a magical power or a cultural and political empowerment created by the proud display of what was once underrated or reductively objectified? Harris sees *Fetish 1*, which also uses a human figure, as operating at the crossroads between art and religion, and makes a distinction between Stout's use of the term and the derogatory implications of the past, but his distinction raises as many questions as it answers. "It is a fetish in the sense of animation and power but not in the sense of paganism and idolatry."[33]

It is worth detouring briefly at this point to the work of the Native American performance artist James Luna, whose work provides an instructive point of comparison. His *The Artifact Piece* also makes his own body the object on display—in this case his live body, lying in a museum display case. His point is more a secular and didactic one about the representation and place of Indians, and in this regard he is similar to Fred Wilson as well as to the Indian artist Jimmie Durham. Luna's *End of the Frail*, for instance, is in ironic interplay with the earlier iconic sculpture *End of the Trail*, but his comments in an interview are interesting in reflecting what is perhaps a significant difference between some Indian and African American artists. Asked about the relation of his performances to rituals, he says, "I don't think I could do that. I couldn't show a ritual. I couldn't get a ritual and tear it up and show it as art. That would go against all of my personal beliefs." He acknowledges that in some sense his performances are rituals "because they are a process, and they involve a lot of things that are in a ritual that people don't realize." He presents "concepts of rituals without presenting ritual, Indian ritual."[34] The important distinction here, I think, is that Luna, like many Indian artists and writers, has a stronger sense of the provenance and ownership of ceremonial and ritual performances and objects than do African American artists like Saar and Stout. There is a greater reluctance to use them in the ways they use conjure or voodoo, and this relates to a wider distinction in views on the ownership of cultural and spiritual "property"—an issue to which I will return.

As well as using African parallels, Stout regularly collects and uses material from the African American conjure tradition, but once again it is worth looking at the actual claims being made for what she is doing. As an imaginary background for some of her work, she has developed the figure of Colonel Frank, a traveler who sends souvenirs and postcards back to Dorothy, a conjure woman whose conjuring table and other possessions Stout displays in her work. The relationship, which seems to involve Dorothy's longings and her attempts to gain power and meaning from disconnected exotic as well as familiar objects, also echoes the colonial background of collecting. Stout creates closed compartments within her work in which she has placed material that remains inaccessible to the viewer, and this reflects her fascination with similar practices in African *nkisi* bags. "Just the fact that there is something in there that I don't know about. That whole sense of mystery that a lot of these pieces have." As Harris says "mystery stimulates her imagination"[35]—and, I would add, ours too. As with Betye Saar, the power is created by multivalence and multiple significations moving across fields of the religious and the artistic, but also the exotic and the nostalgic, and I add these two latter categories not to challenge the importance or legitimacy of the religious element, but to insist on the full nexus of values in which these works, like the New Age artifacts to be discussed later, are consumed. This rather generalized sense of spiritual power does allow her to make connections with Indian and other traditions. She comments that "I'm attracted to spiritual societies. . . . It (spirituality) seems like a means of survival in a world that you can't always understand."[36]

Harris argues that "Stout's work straddles the line between art and efficacy, between life and fantasy,"[37] and her work certainly contains numerous pieces explicitly exploring and presenting objects as having religious roles or power, such as *Ancestral Power Object* and *Her Medicine Cabinet*. As well as specifically African material, she regularly uses African American material, as in *Headstone for Marie Leveau*, and she makes extensive use of the combined magical root and mythological figure of High John the Conqueror. Her use of this figure can be compared with that in Alison Saar's *Conkerin' John*, which is described by Lucy Lippard as "a proud stylized male figure—half real, half-mythical—rising from a massive tangle of roots in a monumental version of the magic charms and vernacular art made by African American artists throughout the South."[38]

One particularly interesting example of this use of African American heritage is her use of Robert Johnson. In Johnson we have a figure of increasingly mythic proportions, approaching those of High John. His prowess as a blues musician has been increasingly given a supernatural resonance because of the legend of his crossroads encounter and the Faustian pact from which he derived his musical powers. Her installation *Dear Robert, I'll See You at the Crossroads* involved a reconstructed juke joint and assemblages of iconic objects, such as the piece *Me and the Devil Blues,* which includes letters from Stout written to Johnson. Her book of the same name also includes work from a project on *Madam Ching* based on a mysterious woman from Stout's youth. Though she uses materials from hoodoo and voodoo, describes her visits to New Orleans when by chance she came across Marie Laveau's tomb as revelatory,[39] and seems to see conjure as playing a role in her life, she seems to consistently shy away from ascribing actual magical efficacy to objects in the accompanying interviews. The power comes, she says, through our associations, and what we project on to the objects through our belief. Asked whether objects "contain their own power," she says, "I think objects can be that way because of the meanings we attach to them or to what we know of them. . . . Any object only has the power we attach to it." A very old object attracts her because "hands have touched it before mine. . . . It has power because of the spirit of what this thing has seen or withstood." On the other hand, when she uses an object and can "make it look old," it "evokes a feeling of the past." She sees these as "two different kinds of power. One that is actually old and then something I make look old. There is a power in being able to take something and make it into something else. To make something from nothing."[40] These seem to me to be deliberately limited and secular/aesthetic claims. Similarly, when asked how she feels about being seen as a conjurer she says only that it is "interesting,"[41] but she does not claim healing or other powers, except in the most general sense. Though fascinated by Marie Laveau and other conjure women, she does not claim to be doing the same through her art.

Writing on Stout, Marla Berns sees the crossroads as emblematic of the intersection of the material and spiritual. Asked about the possibility of life-changing power gained at the crossroads through a pact with the devil, though, Stout is once again non-committal ("I don't know") even though she had already known of and used Elegba in her work before encountering Johnson. In her letter to Johnson, Stout aspires to his capacity for unmediated expression. "I envy you, being able to both play the guitar and sing because both are more direct than my way of making art." She wants to be able to just "play and sing what I'm feeling. . . . It's really hard to make this into a three-dimensional object. . . . sometimes a little can get lost in the translation."[42] Berns's commentary on the project claims that "Conjuration and blues music are two cultural strategies that have been deployed by Diasporic Africans seeking to move from a position of oppression to one of control."[43] This certainly describes the rich mix of materials used by Stout here, but it leaves open the question of whether they are the same sort of cultural strategy, and how similar it is to Stout's aesthetic of assemblage.

This joint use of blues music and conjure as twin African American resources is found in Arthur Flowers's novel *Another Good Loving Blues*, which features a conjure man and a conjure woman, and a blues singer, all of whom have distinctive and positive ways of taking control of the hardships and vicissitudes of their lives. Melvira the conjure woman and Luke Bodeen the bluesman each have to come to terms with traumas, including having to deal with the aftermath of a lynching, and they are finally reconciled in a place called Taproot. The book draws, perhaps rather too easily and uncritically, on the conventional idealizations of blues music and conjure in a world of romance and folktale rather than of realism, but through the figure of Mr. Hootowl, Flowers explores more fully the nature of conjure. Hootowl has many of the traditional accoutrements of a conjure man, including a snake-headed walking stick, and he has traveled widely and seen the full variety of African religions as they have developed in the Americas—Obeah in Jamaica, Santería in Cuba, voodoo in Haiti and candomblé in Brazil. Through him Flowers distinguishes North American hoodoo from all of these, through its more pragmatic approach. "The more he was exposed to the extent of the African Way in the New World, the prouder he became of being a hoodooman. He realized that he was part of a family of African religions and, though clearly hoodoo had lost more of its religious power than any of the others, neither was it burdened with outdated religious dogma and mythology." He goes on to reject animal sacrifice and African fears of "spiritharm,"[44] but this is not to suggest that hoodoo is powerless. "Ravenous with the hunger of the sorcerer for power of any sort, spiritual, personal and temporal, he systematically drew strands of power unto himself."[45] A visitor to the town, none other than Zora Neale Hurston who has a cameo role in the book, asks Hootowl why, if religions have many of the same ingredients anyway, he doesn't choose the more acceptable path of Christianity. "Because," he tells her, "the hoodoo way is our slice of Godhome. Whatever we have kept of our African soul we have kept in hoodoo. The soul of a human race born in Africa."[46]

One of the most sustained critical engagements and strongest claims for the importance of spirit in African American culture, has come from the literary critic Houston Baker. His claim that over the years what he calls "spirit-work" has sustained African American culture is supported by readings of a range of writers. An important aspect of his larger revisionist approach to the Harlem Renaissance, which stretches over several books, is the way he identifies and revalues modes of endurance and resistance that may not have been recognized as such. His ideas of "mastery of form" and "deformation of mastery," for instance, aim to allow us to judge some of the strands of African American culture by different criteria from those of international modernism. Within this strategy the word "spirit" has a particular importance for Baker. In *Workings of the Spirit*, a study that goes beyond the 1920s, he argues that there is "a *sui generis* cultural spirit at work in quite specific ways in Afro-American women's expressivity."[47] Here "spirit" could have a fairly general connotation, as it does when he talks of "the workings of the expressive spirit in Afro-American culture," but Baker makes a different claim when he compares the "spirit work" of African American women writers with the traditions of voodoo and conjure, even claiming that "a poetics of Afro-American women's writing is, in many ways, a phenomenology of conjure."[48]

Here the word "phenomenology" is as important as the word "conjure," in that Baker is developing a phenomenological approach specifically to address the problem of how the spiritual or ideal is articulated and has efficacy in the world of matter. He describes the distinctive use of "felicitous images of the workings of a spirit,"[49] which operate (and here he follows Gaston Bachelard) to create an intersubjectivity, that brings into being and sustains community and belief. In other words, he uses phenomenology to assert subjectivity's power to influence the world rather than being merely a byproduct of the material world and of language. How finally satisfactory this is as an answer to the deconstructive critiques of presence is another matter, but what is important to explore here is his bold move in relating this fairly general defense of consciousness and the powers of art to the powers of conjure.

My argument is that there is a crucial slippage in Baker's description. On the one hand, he describes the powers of imagination and art as *like* conjure in their ability to transform lives and regulate people and cultures who subscribe to the same beliefs, while on the other hand he equates art with the actual practices of conjure, with its claims to direct physical efficacy. Baker claims that "The secret of the conjurer's trade is imagination which can turn almost anything into a freeing mojo, a dynamic 'jack' or a cunning conjure bag." All sorts of objects "can serve the conjurer as *bricoleur*, enabling her to escape oppressively overdetermined meanings."[50] His is a powerful account of the ways in which abjected aspects of African American life are reworked, and he links this directly with the art of storytelling and Hurston's own imaginative transformation of the ethnographic report expected of her in *Mules and Men*. It is, of course, true that a great deal of the action of conjure as *pharmakon* is at this interpersonal and imaginative level, but Baker seems to play down any other levels. As we have seen, other commentators, like Chireau, have also been loath to do this, as it seems to be tidying away all the irrational claims of magic, which are so important, even if hard to handle. Baker does perhaps point to this when he says that "The powers of conjure to provide guidelines, controls, motivation, and remedies for a black vernacular community grow out of the ancient, authentic African origins of its practices. These powers are mightily enhanced, however, by the poetic image of conjure in Afro-American culture."[51]

This suggests a two-level process in which the African and folk-originated practices (which might include actual physical healing practices under the term "remedies") are then used imaginatively and played back into the culture through positive accounts and celebrations of their power, but in his account of Hurston, in his insistence on conflating conjure and storytelling, he actually elides her own ambivalence and reticence about the powers of conjure—and particularly of voodoo, since he barely mentions *Tell My Horse*.

My skeptical approach here may seem rather limited, but I am not insisting on clear-cut divisions between magic and art so much as asking just what Baker is claiming for conjure and "spirit-work." In a chapter of his earlier book, *Afro-American Poetics: Revisions of Harlem and the Black Aesthetic*, titled "Lowground and Inaudible Valleys: Reflections on Afro-American Spirit Work," he argues that we need to recognize the primacy of race and to be aware that African American writers are drawing on a racially derived rather than a universalist idea of art. He insists that the effort, for artists like Jean Toomer, was to "capture the sound of a racial soul and convert it into an expressive product equivalent in beauty and force to Afro-American folk songs or ecstatic religious performance."[52] Discussing *Cane*, he says that "the ancestral spirit of the race is designated by the term *soul*. Mediumistic contact with this soul is almost always coded in terms drawn from a Judeo-Christian tradition," though he does note Toomer's use of African elements, such as in the invocation of "juju men, gree-gree, witch-doctors" in his atavistic description of Carma, on the Dixie Pike, which "has grown from a goat path in Africa."[53]

It is not just that Toomer uses trance and ecstatic states of mind as his subject matter or as instances of a larger experience of "soul" or "spirit." In Baker's view *Cane* is "infused with what we can call a religious, mystical, or entranced force antagonistic to 'art,'" after Toomer's experiences in Georgia had transformed him from modern artist to "an Afro-American medium."[54] Baker grounds transcendent experiences in a hinterland of folk experience and culture (what he calls lowground), so that "the trance, in a word, is dependent upon folk sounds for its very inducement."[55] The invocation of folk *sounds* here refers more to vernacular expression in general than to music, but implicitly it resonates with the widespread appeal to music and orality as privileged areas of African American expression.

The twin invocation of music and magic is a powerful rhetorical tool in the African American context, and I want to continue to question just what claims are being made for the power of music and its relation to spirit. In a piece called, appropriately enough for this book, "Body and Soul," Al Young has described first hearing Coleman Hawkins's classic version of that song in 1939, and his sense of the music's puzzling transcendence. "I knew what a body was, but what was a soul? Was it like a breeze?" Finally he has an image of it as an essence. "Essence in this instance is private song, is you hearing your secret sorrow and joy blown back through Coleman Hawkins, invisibly connected to you and played back through countless bodies, each one an embodiment of the same soul force."[56]

In this almost Neoplatonic view, music is an expression of an ideal form, finding a fleeting identity in matter that it is also transcending, but Young's vision of the music being played back through countless bodies is important, because it invokes an African American community and continuity that physically persists. This potential solidarity of many thousands gone, the idea of the material bodies in which black cultural nonmaterial resources have been carried and handed down, suggests something that is both material and nonmaterial. The idea of African American music acting as a spiritual link across generations has a strong political and cultural resonance, but it has also been questioned for the risk it runs in essentializing and idealizing music and its role. Ronald Radano, for instance, has argued that for the Black Aesthetic critics, music was made to act as the signifier of what he calls "a primordial African-based culture." In fact, he says, they were more interested in literature, with the result that music really functioned in their writings and speeches as "a supplement, an exoticized Other that enhanced the sense of mystery and spirit informing the stable grounds of the text." While he accepts that later critics have made this more complex he is still uneasy with a tendency on the part of Gates and Baker to what he calls "an ahistorical devotion to a 'vernacular' grounding that is reformulated in the postmodern lexicon of elusiveness: signifyin(g), the blues matrix, etc."[57]

What I am particularly interested in here are the spiritual claims made for music, and how far the word "spirit" is being stretched. Amiri Baraka's commitment to African American music, evidenced not only in the pathbreaking *Blues People* of 1963 and the later collections *Black Music* of 1967 and *The Music* of 1987 but also in numerous poems and essays, is clear, and what runs through it is an investment in aspects of African American music as the site of an original and continuing cultural essence or resource—what he has called in an important essay "The Changing Same." In Baraka we find on one hand the idea of music as an expression of its cultural context, something that reflects and expresses the specificity of place and time, of roots and routes. In this way it creates solidarity and tells the tales of the tribe. But on the other hand, we find the belief in its capacity to go beyond this people and this time. Baraka sees in the New Music and in Albert Ayler and Coltrane, for instance, something else related to the surviving religious traditions, and he calls these musicians "God-seekers." Though the new music may have begun by defining itself in social comment, "Once free, it is spiritual. But it is soulful before, after, any time, anyway."[58]

In this way the music is transcendent of the conditions of its production and contains an aspiration toward something more.[59] In a recording with Hugh Ragin and David Murray, Baraka recites a poem, "Message from Sun Ra," in which the message is "The world is in transition, your world and your condition."[60] In keeping with Sun Ra's claims, it is supposedly in "Jupiter-language," and I would suggest that this use of Sun Ra demonstrates Baraka's refusal to give up on the idea of an alternative spirit world.[61] There is a clear awareness in his work of the ways in which cultural expression is more than its determinant elements.

What is encumbered sings to

change its meaty box. The dirt

is full of music.[62]

The language and imagery of the Black Arts movement draws heavily both on conjure and music. For instance, the title of Larry Neal's *Hoodoo Hollerin' Bebop Ghosts* brings together music and magic, and his poem "Fragments from the Narrative of the Black Musicians" uses lines from blues songs and references to cakewalk as well as to Legba. The poem is an invocation of ancestral powers, culminating in a celebration of male sexual potency and fertility, and as a part of his deliberate rehabilitation of earlier primitivist stereotypes, Neal, like Ishmael Reed, invokes Vachel Lindsay's poem:

Congo, the hoodoo man, haunts these cabins, words mesh into night.

He works spells; his spirit runs in deep rivers

And sings in shadow trees, runs deep rivers

And sings in shadow trees. [63]

Using much of the same imagery as the Black Arts writers, but with a different view of the Black Aesthetic, Ishmael Reed powerfully develops the conjunction of music, magic, and African American history, incorporating postmodern and post-structuralist critiques of essentialism. His novel *Mumbo Jumbo* revisits, from the standpoint of the 1970s, many of the themes of the 1920s and early 1930s treated in Chapter 3 and it also complements Baker's revisionist account of the Harlem Renaissance by emphasizing the continuities and importance of voodoo and hoodoo elements, which he makes central to African American cultural survival. Drawing on later accounts of voodoo and Haiti, he gives it more political resonance as a movement of resistance than Hurston did in her accounts. This stress on voodoo and its African roots also entails a radical devaluation of the role of Christian spirituality and its cultural forms. "I've decided that gospel music is just a front for voodoo. Mahalia Jackson had a difficult time getting her brand of gospel over to orthodox ministers. And I think when they're praising Jesus, they're really singing about Legba or someone like that . . . Damballah. The rhythms are voodoo. The genius of voodoo is its camouflage."[64]

In the novel, Reed uses the idea of a mysterious force, "Jes Grew," which is intangible like spirit, but expresses itself in the most subversive bodily ways through rhythm and dance. In this way he takes over the idea of spirit possession for his own ends.[65] One character, Papa La Bas, described as "noonday Hoo-Doo, fugitive-hermit, obeah-man, botanist, animal impersonator, 2-headed man, You-Name-It," recalls for modern students the rise of Jes Grew as a movement of black cultural expression, starting in New Orleans.[66] This contagious movement, which caused people to dance and feel possessed by a spirit, reached epidemic proportions in the so-called Jazz Age of the 1920s before being defeated, at least temporarily, by the forces of conformity and authority, which tried to control or co-opt the movement. Papa La Bas evokes, through his name, the African figure of Legba as well as Haitian voodoo, and he is engaged in a struggle with those forces determined to stamp out or usurp Jes Grew's powers. These opposing forces include a figure, Hinckle von Vampton, modeled on Carl Van Vechten and a black stooge of the white authorities referred to as the Talking Android.

Clearly, through the idea of the contagion of Jes Grew in the Twenties, Reed is referring to jazz and related African American music. He takes the term from James Weldon Johnson's description of the development of ragtime,[67] and the names of African American musicians are scattered throughout the book, but the book also invokes a much larger time frame, because this particular epidemic of Jes Grew is only the latest manifestation of a force that goes back to Africa at least. Reed traces it back to Osiris, "the man who did dances that caught-on,"[68] and describes how this benevolent spiritual force, embodied in a range of figures including Dionysus and Thoth, was suppressed by Set and the Atonist Order. Reed's anachronistic description of mythical and historical figures has the effect of erasing historical differences and emphasizing the continuities of spiritual expression, but it is also typically postmodern in its playful pastiches and parodies of history. A good example would be his treatment of Moses. Like Hurston, Reed offers a revisionist view of him, but whereas she was concerned to make her portrayal consistent with arguments about the role of Africa and Egypt, his approach is more anachronistic and less concerned with being realistic. In his version, for instance, Moses plays guitar. Hearing that Jethro plays the most authentic music ("the heaviest sound") he borrows it, but fails to learn the words that would give it its full meaning, so that when he plays it, it fails to have its full effect.[69] The idea of words that could complement the music, a text that Jes Grew needs to fulfill its mission, is fundamental to the novel. One of the epigraphs to the novel reads, "So Jes Grew is seeking its words. Its text. For what good is a liturgy without a text?" and this reflects Reed's and other writers' mission to express in written form the strengths of the oral vernacular tradition in its many manifestations, including narrative, music, and conjure.[70]

While in many ways Reed's book takes up the themes of the Harlem Renaissance, and makes Harlem of the twenties a place of promise and ferment, his positive emphasis on conjure and jazz goes well beyond many of the artists of that time, and certainly beyond the rather cautious approach of Locke's *The New Negro*.[71] Reed quotes from J. A. Rogers's essay in that volume, which compares jazz's "epidemic contagiousness" with measles.[72] Rogers's view is ambivalent, and he does see great possibilities once jazz has been refined or developed, but the terminology of plague is revealing. While Reed's own vision of an apocalyptic wave of energy that transforms Western society is comic and fantastic, and the panic responses of his characters are meant to be ridiculous, the link between changes in music and dangerous transformations in society was indeed regularly made.[73]

In his positive view of the new music and of conjure Reed is closer to Hurston than the more elitist members of the Harlem Renaissance, and *Mumbo Jumbo* can in fact be read as an implicit dialogue with many of her concerns. It also exhilaratingly engages with the larger treatment of the primitive in the era, with allusions to Freud and at the attempts to contain the magical and primitive within museum cases and categories. Europe, he tells us, could "no longer guard the 'fetishes' of civilizations which were placed in the various Centers of Art Detention located in New York."[74] His use of the term fetish here is a swipe at Europe's irrationality more than anything else, and is reminiscent of Marx's rhetorical uses of the language of fetish and superstition. In his celebratory description of "the HooDoo of VooDoo" and its "bleeblop essence," Reed describes its opponents as "Black and White Atonists, Europe the ghost rattling its chains down the deserted halls of their brains."[75]

Marx's famous phrase about the specter of revolution that is haunting Europe seems here to be reversed so that Europe is now the specter haunting and hindering the present, and this same passage is quoted approvingly by Nathaniel Mackey,[76] whose own writings constitute one of the most searching and self-conscious treatments of music and spirit, and to whom I devote the rest of this chapter. Mackey's ongoing series of novels with the collective title *From a Broken Bottle Traces of Perfume Still Emanate* features a narrator who plays in jazz ensembles variously known as the Mystic Horn Society, the Deconstructive Woodwind Chorus, the Crossroads Choir, and the Boneyard Brass Octet, and much of the writing is directly about their performances.

The novels are made up entirely of letters from the protagonist, who signs himself "N.," to someone only known as "Angel of Dust." In this name we see the typical conjunction in Mackey of spiritual and material, heavenly and earthy, and the letters reflect these concerns. As we join their dialogue in the first novel, Angel of Dust has apparently been insisting on the need for a clear belief in an original source (like a religious faith in God or a culturally centered belief like Afrocentrism) and has asked N. to distinguish between what comes *from* a source and what is *about* a source—between "what speaks of speaking of something, and what (more valuably) speaks *from* something, ie where the source is available, becomes a re-source rather than something evasive, elusive, sought after." N. responds in his letter with a defense of his focus on loss and absence rather than the assertion of presence. "We not only can but should speak of 'loss' or . . . speak of *absence* as unavoidably an inherence in the texture of things." His "pre-occupation with origins and ends is exactly that: a pre- (equally post-, I suppose) occupation." He distinguishes between the supposed solidity of Angel's world and "the world my 'myriad words' uncoil." His world is not "insubstantial, unreal or whatever else. Only an other (possibly Other) sort of solidarity." It is "an unlikely Other whose inconceivable occupancy glimpses of ocean beg access to." And he ends the letter by insisting, "Not 'resource' so much for me as re:Source."[77]

The distinction here is an important one, even if it seems willfully abstruse. If we assume that there is a point of origin and absolute presence that precedes and transcends the day-to-day world of our material senses—a God—then artists and others may be able to access that spirit or power and speak, or be spoken through, from the source. On the other hand, if we take a poststructuralist or deconstructionist view that questions such claims for presence, then all we can ever do is write *about* it and in doing so bring into being or sustain a flickering sort of presence created through the processes of difference and deferral inherent in representation itself.[78] What is crucial is that to insist on absence is not to reject all dealings with the idea of presence as a resource, but to see the two terms in a dynamic relation, with the idea of source and spirit being questioned and historicized rather than taken for granted. Mackey is aware of the importance of being able to claim a historical/geographical origin in Africa and connect up with it, but he approaches with caution the merging or eliding of this with the idea of a cultural and hence a spiritual wholeness. Instead, he explores the lack of wholeness. He wants to foreground those black linguistic and musical practices that emphasize process and invention rather than a return to a supposedly fixed identity or essence, and he wants "a countertradition of marronage, divergence, flight, fugitive tilt."[79]

He directs attention to the formal processes by which black artists have dismantled the limiting labels of identity, which for him means focusing on lack rather than on a presumed spiritual plenitude.[80] In his second letter to Angel of Dust, the character N. introduces the idea of a physical lack. "However much I may in the end/beginning turn out to have been courting a 'lack' I intend to keep that tail-biting lizard in mind. Aren't we all, however absurdly, amputees?"[81] The idea of lack and severance here is an important one in Mackey. From the Caribbean writer Wilson Harris, he takes the idea of music operating like a "phantom limb" for peoples of the African diaspora. Harris saw music as a powerful cultural resource because it was a powerful and resonant reminder of what had been lost in the destruction of cultures and people in slavery and its aftermath, and he described this in figures of loss, amputation, and absence—an idea taken up powerfully by later writers.

Saadiya Hartman sees the recognition of loss as "a crucial element in redressing the breach introduced by slavery. This recognition entails a remembering of the pained body, not by way of a simulated wholeness but precisely through the recognition of the amputated body in its amputatedness, in the insistent recognition of the violated body as human flesh, in the cognition of its needs and in the anticipation of liberty. In other words, it is the ravished body that holds out the possibility of restitution, not the invocation of an illusory wholeness or the desired return to an originary plenitude."[82] For Harris, music is a reminder of what had once been there. It is a reminder of absence that is a feeling of presence—as if the leg is still there. We could say it is an absence felt as a presence, or a feeling of presence that points toward an absence. So, though "phantom" usually suggests illusion or unreality, Mackey wants to exploit its more challenging and critical implications.[83]

The word "phantom" "is a relative, relativizing term that cuts both ways, occasioning a shift in perspective between real and unreal," and the phantom limb "reveals the illusory rule of the world it haunts."[84] In other words, the awareness of absence, expressed as a false presence can be a sort of resource in itself. "The phantom limb is a felt recovery, a felt advance beyond severance and limitation that contends with and questions conventional reality." It is "a feeling for what is not there that reaches beyond as it calls into question what is. . . . The phantom limb haunts or critiques a condition in which feeling, consciousness itself, would seem to have been cut off."[85] This means that music can function to reveal a spiritual dimension that is experienced as something physical but points to more than itself. "The world, music reminds us, inhabits while extending beyond what meets the eye, resides in but rises above what is apprehensible to the senses." This is not the same, though, as saying that when we listen to music we enter a separate spiritual realm or experience a spiritual presence, because what interests Mackey is the way in which its effects are associated with absence and loss.[86] Music is a pointing *toward* rather than an expression *of* that other world. Mackey's poem "Grisgris Dancer" is based on an Afro-Caribbean figure whose use of what were called fetishes or gris-gris or charms has been melodramatically and negatively presented as a form of malign superstition by white observers. The practices of the "backwardswalking / twoheaded / woman" address

All the gathered

ache of our

severed selves,

all the

windowless light

but do not offer any simple solace or remedy for it.[87]

He refers to the Kaluli people of Papua New Guinea, who see song as "a complaint and a consolation." In this view we are all orphans but "in back of 'orphan' one hears echoes of 'orphic,' a music that turns on abandonment, absence, loss. . . . Think of the black spiritual 'Motherless Child.' Music is wounded kinship's last resort."[88] Music, then, can be a phantom reminder of what is not here, but it is still playing a positive role in keeping alive in the mind a utopian possibility. And of course black music has also pointed beyond the present and actual in more direct historical ways as a response to slavery and oppression, so this reaching or pointing beyond has both a social and a metaphysical dimension.[89]

It is typical of Mackey to refuse to separate out the social and the theoretical. The musical phenomenon of call and response, for instance, is usually seen as an expression of a social relation as well as a musical form, but Mackey has another take on this. As well as the communal context and the relation between individual and group in communal assent, he wants to look at the ways in which "*assent* can be heard to carry undertones or echoes of *ascent* (*accents* of ascent)."[90] He also refers to this in an account of a performance in *Bedouin Hornbook* when he describes the flute-player fulfilling for a moment the dreams of the oppressed. "An almost clandestine appeal, its claim was that were there no call the response would invent one."[91] This could be taken at the social level, suggesting that revolution comes from below, that the people create and call into being their leader, but it also connects up with the idea that it is only through and within our mundane condition of belatedness that we actually bring into being what is supposed to have been there from the beginning, namely the primary or originary. But we may only experience this is as phantom or ghost, rather than as pure or unmediated soul or spirit, since the sublime can only be seen as an aesthetic phenomenon—the creation of an effect, rather than the actualization of a spiritual presence.

In his fiction Mackey literalizes these ideas, often to comic effect. He refers to a tenor player whose solo has a " 'phantom' reach" and then typically brings this down to earth with humor by suggesting that he perhaps achieved this by smoking a joint soaked in embalming fluid.[92] Equally he plays with the idea of music as transcending itself, when one member of the band, Penguin, seems to create balloons from his horn. These float above the band, borne aloft by circular breathing, and contain a message, like those above the characters' heads in comic strips. This creates a sensation, with audiences not sure what they've actually seen, and the band is not sure what is happening, either, but the narrator typically improvises on it and on the idea of a balloon, in a way that is both highly intellectual and abstract and at the same time led by sound—something that we could trace back to one of his poetic influences, Robert Duncan, and his tone leading and punning.

In the novel Mackey has already performed a set of improvisations and variations on the name of a member of the band, Penguin—a flightless bird, whose wings are just stubs, or nubs—just quills and feathers—which are related to pens and writing. This is itself related to a recurrent dream of a figure of a woman drummer called Penny. He then performs a similar flight of improvisation on the word "balloon," which he sees as B'Loon (as in B'Fox or Brer Fox, as well as the African form of many names), and he relates this to the water bird, the loon, which is associated with Native American Earthdiver myths, in which the loon dives deep to be able to bring up some mud, which grows to become our world. So we have a conjunction of aerial flight, with its associations of transcendence, with the lowest and most earthly. "Are the balloons mud we resurface with, mud we situate ourselves upon, heuristic precipitate, axiomatic muck, unprepossessing mire?"[93]

Mackey's concern, then, is with music's power to link the material and the spiritual by pointing toward something not only physical. In some ways, this may seem a conventional enough claim for music as having transcendent dimensions, but Mackey has an important twist in *formal* terms here. For him the reaching beyond does not happen by abstraction, by achieving a Platonic or pure form that is greater than the actual sound. It is not through a transcending of the material thing, the sound, and achieving a purity that is independent of the sounds heard, as for instance, in Eliot's idea of music in *Four Quartets*. Instead, the effect is achieved by stressing and stretching the sounds themselves. For example, if you exaggerate the *sounds* of the words, such as the sibilants, as you speak, you are stressing the materiality of the sound and reaching to the edge of its signifying system. You draw attention to the material sounds not to the semiotic system by which you are being understood. Similarly, to stretch to the very edge of an instrument's or voice's range, or beyond, is to risk losing meaning (interfering with the semiotic system of music) but also, paradoxically, sometimes to create the sense of pointing toward something else outside or beyond it. It is this that can give the sense of yearning, or aspiring—in other words, the effect of the sublime. For instance, when a voice or an instrument soars and strains, we become aware of the physical medium, but we are also directed beyond it. Mackey's narrator talks for instance about the role of the falsetto, and he puns on the idea of the "strangulated tenor." Talking about Al Green, he says "I've long marveled at how all his going on about love succeeds in alchemizing a legacy of lynchings—as though singing were a rope he comes eternally close to being strangled by." He describes this as a "metavoice," bearing the weight of "a gnostic transformative desire to be done with the world." The "false" voice "creatively hallucinates a 'new world.'" "What is it in the falsetto," he asks, "that thins and threatens to abolish the voice but the wear of so much reaching for heaven?" Not just the falsetto, but the moan and the shout can explore "a redemptive unworded world."[94]

It is the breaking and stretching, what he calls the rasp and creak of sound and forms under pressure, that interests him, and he mentions, for instance,

Rahsaan Roland Kirk's many voicings and breathings over the flute as he is playing. He also develops the idea, related to the idea of the phantom, of a language or a sound being corrupted, or invaded from outside. In Coltrane he finds sometimes an "unruly agonistic sound in which it seems that the two articulations are wrestling with one another, that they are somehow one another's contagion or contamination."[95] This is not dialogical, or call and response in any communal sense, but something that threatens or promises to pollute or to transform the intended sound. He links this elsewhere to possession as this is found in voodoo, where one is said to be "ridden" by a spirit, or *loa*, like a horse. In his poem "Ohnedaruth's Day Begun" he describes such a state of possession in a jazz musician:

We play "Out of

This World" instead, the riff hits

me like rain and like a leak in my

throat it won't quit. No reins whoa

this ghost I'm ridden by[96]

He mentions elsewhere that the poem was written for John Coltrane ("Out of This World" is a Coltrane number and of course is a very appropriate title for this theme), and he refers to "a surge, a runaway dilation, a quantum rush you often hear in Trane's music, the sense that he's driven, possessed—*ridden*—as it's put here."[97] The idea of being "transported," in all its senses, is taken up and developed in Mackey's poetry. In "Song of the Andoumboulou" he uses the idea of a train journey to express, traditionally enough, the idea of a movement or quest for something perhaps unattainable. The train is variously located in Spain and then in Brazil but is often more abstract.

It was a train we were on

peripatetic tavern we

were in, mind unremittingly

elsewhere, words meaning

more

than the world they

pointed at, asymptotic

tangent, Ahtt it

was called.[98]

The vehicle is less important than its ability to go beyond the limits of earth.

was a boat we were on, bus we were

on, sat on a train orbiting abject

Earth

As well as suggesting Sun Ra's use of images of space travel, which included orbiting monorails and satellites, this also invokes the African American use in sermons of the gospel train, and the underground railroad referred to obliquely in spirituals:

Would-be train we'd

Heard about in sermons, songs, to ride

was to bid exile goodbye. Ride meant to

be done with waiting

And he folds this into more jazz-based references:

Gnostic sleeper stowed

Away on

The boat we rode, runaway sunship, Trane's

Namesake music's runaway ghost.[99]

Mackey, then, is fascinated by the impurities, by the edges of the medium where it becomes invaded by something else and where we feel the rasp and creak, the physical characteristics of the medium itself. Olly Wilson has identified what he calls a "heterogeneous sound ideal" informing a great deal of African American music. According to Wilson, whereas Western music has aimed increasingly for a blending of sounds, African and African American music has sought a wide range of contrasting timbres, even within a single line, to create a different texture, and this can involve the full continuum of vocal sounds ranging from speech to song.[100] Mackey puts this in a more formal and theoretical context in arguing that it is on the edges, where it is most stretched and threatened, that we are aware of both the absolute materiality of the sound and its capacity to point toward something more.

Mackey refers several times to the striking description by the Dogon people of the sound made by the shuttle and block in the process of weaving as the "creaking of the Word." This is because for them the creation of cloth and the creation of language are intimately related. The anthropologist Marcel Griaule was told that "As the threads crossed and uncrossed, the two tips of the Spirit's forked tongue pushed the thread of the weft back and forth, and the web took shape from his mouth in the breath of the second revealed Word. For the Spirit was speaking while the work proceeded. As did the Nummo in the first revelation, he imparted his Word by means of a technical process, so that all men could understand. By so doing he showed the identity of material actions and spiritual forces, or rather the need for their cooperation."[101] Thus the web of language is not just a figure of speech, nor even a metaphor *for* speech, but an assertion of the unity of the material and the immaterial, cloth and word, textile and text.

What attracts Mackey here is not just the idea of the inextricability of material and spiritual, but the idea of friction, of strain or incompleteness in this fusion. "It is the noise upon which the word is based, the discrepant foundation of all coherence and articulation, of the purchase upon the world fabrication affords. Discrepant engagement, rather than suppressing or seeking to silence that noise, acknowledges it." This "antifoundational acknowledgement of founding noise"[102] is, I think, fundamental to his scrupulously post-structuralist stance, so that Michael Harper's description in the preface to Mackey's *Eroding Witness* of Mackey making and restoring disparate connections and working toward "the reconstruction of a spiritual wholeness despite the fragmentation of the body" may be going further than Mackey himself would, in its suggestion of a unity to be returned to. Mackey's own poetry employs a number of techniques which decenter a self or single point of control and allow for "the cultivation of another voice, a voice that is other than that proposed by one's intentions, tangential to one's intentions, angular, oblique. . . . That sliding away wants out."[103]

The idea of voice is crucial here in its implication—its invocation—of presence, and Mackey is interested in the ways in which that voice can be influenced and informed by more than the conscious self. Like a number of American poets, he refers to Lorca's use of the *duende*, which he describes as "a kind of gremlin, a gremlinlike, troubling spirit" that can inhabit or haunt the artist. It is heard or overheard in the deepest and most disturbing parts of the work, is beyond mere technique, and is the expression of spirit.[104] But Mackey stresses two aspects, which others often don't. One is the idea of dissonance, what he describes as "trouble in the voice." It has to do with "trouble, deep trouble," and ultimately unredeemable loss and death. The other important aspect is its racial dimension. In an essay in which he invokes the possible Egyptian origins of gypsies, Mackey refers to Lorca working with "the black aesthetic of Spain." He recalls the advice given to Lorca by a gypsy singer ("What you must search for and find is the black torso of the Pharoah"), and

Lorca's statement that "All that has dark sounds has *duende*" (or it could be black sounds, depending on the translation, as Mackey points out).[105]

Some time before, in an essay published in 1954, Ralph Ellison made very similar points, explicitly linking flamenco music to blues and other forms of African American music. He described Spain as "neither Europe nor Africa but a blend of both" and found in Andalusian gypsy music qualities that, like those of jazz, are not the result of "primitivism" but of "an aesthetic which rejects the beautiful sound sought by Western classical music." The gypsies, like the slaves, retain an awareness of "the physical source of man's most spiritual moments" and flamenco is like the blues in the way it works in the music to mock the despair expressed in the lyric. It "expresses the great human joke directed against the universe," namely that "though we be dismembered daily we shall always rise up again."[106] Here Ellison invokes the Christian myth of the resurrection, but as a model of human survival, a stance toward suffering, rather than a transcendence—and the reference to dismembering clearly links with Mackey's ideas.

Mackey's work is a deliberate and often witty challenge to the idea of spirit or source as something outside and separate from the material realm, something to be achieved through leaving or transcending the physical. In other words, he insists on Body *and* Soul rather than Body *or* Soul. To do this he draws on and contributes to the rich expressions of this in African American culture, but he also uses post-structuralist theory to avoid the essentialism and exceptionalism that haunt many claims for African American music. He is then able to demonstrate how African Americans have created a powerful aesthetic that combines spiritual power with concrete realities, which finds spirit at the edges of the ordinary, and at the heart of the earthly, in the mud of the earth-diving loon, and in the Angel of Dust.

Chapter 5

The Return of the Fetish

In the last chapter I dealt with some uses of the legacy of conjure and music by African American artists and writers, and the claims made for that legacy as a continuing resource for their community. The question of the wider relevance or applicability of these forms was not my main focus, but I want to begin this chapter by making a bridge with Native American concerns with spiritual and cultural continuity through the figure of Robert Johnson, as used by Renée Stout and Sherman Alexie, before moving on to show how the concern with spiritual legacy takes rather different forms in a Native American context.

The high visibility of Johnson today is largely the result of the Blues Revival of the 1960s, in which a new generation of white enthusiasts rediscovered early bluesmen and invested them with the glamour of authenticity and hard living. In Johnson's case the legends of his existential encounters at the crossroads also lent him the mystique of black magic. This mythology linked him to his supposed cultural and religious roots but presented his situation and music as universally applicable and appealing, and contributed to a larger conception of the blues as a form or feeling that transcended race.[1] This cross-cultural iconicity is strikingly exploited in Sherman Alexie's *Reservation Blues*, in which the figure of Robert Johnson turns up on the Spokane Indian reservation with his guitar. The novel is prefaced with the lyrics of one of Johnson's most famous songs ("I went down to the crossroad / fell down upon my knees") together with a quotation from jazz musician Charles Mingus, reflecting the resolutely mixed and nontraditional tone of the book. Johnson goes for help to Big Mom, a rather mysterious, and spiritually powerful Spokane woman, while his guitar, which has the power to travel on its own, and inspire those who play it, triggers the success of an inexperienced group called Coyote Springs, made up of Spokane Indians and two part-Flathead women.

Their music is not traditional, as Alexie stresses, but is an "all-Indian rock and blues band." When they appear in public a "lot of New Agers showed up with their crystals, expecting to hear some ancient Indian wisdom and got a good dose of Sex Pistols covers instead."[2] The band eventually fails after being flown to New York to audition by white agents, whose names, Sheridan and Wright, suggest the U.S. Army generals of the last century. (Wright, in fact, seems to have been responsible for shooting the horses of the Spokane people, and the screams of these horses recur through the book, as I will show later.) Though they reject the band, the producers latch on to the two white groupies and backup singers, who are then packaged to offer all the acceptable aspects of Indianness for a mass market. Alexie gives us the lyrics of their song, which manage to ring all the conventional changes on traditional Indian themes that have become clichés in popular representations.

Can you hear the eagle crying?
I look to the four directions
And try to find some connection
With Mother Earth, Mother Earth
. . . .
And my hair is blonde,
But I'm Indian in my bones
And my skin is white,
But I'm Indian in my bones.[3]

There are echoes here of the Modernist imitations of Indian song discussed in Chapter 3, as well as New Age imitations, and Alexie is clearly critical of this sort of white expropriation and essentialism, but he is also wary of essentialism as it operates from within the Indian community. He gives us the text of an open letter in the local press that criticizes the group's ability to represent the Spokane tribe. "Do we really want other people to think we are like this band? Do we really want people to think that the Spokanes are a crazy storyteller, a couple of irresponsible drunks, a pair of Flathead Indians and two white women? I don't think so."[4] There is surely some self-reflexive irony here about Alexie's own project in this book, which expresses the irredeemably modern and mixed nature of Indian identity in ways that go beyond traditional definitions of Indian community. In a very positive review of the book, Leslie Silko pinpoints this issue and finds an inevitable ambivalence about the guitar and the gift it represents, which is "a talent or gift that consumes individuals and calls them away from the community. Alexie's version of Robert Johnson, on the run to escape the music, his hands burned and scarred by the guitar, casts an ominous light on talent."[5]

At one point, Thomas, the main character, hears Robert Johnson's voice sounding across the reservation. "Then the music stopped. The reservation exhaled. Those blues created memories for the Spokanes but they refused to claim them. Those blues lit up a new road, but the Spokanes pulled out their old maps. Those blues churned up generations of anger and pain: car wrecks, suicides, murders. Those blues were ancient, aboriginal, indigenous."[6] This is a complicated passage, not least in what it claims for the blues. It may seem to be lamenting the failure of the Spokanes to move forward and to adapt and adopt, but it does so by implying that the blues are indigenous anyway. This would mean that Alexie is in danger of using the blues in the same universalizing way as the white women in their song quoted above use ideas of Indian-ness. Another way of reading it is to see Alexie as using the blues to point to a fundamental hybridity in America rather than trying to replace one original purity or indigeneity with another.[7] If we combine the passage with the con-clusion of the book, we can perhaps see what survives Alexie's ironic dismissals of essentialist conceptions of Indian identity.

At the end of the novel, Thomas and the remains of the band leave the reservation for the city after the suicide of one of their members. Robert John-son remains with Big Mom, who sits in her rocking chair "measuring time with her back and forth, back and forth, back and forth there on the Spokane In-dian Reservation. She sang a protection song, so none of the Indians, not one, would forget who they are." At one level then, there is a contrast between lin-ear movement in the trip to the city, which expresses the new, and a timeless or cyclic movement, back and forth, that conserves, but in fact on the road to the city the band are accompanied by the shadow horses that have recurred through the novel and whose slaughter by soldiers in the last century represents white oppressions of the past. Big Mom seems to have re-created them, and the remaining members of the band in the car "sang together with the shadow horses: we are alive, we'll keep living. Songs were waiting for them up there in the dark. Songs were waiting for them in the city. Thomas drove the car through the dark. He drove. Checkers and Chess reached out of their windows and held tightly to the manes of the shadow horses running alongside the blue van."[8]

There is clearly an attempt here to blend together the traditional and the modern, to refuse the dichotomies within which Indians and Indian culture have been (mis)represented, but it is arguable whether this foregrounding of the mythic and traditional quite reflects the book as a whole, or indeed its par-ticular strengths. How viable is it to rehabilitate or reappropriate images that are already so heavily overdetermined within such a hybrid and postmodern novel and expect them to carry an ultimately redemptive charge? Alexie is scornful of the "New Agers" and their simplistic expectations of Indian spiri-tuality, and his eclectic postmodernism and embrace of hybridity raises the question of which sort of syncretisms are acceptable and which are not. In Chapter 1 I referred to Chrétien Le Clercq's scornful account of an Indian woman who had incorporated Native and Christian elements into a cross, but in Alexie's novel the priest on the reservation is pleased and amused by a dream catcher that has been made to incorporate rosary beads in an intricate network.[9] We could even argue that such syncretism points back to an activity so fundamental as to be itself indigenous and aboriginal, as well as forward to New Age appropriations, in ways that raise difficult questions about the trans-latability and commercial and cultural circulation of spirituality.

Throughout the book, I have been exploring the nexus of ideas that have run through anthropological, theological, and popular discourses about matter, spirit, and race, focusing on key words such as "fetish" and "totem." In dealing with contemporary African American artists in Chapter 4, I showed how there have been some reclamations of the materiality of the fetish and conjure, as well as some debatable claims for the generalizability of spirit. When we turn to Indian artists we find a comparable but crucially different picture, one that requires me—yet again—to return to the fetish and some other nineteenth-century formulations as a context for New Age and contemporary Indian treatments of spirituality. This will give me the basis on which finally to move to the work of Leslie Silko, whose writings seem to me most profoundly to pull together most of the strands of my inquiry.

While the term "fetish" has now been almost entirely abandoned in its original usages and referents and has migrated to broader psychological and cultural usages, I want to focus on one rather odd survival of the term, which is its use to describe the small stone sculptures in animal forms made by the Zuni Indians of New Mexico and known as Zuni fetishes. The term "fetish," or "fetich," to describe these stone objects can be traced specifically to Frank Hamilton Cushing's *Zuni Fetiches*, which I discussed in Chapter 1, but this now seems to be one of the few places in America, or indeed anywhere in the world, where the word fetish is still used widely and nonpejoratively to describe a religious object. Numerous nonscholarly books, glossy catalogs, and Web sites deal with these Zuni fetishes as objects of spiritual, artistic, or decorative worth, and the objects themselves are widely available at galleries and by mail order, and I want to use them to follow up more broadly the New Age appropriations and commodifications of Indian spirituality.

Hal Zina Bennett's *Zuni Fetishes: Using American Objects for Meditation, Reflection and Insight* offers a generalized pantheistic view of nature, which he presents as the Indian one, and it offers a good example of what some collectors think they are acquiring. He uses fetishes as "guidance toward enjoying a more loving relationship with nature, with this beautiful blue planet that is our Mother."[10] Accordingly, he feeds the fetishes in the traditional way and treats them as animated. In a New Age mixture of executive and religious language he tells us of having a "conference" with his fetishes to get guidance. Other books—glossy catalogues with price-guides, and texts which exemplify the mixture of spiritual and aesthetic idealization of the Indians of the Southwest—reveal more of the commodity aspect. Thus, although the term "fetish" is preserved in this one instance, it has lost any of the danger of magic or materiality. What we have left is both a commodification of the fetish and commodity fetishism.[11]

In the context of New Age activities, the sheer exchangeability of the spiritual is crucial, and it has an intimate connection with material exchange through that ultimate point of exchangeability, the commodity. New Age objects are supposedly translatable and adaptable because they all have spiritual power, but what really makes them interchangeable and exchangeable is that they are all commodities in the same market. The circulation in a "free market" of objects that are interchangeably "spiritual" not only blurs distinctions between different religious traditions but has the overall effect of obscuring the material differences of economic and political power between buyers and the people they borrow from. As Philip Deloria puts it, "The presence of multicultural images and statements, however, lets Indian players [whites identifying with Indians] claim a sincere but ultimately fruitless, political sympathy with native people."[12] The alternative economic image to this one of free-market exchange is one that sees spirituality as a form of property, and New Age activities as unwarrantable appropriation. Vine Deloria has deplored the arrogant assumption that "there is nothing that Indians possess, *absolutely nothing*—pipes, dances, land, water, feathers, drums and even prayers—that non-Indians cannot take, whenever and wherever they wish."[13]

A similar text to Bennett's is a spiritual self-help publication, *Totems*, which offers a detailed guide to the identification and use of what the subtitle describes as "the transformative power of your personal animal totem." The first chapter introduces "our animal companions on Turtle Island," but in spite of the title the power is not entirely based around Indian materials. Here all spiritual terms are grist for the author's mill. All cultures have "sensed an unknown force that underlies all paranormal phenomena." This is *mana*, the Hindu *prana*, the Sufi *baraka*, the Chinese *chi*, Japanese *ki*, and Old Norse *wodan*, and in addition "various Native American tribes chant its name as *wakan, manitou*, or *orenda*." Contact with these "spirit helpers" will allow access to supernatural power, and "through your animal totems, you may well discover that your disciplined use of the *mana* will be of inestimable value enabling you to . . . soar into higher spiritual dimensions."[14]

The use of the word "totem," to suggest some object of atavistic attachment, as it is used here, has taken it well beyond Indian associations, and in fact this practice was already widespread before it was pressed into New Age service. The African poet Léopold Senghor could write more than half a century before in a poem called "The Totem":

I must hide him deep in my veins

The Ancestor with the skin of a tempest streaked by lightning and thunder

My Guardian-Animal, I must hide him

Lest I burst the dam of scandals.

Here the idea of a guardian spirit has been combined with the Africanist assertions characteristic of the Negritude movement, so that, far from being a donor spirit, as in North America, the totem seems to represent an original atavistic racial essence. In the same vein, in a collection of plays "from the Black World Repertory" published in 1989 under the title *Totem Voices*, the editor sees song and other art forms resurrecting "our totemic relationship to the ancestors."[15] We also find the term used in the visual arts in the same way to invoke universal or archetypal beliefs or fears, as in the painter Jackson Pollock's expression of elemental mythic and ritual processes in two pieces called *Totem* 1 and 2.[16] The African American painter Norman Lewis's *American Totem* suggests a more ironic use of the term, particularly if we see, as some have done, racial implications and echoes of a KKK mask in his painting.

But the problems raised by the translatability of spiritual terms or properties cannot simply be solved by closing the borders. As with the larger question of Indian identity, protectionism can itself be a dangerous trap and Indian writers and intellectuals have themselves grappled with the issue.[17] The too-easy melding of disparate cultural or religious values under the umbrella of the "spiritual" can also take place under Indian auspices, and for idealistic as well as commercial reasons, and it may be hard to disentangle the various agendas. We have seen Alexie's appropriation of blues music in his novel, and he explores the issue elsewhere, as in his short story "Because My Father Always Said He Was the Only Indian Who Saw Jimi Hendrix Play 'The Star-Spangled Banner' at Woodstock." Much more problematic is a book like Ed McGaa Eagle Man's *Mother Earth Spirituality: Native American Paths to Healing Ourselves and Our World*. This could be seen in the tradition of Black Elk's mission to share and extend a Native vision and philosophy, or as a commercial bastardization of Indian values. The book's biographical details are at pains to stress McGaa's authenticity as Sioux and his firsthand knowledge of Sioux religion (supported by a statement on the cover from the anthropologist William Powers), but the overall aim of the book is much more broadly based and inclusive, as indicated by the "our" of the title and jacket endorsements from New Age and Rainbow Tribe figures. The result is a numbing level of generality combined with a vague optimism. "As people evolve spiritually in this modern age, with its great gift of communication, more and more of the deeper-thinking ones of all walks of life and all races are realizing and agreeing and meeting together without all the age-old religious narrow-mindedness that held back spiritual and environmental progression. The end result will be harmony for us all."[18]

There is an assumption throughout of the translatability of ideas and of languages, and there is even a four-page "Lakota Mother Earth Relationship Word List," which offers words "that may be heard in ceremony or that are associated with Sioux spirituality." An example of how these might be used in this new ecumenism is offered in another of the appendixes to the book, a prayer by "Bright Earth Warrior (Judith Flavia), one of my rainbow friends," which incorporates many of these words into a "Prayer to the Six Powers of the Universe." My interest here is not in the authenticity or the spiritual depth, or otherwise, of such ventures, but in the assumptions about *translatability* and the role that Native words play in equating to, or filling out, the empty concept of "spirituality." This question of translation has long concerned missionaries as well as anthropologists. For earlier Christian missionaries, the issue was how to convert Indian terms and Indian subjects into Christian ones, and even the translation of the Gospel *into* Indian languages was all in the interest of a spiritual translation or conversion *from* Indian into Christian.

More recent Christian thinking, though, has given much more attention to a two-way exchange, sometimes called inculturation, by which Christianity itself would be changed. This would offer, in the words of the Choctaw Reverend Steve Charleston, "a new vocabulary in dealing with what we have been describing as a Native spirituality," which could provide part of the basis for a new contemporary Christian theology. "Instead of Western writers hacking away at a Native spirituality, we would begin to see the emergence of more theologians from within the Native community itself."[19] He sees the blanket term "spirituality" as blocking recognition of the distinctive qualities of Native American Christianity, and in a later piece he extends the attack on spirituality from a boldly argued materialist perspective. Charleston pinpoints the way in which Native tradition and religion have been restrictively characterized "by reference to a single symbol system (almost to a single word). . . . The words we use as Native People when we speak theology are the words of *spirituality*. They are words that speak in the poetic cadence of mysticism." This language, with its use of ideas of Mother Earth and its assertion of an indigenous tradition and continuity, has been useful and has given Indians "a persuasive presence in communicating our symbols . . . to a larger audience." The success of this can be judged by the extent to which this language of spirituality has been taken up and Native people have become "icons in the self-generated mysticism of Western civilization."[20]

What is needed now, though, given what Charleston sees as the increasing multinational pressures that will destroy any remaining Native autonomy and sovereignty, is a new set of symbols for Native people, in which economic and political power can be properly addressed. This may initially seem odd, because "we have confined ourselves to the soft syllables of spirituality," but "it is as much a part of our traditional vocabulary as *Mother Earth*. What I have described as *commonality* . . . is the ground of our economic theory and, therefore, the complement to our spirituality. It is, in fact, the material out of which that spirituality is fashioned." It is in finding linguistic reference points that can act as "a strong *translation code* to other cultures"[21] in the way that spirituality has done that Native culture stands its best chance of speaking authoritatively from its own values and connecting with others internationally.

This is an intriguing proposition. There are many other explorations of ways in which religious values need to be articulated in a manner that avoids the traps of spirituality, but few with this clear materialist emphasis. In 1974 the artist Jimmie Durham made a provocative, and I think still relevant, attempt to describe Indian spirituality in terms of Marxism and to argue that it is in fact much closer to a genuinely materialist approach than it is to what is called spirituality in America. In his essay "American Indian Culture: Traditionalism and Spiritualism in a Revolutionary Struggle," he argued that Indian religion is rooted in the earth and in the material world experienced as part of a whole. This is totally different both from spirituality conceived of as an escape from the material world and materialism conceived of as an attachment to objects as commodities mediated by money, as in modern capitalism. He is aware of the apparent contradiction of defending Indian traditionalism against spirituality, but this is because the term has been totally compromised, and he wants to reclaim the activist political dimensions of spiritual movements like the Ghost Dance and insist on the rootedness of Indian spirituality in many of the same ways as Charleston.[22]

In Chapter 1, I described the adoption of a number of Native terms to represent more general concepts developed by anthropologists, and even the competition among terms such as *manitou* and *orenda*. The assumption was that even diverse Indian cultures shared common religious conceptions not accessible through European terms, and we can see a similar assumption in some recent defenses of the specificity of Indian religion. Viola Cordova, for instance, has argued that Europeans have not been able to understand the term *Usen* (as used by Apache and Athabascan people of the Southwest), but she treats it as commensurable with other Native terms, as part of a shared pan-Indian concept. "The Blackfoot speak of *natoji*, the Sioux of *wakan tanka*, the Navajo of *nil'ch'i*, and the peoples of the northeastern United States have the term *manitou*. In all circumstances the term signifies something 'of a substance, character, nature, essence, quiddity beyond comprehension and therefore beyond explanation, a mystery; supernatural; potency, potential.'"

Usen may or may not contain all the features of other groups, but it does, according to Cordova, "encompass the notion of something that simply is, that remains unidentifiable, mysterious, 'supernatural' in the sense that it is beyond pointing to."[23] She argues that Western thinkers (from which she rather improbably excludes Greeks and Romans, since they apparently recognized a dynamic rather than a static universe) are incapable of understanding such notions and have only been able to substitute an inadequate substitute characterized as the "Great Spirit." For her, then, it is not merely multiplicity that is being suppressed within the idea of the monotheistic God, but something altogether more inexpressible, and she invokes B. L.Whorf's idea of linguistic relativity to suggest the impossibility of translating it.

Within the Western tradition, though, what is "beyond pointing to" has had an important role in Romantic thought through the idea of the sublime; indeed, Indians and their relation to nature have been extensively treated in these terms. More recent deconstructive approaches have stressed the psychological and linguistic rather than the religious dimensions of the concept. Rather than seeing the sublime as referring to an ineffable presence whose existence is assumed but, by definition, never grasped, the sublime has been approached in more skeptical and deconstructive terms, as a linguistic operation, the product of the breakdown of signification itself, which *creates* a "sublimity-effect" rather than *representing*, or failing to represent, an actual state. We may be reminded of Nathaniel Mackey's distinctions about source and re-source discussed in the previous chapter. In any case, the description of a term like *Usen* in terms of the unrepresentable and inexpressible runs the risk, ironically, of bringing it into the potentially exoticizing terms of the Western sublime while trying to shield it from co-optation by the generalizing assumptions of universal translatability implied by the term "Great Spirit," thus substituting one homogenizing category for another.[24]

These are difficult issues, which are given added resonance and urgency in a context of disputes over the illegitimate appropriation and commodification of ideas and cultural properties in general, and I want to turn finally to the work of Leslie Silko, which constitutes perhaps the most powerful and sustained engagement with this and many of the other concerns of my study. Throughout her writings she has brought religious beliefs and political actualities and actions into fascinating conjunctions and has approached head-on the question of how they are reconciled or interact. In addition, her writing raises the question of the significance of the tribal and local in relation to a larger world, and of specific tribal beliefs in relation to other religions. In *Ceremony*, the Laguna myths frame and include the historical events both formally, in that the myth enfolds the historical narrative at the beginning and end of the text, and thematically, as when the grandmother reflects that she feels she has heard the whole story before. The healing ceremony for Tayo works at the local Laguna level in defeating the "witchery" that has infected him and the community, but Silko's use of the uranium mine as a site of witch activity encourages us to generalize out to an international level, where the web of interconnections links American wars overseas with the situation of Indians at home. Similarly, the insistence that the ceremonies must change in order to survive, together with the elements of hybridity in the book, runs counter to any idea that religious transcendence would mean a retreat from the world or from contemporary realities. The complex balance achieved by Silko in this book has been widely acclaimed,[25] but her next novel, *Almanac of the Dead*, took this sense of intersecting realms much further, and in controversial and challenging ways.

Within *Almanac of the Dead*'s huge panoramic sweep there are a number of key revisions of the themes of earlier Indian literature. One is a geographical reorientation, in which the South becomes the locus of power and hope. This is linked to the idea of a social and religious movement that will transform the conditions of Indians, and through a revolutionary army will replace the present relation to the South, one based on the traffic of drugs and people, with a more human interrelation. The actualization of this new history is linked to the rewriting/reconstituting of the lost records and memories contained in the fragmentary text referred to as the "Almanac of the Dead." Silko's conception of this new historical movement also involves another revision to the themes of Indian literature in her treatment of race. While Silko has already explored Indian-white racial and cultural hybridities, in this book she includes an African American, Clinton, along with the Indian revolutionaries.

Predictably, though, I want first to approach her work through her treatment of fetishism, which actually links these major themes, not least because Silko draws on the full range of shifting discourses about spiritual and magical power that I have been exploring throughout this book. One of the central themes, explored through the Laguna Indian Sterling, is the immaterial power of objects—the original idea of fetishism. Sterling has been punished by his own people for allowing white outsiders to photograph a stone formation that had appeared suddenly near the uranium mine. This formation had the appearance of a serpent and was seen by the local people as representing the return of the old snake that had disappeared from its traditional home at the lake and that gave Laguna its name. Though nothing tangible was removed when it was photographed, and the whites had not even understood the significance of what they saw, the exposure had represented desecration to the tribe and triggered painful memories of a much earlier theft of stone figures, which had subsequently made their way into a museum collection. For the people, "these were not merely carved stones, these were *beings* formed by the hands of the kachina spirits."[26]

Elsewhere in the novel, the traffic of objects is related to the larger traffic of drugs from the South, which itself is part of Silko's uncompromising exploration of the logic of capitalist supply and demand that can and does extend to trade in bodies, body parts, and pornographic images of the abuse of bodies, as well as drugs. She stretches the idea of the exchange of commodities to its ultimate, so that absolutely anything becomes a commodity, and in this vision the consumers become figures of nightmare, literally vampires and cannibals. Crucial for my larger concerns here is the way that she has taken on the idea of commodity fetishism at its most fundamental level and has reinstituted the material human body, not only as the source of labor occulted and effaced in the commodity, but as an object for sale and circulation in itself. What she adds are extra dimensions of fetishism taken from the Freudian analysis of displaced sexuality.

In an intriguing discussion of the novel that chimes with many of my own concerns, Ami Regier argues that rather than seeing fetishism as an outmoded or primitive system of thought, Silko "presents fetishism as a problematized touchstone of cultural difference where tribal and European points of view are laden with histories of cultural politics."[27] In other words, Silko combines the old conception of fetish as magical or animated object (and we do have a stone fetish in the book, an opal "dressed" in red wool and feathers and coca leaves)[28] with the tools developed by Marx and Freud for examining the false ascriptions of value in modern society. In particular, she engages with Marx through the revolutionary Angelita, who makes a case for "Marx, tribal man and story-teller." According to her, he "understood what tribal people had always known: the maker of a thing pressed part of herself or himself into each object made. Some spark of life went from the maker into even the most ordinary objects. Marx had understood the value of anything came from the hands of the maker."[29] Here Angelita is explaining Marx's labor theory of value in terms of animism, which means she is performing a parallel but reverse operation to Marx's own adroit use of the metaphor of animation and enchantment in his critique of commodity fetishism. Whereas he argues that objects as commodities in capitalism take on false properties and are falsely seen as having a life of their own by having their processes of human production occluded, here Angelita transforms Marx's economic analysis—that labor creates value—by literalizing his metaphor of value as human life. This is a positive use of what has often been criticized as Marx's humanism—his privileging of use value and labor value as outside and prior to the sphere of exchange and circulation.[30]

Regier makes the point that Marx's approach, which is to demystify, to explain an illusion, may be useful for analysis, but in a revolutionary situation it may not be as useful a resource as the older idea of fetishism. This is because the older idea retains a belief in a power that could be used, particularly by those without conventional power, and could therefore mobilize people into action through belief. Angelita's account of Marx gives one way of representing him in terms of religious animistic belief, but this still leaves the question of whether Silko, as opposed to Angelita, is doing this, and if so how convincing it is. Regier argues that "Silko links the oracular fetish to the commodity fetish in order to problematize Marx's comparison of capital's operations to tribal fetishisms; instead of covering up social constructions of value and meaning, her comparatively presented fetishisms reveal their operations."[31] Certainly, in the novel we do have a whole range of beliefs in the power or animation of objects, which move among the different definitions of fetishism, and one of the most powerful effects of Silko's use of the various sorts of fetishistic belief in the book is that the modern secular world is shown to be shot through with irrational and grotesque forms of belief, fuelling monstrous actions. The modern commercial world of globalization and multinational capital, far from having moved beyond the simple superstitions of primitive beliefs (or fetishism in its original meaning), is riddled, in Silko's account, with the most extreme forms of what in *Ceremony* she called "witchery"—the world of nightmare in which cannibal and vampire creatures prey on human beings.

In this respect *Almanac* could be seen as offering a dramatic realization of Michael Taussig's analysis of the workings of capitalism in South America. He has shown how native perceptions of the operations of capitalism and commodity fetishism are couched in terms of animism, and instead of dismissing this way of describing it as superstitious and inaccurate, he has demonstrated how it illuminates Marx's original insights and actualizes his metaphors. In *Shamanism, Colonialism and the Wild Man*, Taussig refers to a "resurgent animism" that "makes things human and humans things" through the creation of a state of terror created by international capitalism which binds together Indians, African Americans, and Europeans through the fetishism of commodities.[32] The Native way of describing the operation of capitalism in animist terms, rather than being dismissed as superstitious, is shown to accurately expose the magical thinking behind the commodity fetishism of the capitalist operators.

In Silko's novel, the Mexican businessman Menardo is an example of the irrational faith in modern technology to the point of fetishism. His obsessive desire for absolute security goes beyond the armed guards, and even private armies, that he is selling to others under the package of "Universal Insurance." Silko shows how his (irrational) faith in the powers of his high-tech bulletproof vest merges with other more Freudian forms of sexual fetishism involving the vest itself. She makes the parallel with the fetish clear through the figure of Tacho, who eventually shoots Menardo, and who represents Indian spiritual continuity through his communications with macaws and his care for the opal stone that he finds and treats as an animated spirit. He sees himself as chosen by the spirits of the macaw and opal. "Blood: even the bulletproof vest wanted a little blood. Knives, guns, even automobiles, possessed 'energies' that craved blood from time to time. Tacho had heard dozens of stories that good Christians were not supposed to believe. Stories about people beaten, sometimes even killed, by their own brooms, or pots and pans. . . . Airplanes, jets, and rockets were already malfunctioning, crashing and exploding. Electricity no longer obeyed the white man. The macaw spirits said the great serpent was in charge of electricity. The macaws were in charge of fire."[33]

A shirt that promises protection inevitably evokes the shirts associated with the Ghost Dance religion in some of its manifestations on the Great Plains, which were supposed to protect their wearers. The idea of the Ghost Dance and the Prophet's prediction of the sweeping away of Europeans and the restoration of what they had destroyed becomes a key theme as the book progresses, but through one of her characters Silko makes a crucial distinction between Menardo's belief and that of the ghost dancers. One of the Indian activists, Wilson Weasel Tail, addresses the question of the practical effectiveness of the Ghost Dance. Anthropologists, he says, argue that the Ghost Dance lost credibility when the ghost shirt did not stop bullets and Europeans did not disappear. "But it was the Europeans, not the Native Americans, who had expected results overnight; the anthropologists, who feverishly sought magic objects to postpone their own deaths, had misunderstood the power of the ghost shirts. Bullets of lead belong to the everyday world; ghost shirts belong to the realm of spirits and dreams. The ghost shirts gave the dancers spiritual protection while the white men dreamed of shirts that repelled bullets because they feared death.[34] In fact, he insists that the Ghost Dance did not end at Wounded Knee but continues today. The false trust in physical protection described by Weasel Tail is Menardo's mistake, of course, but Silko is making a broader point about material and spiritual "security," and this relation between spiritual and material effectiveness has a more general and perhaps problematic resonance in the book. The last section of the novel describes the coming together in Tucson of a range of different revolutionary groups within the protective disguise of a New Age "International Holistic Healers Convention." Thus, within the bland and commercial appropriations of spirituality I have outlined earlier in this chapter, Silko describes something much more powerful and oppositional taking shape.

As well as this set piece at the end there are other examples in the novel of the way that the trade in occult or magical materials could operate as a sort of parallel to the drugs trade in feeding a need that white America does not like to acknowledge. Tacho's twin brother, El Feo, recalls how a village of witches in Mexico had become wealthy "because they had tapped into the great inter-American market for 'Inca secrets' and 'Aztec magic.' European descendants on American soil anxiously purchased indigenous cures for their dark nights of the soul on the continents where Christianity had repeatedly violated its own canons."[35] Along with Mayan and Yacqui revolutionaries committed to armed struggle and others who feel that white society's sicknesses and ecological irresponsibility will cause its own implosion and self-destruction, we have the interesting figure of Clinton, an African American Vietnam vet who has been slowly gathering together a movement deliberately made up from a synthesis of racial histories and beliefs.

Clinton is a significant figure in the novel, especially for my purposes, because of his attempts to fuse Indian and African American concerns. He worships African deities, particularly Ogoun, but he also has Cherokee ancestry and is fascinated by the connections and collaborations of escaped slaves and Indians throughout the Americas. He sees that "certain of the African gods had located themselves in the Americas as well as Africa: the Giant serpent, the Twin Brothers, the Maize Mother, to name a few. Right then the magic had happened: great American and great African tribal cultures had come together to create a powerful consciousness within all people." This was an inclusive movement. "Damballah excluded no-one," but Clinton believes that the fundamentally peaceful gods of Africa became transformed because of the harshnesses of the American experience. "Ogoun was no gentleman-warrior here; Ogoun was the guerilla-warrior of hit-and-run and scorched earth and no prisoners."[36]

He wants to mobilize a combined force against white America and is particularly fascinated by the black Indians of New Orleans' Mardi Gras parades, which I referred to in Chapter 3.[37] His broadcasts describe and celebrate a fusion of African and American, which seems to owe much to Haitian voodoo. (Silko in fact describes Voodoo as "a new indigenous American religion" and speaks of Hurston's "wonderful" book, *Tell My Horse*.)[38] Clinton envisages Damballah, great serpent of the sky and keeper of all spiritual knowledge, joining the giant plumed serpent Quetzalcoatl. At the Holistic Healers convention, one of the key speakers is the so-called Barefoot Hopi, who makes the prophecy that the sacred twins will be coming from the South. "In Africa and in the Americas too, the giant snakes, Damballah and Quetzalcoatl, have returned to the people." The snakes tell the people, he says, that "millions will move instinctively; unarmed and unguarded they will begin walking steadily north, following the twin brothers."[39]

As some of the many thematic and plot strands of the novel come together at the convention there is a suggestion of an apocalyptic ending, in which the changes prophesied will actually happen, but at the end the various characters go their own way. Clinton is last seen heading for Haiti after visiting "some of his Black Indian cousins in New York."[40] In his notebook he has noted down instances of Indian-black collaborations and support in resistance to oppression from the sixteenth century onward, and Silko actually devotes several pages of her book to the extensive list. For him, "Nothing could be black only or brown only or white only any more. . . . This was the last chance the people had against the Destroyers, and they would never prevail if they did not work together as a common force."[41] The very fitful nature of any "common force" involving Native American and African Americans over the years, whether politically activist or cultural, can be seen as a product of the larger racial divisions that my book has been exploring. This is not to say, of course, that there have not been political and cultural liaisons, as Clinton's list suggests, but that the languages and concerns often seem even now to operate in parallel rather than together.[42]

In the final section of the book, though, Sterling returns to Laguna, where he finds that the stone serpent is now "looking south, in the direction from which the twin brothers and the people would come."[43] How hopeful or satisfactory we find this ending may depend on how we weight the spiritual and political potentialities invoked. One early skeptical review complained that Silko's "premise of revolutionary insurrection is tethered to airy nothing. . . . The appeal to prophecy cannot make up the common-sense deficit."[44] It could be argued that the novel is trying to bridge the clear gap assumed here between the practical and political, and that the complex interplay of belief systems centering around the power of objects is Silko's way of exploring, if not bridging, the gap. Still, it is not necessarily a reductive approach to ask about the material efficacy and impact of beliefs, and the relation of prophecy to history. In her first novel the mythic dimension of the Laguna stories and myths were presented as containing the historical realm, even if they needed to change within that same realm if they were to survive. In *Almanac* the relation is more fully articulated, and the end of the novel seems to allow room for more political action, with mythic elements, like the snake, figuring historical change to come, but we might still feel this remains inconclusive.

One way to approach this is to return to the use of the Ghost Dance. One of its original aims seems to have been the very tangible one of bringing back the buffalo, and David Moore has pointed to the widespread invocation of this by a range of contemporary writers including Gerald Vizenor, Linda Hogan, and James Welch as an instance of the urge to "dream the world into harmony."[45] Seen from the viewpoint of linear history, such "dreaming" can only be seen as an escapist or nostalgic fantasy, or at best a utopian ideal, but Moore is intent on showing how, if history is seen as cyclic, the return of the buffalo is not impossible at all. He cleverly juxtaposes these literary and imaginative dimensions with details of the actual regeneration of buffalo herds and the increasing evidence that a return of the buffalo makes realistic ecological sense, so that his essay itself makes it difficult for us to separate out too simply the ideal and the real, or the spiritual and the material. "The return of the buffalo, and of the Ghost Dance that invoked that return, are as radically revisionary of the American national narrative as is the notion of tribal sovereignty coexisting in a nation like the United States." It is a logical and practical impossibility from one point of view, which can and must work from another.

In Chapter 3 I quoted the white anthologist Brandon flippantly dismissing the idea of the magical power of the Ghost Dance poetry ("we don't want the buffalo, we only want the poetry"). Moore's essay offers a powerful rejoinder to such attempts to make hard and fast distinctions, and it can provide a way of reading not only the end of Silko's novel, but the end of Alexie's *Reservation Blues* discussed earlier in this chapter. The horses that reappear to accompany the band, running with their car, are reincarnations of those Spokane horses slaughtered by the orders of General Sheridan, and Moore quotes Sheridan's insistence that to "kill, skin, and sell until the buffalo is destroyed" was the only way to "allow civilization to advance."[46]

In *Gardens in the Dunes* of 1999 Silko returns again to the Ghost Dance, but in a different historical context. The novel is set in the time of the original Ghost Dance and records the scattering of Indian communities in the Southwest by following the lives of the Sand Lizard family of a young girl named Indigo and her mother and sister.[47] The parallel and gradually coalescing spiritual experiences of the white woman Hattie and the young girl Indigo in their encounter with pre-Christian European religions are contrasted with a heartless and reductively rationalist masculine world of science and commerce. Though the spiritual experiences in the novel are presented as timeless, or transcending any particular historical moment, Silko is also careful to situate the action historically, at points where the various developing forms of Western scientific inquiry (comparative religion and botany) intersected with indigenous belief systems. These were themselves undergoing profound change as a result of larger economic and political forces associated with colonialism and the workings of international capital. Whereas Indigo relates to nature with a childlike directness, reveling in the physical sensations of color and smell and loving some animals like people, Hattie's husband Edward is a scientist and collector concerned with the propagation and hybridization of plants for commercial exploitation. Through his unsuccessful ventures, Silko gives a historical dimension to the concept of hybridity, showing how plant collecting and taxonomy were related to commerce and to European control of the resources of the rest of the world. In the novel, mining and plant collecting are fuelled by the same exploitative motives, since Edward's illegal activities in Brazil and Corsica all involve the collection of specimens for commercial exploitation.

The idea of hybridity also has a racial dimension, though, which is reflected in the threatening presence of a woman who is part Mayan and part African. Edward is inexplicably frightened by a chance encounter with such a woman in Tampico and only later hears stories from the sailors about the Black Indian of Tampico, who can call down storms upon ships, causing them to be wrecked. She remains a shadowy figure, and Silko leaves her actual power or nature unresolved, but there are also more positive images of hybridity and mixed blood. Sister Salt's lover and business companion, Big Candy, is African American and has memories of tales of the Redstick Indians who adopted escaped slaves. He and Sister Salt produce a child, and he is instrumental, though unknowingly, in furthering the Yacqui resistance. This more political strand of the story, in the shape of Delena, a mysterious freedom fighter-cum-exoticized fortune-teller, seems only sketchily integrated, with the result that, though this material does resonate with *Almanac of the Dead*, the main thrust of the novel is quite different and focuses more on the connections with diverse strands of European religions.

Ami Regier sees Silko's use of other religions as an aspect of her advocacy of hybridity and syncretism,[48] which represent the way forward for Indigo and her fellow survivors of colonialist expansion. She focuses on Silko's use of the Ghost Dance and its capacity to be adaptable to many purposes by different tribes, including the Mormons, who appear in the novel. Regier links this with the transnational sweep of the novel and James Clifford's concept of "traveling cultures" and argues that in highlighting the pre-Christian elements in Christianity, Silko is also showing that even the supposed center is always and already deeply hybrid—an idea reinforced by the early images of animal and human hybrid forms that Hattie and others find.

Regier's enthusiasm for the instability and creativity found in the hybrid and transnational space created in the novel extends to its revolutionary potential, but it is here, I think, that the precise nature of her claims needs to be pinned down. As she points out, the end of the novel presents a Ghost Dance (though

Silko's characters always refer to it as the coming of the Messiah), the culmination of which, on the fourth day, is prevented by the arrival of the police and soldiers. At this point a half-crazed Hattie, believing in the coming of the Messiah, burns down part of the nearby town of Needles, and Regier sees this fire as a "metonym" of the millenarian change promised in the Ghost Dance. Silko has clearly brought the events into conjunction for this purpose, but here, as in *Almanac of the Dead*, in specifying the actual relation of ceremony to political or practical consequences, Silko is perhaps more cautious than Regier's account might suggest. Regier's essay in fact makes close links between Silko's own writing and the effects claimed for a Ghost Dance when she argues that "Written narrative may function as a ghost of the Ghost Dance carrying out the oral tradition's revolutionary work in latter-day performative forms that are magically real enough to be powerful."[49] But what does this last phrase really mean? We could read it as saying that the book is powerfully persuasive as writing, and that therefore, *like* the ceremony, it may have effects on people and change the world through their actions, but I am not sure that Regier is not implying a lot more with the word "magically."

It may seem pedantic to focus on what I see as a slippage between different sorts of claims here, but I think it points to a larger issue. This is the simultaneous situating of Silko within a post-structuralist framework of hybridity and transnationalism and a traditional Indian one of rooted and local spiritual truths. The former context would suggest an absence of any absolute claims for a rooted or essential position of truth, while the second would not. Traditional and indigenous peoples may reasonably suspect any celebration of diasporic and transnational identity if it is going to be used to challenge their unique and local rights and values, as writers like Elizabeth Cook Lynn have argued. It is for this reason that Silko's position may be more ambiguous than Regier suggests, but this is linked to another issue. What sort of common ground would these hybrid formations have that would bring them together in revolution or unified belief?

Silko's use of the Ghost Dance inevitably raises questions about the particular and general meaning of religious visions. She describes the Sand Lizard people as one of many groups influenced by the Paiute prophet Wovoka's original vision.[50] Recent work has allowed us a fuller picture of Wovoka and the Ghost Dance than the early white panic reactions to it as a militant movement, but even at the time James Mooney for one recognized its underlying similarities with other religious movements. His account, from which Silko seems to have borrowed in adapting some songs, is both a powerful recognition of the material reasons for the dissatisfactions and longings that would find expression in a shared prophetic movement and an insistence on the common elements in all religions. "The systems of our highest modern civilizations have their counterparts among all the nations, and their chain of parallels stretches backward link by link until we find their origin and interpretation in the customs and rites of our own barbarian ancestors, or of our still existing aboriginal tribes."[51]

This is an expression of the comparativist impulse I have traced in earlier chapters, as is his comment that "the doctrines of the Hindu avatar, the Hebrew Messiah, the Christian millennium, and the Hesûnanin of the Indian Ghost Dance are essentially the same, and have their origin in a hope and longing common to all humanity."[52] Michael Elliott has argued that the narrative frame that Mooney provides runs counter to the evolutionary assumptions of unilinear progress, implying a cyclic return, which has more in common with Silko's approach.[53] He points to an impulse to present the "real" in the late nineteenth century, and the development of modes in which to do it, namely realism and ethnography, which are at odds with powerful counter-impulses that want to preserve the area of the unreal. Thus, although Mooney makes the comparative connections with Christianity and is sympathetic to the impulses of the Ghost Dance, he does not himself subscribe to the belief in its supernatural power, and this is where he makes an interesting complement to Silko. In Mooney there is the ethnographic impulse to present what he sees as the unvarnished reality, which means presenting ghost dancers accurately and voicing their grievances, but not necessarily accepting their terms of belief. Mooney is totally confident in explaining away the magical or supernatural elements. He reports background information about the occurrence of an eclipse that "seems to explain the whole matter" and in the process to undermine the validity of Wovoka's vision of the death of the sun. Similarly, he reports the views of two Indian witnesses, the skeptical Cheyenne Tall Bull, a man "of good hard sense and disposed to be doubtful in regard to all medicine men outside of his own tribe," and the Arapaho Black Coyote, "of contemplative disposition, much given to speculation on the unseen world." After Wovoka had waved a feather over his hat, the latter had seen "the whole spirit world" where the former had seen "only an empty hat." Mooney stresses that to his knowledge "both men were honest in their statements,'" but the tone of the rest of Mooney's account leaves little doubt that he himself sees Wovoka as ultimately a powerful hypnotist.[54]

Mooney's own Irish origins have been cited as a relevant factor in his political sympathy with the oppressed Indians. He does also record resorting to traditional Irish magical practices himself in an engagement with a shaman, but even there he is still ultimately the detached inquirer and collector.[55] Nevertheless, his reading of the Ghost Dance as expressive of political as well as millenarian longings, and his emphasis on Plains manifestations of the movement, does take the political and secular dimensions more seriously than elsewhere.[56] For instance, the Second Annual Meeting of the American Folklore Society in 1891 heard a paper from Alice Fletcher on "The Indian Messiah" that stressed the traditional roots of the new "craze" in trances and dancing. While Fletcher acknowledges the demoralization and poverty of its practitioners, she has no sense that this could be an empowering movement. She insists that it is "confined exclusively to the uneducated" and has been used by "the non-progressive and turbulent elements" and the "conjurers, dreamers and other dangerous persons" for their own ends.[57] Mooney's account, by contrast, noted the importance of returned pupils from boarding schools, whose writing skills helped to spread the message, and their role also suggests how much more complex the movement was, at least in some of its forms, than an expression of regressive longing.[58] Fletcher seemed to reflect the general view, with Boas describing such crazes as "a nervous disease." Members generally responded in comparativist mode by citing parallels from around the world, including one intriguing parallel with an outbreak among African American slaves in Kentucky, who believed General Fremont was about to appear to deliver them from slavery. The member making this parallel did comment on the frequency of such ideas among "oppressed or subjected races," but this served only to reinforce the idea that superstition and gullibility were evils to be eradicated along with such unfortunate conditions.[59]

Silko restricts herself in *Gardens in the Dunes* to the Southwestern occurrences, and does not bring out the political dimensions in the way she does in *Almanac of the Dead*. By presenting the Ghost Dance mainly as experienced by a child, the visionary and prophetic aspects are foregrounded, and it is these elements that Indigo recognizes in the other religions she encounters. Other characters make the comparative connections more explicitly. Sister Salt recognizes the same ideas in a description of the Valley of Bones from Ezekiel, which she reads out in a fortune-telling exercise. "Here it was even in the Bible—everything Wovoka said was true."[60] The conjunction in this scene of Tarot cards and Ezekiel, and, in the European scenes of the novel, of Celtic and Arthurian Grail legends, and sacred groves and circles, in fact strongly suggests the comparative mythology that influenced Modernist writers, most notably Eliot's *Waste Land* and its acknowledged debt to Jessie Weston.

Drawing in many ways on the conventions of the nineteenth-century sentimental novel, *Gardens in the Dunes* revolves largely around women and their sensibilities and vulnerabilities in their society. Through the travels of Indigo with her white guardians, we are introduced not to a modern scientific Europe but to one of pre-Christian survivals and syncretisms surviving in old gardens, buildings, and beliefs. Aunt Bronwen shows them Celtic and pre-Christian stones and implies in her eccentric way that they move and have medicinal power of their own.[61] She warns them of the dangers of destroying sacred circles and their groves, and there is a symbolic link with Edward's ill-fated attempts to collect valuable minerals from a meteor site, where he finds an iron meteorite wrapped in feathers and cotton. Here we have the animated stone—the fetish that I have discussed at length earlier and that Silko has used in a different form (an opal dressed in feathers and coca leaves) in *Almanac of the Dead*. The power residing in stones or associated with them is something that has continued to fascinate Silko, in short stories, memoirs and essays.[62] In one essay for instance, she asserts that "A rock shares this fate with us and with animals and plants as well. A rock has being and spirit, although we may not understand it. The spirit may differ from the spirit we know in animals or plants or in ourselves. In the end we all originate from the depths of the earth,"[63] and in an interview she refers to herself as a "stone-worshipper."[64]

The underlying common ground invoked in the novel is of a spiritual presence experienced through visions and stone remnants of Celtic and other pre-Christian religions across Europe, which the Christian church has continually, and unsuccessfully, attempted to eradicate. Here the figure of Hattie becomes central, in that she has visions and sensations that allow her (and the reader) to connect up her ideas with various pre-Christian survivals in the form of Roman and Celtic remains. Her visions are often linked to stones and light: a strange light she experiences in her aunt's garden in Somerset, a recurrent dream of a stone, and an experience of light in Corsica when she and Indigo join Christian believers who have been attracted to a schoolhouse wall where an image of Mary is supposed to have appeared. She sees a glow that "grew brighter with a subtle iridescence that steadily intensified into a radiance of pure color that left her breathless, almost dizzy."[65] She half-doubts her experience ("was it an odd reflection off metal or glass? . . . But here she was with dozens of witnesses!") but Indigo and the local Christians see much more. Indigo has been waiting for the return of the Messiah, because she was removed from her people, who were at that time practicing the Ghost Dance and dancing for the coming of the Messiah. Looking at the wall, she sees "tiny reflections glitter on the surface of the whitewashed plaster that she recognized as the flakes of snow that swirled around the dancers the last night when the Messiah appeared with his family."

Hattie has already experienced the repressive force of academic orthodoxy as a would-be student of Christian heresies at Harvard. Her thesis attempted to demonstrate through a reading of the Gnostic Gospels that the Bible as we know it, which provides the basis for Christian faith, is actually premised on the exclusion of many disparate texts and divergent ideas. The response of her seniors is to deny the reliability of the other Gospels and to see them as heretical. Silko brings out the gender implications—she is rejected as much as anything because she is a woman and therefore not taken seriously at an intellectual level—but concentrates more on the prospect that such overlooked texts open up, of an original Christianity that would share much more with "primitive" and other religions than the present orthodoxy. Though this idea is rejected by Hattie's committee, it is fundamental to the action and structure of Silko's novel. *Gardens in the Dunes* offers another take on some of the nineteenth-century concerns over the legitimacy of religious and magical claims, and Silko manages to demonstrate the conjunction of such debates with the operations of political and economic power in the period from the viewpoint of the marginalized and powerless.

Thus, Silko's use of Gnosticism is in many ways fundamental to the novel in the glimpse it offers of a religion based on unmediated vision rather than dogma,[66] but her dramatization of these shared or comparable visionary experiences prompts questions about what exactly the link is. Does everyone experience the same unmediated vision, or does each local community need to clothe it in its own imagery or language? In which case, how do we know it is the same? Brewster Fitz provides some helpful close analysis of the ways in which Silko presents religious experiences, by focusing on her use of the idea of glossolalia or speaking in tongues, a form of communication that transcends any specific local language and obviates the need for translation. The crucial thing about it is not that everyone shares a metalanguage, but that each person hears the message in his or her own language. We can see this as miraculous because it both allows and affirms difference while transcending them, rather than making everyone the same in order to affirm a single truth, as missionaries had to do. In other words, it gets over the problem of translation and of the reduction of experience to terms common—and general—enough to be readily translatable.

Fitz looks very carefully at how the actual communication is taking place in the novel between characters speaking different languages and gives close readings of scenes where a communion of spiritual perception and understanding seems to be taking place. In wanting to pin down just what is happening, he is, I think, probing at the heart of the larger claims of the book. He questions how characters and readers actually know what experience or understanding is being shared, that is, what sort of actual communication is taking place across languages, and he asks a question that can also apply to the communicability and translatability of the spiritual experiences that are presented as uniting them. "Is the close reader who asks questions from a realistic point of view a traitor to a text that is constructed around the dream of unmediated communication and epistemological communion?"[67] As I have shown earlier, this is a crucial question that needs also to be asked about the syncretism of New Age spirituality, in that its claims to be able to use very disparate traditions seem often to depend on assuming that what is being experienced can be fused together and subsumed under a general umbrella of "spirituality." Thus the invocation of spirituality itself becomes a way of not having to address questions of cultural translatability. Interestingly, Ami Regier seems to read the scene where speaking in tongues seems to be taking place rather differently. She explains away Indigo's view of it as "a child's vision of cross-cultural perception and understanding," which is to secularize the scene considerably and remove the possibility of something miraculous taking place.[68]

So Silko presents us with a set of images for the reader, and experiences for the characters, which makes connections across cultures and belief systems and suggests continuity and growth, even though the novel is set historically at the lowest point in Indian fortunes. Ultimately the sisters are reunited and the gardens are restored. The gladiolus bulbs, which Indigo brings back and which are initially dismissed as useless, turn out to be edible as well as beautiful (combining the material and spiritual), and though the old sacred rattlesnake that guarded the well has been killed, the book ends with a new snake appearing, and the words "Old Snake's beautiful daughter moved back home." Natural (and female) forces have reestablished continuities, so that even if the interruption of the Ghost Dance has prevented the Messiah from coming in that particular form, the implication is that the same spirit is evident elsewhere. This ending echoes the conclusion of *Almanac of the Dead*, and Silko has written of her retrospective realization that she had had to write *Almanac of the Dead* "in order to figure out for myself the meaning of the giant stone snake that had appeared near the uranium mine in 1979."[69] In fact, it is striking that all three of her novels end with the same ingredients in different conjunctions: the snake, stones, the return to a source, and the vexed question of what sort of material efficacy the spirit can exert.

Silko ends, as I will, with stones and the belief in their power. I began with fetishism, which was regularly dismissed as the worship of "stocks and stones," and I end, through Silko, with the conjunction of these same beliefs with New Age practices. By insisting on trying to pin down just what is being claimed in a range of discourses in which words like spirit, magic, and fetish are used— by taking literally the claims, and by questioning how far such words are used metaphorically—I have tried to show the underlying intellectual and political agendas and their relation to ideologies of race. The bringing together of such widely disparate material in this book has run the risk of ironing out important differences between African American and Indian histories and cultures, but my gamble has been that through such new conjunctions we might not only see new similarities but also reveal some of the ideological assumptions that have put such comparisons out of court. The other risk, outlined in the introduction, is related to questions about the usefulness or appropriateness of a radically skeptical approach to the discourses of magic and spirit. Does such an approach mean simply that we miss the point and end up like a tone-deaf critic at a concert—logical but ultimately pointless, and in the process managing to give offense to those who *can* hear the music? Perhaps, but my hope is that by bringing to the contemporary discourses of the later chapters the same approaches I used to critique what might seem the outdated debates of earlier centuries, we might be able to see continuities that can help us to sort out just what is involved in claims for spirituality and spiritual efficacy as they become inevitably entangled with issues of race.

Notes

Introduction

1. I make the usual acknowledgment of the problems and pitfalls of racial terminology. In the absence of any agreed or wholly acceptable terms I will use "Indian," "Native American," "Native," and "American Indian" interchangeably; "African American," except where I am repeating a period use of "Negro"; and "white" or "European," with all their inadequacies.

2. See particularly the still-groundbreaking work of Jack D. Forbes, *Black Africans and Native Americans: Color, Race and Caste in the Evolution of Red-Black Peoples* (Oxford: Basil Blackwell, 1988), and the extensive work of Daniel Littlefield over many volumes. See also William Loren Katz, *Black Indians: A Hidden Heritage* (New York: Atheneum, 1986). Among a growing number of studies of particular groups, see Karen I. Blu, *The Lumbee Problem: The Making of an American Indian People* (New York: New York University Press, 1980); Kenneth W. Porter, *The Black Seminoles: History of a Freedom-Seeking People* (Gainesville: University Press of Florida, 1996); Katja May, *African Americans and Native Americans in the Creek and Cherokee Nations, 1830s to 1920s: Collision and Collusion* (New York: Garland, 1996); Lisa Bier, *American Indian and African American People, Communities and Interactions: An Annotated Bibliography* (Westport, Conn.: Praeger, 2006).

3. Jon Butler, *Awash in a Sea of Faith: Christianizing the American People* (Cambridge, Mass.: Harvard University Press, 1990), 156.

4. William Knox, *Three Tracts Respecting the Conversion and Instruction of the Free Indians and Negroe [sic] Slaves in the Colonies, Addressed to the Venerable Society for the Propagation of the Gospel* (London, 1768), 6.

5. Knox, *Three Tracts*, 9, 10.

6. Knox, *Three Tracts*, 16–17.

7. Joseph Holt Ingraham, *Lafitte, the Pirate of the Gulf* (London: J. S. Pratt, 1845), 128–29.

8. Ingraham, *Lafitte, the Pirate of the Gulf*, 61.

9. Ingraham, *Lafitte, the Pirate of the Gulf*, 173.

10. One other striking comparison of the mental and moral capacities of the different races that is set against the politics and policies of Removal and slavery, and chimes with Knox and Ingraham, comes from Alexis de Tocqueville's account in *Democracy in America* of an encounter with two women, one Indian and one African American, who are looking after a rather demanding young white boy. The Indian woman is proud and self-contained, while the Negro is subservient and seemingly without an identity of her own, other than the one that has been created by her powerless situation, and

Tocqueville sees this triangle of relations and capacities as reflecting the larger national situation. See my "The Red and the Black: Autobiography and the Creation of Mixed Blood Identity," in *Writing and Race*, ed. Tim Youngs (London: Pluto Press, 1995).

11. Joseph Mitchell, *The Missionary Pioneer, or A Brief Memoir of the Life, Labours and Death of John Stewart (Man of Colour) Founder, under God of the Mission among the Wyandotts at Upper Sandusky, Ohio* (New York: J. C. Totten, 1827), 68.

12. The earliest such account, that of John Marrant, identifies him as "Black" in the title but makes no further mention of his race at all. *A Narrative of the Lord's Wonderful Dealings with John Marrant, a Black (Now Going to Preach the Gospel in Nova Scotia). Taken down from his Own Relation, Arranged, Corrected and Published by the Rev. Mr. Aldridge* (London, 1785). Karen Weyler has argued that early accounts such as this need to be seen in the context of an eighteenth-century view, in which race is an unstable concept moving between an entity defined by culture and geographical location to something defined by appearance, skin, and intellectual qualities, as in the nineteenth century. Karen Weyler, "Race, Redemption, and Captivity in the Narratives of Briton Hammon and John Marrant," in *Genius in Bondage: Literature of the Early Black Atlantic*, ed. Vincent Carretta and Philip Gould (Lexington: University Press of Kentucky, 2001).

13. William Apess, *A Son of the Forest and Other Writings*, ed. Barry O'Connell (Amherst: University of Massachusetts Press, 1997), 46. See Laura E. Donaldson, "Son of the Forest, Child of God: William Apess and the Scene of Postcolonial Nativity," in *Postcolonial America*, ed. Richard C. King (Urbana: University of Illinois Press, 2000), and "Making a Joyful Noise: William Apess and the Search for Postcolonial Method(ism)," in *Messy Beginnings: Postcoloniality and Early American Studies*, ed. Malini Johar Schueller and Edward Watts (New Brunswick, N.J.: Rutgers University Press, 2003). Donaldson's work here and in her forthcoming book demonstrates the many ways in which Christianity was creatively adapted and transformed to play an integral part in the political and spiritual life of Indian communities.

Chapter 1

1. For an indication of such uses, which are beyond the terms of this study, see Roy Ellen, "Fetishism," *Man*, n.s., 23, 2 (1988): 213–35; William Pietz, "Fetish," in *Critical Terms for Art History*, ed. Robert S. Nelson and Richard Schiff (Chicago: University of Chicago Press, 1996), 197–207; Laura Mulvey, "Some Thoughts on Theories of Fetishism in the Context of Contemporary Culture," *October* 65 (1993): 3–20; Steven F. Kruger, "Fetishism, 1927, 1614, 1461," in *The Postcolonial Middle Ages*, ed. Jeffrey Jerome Cohen (New York: St. Martin's Press, 2000).

2. His work consists of a string of remarkable essays. See especially William Pietz "The Problem of the Fetish," parts 1, 2 and 3, *Res* 9 (1985): 5–17; *Res* 13 (1987): 23–45; Res 16 (1988): 105–23; "The Fetish of Civilisation: Sacrificial Blood and Monetary Debt," in *Colonial Subjects: Essays on the Practical History of Anthropology*, ed. Peter Pels and Oscar Salemink (Ann Arbor: University of Michigan Press, 1999); "Death of the Deodand: Accursed Objects and the Money Value of Human Life," *Res* 27 (1993): 97–108.

3. Pietz, "'The Problem of the Fetish, Part 1," *Res* 9 (1985): 7.

4. See Margaret T. Hodgen, *Early Anthropology in the Sixteenth and Seventeenth Centuries* (Philadelphia: University of Pennsylvania Press, 1964).

5. William Bosman, *A New and Accurate Description of the Coast of Guinea* (London, 1705), 148.

6. John Atkins, *A Voyage to Guinea, Brazil, and the West Indies in His Majesty's Ships the Swallow and the Weymouth* (London, 1735), 84.

7. Bosman, *A New and Accurate Description*, 150.

8. Frank E. Manuel, *The Eighteenth Century Confronts the Gods* (Cambridge, Mass.: Harvard University Press, 1959), 130. See also Francis Schmidt, "Polytheisms: Degeneration or Progress?" *History and Anthropology* 3 (1987): 9–60.

9. David Hume, *The Natural History of Religion*, in *Dialogues and the Natural History of Religion*, ed. J. C. A. Gaskin (Oxford: Oxford University Press, 1993), 136.

10. Hume, *The Natural History of Religion*, 158

11. Moshe Halbertal and Avishai Margalit, *Idolatry* (Cambridge, Mass.: Harvard University Press, 1992), 3.

12. Pietz, "The Problem of the Fetish, Part 2," 23.

13. Henry Krips, *Fetish: An Erotics of Culture* (Ithaca, N.Y.: Cornell University Press, 1999), 58.

14. Father Joseph de Acosta, *The Natural and Moral History of the Indies*, repr. from the English edition, trans. Edward Grimston (1604), ed. Clement R. Markham (London: Hakluyt Society, 1880), 302, 304–5.

15. Charles de Brosses, *Du Culte des dieux fétiches, ou parallèle de l'ancienne religion de l'Égypte avec la religion actuelle de Nigritie* (Paris, 1760), 182 (my translation).

16. De Brosses, *Du Culte*, 183.

17. De Brosses, *Du Culte*, 83–84.

18. August Comte, *The Positive Philosophy* (1830–32), trans. and condensed by Harriet Martineau (New York: Calvin Blanchard, 1855), 545, 548.

19. Comte, *The Positive Philosophy*, 549. This had already been addressed as a linguistic question by missionaries and later by those concerned to show that the original language was poetry. It is an idea that recurs in descriptions of American Indians and continues at the heart of Romantic views of poetry.

20. "There was, first of all, this juggler's Ouahich, which was a stone of the size of a nut wrapped in a box which he called the house of his Devil. Then there was a bit of bark on which was a figure, hideous enough, made from black and white wampum, and representing some monster which could not be well distinguished, for it was neither the representation of a man, nor of any animal, but rather in the shape of a little wolverine, which was adorned with black and white beadwork. That one, say the jugglers, is the master Devil, or Ouahich." Chrétien Le Clercq, *New Relation of Gaspesia, with the Customs and Religion of the Gaspesian Indians* (1691), trans. and ed. William F. Ganong (Toronto: Champlain Society, 1910; repr., Westport, Conn.: Greenwood Press, 1968), 221, 222.

21. Joseph-François Lafitau, *Customs of the American Indians Compared with the Customs of Primitive Times* (1724), trans. and ed. William Fenton and Elizabeth Moore (Toronto: Champlain Press, 1974), vol. 1, 243.

22. Lafitau, *Customs of the American Indians*, vol. 2, 210.

23. Lafitau, *Customs of the American Indians*, vol. 2, 178. For a similar use of the term, see the description in *The Jesuit Relations and Allied Documents: Travels and Explorations of the Jesuit Missionaries in New France, 1610–1791*, trans. and ed. Reuben Gold Thwaites (Cleveland: Burrows Brothers, 1896–1901), 22, 319. After baptism, one Algonquin surrenders the "last Relic of his superstition. This was a Stone, which they consider very precious, wrapped up in fine Down." Found in the throat of an elk and treasured as a support, it is eventually given up in response to the missionary's question. According to the Algonquin "He asked me if I had not some little Manitou about me: I said that I had not. I lied; I was still attached to that superstition which I now detest."

24. Lafitau, *Customs of the American Indians*, vol. 1, 179.

25. Editors Fenton and Moore in their English edition insert the subheading of "Fetishes or Charms" to the section quoted above in which Garnier and Lafitau exam-

ine the Indian objects, without indicating, as they customarily do, that this is their own insertion. Presumably this is the influence of de Brosses, whom they discuss in their introduction.

26. De Brosses, *Du Culte*, 10.

27. G. W. F. Hegel, *The Philosophy of History* (1837), trans. J. Sibree (New York: Dover, 1956), 93. For an account of relevant aspects of the European representation of Africa, see Christopher L. Miller, *Blank Darkness: Africanist Discourse in French* (Chicago: University of Chicago Press, 1985). Miller is illuminating on de Brosses, but as with Pietz, there is no sense in his account that de Brosses refers to anywhere but Africa.

28. Edward Burnet Tylor, *Primitive Culture: Researches into the Development of Mythology, Philosophy, Religion, Language, Art and Custom* (1871) (repr., New York: Henry Holt, 1889), vol. 1, 424. For a broader context, see George W. Stocking, Jr., *Victorian Anthropology* (New York: Free Press, 1987).

29. Tylor, *Primitive Culture*, vol. 2, 144.

30. Tylor, *Primitive Culture*, vol. 2, 168.

31. A metaphorical relation is based on likeness, whereas a metonymic relation is based on contiguity, or part-whole connection. Thus an image of a saint is like him or her but does not partake of any of the saint's actual being, whereas a finger or other relic is a part of a lost whole.

32. Tylor, *Primitive Culture*, vol. 1, 169.

33. Tylor, *Primitive Culture*, vol. 1, 113, 112. Frazer was later to systematize these relations, in his tripartite distinction of magic, religion, and science and the category of sympathetic magic. Wouter J. Hanegraaff's "The Emergence of the Academic Science of Magic: The Occult Philosophy in Tylor and Frazer," in *Religion in the Making: The Emergence of the Sciences of Religion*, ed. Arie L. Molendijk and Peter Pels (Leiden: Brill, 1998), has some excellent insights into the status of magic and religion in the period.

34. See Tomoko Masuzawa, "Troubles with Materiality: The Ghost of Fetishism in the Nineteenth Century," *Comparative Studies in Society and History* 42, 2 (2000): 242–67, which takes a similar approach to mine here.

35. Peter Pels, "The Spirit of Matter: On Fetish, Rarity, Fact and Fancy," in *Border Fetishisms: Material Objects in Unstable Places*, ed. Patricia Spyer (New York: Routledge, 1998), 91.

36. Tylor, *Primitive Culture*, vol. 2, 152.

37. Tylor, *Primitive Culture*, vol. 1, 426. Tylor describes the presence at spiritualist meetings of "a set of Indian and negro child-spirits" which he traces to the movement's roots in America. In a rather comic encounter, we are told, "Rosie talked what she called Ojibwy Indian and I called gibberish. I asked her the word for stone[,] which was nothing like the real word." Quoted in George W. Stocking, Jr., "Animism in Theory and Practice: E. B. Tylor's Unpublished 'Notes on "Spiritualism"'" *Man* 6 (1971): 94. For an American instance of this use of Indians as spirit identities, see Cora Richmond, *Ouina's Canoe and Christmas Offering, Filled with Flowers for the Darlings of the Earth, Given through her Medium, 'Water Lily' (Mrs Cora V. L. Richmond)* (Ottumwa, Iowa: D. M. and N. P. Foz, 1882), which is a mixture of poems and stories recycling Indian stereotypes.

38. Karl Marx, *Capital: A Critique of Political Economy*, trans. S. Moore and E. Aveling, 3 vols. (London: Lawrence and Wishart, 1970), vol. 1, 70–72. For discussion of Marx's use of fetishism, see Maurice Godelier, *Perspectives in Marxist Anthropology* (Cambridge: Cambridge University Press, 1977); William Pietz, "Fetishism and Materialism: The Limit of Theory in Marx," in *Fetishism as Cultural Discourse*, ed. Emily Apter and William Pietz (Ithaca, N.Y.: Cornell University Press, 1993); Jean Baudrillard, *For a Critique of the Political Economy of the Sign* (St. Louis: Telos Press, 1981), 8–101. See also Jacques Derrida, *Spectres of Marx: The State of the Debt, the Work of Mourning and the New International*

(New York: Routledge, 1994), for a further discussion of questions of materiality and Marx's legacy. Perhaps the most interesting anthropological development of these ideas, focusing on the extent to which native beliefs in a magically animated world of objects might actually offer a conceptual tool for the understanding of capitalist exploitation, has been in the work of Michael T. Taussig. See for example *The Devil and Commodity Fetishism in South America* (Chapel Hill: University of North Carolina Press, 1980). For an appraisal and a rather different application of these ideas, see Peter Gose, "Sacrifice and the Commodity Form in the Andes," *Man*, n.s. 21, 2 (1986): 296–310. More recent skeptical accounts of the enthusiasm for analyses based on concepts of magic and mystification have questioned the tendency stemming back to 1960s radicalism to see politics and power symbolically. See, for instance, Sean McCann and Michael Szalay, "Do You Believe in Magic? Literary Thinking and the New Left," *Yale Journal of Criticism* 18, 2 (2005): 435–68. My skepticism in later chapters about some of the claims made for art and literature in effect amounts to asking the title question of this essay.

39. Rev. P. Baudin, *Fetichism and Fetich Worshippers*, trans. M. McMahon (New York: Benziger Press, 1885), 3. For a characteristic account, see E. J. Glave, *In Savage Africa* (New York: Russell and Son, 1892). Glave was with Stanley on one of his expeditions and refers throughout to "native superstitions" and fetishism and the "fetish-man." "The African of the interior can find no note of sympathy in the world immediately surrounding him. . . . Everything in earth or sky seems to threaten his existence" (78). For evidence of the survival of the pattern of assertion and denial well into the twentieth century, see, for instance, Robert Hamill Nassau, *Fetichism in West Africa: Forty Years' Observation of Native Customs and Superstitions* (New York: Charles Scribner's Sons, 1904), where Nassau is at pains to rebut the allegations of simple object worship. A. B. Ellis's "The Indwelling Spirits of Men," *Popular Science Monthly*, 36 (1890): 794–801, was one of the few instances of comparisons between African and Indian beliefs.

40. Baudin, *Fetichism and Fetich Worshippers*, 81.

41. Baudin, *Fetichism and Fetich Worshippers*, 5–6, 10.

42. Baudin, *Fetichism and Fetich Worshippers*, 103.

43. Baudin, *Fetichism and Fetich Worshippers*, 81.

44. Baudin, *Fetichism and Fetich Worshippers*, 103. The real threat is in fact from the prospect of the "lower and still more vile" figure of the "fetichist turned Mussulman," as the spread of Islam would effectively block Christianity.

45. Heli Chatelain, "African Fetishism," *Journal of American Folklore* 7 (1894): 304.

46. John Long, *Voyages and Travels of an Indian Interpreter and Trader* (1791), ed. Reuben Gold Thwaites (Cleveland: Arthur H. Clark, 1904), 123.

47. Long, *Voyages and Travels*, 124–25.

48. "Each grand family is known by a badge or symbol, taken from nature; being generally a quadruped, bird, fish, or reptile. The badge or Dodaim (Totem, as it is has been most commonly written), descends invariably in the male line." There is no intermarrying between members of "the same symbol," and Warren describes the totem entirely in terms of kinship divisions. *History of the Ojibwa Nation* (Minneapolis: Ross and Haines, 1957), 42.

49. J. F. McLennan, "The Worship of Animals and Plants" *Fortnightly Review* 12 (1869): 422. The second part was published in vol. 13, 1870.

50. See Patrick Wolfe, *Settler Colonialism and the Transformation of Anthropology: The Politics and Poetics of an Ethnographic Event* (London: Cassell, 1999). For the misinterpretations of the original term, see Theresa M. Schenck, "The Algonquian Totem and Totemism; A Distortion of the Linguistic Field," *Papers of the Algonquian Conference* 28 (1996): 341–53. See also W. J. T. Mitchell, "Romanticism and the Life of Things: Fossils, Totems and Things," *Critical Inquiry* 28 (2001): 167–84, who builds a fascinating

argument about the related conceptions of fossil and totem as expressions of different relationships between human and animal worlds in Romantic thought.

51. See Claude Levi-Strauss, *Totemism* (Boston: Beacon, 1963). For an account of the American critiques, see Warren Shapiro, "Claude Levi-Strauss Meets Alexander Goldenweiser: Boasian Anthropology and the Study of Totemism," *American Anthropologist* 93 (1991): 599–610.

52. Michael Taussig argues that in fact he is extensively theorizing the fetish but under the name of totem. *The Nervous System* (New York: Routledge, 1992), 111–40.

53. The earliest descriptions of the distinctive carvings and posts of the area do not use the word "totem." See, for example, Fredric W. Hoxay, ed., *Voyages of the "Columbia" to the Northwest Coast, 1787–1790 and 1790–1793* (Boston: Massachusetts Historical Society, 1941), 69, 234. By the late nineteenth century, however, the term has appeared, as in Aurel Krause's use of it. "An unusual decoration of the house is the heraldic column or totem pole." They show "the heraldic crests of the clans." Aurel Krause, *The Tlingit Indians: Results of a Trip to the Northwest Coast of America and the Bering Straits* (1885), trans. Erna Gunther (Seattle: University of Washington Press, 1956), 89. He gives a footnote to his use of the word "totem," suggesting that it is not yet a common usage: "The word is taken from Algonquin and was introduced by Schoolcraft. According to Max Müller it means 'a family symbol' and was originally pronounced 'ote'" (273). In his glossary, Krause gives "totem pole" as "ku-ti-ga." (249), and describing the Haida, where he notes more totem poles and more rich ornamentation, he notes "a distinction between the one at the entrance of the house, called 'kechen' and those erected in memory of the dead, called 'chat'" (208). By the time of George T. Emmons's accounts in the late 1880s, he is also talking about totem poles and totemic animals, but in his description of the relation to animals he uses the terms "crest" and "heraldic" as synonyms, though the modern editor inserts the word "totem." George T. Emmons, *The Tlingit Indians*, ed. Frederica de Laguna (Seattle: University of Washington Press, 1991), 48, 34, 32. In 1901 Charles Hill-Tout argued, against what were becoming the prevailing assumptions, that the Indians of British Columbia did not in fact fit the pattern of totemism, since the usual expectation in totemic societies of belief in shared sanguineal relations through "a common descent from their totem prototypes" was completely lacking. Instead, what was prominent was the personal, rather than the clan totem, which was "in turn a development of earlier fetishism." *The Origin of the Totemism of the Aborigines of British Columbia* (Ottawa: Transactions of the Royal Society of Canada, 1901), 6.

54. Daniel G. Brinton, *Religions of Primitive Peoples* (New York: Putnams, 1899), 131.

55. Brinton, *Religions of Primitive Peoples*, 161.

56. We find a late example of this in the work of Hartley Burr Alexander. Using the developmental model, and illustrating it through a range of Indian tribes, he does find fetishism and a development toward monotheism, but for him all these stages involve a spiritual awareness of nature. The fundamental mode is animism, and he describes fetishism as "merely highly localized animism." *The Religious Spirit of the American Indian: As Shown in the Development of His Religious Rites and Customs* (Chicago: Open Court, 1910), 6. Even the presence in one of his books of a bizarre illustration titled "Fetish Necklace of Human Fingers" is neither commented on nor allowed to spoil the generally celebratory style. The title tells us all. This is to be about religion and spirit and looks forward to the plethora of New Age books invoking or aping what they call Native American "spirituality." What Alexander calls "the primitive inability to think an abstraction other than concretely" played into the Indians' role as exemplars of Romantic pantheistic belief, where what is concrete and material is seen as natural and aesthetically pleasing, because it is seen as a fragment of a larger less material whole.

Religious Spirit, 49. See also his later book, *The World's Rim: Great Mysteries of the North American Indians* (Lincoln: University of Nebraska Press, 1953). On the development of these views, see Christopher Vecsey, "American Indian Environmental Religions," in *American Indian Environments: Ecological Issues in Native American History*, ed. Christopher Vecsey and Robert W. Venables (Syracuse, N.Y.: Syracuse University Press, 1980). For negative native reactions, see Bron Taylor, "Spirituality, or Cultural Genocide? Radical Environmentalism's Appropriation of Native American Spirituality," *Religion* 27, 2 (1997): 183–215.

57. Thwaites, *Jesuit Relations* 67, 153.

58. Louis Hennepin, *A New Discovery of a Vast Country in America* (1697), ed. Reuben Thwaites (Chicago: McClurg, 1903), 655.

59. Hennepin, *A New Discovery*, 538–39.

60. Hennepin, *A New Discovery*, 641. In W. J. Hoffman's detailed account of the Midewiwin Society of the Ojibwa, this is attributed to Marquette. Bureau of American Ethnology, Annual Report 8 (Washington, D.C.: Smithsonian Institution 1885–86), 155.

61. Hennepin, *A New Discovery*, 208. See also Acosta, who accepts that the Indians have an original knowledge of God. "They commonly acknowledge a supreame Lord and Author of all things, which they of Peru call Viracocha, and give him names of great excellence, as Pachacamac, or pachayachchic, which is the Creator of heaven and earth; and Vsapu which is admirable, and other like names." This, he says, "accordeth well with that which is said of Saint Paul," referring to his discovery of the temple dedicated to the Ignoto Deo, and preachers are therefore able to communicate to the Indians the idea of a supreme deity. Nevertheless, "it hath caused great admiration in me, that although they had this knowledge, yet had they no proper name for God. If wee shall seeke into the Indian tongue, for a word to answer to this name of God, as in Latin, *Deus*, in Greeke, *Theos*, in Hebrew *El*, in Arabike, *Alla*; but wee shall not finde any in the Cuscan or Mexicaine tongues. So as such as preach or write to the Indians use our Spanish name *Dios*, fitting it to the accent or pronunciation of the Indian tongues, the which differ much, whereby appeares the small knowledge they had of God seeing they cannot so much as name him, if it be not by our very name." Acosta, *The Natural and Moral History of the Indies*, 303.

62. Roger Williams, *A Key into the Language of America, or An Help to the Language of the Natives in That Part of America Called New England*, ed. John J Teunissen and Evelyn J. Hinz (1643; repr. Detroit: Wayne State University Press, 1973), 191.

63. Williams, *A Key into the Language of America*, 175.

64. Quoted in Karen O. Kupperman, *Indians and English: Facing off in Early America* (Ithaca N.Y.: Cornell University Press, 2000), 116.

65. Bruce M. White, "Encounters with Spirits: Ojibwa and Dakota Theories about the French and Their Merchandise," *Ethnohistory* 41, 3 (1995): 378. See also Neal Salisbury, *Manitou and Providence: Indians, Europeans and the Making of New England, 1500–1643* (New York: Oxford University Press, 1982), and David Murray, *Indian Giving: Economies of Power in Early Indian-White Encounters* (Amherst: University of Massachusetts Press, 2000).

66. Thwaites, *Jesuit Relations*, 12, 7.

67. See Michael M. Pomedi, *Ethnophilosophical and Ethnolinguistic Perspectives on the Huron Indian Soul* (Lewiston, N.Y.: E. Mellen Press, 1991). See also Kenneth M. Morrison, "Montagnais Missionization in Early New France: The Syncretic Imperative," *American Indian Culture and Research Journal* 10, 3 (1986): 1–23.

68. Gabriel Sagard, *The Long Journey to the Country of the Hurons* (1632; repr., Toronto: Champlain Society, 1939), 170–71.

69. John Steckley, "Brebeuf's Presentation of Catholicism in the Huron Language: A Descriptive Overview," *University of Ottawa Quarterly* 48, 1–2 (1978): 99. (He also points out that as familiarity with the Christian ideas increased, terms like *aki* may have later become more usable.) See also Elisabeth Tooker, *An Ethnography of the Huron Indians, 1615–1649* (Syracuse, N.Y.: Syracuse University Press, 1991), 78 for reference to *oki*.

70. Le Clercq, *New Relations of Gaspesia*, 232–33. I discuss this passage in relation to trade goods and conversion in *Indian Giving*, 190–91.

71. Laura Donaldson, "Making a Joyful Noise: William Apess and the Search for Postcolonial Method(ism)," in *Messy Beginnings: Postcoloniality and Early American Studies*, ed. Malini Johar Schueller and Edward Watts (New Brunswick, N.J.: Rutgers University Press, 2003), 38–40.

72. Le Clercq, *New Relations of Gaspesia*, 145.

73. Le Clercq, *New Relations of Gaspesia*, 152.

74. See Ganong's introduction to Le Clercq, *New Relations of Gaspesia*, 39. See also Russell Barsh's comment that "Long before it took on Christian associations, the equal-sided Mi'kmaw cross was a symbol of the four directions and gave its people wisdom, the strength to survive, and safety on their long voyages." In Bruce Elliott Johansen, ed., *Encyclopedia of Native American Legal Tradition* (Westport, Conn.: Greenwood Press, 1998), 192.

75. Le Clercq, *New Relations of Gaspesia*, 188. In the Bible, see Acts 17:23, "For as I passed by, and beheld your devotions, and an altar with the description TO THE UNKNOWN GOD. Whom, therefore you ignorantly worship, him declare I unto you."

76. Le Clercq, *New Relations of Gaspesia*, 133.

77. See Hodgen, *Early Anthropology in the Sixteenth and Seventeenth Centuries*.

78. For an account of other instances of the cross in America, and their place in debates over original monotheism, see Giuliano Gliozzi, "The Apostles in the New World: Monotheism and Idolatry between Revelation and Fetishism," *History and Anthropology* 3 (1987): 123–48.

79. Quoted in Lafitau, *Customs of the American Indians*, vol. 2, 269.

80. Hennepin, *A New Discovery*, 453.

81. Hennepin, *A New Discovery*, 453.

82. Gerald Vizenor quotes this and compares it with a more recent dictionary definition of the word *manidooke* "to have spiritual power or conduct a ceremony." Vizenor finds here what he calls "the crease of monotheism and dominance." *Fugitive Poses: Native American Indian Scenes of Absence and Presence* (Lincoln: University of Nebraska Press, 1998), 16.

83. Mary B. Black, "Ojibwa Power Belief System," in *The Anthropology of Power: Ethnographic Studies for Asia, Oceania, and the New World*, ed. Raymond D. Fogelson and Richard N. Adams (New York: Academic Press, 1977). Black is building on Irving Hallowell's account of Ojibwa ontology, which points out the difficulties in aligning animate/inanimate distinctions across the Ojibwa and other languages. "What we view as material inanimate objects—such as shells and stones—are placed in an animate category along with persons which have no physical existence in our world view. . . . Since in the Ojibwa universe there are many kinds of reified person-objects, which are other than human but have the same ontological status, these, of course, fall into the same ethnoseme as human beings and into the animate linguistic class." A. Irving Hallowell, "Ojibwa Ontology, Behaviour and World View," in *Culture and History: Essays in Honor of Paul Radin*, ed. Stanley Diamond (New York: Columbia University Press, 1960), repr. in *Teachings from the American Earth: Indian Religion and Philosophy*, ed. Dennis Tedlock and Barbara Tedlock (New York: Liveright, 1975), 147.

84. See Curtis M. Hinsley, "Zunis and Brahmans: Cultural Ambivalence in the Gilded Age," in *Romantic Motives: Essays on Anthropological Sensibility*, ed. George W. Stocking, Jr. (Madison: University of Wisconsin Press, 1989). His fame had some strange spin-offs, as for instance, in something that promises from its cover to be an anonymous dime novel, *Almost a Life: Or Saved by the Indians, a Truthful Story of Life among Our Western Indians* (New York: Healy and Bigelow, Indian Agents, 1879), which has as its first item "Frank Cushing's Story; How the Great Indian Sagwa Saved the Life of the Famous Ethnologist." This turns out to be an extended advertisement for Indian Oil and various herbal remedies supposedly from the Kickapoo Indians, so there is a certain irony that the self-publicist is himself exploited here with claims to a spurious magic.

85. Quoted in Curtis Hinsley, "Hopi Snakes, Zuni Corn: Early Ethnography in the American Southwest," in *Colonial Subjects: Essays on the Practical History of Anthropology*, ed. Peter Pels and Oscar Salemnik (Ann Arbor: University of Michigan Press, 1999), 192.

86. Charles F. Lummis, *The Land of Poco Tiempo* (London: Sampson Low, Marston, 1893), 145–46. For representative earlier negative uses, see Fritz Schultze, *Fetichism: A Contribution to Anthropology and the History of Religion* (New York: Humboldt, 1871).

87. Barbara Tedlock, for instance, uses the term "icon" "out of respect for native points of view." The distinction she is making, as demonstrated in her quotations from the *OED* definitions, is between "a representation of some personage—itself regarded as sacred and honoured with worship" and "an inanimate object worshipped by savages on account of its supposedly inherent magical powers." *Dreaming: Anthropological and Psychological Interpretations* (Cambridge: Cambridge University Press, 1987), 130. This shift is more than terminological insofar as it claims for what was dismissed under the name of "fetishism" the same symbolic uses of objects and representations as in other religions. John Fulbright, dealing with Hopi and Zuni prayer sticks, which have many of the same functions and significance as Cushing's fetishes, avoids the term and follows Tedlock. He wants to move beyond what he sees as the limitations of the mechanical and impersonal causation of magic and allow for intentionality and personal responsibility in the operation of prayer sticks. John Fulbright, "Hopi and Zuni Prayer-Sticks: Magic, Symbolic Texts, Barter or Self-Sacrifice?" *Religion* 22 (1992): 223.

88. J. N. B. Hewitt, "Orenda and a Definition of Religion," *American Anthropologist*, 8, 4 (1902): 38. For a later view, see Hope L. Isaacs, "*Orenda* and the Concept of Power among the Tonawanda Seneca," in *The Anthropology of Power: Ethnographic Studies for Asia, Oceania, and the New World*, ed. Raymond D. Fogelson and Richard N. Adams (New York: Academic Press, 1977).

89. F. W. Hodge, ed., *Handbook of American Indians North of Mexico* (Washington, D.C.: Smithsonian Institution, Bureau of American Ethnology, 1910), bulletin 30, vol. 2, 146.

90. Hodge, *Handbook of American Indians North of Mexico*, 366.

91. For details of nineteenth-century views, see Charles Reagan Wilson, "Shamans and Charlatans: The Popularization of Native American Religion in Magazines, 1865–1900," *Indian Historian* 12, 3 (1979): 6–13.

92. See Clyde Holler, ed., *The Black Elk Reader* (Syracuse, N.Y.: Syracuse University Press, 2000), for recent essays on the production and significance of these texts, and Joseph Epes Brown, *The Spiritual Legacy of the American Indian* (New York: Crossroads, 1987). Recent commentators have shown the development of the term *Wakan Tanka*, translated as "Great Spirit, Great Mystery," as a way of translating the Christian God and presenting Indians as capable of a higher monotheistic belief. See, for instance, Raymond J. DeMallie and Douglas R. Parks, eds., *Sioux Indian Religion: Tradition and Innovation* (Norman: University of Oklahoma Press, 1987), 27–30. Later anthropological overviews have taken care to avoid such ranking according to transcendence, even if not the attempt to find common denominators. In William K. Powers's entry in the

Encyclopedia of Religion under "The Supernatural," he brings together Lakota *wakan*, Algonquian *manitu*, Ponca *xube*, and Comanche *puba* under the idea of sacred power, which he offers in preference to the misleading "medicine." In *Native American Religions: North America. Selections from "The Encyclopedia of Religion,"* ed. Lawrence E. Sullivan (New York: Macmillan, 1989), 23. See also Leroy N. Meyer and Tony Ramirez, "'Wakinyan Hotan': The Inscrutability of Lakota/Dakota Metaphysics," in *From Our Eyes: Learning From Indigenous Peoples,* ed. Sylvia O'Meara and Douglas West (Toronto: Gramond Press, 1996). The refreshing aim of Julian Rice is to "affirm that a godless people can still be a spiritual one." *Before the Great Spirit: The Many Faces of Sioux Spirituality* (Albuquerque: University of New Mexico Press, 1998), 18. He demonstrates not only the ways in which Frances Densmore, John G. Neihardt, Joseph Epes Brown, and others amalgamated a range of different sacred or "wakan" figures into one Great Spirit or Supreme Being on the model of the anthropomorphized Christian God, but also the vitality and validity of the other ways in which Sioux belief operates. "The practical content and energy of Lakota spirituality in most cases derived directly from a confident alliance with an animal spirit rather than from power conferred by the great cosmic entities" (148).

93. H. L. Hosmer, *The Octoroon* (New York: Follett, 1863), 179–80.

94. David Christy, *A Lecture on African Civilization, Including a Brief Outline of the Social and Moral Condition of Africa and the Relation of American Slaves to African Civilisation* (Cincinnati: J. A. and U. P. James, 1850).

95. We do find isolated hints of unorthodoxy, as in the account of "Uncle Jack," who was born in Africa but became an impressive preacher. We are told of his confrontation with a backwoods African American preacher called Campbell, an intriguing figure who insisted that he didn't need a Bible, as most African Americans couldn't read, and burnt it. This seems to have rung alarm bells with white planters, and Uncle Jack was dispatched to refute his arguments. Rev. William S. White, *The African Preacher: An Authentic Narrative* (Philadelphia: Presbyterian Board of Publications, 1843).

96. Mechal Sobel, *The World They Made Together: Black and White Values in Eighteenth-Century Virginia* (Princeton, N.J.: Princeton University Press, 1987), 98.

97. Harry Middleton Hyatt, *Hoodoo–Conjuration—Witchcraft—Rootwork: Beliefs Accepted by Many Negroes and White Persons, These Being Orally Recorded among Blacks and Whites* (Hannibal, Miss: Western Publishing, 1970–80). The only substantial studies before this were that of Newbell Niles Puckett, *Folk Beliefs of the Southern Negro* (Chapel Hill: University of North Carolina Press, 1926), and those by Zora Neale Hurston, to be discussed later. Fieldwork carried out at the same time as Hyatt's research, but under the auspices of the WPA, eventually became available in the many volumes of George P. Rawick, ed., *The American Slave: A Composite Autobiography* (Englewood Cliffs, N.J.: Greenwood Press, 1972), which contains a mass of scattered material on conjure. Two important single volumes published more immediately were Writers' Program, *Drums and Shadows: Survival Studies among the Georgia Coastal Negroes* (Savannah Unit, Georgia Writers' Project, 1940), foreword by Guy B. Johnson (repr.; Westport, Conn.: Greenwood Press, 1973) and Lyle Saxon, Edward Dreyer, and Robert Tallant, eds., *Gumbo Ya-Ya: A Collection of Louisiana Folktales* (Boston: Houghton Mifflin, 1945). The subtitle of the Georgia volume reveals its assumptions, and it is designed rather mechanically, so that folkloric elements mentioned during the informants' vernacular accounts are cross-referenced, without any analysis, to a large appendix made up of quotations from African and West Indian sources, ranging from early travelers and missionaries to Melville Herskovits on Haiti. For works that treat conjure usefully within the larger framework of African American religion and culture, or that devote a section to this topic, see Albert J. Raboteau, *Slave Religion: The "Invisible Institution" in the Antebellum South* (Oxford: Oxford University Press,

1978), 75–87, 275–88; Philip D. Morgan, *Slave Counterpoint: Black Culture in the Eighteenth-Century Chesapeake and Low Country* (Chapel Hill: University of North Carolina Press, 1998), 620–27; Michael A. Gomez, *Exchanging Our Country Marks: The Transformation of African Identities in the Colonial and Antebellum South* (Chapel Hill: University of North Carolina Press, 1998), 49–50, 283–90: William D. Piersen, *Black Yankees: The Development of an Afro-American Subculture in Eighteenth-Century New England* (Amherst: University of Massachusetts Press, 1988), 74–86; Lawrence Levine, *Black Culture and Black Consciousness: Afro-American Folk Thought from Slavery to Freedom* (Oxford: Oxford University Press, 1977), 55–83.

98. David H. Brown, "Conjure/Doctors: An Exploration of a Black Discourse in America, Antebellum to 1940," *Folklore Forum* 23, 1/2 (1990): 5.

99. Brown, "Conjure/Doctors," 26.

100. He refers to the work of Tambiah and Comaroff, among others, but the issue is at the heart of what was known as the rationality debate of the 1960s and 1970s, which was itself a revisiting of the discussions of the "primitive mind" of Levy Bruhl and others at the beginning of the century.

101. Grey Gundaker, *Signs of Diaspora/Diaspora of Signs: Literacies, Creolization, and Vernacular Practice in African America* (New York: Oxford University Press, 1998), 22.

102. This also relates to Harryette Mullen's argument about what she calls "visionary literacy," in which she challenges the easy opposition of oral and literate, the oral being the privileged area of African American expression. This is based, she says, on false assumptions in that it ignores Islamic traditions of Africa, but more broadly she wants to argue for connections between African spirit writing and African American techniques and traditions of spiritual power. "African Signs and Spirit Writing," *Callalloo* 1, 3 (1996): 670–89. See also Aldon Lynn Nielsen, *Black Chant: Languages of African American Modernism* (Cambridge: Cambridge University Press, 1997), 3–37, for the ramifications of these ideas in contemporary writers.

103. Quoted Theophus H. Smith, *Conjuring Culture: Biblical Formations of Black America* (New York: Oxford University Press, 1994), 121. See Lerone Bennett, *The Negro Mood* (Chicago: Johnson, 1964). For a parallel work that wants to justify blues by showing they are ultimately spiritual, see James H. Cone, *Spirituals and the Blues* (New York: Orbis Books, 1991). There is a more extended treatment of this theme in the novel by Arthur Flowers discussed in Chapter 4.

104. Brown, "Conjure/Doctors," 31.

105. Yvonne P. Chireau, *Black Magic: Religion and the African American Conjuring Tradition* (Berkeley and Los Angeles: University of California Press, 2003), 54.

106. Chireau, *Black Magic*, 40–41, 47.

107. See Rachel E. Harding, *A Refuge in Thunder: Candomblé and Alternative Spaces of Blackness* (Bloomington: Indiana University Press, 2000), 27–33, 147–56. In her use of Pietz's stress on the materiality of the fetish to apply to the objects and general orientation of *candomblé*, as well as her stress on the material bodies of the slaves, she offers a parallel approach to that taken here. In contrast to the more elaborate and systematic syncretic religions of the Caribbean and Latin America, conjure may look rather thin—a patchy collection of practices designed for instrumental effect, rather than a system of belief—but my argument is that it is the balance of system and pragmatic flexibility that is of particular interest. For studies of these syncretic aspects, see, for example, Bruce Jackson, "Another Kind of Doctor: Conjure and Magic in Black American Folk Medicine," in *African-American Religion: Interpretive Essays in History and Culture*, ed. Timothy E. Fulop and Albert J. Raboteau (New York: Routledge, 1997), and George J. McCall, "Symbiosis: The Case of Hoodoo and the Numbers Racket," in *Mother Wit from the Laughing Barrel*, ed. Alan Dundes (Jackson: University Press of Mississippi, 1990),

420. F. Roy Johnson's *The Fabled Doctor Jim Jordan: A Story of Conjure* (Murfreesboro, N.C.: Johnson, 1963) fails to go very far into the sort of syncretism involved, but it is clear that Jordan combined healing of various sorts with advice and successful business. His funeral was held at a Baptist church, and Jordan apparently "never walked with 'ole Satan but with the Lord" (1). Johnson sees conjure as coming from Indian and European as well as African sources.

108. Eugene D. Genovese, *Roll Jordan Roll: The World the Slaves Made* (New York: Vintage Books, 1976), 222, 223. John Dollard saw it still operating in this way in the 1930s. "Magic accepts the status quo; it takes the place of political activity, agitation, organization, solidarity or any real moves to change status." For him it offered only psychological efficacy. It was "a control gesture, a comfort to the individual, an accommodation attitude to helplessness." *Caste and Class in a Southern Town* (New York: Doubleday, 1937), 263. See Norman E. Whitten, Jr., "Contemporary Patterns of Malign Occultism among Negroes in North Carolina," *Journal of American Folklore* 75 (1962): 311–25, for further views of magic as having a fundamentally accommodationist function. His overall argument is at odds with Herskovits in that he sees conjure in the context of a pattern of magical thought brought to the Piedmont by seventeenth- and eighteenth-century Europeans.

109. Frederick Douglass, *Narrative of the Life of Frederick Douglass, an American Slave* (1845; repr., New York: Dolphin Books, 1963), 72, 73.

110. Frederick Douglass, *My Bondage and My Freedom* (1855; repr., New York: Dover, 1969), 238.

111. Douglass, *My Bondage and My Freedom*, 241.

112. Harryette Mullen perhaps overstates the case in saying that Douglass "progressively dissociates himself from this superstitious belief in the power of ritual object." "African Signs and Spirit Writing," 678.

113. Walter C. Rucker, *The River Flows On: Black Resistance, Culture, and Identity Formation in Early America* (Baton Rouge: Louisiana State University Press, 2006), 141.

114. Chireau, *Black Magic*, 67. Harryette Mullen points to the ways in which what she calls visionary literacy, which was different from the literacy demonstrated by Douglass and involved "reading" signs and hieroglyphs, was involved in the beliefs and actions of Nat Turner. "African Signs and Spirit Writing," 678–79. William Wells Brown also mentions consulting a diviner. On spirit-writing and its relation to African American rebellions, see also Gundaker, *Signs of Diaspora/Diaspora of Signs*, 178.

Chapter 2

1. Peter Pels, "Occult Truths: Race, Conjecture, and Theosophy in Victorian Anthropology," in *Excluded Ancestors, Inventible Traditions: Essays toward a More Inclusive History of Anthropology*, ed. Richard Handler (Madison: University of Wisconsin Press, 2000), 37.

2. Quoted in John D. Kerkering, *The Poetics of Racial and National Identity in Nineteenth-Century American Literature* (Cambridge: Cambridge University Press, 2003), 169.

3. Kerkering, *Poetics of Racial and National Identity*, 174. Much earlier, in 1853, J. D. B. De Bow speculated about the connections between the Negroes' propensity to tuberculosis and their superstition. He even created a condition connected with this, "*Drapetomania*, or the disease causing Negroes to run away," which could be prevented by keeping them submissive and properly cared for. Quoted in Brown, "Conjure/Doctors," 15.

4. Susan Gillman, *Blood Talk: American Race Melodrama and the Culture of the Occult* (Chicago: University of Chicago Press, 2003), 6.

5. Werner Sollors quotes Emma Hardinge's *Modern American Spiritualism*: "It is a glorious indication of the bright transfiguration which death effects in our human weaknesses and vices, to find the red man, whose highest earthly virtue is revenge . . . almost invariably performs, in the modern spiritual movement, the high and blessed function of the benevolent Healer." In "Benjamin Franklin's Celestial Telegraph, or Indian Blessings to Gas-lit American Drawing Rooms," *American Quarterly* 35, 5 (1983): 480.

6. Russ Castronovo, "The Antislavery Unconscious: Mesmerism, Vodun and 'Equality,'" *Mississippi Quarterly* 53, 1 (1999): 41.

7. Nathan Francis White, *Voices from Spirit-land* (New York: Partridge and Brittan, 1854), x.

8. White, *Voices From Spirit-land*, 89.

9. Paschal Beverly Randolph, *The Wonderful Story of Ravalette* (New York: Sinclair Tousey, 1863), iv.

10. Randolph, *The Wonderful Story of Ravalette*, 9, 13.

11. Randolph, *The Wonderful Story of Ravalette*, 17, 19, 20.

12. Clara Louise Burnham, *Sweet Clover: A Romance of the White City* (Boston: Houghton, Mifflin, 1894), 201.

13. Marietta Holley, *Samantha at the World's Fair, by Josiah Allen's Wife* (New York: Funk and Wagnall, 1893), 372. Encountering the Iroquois village the narrator produces a comically stereotyped reaction, mourning the disappearance of the Indians. "And poor things! Where be they now? Passed away. Their canoes have gone down the stream of Time, and gone down the Falls out of sight. But to resoom." And so she moves swiftly on to the Yucatan exhibit (374). One irony here is that a number of Iroquois were actually brought to Chicago to occupy the village, so it was not meant entirely to reinforce the idea of the Vanishing Indian. See also Robert W. Rydell, *All the World's a Fair: Visions of Empire at American International Expositions* (Chicago: University of Chicago Press, 1984).

14. Eric J. Ziolkowski, *A Museum of Faiths: Histories and Legacies of the 1893 World's Parliament of Religions* (Atlanta: Scholars Press, 1993), 321. See also Richard Hughes Seager, ed., *The Dawn of Religious Pluralism: Voices from the World's Parliament of Religions, 1893* (LaSalle, Ill.: Open Court, 1993), and John H. Barrows, *The World's Parliament of Religions* (Chicago: Parliament, 1893).

15. See Ronald Niezen, *Spirit Wars: Native North American Religions in the Age of Nation Building* (Berkeley and Los Angeles: University of California Press, 2000), on her collecting, and David W. Stowe, *How Sweet the Sound: Music in the Spiritual Lives of Americans* (Cambridge, Mass.: Harvard University Press, 2004). For the larger picture, see Joan Mark, *A Stranger in Her Native Land: Alice Fletcher and the American Indians* (Lincoln: University of Nebraska Press, 1988).

16. Charles Eastman, "Sioux Mythology," in *International Folklore Congress of the World's Columbian Exposition* (Chicago: Charles H. Sergel, 1898), vol. 1, 225. A shorter version was also published in 1894 in *Popular Science Monthly*, repr. in William M. Clements, *Native American Folklore in Nineteenth Century Periodicals* (Athens, Ohio: Swallow Press, 1986).

17. Simon Pokagan, "Indian Superstitions and Legends," in Clements, *Native American Folklore*, 251–52.

18. Quoted in Timothy Hall Breen, "The Conflict in *The Golden Bough*: Frazer's Two Images of Man," *South Atlantic Quarterly* 66, 2 (1967): 185.

19. See E. P. Evans, "Recent Recrudescences of Superstition," *Appleton's Popular Science Monthly* 48, no. 1 (1895). For a more benign view, see Agnes Repplier, "On the Benefits of Superstition," *Atlantic Monthly*, August 1886: 177–86, who questioned the easy dismissal by the new rationalists of the vaguer areas of doubt, which would allow the imagination to grow.

20. Brad Evans, *Before Cultures: The Ethnographic Imagination in American Literature, 1865–1920* (Chicago: University of Chicago Press, 2005), 7. See also Lee D. Baker, *From Savage to Negro: Anthropology and the Construction of Race, 1896–1954* (Berkeley and Los Angeles: University of California Press, 1998), 73–74.

21. Zitkala Ša ,"Why I Am Not a Pagan," *Atlantic Monthly* 90 (1902): 803

22. Zitkala Ša, "Why I Am Not a Pagan," 802–3.

23. Zitkala Ša, *American Indian Stories* (1921; repr., Lincoln: University of Nebraska Press, 1985), 107.

24. Zitkala Ša, "The School Days of an Indian Girl," *Atlantic Monthly* 85 (1900): 193.

25. Though the story is actually about skullduggery between white colonials on a sugar plantation, a visit to the "obi man," "a time-worn fragment of Ethiopian humanity," is included to add local exoticism. In his house, "filth and mystery and darkness blend in grim combination." A curtain hides "Arcanum—the Chamber of Horrors, or Holy of Holies, whichever your attitude towards obeah inclines you to call it." Eden Phillpotts, "The Obi Man," *Harper's Weekly*, July 1, 1893: 617. Phillpotts's many novels include a number that skirt around the subject of obeah. *The Golden Fetich* (New York: Dodd, Mead, 1903), for instance, flirts with what one character calls "some mumbo-jumbo foolery of niggers."

26. "Is Everybody Superstitious?" *Harper's Weekly Magazine*, October 21, 1893: 1016. It is interesting to compare this stance with the case now more likely to be made for folklore studies, which tends to look nonjudgmentally at all sorts of beliefs with a view to seeing what function they are fulfilling. Marilyn Motz has argued that folklorists are well placed to put into practice the recent formulations about the practice of belief in everyday life from Michel de Certeau, Derrida, and others. "The Practice of Belief," *Journal of American Folklore* 111 (1998): 339–55. See also Patrick B. Mullen, "Belief and the American Folk," *Journal of American Folklore* 113 (2000): 119–43.

27. Jon Cruz, *Culture on the Margins: The Black Spiritual and the Rise of American Cultural Interpretation* (Princeton, N.J.: Princeton University Press, 1999), 178, 179.

28. Cruz, *Culture on the Margins*, 127.

29. William Wells Newell, " On the Field and Work of a Journal of American Folk-Lore," *Journal of American Folklore* 1 (1888): 5. The differences between the more inclusive and less critical approach of the folklorists and the more hierarchical concerns of the religionists with more spiritualized expressions of belief are clear in Andrew Lang's sharp critiques of Max Müller and his concern for "higher" religions. See Andrew Lang, *Custom and Myth* (1884; repr., London: Longmans, Green, 1910).

30. John W. Richards, though, sees the effect of the adoption of the Negro within the European categories of "folk" as having the effect of minimizing and distorting the distinctive African legacy. "African-American Folklore in a Discourse of Folkness," *New York Folklore* 18 (1962): 73–89.

31. Eric Lott, *Love and Theft: Blackface Minstrelsy and the American Working Class* (New York: Oxford University Press, 1995), 3.

32. At the level of popular belief and practice, Indians and African Americans had long been credited with powers that were officially dismissed. In an entry to his diary of 1799, William Bentley records attending the funeral of Jude, an African woman who had been "long celebrated at Twisse's as a Fortune teller & in this age of illuminatism has had ample encouragement." *The Diary of William Bentley* (1902; repr., Gloucester, Mass.: Peter Smith, 1962), vol. 2, 302. He also refers to "a pretended Indian doctor" arrested in connection with a murder (vol. 1, 37) and complains of the general gullibility of the people. "To show that superstition is not done away, a Continental Soldier with his maple rods was with me to borrow a bible & Psalm Book with a benediction to recover some chests of money upon the Neck. After his usual superstitions I granted

him a bible and psalms at his wishes. . . . What progress we have made while we still have our Conjurers &c in full credit." Vol. 3, 358. See also Ignatius Lewis, *The New Fortune Book of OBI or West Indian Astrologer, by Ignatius Lewis, the Jamaican Seer of Colour* (London, 1823), and Chloe Russell, *Complete Fortune Teller and Dream Book by Chloe Russell, a Woman of Colour of the State of Massachusetts, commonly termed the Old Witch or Black Interpreter* (Boston, 1821). For texts invoking Indian magic and medicine, see Daniel Gardner, *A New System of Indian Doctoring* (Windsor, Vt.: Statesman Office, 1839); Benjamin B. Walker, *The Indian Practice of Medicine, Being a Treatise Divested of Professional Terms, on the Nature, Causes, Symptoms and Treatment* (Louisville, Ky.: John C. Noble, 1847). A staple of magical practices, George Hohman's *Der Freund in der Noth* was published as George Hohman, *Pow-Wows; or The Long Lost Friend*, even though nothing in the book even refers to Indians, and it is important generally to treat these texts skeptically as largely if not entirely the product of white agendas. See also William D. Piersen, "Black Arts and Black Magic: Yankee Accommodations to African Religion," in *Wonders of the Invisible World: 1600–1900*, ed. Peter Benes (Boston: Annual Proceedings of the Dublin Seminar for New England Life, 1995).

33. James Melville Beard, *K.K.K. Sketches, Humorous and Didactic* (Philadelphia: Claxton, Remsen and Haffelfinger, 1877), 65.

34. Beard, *K.K.K. Sketches*, 69.

35. William D. Piersen, *Black Legacies: America's Hidden Heritage* (Amherst: University of Massachusetts Press, 1993), 151.

36. Elliot J. Gorn, "Black Spirits: The Ghostlore of Afro-American Slaves," *American Quarterly* 36, 4 (1984): 553, 559. See "The Ghostly Legend of the Ku-Klux Klan," *Negro History Bulletin*, 14 (February 1951), repr. in *Mother Wit from the Laughing Barrel*, ed. Alan Dundes (Jackson: University Press of Mississippi, 1990), 586–94. For an interesting later discussion that identifies the white stratagem, but still implicitly accepts that blacks were more susceptible to superstition, and were outgrowing it, see the labor leader A. Philip Randolph's account of attempts to intimidate him by playing on his supposed superstition in "The Human Hand Threat," repr. in Dundes, *Mother Wit*, 397–401.

37. Edward E. Pollard, *Black Diamonds Gathered in the Darkey Homes of the South* (New York: Pudney and Russell, 1860), x.

38. Joel Chandler Harris, "Plantation Music," *The Critic* 3, 95 (1883) 505–6: repr. in *The Negro and His Folklore in Nineteenth-Century Periodicals*, ed. Bruce Jackson (Austin: University of Texas Press, 1967), 178, 180.

39. Joel Chandler Harris, *Nights with Uncle Remus: Myths and Legends of the Old Plantation* (1883), ed. John T. Bickley and R. Bruce Bickley (New York: Penguin, 2003), 32.

40. Harris, *Nights with Uncle Remus*, 11.

41. Thomas Wentworth Higginson, "Negro Spirituals," *Atlantic Monthly* 19 (1867): 685.

42. Cruz, *Culture on the Margins*, 158. See also Mieke Bal, "Telling Objects: A Narrative Perspective on Collecting," in *The Cultures of Collecting*, ed. John Elsner and Roger Cardinal (London: Reaktion Books, 1994).

43. Harris, *Nights with Uncle Remus*, 349.

44. Juniper Ellis, "Enacting Culture: Zora Neale Hurston, Joel Chandler Harris, and Literary Ethnography," in *Multiculturalism: Roots and Realities*, ed. C. James Trotman (Bloomington: University of Indiana Press, 2002).

45. Joel Chandler Harris, *Uncle Remus, His Songs and Sayings: The Folklore of the Old Plantation* (New York: D. Appleton, 1881), 133.

46. Harris, *Uncle Remus, His Songs and Sayings*, 134.

47. Harris, *Uncle Remus, His Songs and Sayings*, 136. Harris reprints the whole of this song in the "Songs" section of the book, and he includes the following forceful verse in another song.

De ole bee make de honeycomb,

De young bee makes the honey,

De niggers make de cotton en co'n,

En de w'ite folks gits de money

48. Harris, *Nights with Uncle Remus,*137.

49. Reprinted in R. Bruce Bickley, Jr., ed., *Critical Essays on Joel Chandler Harris* (Boston: G. K. Hall, 1981), 48.

50. Joel Chandler Harris, *The Bishop and the Boogerman* (New York: Doubleday, Page, 1909), 127.

51. Harris, *The Bishop and the Boogerman*, 115.

52. My assumption is that Harris here and in the Remus stories is not deliberately critiquing his own society's values, but for a strongly made counterargument, see Robert Cochran, "Black Father: The Subversive Achievement of Joel Chandler Harris," *African American Review* 38, 1 (2004): 21–34. Though he does not deal with this novel at all, Cochran does cite Harris's dismissive reference to the "Bugaboo of Social Democracy," which is making a "problem out of something which never had an existence" (27), which does suggest the "boogerman" of this story.

53. Harris, *The Bishop and the Boogerman*, 112–13.

54. Harris *The Bishop and the Boogerman*, 123.

55. Avery F. Gordon, *Ghostly Matters: Haunting and the Sociological Imagination* (Minneapolis: University of Minnesota Press, 1997), 8. For a discussion using Derrida's ideas of haunting, see my "Cultural Sovereignty and the Hauntology of American Identity," in *Mirror Writing: (Re-)Constructions of Native American Identity*, ed. Thomas Claviez and Maria Moss (Berlin: Galdsa—Wilch Verlag, 2000).

56. Joel Chandler Harris, *Free Joe and Other Georgian Sketches* (New York: P. F. Collier, 1887), 3, 4.

57. The compulsion to preserve and fix a mythical past and the processes of denial and assertion are clearly shown in Harris's introduction to a volume of poems and paintings, *Bandanna Ballads*. He praises the portraits of slaves, which are evidence of a past society in which real nobility did exist. "Whatever the negroes are now, whatever they may become in the cold-storage conditions of our commercial environment, these portraits present unimpeachable evidence of what they were. The art with which the facts are set forth is so felicitous in its touch, so faithful and so informing, that it goes deeper than character and individuality; it revives and resurrects the period; in some mysterious way it restores the atmosphere and color of the period." The imagination "makes its creations more real than life itself." Howard Weeden, *Bandanna Ballads* (New York: Doubleday & McClure, 1899), ix, xii–xiii.

58. Charles C. Jones, *Negro Myths From the Georgia Coast* (Boston: Houghton, Mifflin, 1882), 151, 152, 153. Jones argues that Harris unjustly ignored the Sea Islands in favor of middle Georgia. Jones had earlier written on the Indians of Georgia, which reflects his anthropological as well as antiquarian interests. He follows the general template of his time, in which idolatry is an advance on fetish worship, seeing idols as "denoting not only the entity of a religious idea, but also the cooperation of something like art and imagination," but he is at pains to insist that the Georgia tribes went beyond this stage to one "more elevated and expansive in its character," namely "a devotion which, ignoring the intervention of idols, recognizes the existence of a Supreme Being, a Great Spirit, or of two controlling divinities—the one of good and the other of evil." *Antiquities of the Southern Indians, particularly of the Georgian Tribes* (New York: D. Appleton, 1873), 414–15. See also Ambrose E. Gonzalez, *The Black Border: Gullah Stories of the Carolina*

Coast (Columbia, S.C.: State Company, 1922), a collection of stories, mostly written in 1892 in response to Harris. Where Jones's book, which he dedicates to the "family servants" and their "warm fidelity and affection," seems indulgent towards his subject, Gonzalez leaves us in no doubt of his views. "Out of this fetid armpit of the Dark Continent came the first black bondsmen to curse the western world" (7).

59. William Welles Newell, "Review of *Negro Myths of the Georgia Coast*," *Journal of American Folklore* 1, 2 (1988): 170.

60. S. M. Park, "Voodooism in Tennessee," *Atlantic Monthly* 64 (1889): 379. It is also worth noting that this was at the same time that Chesnutt's tales of the conjure woman were first appearing in the same magazine.

61. The changing representation over the centuries of a famous sorcerer may also reflect this. Described consistently as an Indian by her Puritan contemporaries, Tituba, the servant at the center of the Salem witch trials, was gradually transformed into an African in later commentaries, so that by the time Arthur Miller, in *The Crucible*, portrayed her as a credulous black slave she was fulfilling a larger assumption about the role of magic in African as opposed to Indian religions. This was not necessarily present in earlier centuries, when, for the Puritans and Jesuits, Indians were as much associated with magic as Africans. See Peter Benes, ed., *Wonders of the Invisible World: 1600–1900* (Boston: Boston University, 1995), 17–52. There is a general agreement that Tituba came from Barbados and may have learned these beliefs in the mixture of cultures there, but the resistance to leaving her an Indian in later representations reflects the desire to separate out the appropriate religious propensities of the races. See Chadwick Hansen, "The Metamorphosis of Tituba, or Why American Intellectuals Can't Tell an Indian Witch from a Negro," *New England Quarterly* 47, 1 (1974): 3–12; Elaine G. Breslaw, *Tituba, Reluctant Witch of Salem: Devilish Indians and Puritan Fantasies* (New York: New York University Press, 1996), and Vera Smith Tucker, "Purloined Identity: The Racial Identity of Tituba of Salem Village," *Journal of Black Studies* 30, 4 (2000): 624–34.

62. A question Harris addresses in the introduction to his first book, and again in the extended introduction to *Nights with Uncle Remus*, is the geographical origin of the animal stories. Against suggestions from other folklorists, notably John Wesley Powell, he insists on an African origin rather than an American Indian one. See Evans, *Before Cultures*, 51–81. For one of the very few articles to deal with Indian and African American religion in any comparative way at the time, see A. B. Ellis, "Evolution in Folklore: Some African Prototypes of the 'Uncle Remus' Stories," *Appleton's Popular Science Monthly* 48, 1 (1895): 93–104. James Mooney in his account of Cherokee myths in 1897 referred to the strikingly similar role of the rabbit as mischief maker. He thought Indian-Negro cross-influence likely, given the fact that Indians were also enslaved, and consequently intermingling, but his reasoning reveals the standard racial categorizations of the time. "The negro, with his genius for imitation and his love of stories, especially of the comic variety, must undoubtedly have absorbed much from the Indian in this way, while on the other hand the Indian, with his pride of conservatism and his contempt for a subject race, would have taken but little from the negro." James Mooney, *Myths of the Cherokees*, Nineteenth Annual Report of the Bureau of American Ethnology, 1897–98 (Washington, D.C.: Washington Printing Office, 1900), part 1, 232. See also Florence E. Baer, *Sources and Analogues of the Uncle Remus Tales*, FFC, no. 228 (Helsinki: Suomalainene Tiedeakatemia, 1980), and Jay Hansford C. Vest, "From Bobtail to Brer Rabbit," *American Indian Quarterly* 24, 1 (2000): 19–43, who argues once again for Native American origins but also points out that the particular racial categorizing in the United States meant that racially mixed people would often be regarded as black, thus obscuring cultural as well as racial origins.

63. Mary Alicia Owen, *Old Rabbit, the Voodoo and Other Sorcerers: Voodoo Tales as Told*

among the Negroes of the Southwest (New York: Putnam's Sons, 1893), 8. Jeanette Robinson Murphy in 1899 describes a conjure woman who sells red flannel luck balls, which are to be worn next to the skin on the right side. "I was so fortunate as to discover the contents of one of her balls. Corn, twine, pepper, a piece of hair from under a black cat's foot, a piece of rabbit's foot, and whiskey—all put into a red flannel bag. This was all inclosed in a buckeye biscuit." "The Survival of African Music in America," *Popular Science Monthly* 55 (1899): 60–72, repr. in Jackson, ed., *The Negro and His Folklore*, 335. Other examples of this trope occur in an anonymous article in an early issue of the *Journal of American Folklore*, which itself exemplifies the rather uncritical collecting urge. It quotes from a report from the *Times* of Selma, Alabama, of May 1884, which strikes the tone of detached curiosity. "We have before us something of a curiosity in the shape of a voudoo or conjure bag." An expression of "that lowest order of superstition common to the race since the birth of their most ancient forefathers" this "bundle of trash" contains a rabbit's foot, and various roots and herbs. "Concerning Negro Sorcery in the United States," *Journal of American Folklore* 3, 11 (1890): 281–87. The article also mentions a rabbit foot given to Grover Cleveland "as a talisman," from a rabbit that was shot on the grave of Jesse James.

64. Owen, *Old Rabbit*, vi.

65. Mary Alicia Owen, *The Daughter of Alouette* (London: Methuen, 1902), 163.

66. Mary Alicia Owen, "Among the Voodoos," in *International Folklore Congress of 1891*, ed. Joseph Jacobs and Alfred Nutt (1892), 233.

67. Owen, "Among the Voodoos," 241.

68. Owen, "Voodooism," in *International Folklore Congress of 1891*, 317.

69. Owen, "Among the Voodoos," 239.

70. She describes the founding god of Voodoo as "Old Grandfather Rattlesnake, who in America takes the place of the Green Serpent of African tradition," which suggests an Indian influence not mentioned in her descriptions of Voodoo from New Orleans ("Voodooism," 322). For Indian material, see also her more academic *Folklore of the Musquakie Indians of North America and Catalogue of Musquakie Beadwork and Other Objects in the Collection of the Folk-Lore Society* (London: David Nutt, 1904).

71. Mary Alicia Owen, correspondence, November 27, 1895, and September 20, 1895, Pennsylvania Historical Society.

72. W. E. B. DuBois, "The Religion of the American Negro," in *The New World: A Quarterly Review of Religion, Ethics and Theology* 9 (1900): 614–25.

73. W. E. B. DuBois, *The Souls of Black Folk*, ed. Henry Louis Gates, Jr., and Terri Hume Oliver (New York: Norton, 1999), 123. I am quoting from the book rather than the article as the more readily available source.

74. DuBois, *Souls of Black Folk*, 124, 125.

75. W. E. B. DuBois, *The Quest for the Silver Fleece* (Chicago: A. C. McClurg, 1911), 46.

76. DuBois, *Quest for the Silver Fleece*, 372.

77. DuBois, *Quest for the Silver Fleece*, 75.

78. DuBois, *Quest for the Silver Fleece*, 373, 209.

79. Evans, *Before Cultures*, 184.

80. DuBois, *Souls of Black Folk*, 147.

81. Charles Peabody, "Notes on Negro Music," *Journal of American Folklore* 16 (1903): 148.

82. The fact that this takes place on the Stovall plantation near Clarksdale, where Alan Lomax was later to record Muddy Waters, means that this may be the earliest description of the blues. Robert Palmer describes Peabody's as the first account of black music in the Delta in *Deep Blues: A Musical and Cultural History of the Mississippi Delta* (New York: Penguin, 1981), 24.

83. James Weldon Johnson, *Along This Way: The Autobiography of James Weldon Johnson* (1933; repr., New York: Penguin, 1990), 318.

84. Ronald Radano, "Denoting Difference: The Writing of the Slave Spirituals," *Critical Inquiry* 22 (1996): 508–9.

85. Pauline Hopkins, *Of One Blood* (published in serial form from 1903; repr., London: X Press, 1996), 4–5.

86. The term is from William James, but Hopkins attributes it to an invented author. Cynthia Schrager argues that for both DuBois and Hopkins, the various discourses on psychology and psychic forces "offered a ready language with which to attempt a representation of African American subjectivity." "Pauline Hopkins and William James: The New Psychology and the Politics of Race," in *The Unruly Voice: Discovering Pauline Elizabeth Hopkins*, ed. John Cullen Gruesser (Urbana: University of Illinois Press, 1996), 189. See also Susan Gillman, "Pauline Hopkins and the Occult: African-American Revisions of Nineteenth-Century Science," *American Literary History* 8, 1 (1996): 57–82. She argues that Hopkins uses nineteenth-century sciences in conjunctions that release possibilities for exploring race rather than just defining it in restrictive ways. The idea of excavating the past (archaeology) is linked in the book to opening up the psyche, bringing to light the hidden self (psychology) and the unexplored mental and occult capacities of the mind.

87. Hopkins, *Of One Blood*, 63.

88. Hopkins, *Of One Blood*, 67.

89. Hopkins, *Of One Blood*, 122.

90. Jennie A. Kassanoff, "'Fate Has Linked Us Together': Blood, Gender, and the Politics of Representation in Pauline Hopkins's *Of One Blood*," in Gruesser, *The Unruly Voice*, 176.

91. A Hopkins short story that does not deal directly with race, "The Mystery within Us," appeared in *The Colored American* and dealt with the positive uses of magnetism and electricity to pass on messages from beyond the grave.

92. Pauline Hopkins, *Contending Forces: A Romance Illustrative of Negro Life in North and South* (1900; repr., New York: Oxford University Press, 1988), 199.

93. On the cover of Mary Owen's book was a rabbit and an old woman of color, but also an Indian feather. Charles Colcock Jones's collection also has a rabbit. It is hard to overestimate the importance of the Harris volume, even as late as the 1920s. The cover of the original edition of Hurston's *Mules and Men* had Miguel Covarrubias's sketch of an alligator, which appears in the text itself to illustrate a tale of Brer Dog and Brer 'Gator, and Franz Boas began his preface to Hurston's book by referring to Uncle Remus.

94. Charles W. Chesnutt, "Superstitions and Folk-Lore of the South," *Modern Culture* 13 (1901), repr. in *Charles W. Chesnutt: Essays and Speeches*, ed. Joseph R. McElrath, Jr., Robert C. Leitz, and Jesse C. Crisler (Stanford, Calif: Stanford University Press, 1999), 155.

95. Charles W. Chesnutt, "Post Bellum, Pre-Harlem," *Crisis* 40 (1931): 193.

96. Charles W. Chesnutt, *The Conjure Woman and Other Conjure Tales*, ed. Richard H. Brodhead (Durham, N.C.: Duke University Press, 1994), 10.

97. Chesnutt, *Conjure Woman*, 52.

98. Chesnutt, *Conjure Woman*, 53.

99. Chesnutt, *Conjure Woman*, 49. The term was also reported by Jeanette Robinson Murphy in 1899, in a description of spirituals from a Kentucky woman: "Dese spirituals am de best moanin' music in de world, case dey is de whole Bible sung out and out. Notes is good enough for you people but us likes a mixtery." "Survival of African Music in America," 329.

100. The easy conjunction of conjure and Christianity—of material magical practices and high Christian spirituality—is also reflected in Chesnutt's article on superstition when he describes Aunt Harriet using a magic charm, as dictated to her by a voice that came in her sleep. "Dat voice," she says, "wus de Spirit er de Lawd talkin' ter me," but then Chesnutt insists on a practical explanation and dismisses the spirit voices as her "vagrant imaginings." "Superstitions and Folklore," 158.

101. Eric J. Sundquist brings out the Christian dimensions of the story, which include not only the Eucharist but the idea of slaves as the descendants of Ham. *To Wake the Nations: Race in the Making of American Literature* (Cambridge, Mass.: Harvard University Press, 1993), 382. Adam Gussow links the prevalence of lynchings in the post-Reconstruction 1890s with much of the new subject matter of the blues, which were also appearing at this time. He argues that, though not explicitly referred to, lynchings form an important undercurrent in the blues' concern with issues of violence as well as sexuality, which is not to be found in the already established forms of spirituals and work songs.[101] With the end of slavery, he suggests, there is a changing view of the physical body of the slave. No longer property, it is subject to a different disciplinary regime, and one that comes to include spectacle lynchings, where the body is expendable, to be consumed and transformed in what comes close to ritual sacrifice. Adam Gussow, *Seems Like Murder Here: Southern Violence and the Blues Tradition* (Chicago: University of Chicago Press, 2002).

102. Chesnutt, *Conjure Woman*, 135.

103. Some recent critics have shown how this view of interrelatedness is put at the service of what we would now call an ecological vision by Chesnutt. The stories deal with the linked productivity of land and black labor in slavery and later, as the Northerner John rationalizes the vineyard—if not its genius loci in the form of Julius.

104. Chesnutt, *Conjure Woman*, 185.

105. Chesnutt, *Conjure Woman*, 124.

106. Chesnutt's exploration of interracial obligations and denials in *The Marrow of Tradition* takes place against the background of a violent riot and the actions of a lynch mob, and in *The Colonel's Dream* he tersely describes a lynching. "A rope, a tree—a puff of smoke, a flash of flame—or a barbaric orgy of fire and blood—what matter which? At the end there was a lump of clay." *The Colonel's Dream* (1905; repr., Upper Saddle River, N.J.: Gregg Press, 1968), 277. The clay here might also remind us of the eating of clay in the story "Lonesome Ben," another transformation of a human being into inanimate matter.

107. William L. Andrews, *The Literary Career of Charles W. Chesnutt* (Baton Rouge: Louisiana State University Press, 1980), 54.

108. Chesnutt, *The Colonel's Dream*, 273.

109. Russell, *Complete Fortune Teller and Dream Book*. The Boston Atheneum copy has a drawing of Chloe Russell, which is reprinted in Yvonne Chireau's *Black Magic: Religion and the African American Conjuring Tradition* (Berkeley and Los Angeles: University of California Press, 2003). The Library Company of Philadelphia's copy includes a preamble to the body of the book giving the details of Chloe's past life, in which she describes being captured from Sierra Leone and ill treated. On the verge of suicide, she has a vision of her father and another "bright spirit" who promises her the power to foretell events and prophecy and thereby gain her freedom. The body of the book is made up of love potions and interpretations of dream symbols, in a genteel language clearly aimed at a white audience. If seen in the context of similar works invoking Indian medicine and charms, we would have at least to question the authenticity of this text, though Chireau seems to accept it. Eric Gardner has presented an edited version of the book, with discussion of its authorship, in "*The Complete Fortune Teller and Dream Book*: An

Antebellum Text by Chloe Russel, A Woman of Colour," *New England Quarterly* 78, 2 (2005). Having located an African American woman called Chloe Russell living in Boston at the time. Gardner attempts to connect the text to her, but the links remain hypothetical and unproven, as he acknowledges.

110. A popular early play, *The Disappointment: Or, the Force of Credulity*, by Andrew Barton, actually Thomas Forrest (1767), satirized the enthusiasm for conjurers and the greed for gold. One of the characters, Raccoon, may be meant to be African American.

Chapter 3

1. Walter Benjamin, *One Way Street and Other Writings*, trans. Edmund Jephcott and Kingsley Shorter (London: Verso, 1979), 227.

2. Rachel O. Moore, *Savage Theory: Cinema as Modern Magic* (Durham, N.C.: Duke University Press, 2000), 73. See also Jill H. Casid, " 'His Master's Obi': Machine Magic, Colonial Violence, and Transculturation," in *The Visual Culture Reader*, ed. Nicholas Mirzoff (London: Routledge, 1998), for a discussion of the use of the magic lantern as part of a paradoxical colonial assertion of rationality over the superstition of colonized people.

3. James Clifford, "Ethnographic Surrealism," in *Predicament of Culture: Twentieth-Century Ethnography, Literature and Art* (Cambridge, Mass.: Harvard University Press, 1988). See also Mariana Torgovnick, *Gone Primitive: Savage Intellects, Modern Lives* (Chicago: University of Chicago Press, 1990), and Elazar Barkan and Ronald Bush, eds., *Prehistories of the Future: The Primitivist Project and the Culture of Modernism* (Stanford, Calif.: Stanford University Press, 1995).

4. Quoted in Ronald Niezen, *Spirit Wars: Native North American Religions in the Age of Nation Building* (Berkeley and Los Angeles: University of California Press, 2000), 183.

5. Quoted in Raymond Corbey, "Ethnographic Showcases, 1780–1930," *Cultural Anthropology* 8, 3 (1993): 166.

6. James Fenton's poem on the Pitt Rivers Museum in Oxford brings out well the disparity between scholarly and popular attitudes. "For teachers, the thesis is salutary / And simple, a hierarchy of progress, culminating / In the Entrance Hall." The schoolchildren, though, are clamoring for the monstrous and magical objects and are more truly at home in "the climate of a foreign logic." *Children in Exile: Poems 1968–1984* (New York: Vintage, 1984), 81.

7. Clifford, *Predicament of Culture*, 136, 199.

8. André Malraux, *Picasso's Mask* (New York: Holt, Rinehart and Winston, 1976), 10–11. It may not be wise to put too much weight on the actual words here, since these are Malraux's recollections of what Picasso said many years before.

9. Quoted in Sieglinde Lemke, *Primitivist Modernism: Black Culture and the Origins of Transatlantic Modernism* (Oxford: Oxford University Press, 1998), 38. For the immediate political context, see Patricia Leighton, "The White Peril and l'Art Nègre: Picasso, Primitivism and Anticolonialism," *Art Bulletin* 72, 4 (1990): 609–30. She points out that there was a strong anticolonialist and anarchist sentiment among artists, which was stimulated by news of colonialist excesses and cruelties, but that their use of masks and other objects still subscribed to the same primitivist assumptions as those they criticized. She quotes an outraged right-wing response to the prospect of a museum for such art in 1912, which sees it as the ultimate perversion of taste. "Below black fetishes, there is nothing." It warns against interest in mosaics and "the ape-statues of the basilica" because "the love of the primitive, in art as in politics, suits the black" (628).

10. Annie E. Coombs, *Reinventing Africa: Museums, Material Culture and Popular Imagination*

in Late Victorian and Edwardian England (New Haven, Conn.: Yale University Press, 1994), 131.

11. See especially James Clifford's account of what he calls "ethnographic surrealism" in *Predicament of Culture*. The surrealists were more interested in Oceania and the Northwest coast of America, and in general in the rich and random juxtapositions both within primitive art itself and within the Western museums that assembled it, than in the abstraction and clean lines that Picasso found in African art.

12. See Aldon Jonaitis, "Creations of Mystics and Philosophers: The White Man's Perceptions of Northwest Coast Indian Art from the 1930s to the Present," *American Indian Culture and Research Journal* 5, 1 (1981): 1–45, and Robert Fay Schrader, *The Indian Arts and Crafts Board: An Aspect of New Deal Indian Policy* (Albuquerque: University of New Mexico Press, 1983). In America the acquisition of objects was much more concentrated on Indian materials. As part of the effort at "salvage ethnography" a vast mass of material was collected from tribes assumed to be vanishing. These were exhibited and incorporated into a larger narrative or framework of national and scientific progress, which served to neutralize the objects and their possible power in their original context. Though museum practices changed, reflecting a move from evolutionary and linear assumptions to an interest in whole cultures, the criteria for inclusion remained much the same, and there were many objects that met neither the ethnographic criteria (which privileged the products of a pure or ancient culture over the hybrid or popular) nor the aesthetic. There are intriguing stray references to the collecting of conjure objects—Zora Neale Hurston describes acquiring a "hand" for Boas, for instance, and there were plans for a museum of similar objects at Hampton—but it seems such things were not usually preserved or collected. The sedentary and more ceremonial cultures of the Southwest may have suffered more depredations from collectors than the hunters of the North, whose spiritual observances involved objects like medicine pouches and bundles that would be less collectible as art, as Niezen suggests, but it is difficult to pin down quite what "value" an object had for the native people in each situation. See Niezen, *Spirit Wars*, 181. In Eliza McFeeley's view, "Zuni was incorporated into the United States not so much by conquerors as by collectors." *Zuni and the American Imagination* (New York: Hill and Wang, 2001), 8. The Northwest coast was heavily mined by collectors but there seems to have been less of an issue about the public display than about who had the right to display objects, as many of them contained or embodied family crests—or totems, to use the borrowed term.

13. Bunny McBride, *Molly Spotted Elk: A Penobscot in Paris* (Norman: University of Oklahoma Press, 1995), 158. Apparently secure in her sense of her own Indian identity and heritage, McBride was willing to perform largely within the forms and roles in which Indians were presented to the general public, but her interest in what other cultures had in common was wide ranging. She describes attending lectures by Marcel Mauss and assisting anthropologists with the mounting of exhibitions at the Trocadéro.

14. There were those at the time who recognized this as an expression of the needs of the West rather than as any sort of expression of a primitive reality. The Documents group, whose members included Michel Leiris and Marcel Griaule as well as Georges Bataille, was fascinated by the conjunction of the aesthetic and ethnographic. Bataille referred to the Negro revue Lew Leslie's Black Birds, which performed in Paris in 1929, not as primal or primitive but as related to the needs of a febrile and ailing Western society: "the blacks who (in America or elsewhere) are civilised along with us and who, today, dance and cry out, are marshy emanations of the decomposition who are set aflame above this immense cemetery: so, in a vaguely lunar Negro night, we are witnessing an intoxicating dementia of dubious and charming will-o'-the-wisps, writing

and yelling like bursts of laughter." Georges Bataille et al., *Encyclopaedia Acephalica* (London: Atlas Press, 1995), 36–37.

15. Johannes Fabian, *Time and the Other: How Anthropology Makes Its Object* (New York: Columbia University Press, 1983).

16. Marsden Hartley, *The Collected Poems of Marsden Hartley, 1904–1943*, ed. Gail R. Scott (Santa Rosa, Calif.: Black Sparrow Press, 1987), 328. See also Townsend Ludington, *Marsden Hartley: The Biography of an American Artist* (Boston: Little, Brown, 1992).

17. See Wanda M. Corn, "Marsden Hartley's Native Amerika," in *Marsden Hartley*, ed. Elizabeth Mankin Kornhauser (New Haven, Conn.: Yale University Press, 2002). For a brief account of Hartley in the context of the American use of the primitive, see Gail Levin, "American Art," in *"Primitivism" in 20th Century Art: Affinities of the Tribal and Modern*, ed. William Rubin (New York: Museum of Modern Art, 1984), 453–74.

18. Leah Dilworth, *Imagining Indians in the Southwest: Persistent Visions of a Primitive Past* (Washington, D.C.: Smithsonian Institution Press, 1996), 189.

19. Marsden Hartley, "Redman Ceremonials: An American Plea for American Esthetics," *Art and Archaeology* 9, 1 (1920): 14.

20. Hartley, "Redman Ceremonials," 12.

21. Hartley, "Redman Ceremonials," 13.

22. Mary Austin, *The American Rhythm: Studies and Reexpressions of Amerindian Songs* (1930; repr., New York: Cooper Square Publishers, 1970), 11. For other similar uses of Indian music by white performers, see Carlos Troyer, *Indian Music Lecture: The Zuni Indians and Their Music* (Philadelphia: Theo. Presser, 1913), who describes the Zuni as "Sun- and Nature-worshippers" with a deeply implanted belief that everything in nature is endowed with a "conscious soul" (19). See also Frederick Burton, *American Primitive Music, with Especial Attention to the Songs of the Ojibways* (New York: Maffat, Yard, 1909).

23. Mary Austin, "The Path on the Rainbow" (1918), repr. in *Literature of the American Indians: Views and Interpretations*, ed. Abraham Chapman (New York: New American Library, 1975), 267.

24. Austin, *The American Rhythm*, 57.

25. Hartley, "Redman Ceremonials," 12–13.

26. Quoted in Amy Koritz, "Re/Moving Boundaries: From Dance History to Cultural Studies," in *Moving Words: Re-writing Dance*, ed. Gay Morris (London: Routledge, 1996), 92. Koritz argues that Graham, in her quest for a distinctively American artistic form, used African rather than African American "disintegrative" movement, but mostly Native American materials drawn from the Southwest. See also Mark Franko, "Aesthetic Agencies in Flux: Talley Beatty, Maya Deren, and the Modern Dance Tradition in *Study in Choreography for Camera*," in *Maya Deren and the American Avant-Garde*, ed. Bill Nichols (Berkeley and Los Angeles: University of California Press, 2001).

27. Austin, *The American Rhythm*, 40.

28. Dilworth, *Imagining Indians in the Southwest*, 199.

29. William Brandon, *The Magic World: American Indian Songs and Poems* (New York: William Morrow, 1971), xiv.

30. David W. Stowe, *How Sweet the Sound: Music in the Spiritual Lives of Americans* (Cambridge, Mass.: Harvard University Press, 2004), 118–31.

31. Quoted in Dilworth, *Imagining Indians in the Southwest*, 200.

32. Zitkala Ša, *Dreams and Thunder: Stories, Poems, and The Sun Dance Opera*, ed. P. Jane Hafen (Lincoln: University of Nebraska Press, 2001). See Michelle Wick Patterson, "'Real' Indian Songs: The Society of American Indians and the Use of Native American Culture as a Means of Reform," *American Indian Quarterly* 26, 1 (2002): 44–66.

33. Major figures were Charles Eastman, Carlos Montezuma, and Arthur Parker, as well as Gertrude Bonnin/Zitkala Ša. For a survey of the movement, see Hazel W.

Hertzberg, *The Search for an American Identity: Modern Pan-Indian Movements* (Syracuse, N.Y.: Syracuse University Press, 1971).

34. Cari Carpenter, "Detecting Indianness: Gertrude Bonnin's Investigation of Native American Identity," *Wicazo Sa Review* (Spring 2005): 150.

35. Charles Alexander Eastman (Ohiyesa), *The Soul of the Indian: An Interpretation* (1911; repr., Lincoln: University of Nebraska Press, 1980), xi.

36. More positively, Scott Pratt argues that Eastman's stance was one of pluralism and compares it with William James and Dewey in its tolerance of different views without reducing them to one epistemological standard. "Wounded Knee and the Prospect of Pluralism," *Journal of Speculative Philosophy* 19, 2 (2005): 158–59.

37. Quoted in Richard J. Powell, *The Blues Aesthetic: Black Culture and Modernism* (Washington, D.C.: Washington Project for the Arts, 1989), 35. In Douglas's original unpublished manuscript, titled "The Harlem Renaissance," he has added, and then crossed out, "These later became early outlines of our spirituals, sorrow songs and blues." Unpublished MS, March 18, 1923, Special Collections, Fisk University Library, Nashville, Tennessee.

38. Quoted in Lemke, *Primitivist Modernism*, 50–51. Malgorzata Irek makes the point that the acquisition by Felix von Luschan of a huge collection of Benin objects made Berlin more influential than Paris. Luschan argued very early for such objects to be seen as art, and refused to use inverted commas around the word, but he did use them for words like "fetish," thus questioning the older European categories. "From Berlin to Harlem: Felix von Luschan, Alain Locke and The New Negro," in *The Black Columbiad: Defining Moments in African American Literature and Culture*, ed. Werner Sollors and Maria Diedrich (Cambridge, Mass.: Harvard University Press, 1994).

39. Quoted in Paul Allen Anderson, *Deep River: Music and Memory in Harlem Renaissance Thought* (Durham, N.C.: Duke University Press, 2001), 210.

40. Published in the same year, Rudolph Fisher's *The Conjure-Man Dies: A Mystery Tale of Dark Harlem* plays on the exoticisms of conjure and voodoo. (The phrase "Dark Harlem" is interesting in this respect.) The conjure man of the title calls himself a "psychist," and his office is described in exotic terms, but he is actually a mixture of cold intellect and African spirit. He is an African king, and we have a very melodramatic description of an African ritual. His belief in the power of the mind as well as material forces to determine events, and his urge to "harmonize psychology with material science," seems to reflect earlier spiritualist writings. *The Conjure-Man Dies: A Mystery Tale of Dark Harlem* (1932; repr., Ann Arbor: University of Michigan Press, 1992), 223, 214.

41. Leo Hamilian and James Vernon Hatch, eds., *Roots of African American Drama: An Anthology of Early Plays, 1858–1938* (Detroit: Wayne State University Press, 1972), 253.

42. Hamilian and Hatch, *Roots of African American Drama*, 261.

43. Gerald Horne, *Race Woman: The Lives of Shirley Graham Du Bois* (New York: New York University Press, 2000), 53, 58. Her father, a minister, went to work in Liberia, so she could be said to have more direct contacts than most (49–50).

44. John Cullen Gruesser, *Black on Black: Twentieth-Century African American Writing About Africa* (Lexington: University Press of Kentucky, 2000), 63.

45. Hamilian and Hatch, *Roots of African American Drama*, 262.

46. Horne, *Race Woman*, 77–78. See also Gruesser's *Black on Black*, which includes photographs of an early performance.

47. Lee Baker has outlined the power struggles within anthropology and the role of Boas, as well as the changing importance given to folklore. *From Savage to Negro: Anthropology and the Construction of Race, 1896–1954* (Berkeley and Los Angeles: University of California Press, 1998). The terms of the African survivals debate, originally characterized by the positions of E. Franklin Frazier and Melville Herskovits are well summa-

rized in Albert Raboteau, *Slave Religion: The "Invisible Institution" in the Antebellum South* (Oxford: Oxford University Press, 1978), 48–55.

48. Baker, *From Savage to Negro*, 144.

49. William S. Willis, Jr., "Franz Boas and the Study of Black Folklore," in *The New Ethnicity: Perspectives from Ethnology*, ed. John Bennett (St. Paul, Minn.: West Publishing, 1975), 327. See also Rosemary Levy Zumwalt, *American Folklore Scholarship: A Dialogue of Dissent* (Bloomington: Indiana University Press, 1988). Michael A. Elliot's *The Culture Concept: Writing and Difference in the Age of Realism* (Minneapolis: University of Minnesota Press, 2002) demonstrates the connections between literary realism and the developing idea of culture produced in Boasian anthropology and ethnographic texts. This focus allows Elliott some useful conjunctions of Indian and African folklore in discussions of Hurston, Chesnutt, and Zitkala Ša, among others.

50. Jon Cruz, *Culture on the Margins: The Black Spiritual and the Rise of American Cultural Interpretation* (Princeton, N.J.: Princeton University Press, 1999), 186.

51. Raboteau, *Slave Religion*, 59.

52. Dona Richards, for instance, expressing a later Afrocentric argument, claims that "Africa survived the middle passage, the slave experience, and other trials in America because of the depth and strength of African spirituality and humanism. This spirituality allowed the survival of African-Americans as a distinctive cultural entity in New Europe." "The Implications of African-American Spirituality," in *African Culture: The Rhythms of Unity*, ed. Molefi Kete Asante and Kariamu Welsh Asante (Trenton, N.J.: Africa World Press, 1990), 205. This spiritual capacity is seen to be in opposition to Western rationalism and secularism. "We are a spiritual people living in a profane society" (228).

53. Fauset's essay on "American Negro Folk Literature" is at pains to separate it out from the dominant influence of Joel Chandler Harris and to stress its communal and anonymous nature. While praising Harris's literary skills, he insists that the dominance given to the storyteller Uncle Remus "contorts the Negro folk tale from its true plane." Alain Locke, ed., *The New Negro* (1925; repr., New York: Simon and Schuster, 1992), 239. He argues that the teller of a folktale was "inconsequential" and "a talking machine might serve the purpose just as well," but his main objection is to the way that Remus is taken to represent a "composite picture of the ante-bellum Negro" that fits comfortably with white assumptions. He sees in the originals less humor and more "moralism, sober and almost grim," and "irony, shrewd and frequently subtle" (241). His own transcribed accounts, at least one of which is from a slave brought to America in 1859, adopt a similar vernacular style to Harris's, but appear to have less editorial shaping and include some untranslated (presumably African) words.

54. Locke, *New Negro*, 359. See Jerry Gershenhorn, *Melville J. Herskovits and the Racial Politics of Knowledge* (Lincoln: University of Nebraska Press, 2004), 63–64.

55. Carole H. Carpenter, "Arthur Huff Fauset, Campaigner for Social Justice: A Symphony of Diversity," in *African-American Pioneers in Anthropology*, ed. Ira E. Harrison and Faye W. Harrison (Urbana: University of Illinois Press, 1999).

56. Hazel Carby contrasts Hurston's approach and her avoidance of the class conflicts of the North with that of Jesse Redmon Fauset and Nella Larsen. She argues that in the search for a tradition connecting Alice Walker back to Hurston a pattern has been established that "represents the rural folk as bearers of Afro-American culture." This has "effectively marginalized the fictional urban confrontation of race, class and sexuality that was to follow *Quicksand*." Hazel V. Carby, "The Quicksands of Representation: Rethinking Black Cultural Politics," in *Reading Black, Reading Feminist: A Critical Anthology*, ed. Henry Louis Gates, Jr. (New York: Meridian, 1990), 88.

57. Hurston worked for Herskovits in the unlikely activity of measuring the heads of

the residents of Harlem. His purpose was to establish the degree of interracial mixing with whites and Indians in order to demonstrate that Negroes were in fact a race. This actually had liberal intentions, even though the methods were uncomfortably close to earlier experiments with racist ends. When she was first working with him he opposed the idea of African survivals, and it has been suggested that watching Hurston's distinctive motor behavior may have been one of the triggers leading Herskovits to change his views. Though he did not see these as physically determined racial traits, he did regard them as echoes and survivals that were passed down through communities in culture. See Gershenhorn, *Melville J. Herskovits*, 66.

58. Gwendolyn Mikell, "Feminism and Black Culture in the Ethnography of Zora Neale Hurston," in *African-American Pioneers in Anthropology*, ed. Ira E. Harrison and Faye W. Harrison (Urbana: University of Illinois Press, 1999), 56. See also Deborah Gordon, "The Politics of Ethnographic Authority: Race and Writing in the Ethnography of Margaret Mead and Zora Neale Hurston," in *Modernist Anthropology: From Fieldwork to Text*, ed. Marc Manganaro (Princeton, N.J.: Princeton University Press, 1990).

59. See Roseanne Hoefel, "'Different by Degree': Ella Cara Deloria, Zora Neale Hurston, and Franz Boas Contend with Race and Ethnicity," *American Indian Quarterly* 25, 2 (2001): 181–202. For Deloria, see Bea Medicine, "Ella Cara Deloria," in *Women Anthropologists: A Biographical Dictionary*, ed. Ute Gacs, Aisha Khan, Jerrie McIntyre, and Ruth Weinberg (New York: Greenwood Press, 1988), 45–50.

60. Carla Kaplan, ed. *Zora Neale Hurston: A Life in Letters* (New York: Doubleday, 2002), 97.

61. Hoefel, "'Different by Degree,'" 184, 191–94.

62. Kaplan, *Zora Neale Hurston: A Life in Letters*, 97. See also Mark Helbling, "'My Soul Was with the Gods and My Body in the Village': Zora Neale Hurston, Franz Boas, Melville Herskovits and Ruth Benedict," *Prospects* 22 (1997): 288–89.

63. Kaplan, *Zora Neale Hurston: A Life in Letters*, 129.

64. See the discussion of Boas's introduction to the volume, and Hurston's elaboration on it, in Brian Carr and Tova Cooper, "Zora Neale Hurston and Modernism at the Critical Limit," *Modern Fiction Studies* 48, 2 (2002): 296–97.

65. Kaplan, *Zora Neale Hurston: A Life in Letters*, 137–39.

66. See Pamela Borden, ed., *Go Gater and Muddy the Water: Writings by Zora Neale Hurston from the Federal Writers' Project* (New York: Norton, 1999) and David Kadlec, "Zora Neale Hurston and the Federal Folk," *Modernism/Modernity* 7, 3 (2000): 470–85.

67. This concern to bring out the completeness of the black world she is talking about goes along with what has been criticized as a pastoral impulse in her work, which directs it away from politics and modernity. Both Sterling Brown and Richard Wright expressed concern about the lack of any acknowledgment by Hurston of the presence of bitterness and violence in the society she portrays. See Robert E. Hemenway, *Zora Neale Hurston: A Literary Biography* (Urbana: University of Illinois Press, 1977), 219, 241.

68. Zora Neale Hurston, *Folklore, Memoirs, and Other Writings* (New York: Library of America, 1995), 981.

69. Zora Neale Hurston, "Hoodoo in America," *Journal of American Folklore* 44 (1931): 319.

70. Hurston, "Hoodoo in America," 319.

71. Jason Berry, *The Spirit of Black Hawk: A Mystery of Africans and Indians* (Jackson: University Press of Mississippi, 1995), 12.

72. Berry, *The Spirit of Black Hawk*, 29.

73. The second Marie Laveau was helped by "Doctor Jim," or "Indian Jim," who, according to Robert Tallant, was "three-quarters Indian, one-quarter Negro," and performed a dance that was "a bizarre combination of the Calinda and an Indian war dance,

performed in tights and with a candle balanced on his head." *Voodoo in New Orleans* (Gretna, La.: Pelican, 1998), 111–12. Berry sees the connection of Indians and African Americans as having a taproot in "a sense of mutual rebellion between two oppressed peoples of Louisiana, each with a spiritual past." Berry, *The Spirit of Black Hawk*, 105.

74. Berry, *The Spirit of Black Hawk*, 64.

75. Hurston, *Folklore, Memoirs, and Other Writings*, 856.

76. Hurston, *Folklore, Memoirs, and Other Writings*, 858.

77. Hurston, *Folklore, Memoirs, and Other Writings*, 855.

78. Hurston, *Folklore, Memoirs, and Other Writings*, 176, 177. See Theophus H. Smith, *Conjuring Culture: Biblical Formations of Black America* (New York: Oxford University Press, 1994), 32 for a discussion of this passage.

79. Hurston, *Folklore, Memoirs, and Other Writings*, 178.

80. Hurston, *Folklore, Memoirs, and Other Writings*, 188.

81. Hurston, *Folklore, Memoirs, and Other Writings*, 260. A similar view is found in Mary Owen's earlier account. To be "strong in de haid," and to have personal power, is more important than the actual mix of ingredients. "Never mind what you mix—blood, bones, feathers, grave-dust, herbs, saliva, or hair—it will be powerful or feeble for good or ill in proportion to the dauntless spirit infused by you, the priest or priestess, at the time you represent the god or 'Old Master.'" "Among the Voodoos," in *International Folklore Congress of 1891*, ed. Joseph Jacobs and Alfred Nutt (1892), 230. Owen's short piece makes an interesting comparison with Hurston. She does not pretend to have been initiated, and presents a predictably stereotyped view of the conjure man.

82. Hurston, *Folklore, Memoirs, and Other Writings*, 195.

83. Hemenway, *Zora Neale Hurston*, 123.

84. Carr and Cooper, "Zora Neale Hurston and Modernism," 302.

85. B. C. McNeil, "Review of *Mules and Men*," *Journal of Negro History* 21, 2 (1936): 225.

86. According to Wendy Dutton, the last things she wrote were on magic. See "The Problem of Invisibility: Voodoo and Zora Neale Hurston," *Frontiers: A Journal of Women's Studies* 13, 2 (1993): 131.

87. Quoted in Hemenway, *Zora Neale Hurston*, 246.

88. See Wade Davis, *Passage of Darkness: The Ethnobiology of the Haitian Zombie* (Chapel Hill: University of North Carolina Press, 1988), 32, and Dutton, "The Problem of Invisibility," 140.

89. For a sense of this, see Maya Deren, *Divine Horsemen: The Living Gods of Haiti* (London: Thames and Hudson, 1953). See also Moira Sullivan, "Maya Deren's Ethnographic Representation of Ritual and Myth in Haiti," in Nichols, *Maya Deren and the American Avant Garde*.

90. Katherine Dunham, *Island Possessed* (Chicago: University of Chicago Press, 1969), 105–6.

91. Dutton, "The Problem of Invisibility," 140.

92. Hurston, *Folklore, Memoirs, and Other Writings*, 397.

93. Hurston, *Folklore, Memoirs, and Other Writings*, 496.

94. See Leigh Ann Duck, "'Rebirth of a Nation': Hurston in Haiti," *Journal of American Folklore* 117 (2004): 127–46, who argues that the awkwardness of Hurston's position stems from the fact that, having celebrated racially identified cultures, she is altogether less happy when she finds this invocation of racial identity used in ways that ignore or mask issues of class, as she sees happening in Haiti. Annette Trefzer also sees Hurston as to some extent trapped within American rhetorical justifications for occupation, but she does also stress Hurston's recognition of the role of the experience and performance of spiritual possession in voodoo as a means of liberation from colonial enslave-

ment. "Possessing the Self: Caribbean Identities in Zora Neale Hurston's *Tell My Horse*," *African American Review* 34, 2 (2000): 299–312.

95. Gwendolyn Mikell, "When Horses Talk: Reflections on Zora Neale Hurston's Haitian Anthropology," *Phylon* 43 (1982): 219.

96. Hurston, *Folklore, Memoirs, and Other Writings*, 398.

97. Hurston, *Folklore, Memoirs, and Other Writings*, 376.

98. Hurston, *Folklore, Memoirs, and Other Writings*, 376.

99. Hurston, *Folklore, Memoirs, and Other Writings*, 530

100. Hurston, *Folklore, Memoirs, and Other Writings*, 427.

101. Martha Jane Nadell, *Enter the New Negroes: Images of Race in American Culture* (Cambridge, Mass.: Harvard University Press, 2004), 110.

102. Hurston, *Folklore, Memoirs, and Other Writings*, 456.

103. See Davis, *Passage of Darkness*, 66, 74. See also the more popularized account of his quest for the zombie poison, *The Serpent and the Rainbow* (London: Collins, 1986), 206–11. See Hans-W. Ackerman and Jeanine Gauthier, "The Ways and Nature of the Zombi," *Journal of American Folklore* 104 (1991): 466–93, which surveys the literature on the zombie, and stresses the widespread knowledge of the phenomenon in Africa as well as Haiti

104. Joan Dayan, *Haiti, History and the Gods* (Berkeley and Los Angeles, University of California Press, 1995), 37. Any fuller discussion of Haitian voodoo is beyond the range of this book, of course. I have retained the less accurate term "voodoo" as the more usual spelling, and the one used by Hurston.

105. Dayan, *Haiti, History and the Gods*, 72. For an account of a related use of the idea of the zombie in South Africa, which also links with Taussig's critique of the mystifications of capitalism, see Jean Comaroff and John Comaroff, "Alien-Nation: Zombies, Immigrants, and Millennial Capitalism," *South Atlantic Quarterly* 101, 4 (2002): 779–805.

106. Dayan, *Haiti, History and the Gods*, 36.

107. Dayan, *Haiti, History and the Gods*, 73–74.

108. Dayan, *Haiti, History and the Gods*, 53.

109. Wilson Jeremiah Moses dismisses the book as a sort of anti-Afrocentrism, comparing it to Ellen Watkins Harper's *Moses: A Story of the Nile* (1869). *Afrotopia: The Roots of African American Popular History* (Cambridge: Cambridge University Press, 1998), 207. In fact, Hurston is more complex than this. It is interesting that contemporary reviews did not even refer to the resonance of the use of Exodus material in spirituals or elsewhere. See Henry Louis Gates, Jr., and K. A. Appiah, eds., *Zora Neale Hurston: Critical Perspectives Past and Present* (New York: Amistad, 1993), 26–29.

110. Hemenway, *Zora Neale Hurston*, 263.

111. Zora Neale Hurston, *Moses, Man of the Mountain* (1939; repr., Urbana: University of Illinois Press, 1984), 147.

112. Hurston, *Folklore, Memoirs, and Other Writings*, 378. The widespread nature of such beliefs can be seen in a comment recorded in Georgia in 1940 from an octogenarion, to the effect that the same magic that Moses had used when he turned his rod to a snake before Pharoah still existed among Negroes. "Dat happen in Africa duh Bible say. Ain dat show dat Africa wuz a land uh magic powuh since de beginnin uh history? Well den, duh descendants ub Africans hab duh same gif to do unnatchul ting." Writers Program, *Drums and Shadows: Survival Studies Among the Georgia Coastal Negroes*, Savannah Unit, Georgia Writers' Project, foreword by Guy B. Johnson (1940; repr., Westport , Conn.: Greenwood Press, 1973), 28.

113. Hurston, *Moses, Man of the Mountain*, 289.

114. Hurston, *Moses, Man of the Mountain*, 171, 172.

115. Hurston, *Folklore, Memoirs, and Other Writings*, 931. Arthur Flowers sees his Viet-

nam vet character, HighJohn, in *De Mojo Blues: De Quest of HighJohn de Conqueror* (New York: E. P. Dutton, 1985) as a direct riposte to Hurston's accommodationist views. See also Patricia R. Schroeder, "Rootwork: Arthur Flowers, Zora Neale Hurston, and the 'Literary Hoodoo' Tradition," *African American Review* 36, 2 (2002): 271.

116. Hurston, *Folklore, Memoirs, and Other Writings*, 922, 923.

117. Eric J. Sundquist, *The Hammers of Creation: Folk Culture in Modern African-American Fiction* (Athens: University of Georgia Press, 1992), 69.

118. Zora Neale Hurston, *Jonah's Gourd Vine* (1934; repr., London: Virago Press, 1987), 59.

119. Hurston, *Folklore, Memoirs, and Other Writings*, 323.

120. Sundquist, *The Hammers of Creation*, 69.

121. Rhythm suggests an activityy rather than a thing, and Nathaniel Mackey makes the point that Hurston calls him "High John de Conquer," not Conqueror, thus exemplifying her own description in "Characteristics of Negro Expression" of the vernacular privileging of the verb over the noun. See Nathaniel Mackey, *Discrepant Engagement: Dissonance, Cross-Culturality, and Experimental Writing* (Cambridge: Cambridge University Press. 1993), 268.

Chapter 4

1. See Shelly Errington, *The Death of Primitive Art and Other Tales of Progress* (Berkeley and Los Angeles: University of California Press, 1998), 49–117. See also Marianna Torgovnick, *Gone Primitive: Savage Intellects, Modern Lives* (Chicago: University of Chicago Press, 1990), and Deborah Root, *Cannibal Culture: Art, Appropriation and the Commodification of Difference* (Boulder, Colo.: Westview Press, 1996).

2. See Stuart Levine, "Sacred Circles: Native American Art and Culture," *American Quarterly* 30 (1978): 108–23.

3. Jimmie Durham, *A Certain Lack of Coherence: Writings on Art and Cultural Politics* (London: Kala Press, 1993).

4. See Ronald Niezen, *Spirit Wars: Native North American Religions in the Age of Nation Building* (Berkeley and Los Angeles: University of California Press, 2000), 161–93.

5. Robert Colescott's two paintings *Les Demoiselles d'Alabama: Desnudas* and *Les Demoiselles d'Alabama: Vestidas* (1985) also closely imitate Picasso's original with subversive intent. Here he projects the sexuality and exoticism that Picasso had associated with Africa back on to Europe by making one of the women into a brassy blonde, and the conjunction of Spain, France, and America in the titles suggests an international and hybrid context in which the original painting and the ideological underpinnings of modernist primitivism can now be seen. See Sieglinde Lemke, *Primitivist Modernism: Black Culture and the Origins of Transatlantic Modernism* (Oxford: Oxford University Press, 1998), 56–57.

6. Maurice Berger, *Fred Wilson: Objects and Installations 1979–2000* (Baltimore: Center for Art and Visual Culture, University of Maryland, 2001), 14.

7. Berger, *Fred Wilson*, 37.

8. Wyatt MacGaffey and Michael D. Harris, eds., *Astonishment and Power* (Washington, D.C.; Smithsonian Institution, 1993), 89.

9. See the picture of a shrine in Eliza McFeeley, *Zuni and the American Imagination* (New York: Hill and Wang, 2001), 113. See also Niezen, *Spirit Wars*, 176.

10. William C. Seitz, *The Art of Assemblage* (New York: Museum of Modern Art, 1961), 6.

11. William Rubin, "Accumulation: Power and Display in African Sculpture," *Artforum* 13 (May 1975): 35–47.

12. It may also combine with Gates's idea of signifying to offer a way of exploring distinctive uses of reference or juxtaposition that are not critical or parodic. For an application of this to music, see Samuel A. Floyd, Jr., *The Power of Black Music: Interpreting Its History from Africa to the United States* (New York: Oxford University Press, 1995), 87–99.

13. David C. Driskell, ed., *African American Visual Aesthetics: A Postmodernist View* (Washington, D.C.: Smithsonian Institution, 1995), 19, 73. See also Judith McWillie et al., *Another Face of the Diamond: Pathways through the Black Atlantic South* (Atlanta: New Visions Gallery of Contemporary Art, 1989).

14. See Robert Farris Thompson, *Flash of the Spirit: African and Afro-American Art and Philosophy* (New York: Random House, 1984), and *The Four Moments of the Sun: Kongo Art in Two Worlds* (Washington, D.C.: National Gallery of Art, 1981).

15. Jane H. Carpenter with Betye Saar, *Betye Saar* (San Francisco: Pomegranate, 2003), 28.

16. Carpenter with Saar, *Betye Saar*, 30.

17. MacGaffey and Harris, *Astonishment and Power*, 33.

18. Mary Schmidt Campbell, *Tradition and Conflict: Images of a Turbulent Decade, 1963–1973* (New York: Studio Museum in Harlem, 1985), 59.

19. Quoted in Lucy R. Lippard, "Sapphire and Ruby in the Indigo Gardens," in *Secrets, Dialogues, Revelations: The Art of Betye and Alison Saar: Essays by Lucy R. Lippard, Ishmael Reed and Judith Wilson*, ed. Elizabeth Shepherd (Los Angeles: Wight Art Gallery, University of California, 1990), 11.

20. M. J. Hewitt, "Betye Saar, an Interview," *International Review of African American Art* 10, 2 (2004): 7, 8.

21. Hewitt, "Betye Saar," 21.

22. Hewitt, "Betye Saar," 3.

23. Hewitt, "Betye Saar," 20.

24. Ishmael Reed, "Saar Dust: An Interview with Betye Saar," in Shepherd, *Secrets, Dialogues, Revelations*, 36, 37.

25. Reed, "Saar Dust: An Interview with Betye Saar," 33. Elsewhere he comments that "hoodoo involved art, people made conjure balls, they made dolls, they used many techniques that we associate with the artist, in making what we call the grisgris. Hoodoo . . . was multimedia." Bruce Dick and Amritjit Singh, eds., *Conversations with Ishmael Reed* (Jackson: University of Mississippi Press, 1995), 54.

26. Reed, "Saar Dust: An Interview with Betye Saar," 33–34.

27. Ishmael Reed, *Conjure: Selected Poems, 1963–1970* (Amherst: University of Massachusetts Press, 1972), 26.

28. Robert Gover, "An Interview with Ishmael Reed," *Black American Literature Forum* 12 (1978): 13.

29. For a useful survey of the many other artists of mixed origins, see Juliette Harris, "The Black-Indian Connection in Art: American Portraits, Soulscapes and Spirit Works." *International Review of African American Art* 17, 1 (2000): 2–40.

30. Quoted in Reed, "Saar Dust: An Interview with Betye Saar," 34.

31. MacGaffey explicitly brings the terms together for discussion in his "African Objects and the Idea of the Fetish," *Res* 25 (1994): 123–31.

32. See Hazel V. Carby, *Race Men* (Cambridge, Mass.: Harvard University Press, 1998), 45–83; Gen Doy, *Black Visual Culture: Modernity and Postmodernity* (London: I. B. Tauris, 2000), 157–203; and Kobena Mercer, *Welcome to the Jungle: New Positions in Black Cultural Studies* (New York: Routledge, 1994), 171–219.

33. Michael D. Harris, "Resonance, Transformation and Rhyme: The Art of Renee Stout," in MacGaffey and Harris, *Astonishment and Power*, 124.

34. Steven Durland, "Call Me in '93': An Interview with James Luna," *High Performance* 56 (1991): 34–39.

35. MacGaffey and Harris, *Astonishment and Power*, 149.

36. Alvia J. Wardlaw and Robert V. Rozelle, eds., *Black Art, Ancestral Legacy: The African Impulse in African-American Art* (Dallas: Dallas Museum of Art, 1989), 293.

37. MacGaffey and Harris, *Astonishment and Power*, 146.

38. Reed, "Saar Dust: An Interview with Betye Saar," 20.

39. She makes the connection, in fact, through reading Tallant's unreliable and sensationalized account, *Voodoo in New Orleans* (Gretna, La.: Pelican, 1998). The parallels with Hurston's journey south reflect a general pattern in which New Orleans represents a spiritual center. Hurston wrote a critical review of Tallant's book.

40. Marla C. Berns, *Dear Robert, I'll See You at the Crossroads: A Project by Renee Stout* (Seattle: University of Washington Press, 1995), 34.

41. Berns, *Dear Robert*, 28.

42. Berns, *Dear Robert*, 25.

43. Berns, *Dear Robert*, 26.

44. Arthur Flowers, *Another Good Loving Blues* (London: Secker and Warburg, 1993), 122.

45. Flowers, *Another Good Loving Blues*, 123.

46. Flowers, *Another Good Loving Blues*, 120. For a discussion of the connection, see Patricia R. Schroeder, "Rootwork: Arthur Flowers, Zora Neale Hurston, and the 'Literary Hoodoo' Tradition," *African American Review* 36, 2 (2002): 263–72. In general Schroeder tends to assume that literary texts are the equivalent to hoodoo practices and does not really explore the implications of treating this connection as more than metaphorical.

47. Houston A. Baker, Jr., *Workings of the Spirit: The Poetics of Afro-American Women's Writing* (Chicago: University of Chicago Press, 1991), 66. Baker has been criticized in some quarters for the sort of privileging of black women that he advances in *Workings of the Spirit*, which is seen as essentializing and too close to earlier reductive treatments of the black female body as sites of subjectivity. See Sharon Patricia Holland, *Raising the Dead: Readings of Death and (Black) Subjectivity* (Durham, N.C.: Duke University Press, 2000), 161, who builds on earlier criticism of Baker from Mae Henderson. It could be argued, though, that some of the writing by women themselves is open to the same charge. In Gloria Naylor's *Mama Day*, for instance, we have two elderly women who practice what seems to be traditional conjure, though it is not named as such. Their power is presented as benign, and they mostly seem to operate as herbalists and wise women, who even have the tacit approval of the white doctor. They need to use their powers to exorcise evil, and doing this involves sacrificing the life of a young man in order to save the life of the novel's protagonist, Cocoa. While what the old ladies practice is not given a name, a neighbor, who is referred to as a hoodoo man, is presented negatively as something of an imposter who relies mechanically on charms and roots. Such is the celebratory view of women's powers in the book that it comes as no surprise that the negative aspects of conjure are shown in a man, and in fact Naylor's book can be seen as exemplifying Baker's argument about women's "spirit-work," at least as well as—and perhaps more programmatically than—the novels he chooses for his study. For a more positive view of the novel, which links it with conjure traditions and literary treatments, see Lindsey Tucker, "Recovering the Conjure Woman: Texts and Contexts in Gloria Naylor's *Mama Day*," *African American Review* 28, 2 (1994): 173–88. Naylor's novel does reflect quite a widespread positive treatment of women's spiritual powers, an

approach that can produce predictably themed work. Bertice Berry's *The Haunting of Hip Hop* (New York: Broadway Books, 2001), for instance, describes the appearance of spirit figures with a drum who have come from the past to warn of the false directions being taken by the protagonist in his music. There are, of course, exceptions. Rainelle Burton's *The Root Worker*, for example, gives an entirely negative view of rootwork, which is shown as exacerbating rather than remedying the abusive relationships within the book. In an interview in a readers' guide included with the novel, Burton describes rootwork as "a corrupt form of beliefs and rites that were—and are still—used by opportunists to feed on human suffering, despair, and hopelessness." *The Root Worker* (New York: Penguin, 2001), 4.

48. Baker, *Workings of the Spirit*, 61, 66.

49. Baker, *Workings of the Spirit*, 66.

50. Baker, *Workings of the Spirit*, 99.

51. Baker, *Workings of the Spirit*, 93–94.

52. Houston A. Baker, Jr., *Afro-American Poetics: Revisions of Harlem and the Black Aesthetic* (Madison: University of Wisconsin Press, 1988), 101. Toomer's own later development into belief in a more universalized and less racially and culturally rooted idea of spirit, which he found in Gurdjieff and later in the Quakers, would seem to take him away from Baker's model here.

53. Jean Toomer, *Cane* (1923; repr., New York: Norton, 1988), 12; Baker, *Afro-American Poetics*, 26.

54. Baker, *Afro-American Poetics*, 108.

55. Baker, *Afro-American Poetics*, 102, 107.

56. Art Lange and Nathaniel Mackey, eds., *Moment's Notice: Jazz in Poetry and Prose* (Minneapolis: Coffee House Press, 1993), 250–51. See also the use made of the Hawkins recording in Jayne Cortez's poem, "No Simple Explanations," which is dedicated to Larry Neal, in *Jazz Fan Looks Back* (Brooklyn, N.Y.: Hanging Loose Press, 2002), 42.

57. Ronald M. Radano, "Soul Texts and the Blackness of Folk," *Modernism/Modernity* 2, 1 (1995): 72, 73.

58. Amiri Baraka, *Black Music* (New York: Apollo, 1968), 193. The ways in which the word "soul" took on particular connotations in the 1960 have been traced in recent accounts. Paul Gilroy indicates some of its resonances. "For me, the value of soul and the idea of soul is that they mark that realm which resists the reach of economic rationality and the commodifying process. Soul is a mark of how that precious, wonderful, expressive culture stands outside of commodification, how those cultural processes and the history in which they stand have resisted being reduced to the status of a thing that can be sold." "Questions of a 'Soulful Style': Interview with Paul Gilroy," in *Soul: Black Power, Politics and Pleasures*, ed., Monique Guillory and Richard C. Green (New York: New York University Press, 1998), 251.

59. This could present a problem for the later Marxist and materialist Baraka, though it could presumably be seen as a form of utopian thinking that at least keeps in the culture an idea of something beyond what currently exists.

60. Hugh Ragin, *An Afternoon in Harlem* (Montreal: Justin Time, 1998).

61. These two aspects of music, the rooting in experience and the capacity to aspire to something else, have been identified by Craig Werner in two strands of music, so that "clarifying realities" is represented by the blues and "envisioning possibilities" is represented by gospel. Craig Hansen Werner, *Playing the Changes: From Afro-Modernism to the Jazz Impulse* (Urbana: University of Illinois Press, 1994), 269. Clearly it is reductive to make too categorical a distinction, the point often being the inextricability of the two aspects, as Graham Lock brings out so clearly in his study *Blutopia: Visions of the Future*

and Revisions of the Past in the Work of Sun Ra, Duke Ellington, and Anthony Braxton (Durham, N.C.: Duke University Press, 1999).

62. Quoted in Nathaniel Mackey, *Discrepant Engagement: Dissonance, Cross-Culturality, and Experimental Writing* (Cambridge: Cambridge University Press), 46.

63. Larry Neal, *Hoodoo Hollerin' Bebop Ghosts* (Washington, D.C.: Howard University Press, 1974), 37.

64. Reginald Martin, "An Interview with Ishmael Reed," *Review of Contemporary Fiction* 4, 2 (1984): 184.

65. Sami Ludwig compares the way that language "informs" or inhabits us and even speaks through us, as well as being spoken, with the *loa*, who rides the "horse" and uses it, but who can also be used by the *houngan* for his own ends. Ludwig sees Reed as the conjurer, or *houngan*, who can control the *loas* (and language) as well as be possessed by them and argues that Reed extends this idea of loas to other things that inhabit us and take our power, like governments and corporations. Reed thereby is able to historicize and make available for use what is otherwise seen as transcendent. Sami Ludwig, "Dialogic Possession in Ishmael Reed's *Mumbo Jumbo*: Bakhtin, Voodoo, and the Materiality of Multicultural Discourse," in *The Black Columbiad: Defining Moments in African American Literature and Culture*, ed. Werner Sollors and Maria Diedrich (Cambridge, Mass.: Harvard University Press, 1994), 329.

66. Ishmael Reed, *Mumbo Jumbo* (London: Allison and Busby, 1988), 45.

67. James Weldon Johnson, ed., *The Book of American Negro Poetry*, rev. ed. (New York: Harcourt, Brace and World, 1959), 12. He in turn, of course, takes the term from Harriet Beecher Stowe's phrase to describe Topsy, who "jes grew."

68. Reed, *Mumbo Jumbo*, 162.

69. Reed, *Mumbo Jumbo*, 183.

70. Reed, *Mumbo Jumbo*, 6.

71. A quite different work, but one that also centers on a spirit quintessentially found or symbolized in music, is Toni Morrison's *Jazz*. It too invokes an indefinable spirit and rhythm, "the click of dark and snapping fingers," which drives life in the Harlem of the twenties forward. In Morrison's case the connections with music are strong but more general, and there is not the use of magic, which connects Reed not only back to Hurston's engagement but to the use in the 1970s of black magic as part of a Black Aesthetic.

72. Reed, *Mumbo Jumbo*, 64.

73. One example, which is sufficiently extreme that it would fit into Reed's comic world almost without change, can be found in a collection of essays from the 1930s from a Roman Catholic columnist, Sir Richard Terry, who felt it necessary to warn his readers of the "subversive influences" within modern music. Modern society, which has degenerated with the decline in Christian belief and the rise of "paganism" is now dangerously vulnerable, and "the White races are just now submerged in a spate of negroid sentiment. 'Hot Jazz,' Fox-trots and Black Bottoms occupy the young folk." Having personal experience of the West Indies he particularly fears the way that "the tired Europe of the twentieth century" is flirting with "degenerate cults," including Voodoo, which use music like jazz as an adjunct. He sees "the white races of two continents succumbing to a musical atmosphere from which intellect has been banished and the senses reign supreme." Unfortunately the "animal noises" and "bizarrerie" are not seen as the threat they really are. "Our healthy-minded English lads and lasses see nothing more in this than a joke. Those of us who have heard and seen 'the real thing' [West Indian voodoo] are in a position to say the 'joke' is a dangerous one." Richard R. Terry, *Voodooism in Music and Other Essays* (London: Burns Oates and Washbourne, 1934), 4, 8, 13, 14.

74. Reed, *Mumbo Jumbo*, 15.

75. Reed, *Mumbo Jumbo*, 152.

76. Mackey, *Discrepant Engagement*, 43.

77. Nathaniel Mackey, *Eroding Witness* (Urbana: University of Illinois Press, 1985), 50. The first letters actually appeared in this collection of poetry, before the novels themselves developed.

78. Mackey does not refer to Derrida, but his work probably offers the most sustained critique of presence that runs parallel to Mackey's.

79. Mackey, *Discrepant Engagement*, 285.

80. Mackey, *Discrepant Engagement*, 275.

81. Mackey, *Eroding Witness*, 54.

82. Saidiya Hartman, *Scenes of Subjection: Terror, Slavery and Self-Making in Nineteenth-Century America* (New York: Oxford University Press, 1997), 74. See also Adam Gussow, *Seems like Murder Here: Southern Violence and the Blues Tradition* (Chicago: University of Chicago Press, 2002), who also uses Hartman.

83. Behind his thinking is a tradition of Marxist critique from Lukács, which includes Frederic Jameson and Michael Taussig. He cites with approval Taussig's *The Devil and Commodity Fetishism in South America*, which itself leads back to Lukács's account of the phantom objectivity created by capitalist commodity-based societies. Taussig focuses on the crossing points between capitalist and noncapitalist peasant societies and the ways in which native supernatural beliefs embody perceptions about the new society that are closed off to it by its own apparent rationality. Taussig is useful to Mackey in demonstrating that what is preserved in beliefs that are dismissed as irrational or superstitious may be an acute critique of capitalism, and one that is unavailable to us precisely because we have ourselves mystified the relation of matter and spirit. It is interesting that the image of the phantom limb is used in another celebrated account of the clash of material and spiritual in capitalism. In *Moby Dick*, Ahab gets the carpenter to put his own leg in the place where Ahab's leg used to be, and where he still feels his leg. "So, now, here is only one distinct leg to the eye yet two to the soul." From this he generalizes to a larger connection between material and spiritual. "How dost thou know that some entire, living, thinking thing may not be invisibly and uninterpenetratingly standing precisely where thou now standest?" In the novel, Ahab's monomaniac quest for an absolute is disastrous, but Melville's account is still ultimately a critique of the material limitations of the factory ship and more broadly of the growing materialism that becomes itself a sort of transcendental absolutism while obliterating others. The book is ultimately critical of the dualism that created the peculiar distortions of both material and spiritual so that they are both empty and destructive, unlike the unity of them in the body, as exemplified in Queequeg's body.

84. Mackey, *Discrepant Engagement*, 236.

85. Mackey, *Discrepant Engagement*, 235. Mackey's explorations here anticipate the more recent discussion of cultural haunting referred to in Chapter 2, though his criticism has been surprisingly neglected. While the idea of a missing limb operates here to suggest a spiritual absence, we find an interestingly different approach in the Ojibway writer Gordon Henry, Jr.'s *The Light People*, where we have not a missing limb, but an actual severed limb discovered and exhibited in a museum. The limb was amputated after frostbite and was not buried, as intended, but left in a tree. Henry's story explores the disciplinary impulses that lead to the categorization of the limb by the museum, once it finds its way there, as evidence of past Indian practices. It becomes part of a whole created by the discipline of ethnography, not of the original Ojibway man and his community.

86. As Devin Johnston puts it, "These figures of ghostliness and absence and incompletion are meant to suggest a spiritual supplement to the world that both invests it with a certain urgency and divests it of any ultimacy." "Nathaniel Mackey and Lost Time: 'The Phantom Light of All Our Day,'" *Callaloo* 32, 2 (2000): 5.

87. Mackey, *Eroding Witness*, 17.

88. Mackey, *Discrepant Engagement*, 232.

89. See Lawrence W. Levine, *Black Culture and Black Consciousness: Afro-American Folk Thought from Slavery to Freedom* (New York: Oxford University Press, 1977), 9–55.

90. Nathaniel Mackey, *Bedouin Hornbook* (Los Angeles: Sun and Moon Press, 1997), 25.

91. Mackey, *Bedouin Hornbook*, 115–16.

92. Mackey, *Bedouin Hornbook*, 118.

93. Nathaniel Mackey, *Atet A.D* (San Francisco: City Lights, 2001), 121.

94. Mackey, *Bedouin Hornbook*, 62, 63.

95. Nathaniel Mackey, "Cante Moro," in *Sound States: Innovative Poetics and Acoustical Technologies*, ed. Adalaide Morris (Chapel Hill: University of North Carolina Press, 1997), 205.

96. Mackey, *Eroding Witness*, 73.

97. Mackey, "Cante Moro," 203. The reference to a leaking of sound here might recall the hostile criticism of Coltrane, of whom one critic said that "his horn actually sounds as if it is in need of repair." Quoted in Cuthbert O. Simpkins, *Coltrane: A Biography* (Perth Amboy, N.J.: Herndon House, 1975), 157.

98. Nathaniel Mackey, *Whatsaid Serif* (San Francisco: City Lights, 1998), 22.

99. Mackey, *Whatsaid Serif*, 100.

100. Olly Wilson, "The Heterogeneous Sound Ideal in African-American Music," in *Signifyin(g), Sanctifyin', and Slam Dunking: A Reader in African American Expressive Culture*, ed. Gena Dagel Caponi (Amherst: University of Massachusetts Press, 1999).

101. Marcel Griaule, *Conversations with Ogotemmêli: An Introduction to Dogon Religious Studies* (London: Oxford University Press, 1965), 28, 29, 73. Mackey does not comment on the problems in using a text created out of a colonial encounter, in which the white anthropologist has shaped the text, and probably some of the conceptions within it. See James Clifford, "Power and Dialogue in Ethnography," in his *Predicament of Culture: Twentieth-Century Ethnography, Literature and Art* (Cambridge, Mass.: Harvard University Press, 1988). For an ethnographic reassessment of the fieldwork, see Walter E. A. van Beek, "Dogon Re-studied: A Field Evaluation of the Work of Marcel Griaule," *Current Anthropology* 32, 2 (1991): 139–67.

102. Mackey, *Discrepant Engagement*, 19.

103. Mackey, "Cante Moro," 201.

104. It is interesting to note that in one of the most imaginative and articulate jazz autobiographies, Sidney Bechet describes a similarly unsettling compulsion. "So many of [the musicians] had something inside them and it wouldn't let them rest. It was like there was something in that song deeper than a man could hear, something he could hear calling from the bottom of his dreams. . . . It was that stirring, all that night sound there was at the bottom of the song all that long way back making itself heard." Sidney Bechet, *Treat It Gentle: An Autobiography* (1960; repr., New York: Da Capo Press, 1978), 204.

105. Mackey, "Cante Moro," 195.

106. Ralph Waldo Ellison, *Collected Essays* (New York: Modern Library, 1995), 8, 10, 11.

Chapter 5

1. See Elijah Wald, *Escaping the Delta: Robert Johnson and the Invention of the Blues* (New York: Harper Collins, 2004), for an overview of the creation of the legend. Though the crossroads metaphor has clear African antecedents, the Faustian pact with the devil also

suggests a European and Christian input that is often ignored. Only Greil Marcus sees it as related to Puritan traditions, and as an element within Johnson. Greil Marcus, *Mystery Train: Images of Rock 'n' Roll Music* (New York: Dutton, 1975).

2. Sherman Alexie, *Reservation Blues* (London: Minerva Press, 1996), 40–41.

3. Alexie, *Reservation Blues*, 296.

4. Alexie, *Reservation Blues*, 175–76.

5. Leslie Marmon Silko, "Bingo Big." *Nation*, June 12, 1995: 859. She also mentions that her favorite Alexie story is "Because My Father Always Said He Was the Only Indian Who Saw Jimi Hendrix Play 'The Star-Spangled Banner' at Woodstock," indicating the interest in cultural mixtures explored in her own work.

6. Alexie, *Reservation Blues*, 174.

7. Douglas Ford, "Sherman Alexie's Indigenous Blues," *Melus* 27, 3 (2002): 210.

8. Alexie, *Reservation Blues*, 306.

9. Ford, "Sherman Alexie's Indigenous Blues," 250.

10. Hal Zina Bennett, *Zuni Fetishes: Using American Objects for Meditation, Reflection and Insight* (New York: Harper Collins, 1993), 14.

11. See Kay Whittle, *Native American Fetish Carvings of the Southwest* (Altglen, Pa.: Schiffer, 1998), and Oscar T. Branson, *Fetishes and Carvings of the Southwest* (Santa Fe, N. Mex.: Treasure Chest Publications, 1976). Charlotte J. Frisbie describes finding in a Santa Fe pawnshop "a small plastic pill bottle labelled 'Tatadeen Fetish Food.' The typed label went on to say 'gathered from corn pollen in Chinle, Arizona by Hosteen John Begay. Feed to your fetish (not included) twice a year.'" This was on sale next to fetishes and medicine pouches made from bearskin and "decorated with chicken and rabbit bones and colored plastic beads." All were selling well. *Navajo Medicine Bundles or Jish: Acquisition, Transmission, and Disposition in the Past and Present* (Albuquerque: University of New Mexico Press, 1987), 454 note 4.

12. Philip J. Deloria, *Playing Indian* (New Haven, Conn.: Yale University Press, 1998), 177.

13. Vine Deloria, Jr., *For This Land: Writings on Religion in America*, ed. James Treat (New York: Routledge, 1999), 265. See also Lisa Aldred, "Plastic Shamans and Astroturf Sun Dances," *American Indian Quarterly* 24, 3 (2000): 329–52, who sees the New Age as primarily a consumerist movement. Laura E. Donaldson has also given an incisive account of the disparate collection of objects from different cultures invoked by the would-be shaman Lynn Andrews. Against such blatant and indiscriminate appropriation she argues the case for the nonexchangeability of cultural property. Thus "the decolonizing work of antifetishism demands nothing less than complete repatriation: the returning of Spider Woman and all her counterparts to their rightful places within Native cultures." "On Medicine Women and White Shame-ans: New Age Native Americanism and Commodity Fetishism as Pop Culture Feminism," *Signs: Journal of Women in Culture and Society* 24, 3 (1999): 693. For a less critical view, see Amanda Porterfield, "American Indian Spirituality as a Countercultural Movement," in *Religion in Native North America*, ed. Christopher Vecsey (Moscow: University of Idaho Press, 1990), who compares the new proponents of Indian spirituality with earlier revitalization movements in the way that they combine elements of white and Indian religions to mount a critique of American culture and its materialism. Though she at one point distinguishes the modern emphasis on nature from the "frankly magical supernaturalism" (160) of earlier prophets, which claimed to have real practical efficacy, she does not really question the term "spirituality" itself.

14. Brad Steiger, *Totems: The Transformative Power of Your Personal Animal Totem* (New York: Harper Collins 1997), 91, 95.

15. Paul Carter Harrison, ed., *Totem Voices: Plays from the Black World Repertory* (New York: Grove Press, 1989), xx.

16. Though Pollock was influenced in other works by Navajo sandpaintings and Northwest Coast Indian art, these particular totem paintings seem to invoke not so much any Indian tradition as a universal psychological level of archetypes following Freud or Jung. See Daniel Belgrad, *The Culture of Spontaneity: Improvisation and the Arts in Postwar America* (Chicago: University of Chicago Press, 1998), 66–67.

17. For a brief summary of the issues, see my account in Eric Cheyfiz, ed., *The Columbia History of Native American Literature in the US since 1945* (New York: Columbia University Press, 2006).

18. Ed McGaa (Eagle Man), *Mother Earth Spirituality: Native American Paths to Healing Ourselves and Our World* (New York: Harper Collins, 1990), 45.

19. Rev. Steve Charleston, "The Old Testament of Native America," in *Native and Christian: Indigenous Voices on Religious Identity in the United States and Canada*, ed. James Treat (New York: Routledge, 1996), 72. See also Paul B. Steinmetz, "The New Missiology and Black Elk's Individuation," in *The Black Elk Reader*, ed. Clyde Holler (Syracuse, N.Y.: Syracuse University Press, 2000).

20. Rev. Steven Charleston, "From Medicine Man to Marx: The Coming Shift in Native Theology," in *Native American Religious Identity: Unforgotten Gods*, ed. Jace Weaver (Mary Knoll, N.Y.: Orbis Books 1998), 158.

21. Charleston, "From Medicine Man to Marx," 167.

22. The essay was used against him and selectively circulated by the FBI, and he has since expressed some regrets about the overtly leftist terminology used to express Indian ideas. Jimmie Durham, *A Certain Lack of Coherence: Writings on Art and Cultural Politics* (London: Kala Press, 1993), 15–19.

23. Viola F. Cordova, "The European Concept of *Usen*: An American Aboriginal Text," in *Native American Religious Identity: Unforgotten Gods*, ed. Jace Weaver (Mary Knoll, N.Y.: Orbis Books, 1998), 27–28.

24. A more cautious approach to the equating of different Indian religions comes from Dennis McPherson and Douglas Rabb, when they question the easy equation of Manitou, *wakan*, and *orenda*. They move beyond the linguistic, not into an inexpressible sublime, but into different forms of cultural experience and expectation. In the process they want to expand the idea of the religious and spiritual beyond the prevailing image of spirituality. "Transformative Philosophy and Indigenous Thought: A Comparison of Lakota and Ojibwa World Views," *Papers of the Algonquian Conference* 29 (1997): 202–10.

25. Paula Gunn Allen expressed doubts about her use of traditional knowledge. See Silko's brief response in Ellen Arnold, "Listening to the Spirits: An Interview with Leslie Silko," *Studies in American Literatures* 10, 3 (1998): 16.

26. Leslie Marmon Silko, *Almanac of the Dead* (New York: Penguin, 1992), 33.

27. Ami Regier, "Material Points of Self and Other: Fetish Discourses and Leslie Marmon Silko's Evolving Conception of Cross-Cultural Narrative," in *Leslie Marmon Silko: A Collection of Critical Essays*, ed. K. Barnett and James L. Thorson (Albuquerque: University of New Mexico Press, 1999), 190.

28. Silko, *Almanac of the Dead*, 478.

29. Silko, *Almanac of the Dead*, 520.

30. See, for instance, Marx's discussions of alienated labor in his early "Economic and Political Manuscripts," repr. in Jon Elster, ed., *Karl Marx: A Reader* (Cambridge: Cambridge University Press, 1986), 35–46. For a critique, see Jean Baudrillard, *For a Critique of the Political Economy of the Sign* (St. Louis: Telos Press, 1981).

31. Regier, "Material Points of Self and Other," 195.

32. Michael T. Taussig, *Shamanism, Colonialism, and the White Man: A Study in Terror and*

Healing (Chicago: University of Chicago Press, 1987), 5. See also Kenneth Surin, "Transform the World, Change Life: Michael Taussig's Poetics of Destruction and Revelation," *South Atlantic Quarterly* 92, 2 (1993): 264.

33. Silko, *Almanac of the Dead*, 512.

34. Silko, *Almanac of the Dead*, 722.

35. Silko, *Almanac of the Dead*, 478.

36. Silko, *Almanac of the Dead*, 417.

37. See also Joseph Roach, *Cities of the Dead: Circum-Atlantic Performance* (New York: Columbia University Press, 1996). Roach suggestively brings together the Ghost Dance, the Mardi Gras performances, and voodoo (202–11). The tradition of the parades also makes an appearance in Ishmael Reed's *Shrovetide in Old New Orleans* (New York: Doubleday, 1978).

38. Ellen L. Arnold, ed., *Conversations with Leslie Marmon Silko* (Jackson: University Press of Mississippi, 2000), 154, 187. There are interesting similarities between Clinton and the Vietnam vet protagonist of Arthur Flowers's *De Mojo Blues: De Quest of HighJohn de Conqueror*, who also wants to find a form of revolutionary healing. His initiation into hoodoo gives him a power that by the end of the novel he seems to be about to use to effect large-scale social change. At one low point he wonders about himself, in terms relevant to my later discussion of Silko, "Is he for real, or just megalomaniacing? Was he just ghostdancing his people down a hardroad to genocide?" (194).

39. Silko, *Almanac of the Dead*, 735.

40. Silko, *Almanac of the Dead*, 742.

41. Silko, *Almanac of the Dead*, 747.

42. Joy Harjo's poem "Reconciliation, a Prayer," read at a memorial for Audre Lorde, is an interesting but fairly unusual expression of common ground. See *Religion and Literature* 26, 1 (1994): 55–64, for the poem and an interview in which she discusses it.

43. Silko, *Almanac of the Dead*, 763. Silko writes of this actual event and the Laguna reactions to it in "Fifth World: The Return of Ma-ah-shra-truee, the Giant Spirit," in *Yellow Woman and a Beauty of the Spirit: Essays on Native American Life Today* (New York: Simon and Schuster, 1996). In the novel, she changes the direction in which the serpent's head is pointing from west to south.

44. Sven Birkerts, quoted in Caren Irr, "The Timeliness of *Almanac of the Dead*, or a Postmodern Rewriting of Radical Fiction," in *Leslie Marmon Silko*, ed. Barnett and Thornton, 223.

45. David L. Moore, "Return of the Buffalo: Cultural Representation as Cultural Property," in *Native American Representations: First Encounters, Distorted Images and Literary Appropriations*, ed. Gretchen M. Bataille (Lincoln: University of Nebraska Press, 2001), 56.

46. Quoted in Moore, "Return of the Buffalo," 63.

47. Silko commented in an interview that she wanted her characters to come from "one of those remnant, destroyed, extinct groups," and had invented this name to represent such a group. See Arnold, *Conversations with Leslie Marmon Silko*, 164.

48. Recent postcolonial celebration of syncretism tends not even to acknowledge what a controversial term this has been in anthropology because of the tendency in the past to efface the damage done to native cultures in the process of forced change, or even to equate such changes with progress toward the values of the dominant civilization.

49. Ami Regier, "Revolutionary Enunciatory Spaces: Ghost Dancing, Transatlantic Travel, and Modernist Arson," *Modern Fiction Studies* 51, 1 (2005): 135.

50. In an interview, Silko mentions an actual Ghost Dance that took place in 1893 in Kingman, which she moves in her novel to Needles.

51. James Mooney, quoted in David W. Stowe, *How Sweet the Sound: Music in the Spiritual Lives of Americans* (Cambridge, Mass.: Harvard University Press, 2004), 128. Stowe's

account of the Ghost Dance and its songs brings out the movement's syncretism and Mooney's reactions.

52. James Mooney, *The Ghost-Dance Religion and Wounded Knee* (1896), abridged ed. (Chicago: Chicago University Press, 1965), 1.

53. Michael A. Elliott, *The Culture Concept: Writing and Difference in the Age of Realism* (Minneapolis: University of Minnesota Press, 2002), 89–123.

54. Mooney, *The Ghost-Dance Religion*, 18, 187.

55. In an exchange with a Cherokee shaman, having passed himself off as a "great conjurer," he is asked for help and is forced to perform. He then "with very impressive ceremonies recited some Gaelic formulas while walking in a circle in the orthodox manner." L. G. Moses, *The Indian Man: A Biography of James Mooney* (Urbana: University of Illinois Press, 1984), 24.

56. See Michael Hittman, *Wovoka and the Ghost Dance* (Lincoln: University of Nebraska Press, 1990).

57. Alice C. Fletcher, "The Indian Messiah," *Journal of American Folklore* 4, 12 (1891): 59–60.

58. See Ronald Niezen, *Spirit Wars: Native North American Religions in the Age of Nation Building* (Berkeley and Los Angeles: University of California Press, 2000), 132.

59. William Welles Newell, "Second Annual Meeting of the American Folklore Society," *Journal of American Folklore* 4, 12 (1891): 6.

60. Leslie Marmon Silko, *Gardens in the Dunes* (New York: Simon and Schuster, 1999), 362.

61. Silko, *Gardens in the Dunes*, 239, 253.

62. In "An Essay on Rocks," she describes a mysterious black shape seen from a distance and her investigation of it. When she finds it, it turns out to be "only a black rock the size of an auto engine alone in the middle of the arroyo half buried in white sand," but she also uses photographs in the essay, and in linked essays she explores the peculiar powers or "magic" of photography, by which it can bring out electromagnetic or other connections between the object and the photographer. For a useful discussion, see Brewster E. Fitz, *Silko: Writing Storyteller and Medicine Woman* (Norman: University of Oklahoma Press, 2004), 31–48.

63. Silko, *Yellow Woman*, 27.

64. Arnold, *Conversations with Leslie Silko*, 166.

65. Silko, *Gardens in the Dunes*, 321.

66. To give the sense of Hattie's shock of recognition, she actually draws on some later discoveries of the Gnostic Gospels at Nag Hammadi in the 1940s, using Elaine Pagels's influential book based largely on these discoveries. See Elaine Pagels, *The Gnostic Gospels* (New York: Random House, 1979). See also Arnold, *Conversations with Leslie Silko*, 164. In fact, though, her account of Hattie's developing ideas is not so anachronistic as this might suggest. There was already an interest in the nineteenth century in those Gnostic materials that were then available, and by the end of the century new discoveries were much debated, both on the fringes of the academy and within it. Silko's account of what Hattie finds in the Coptic scrolls of Dr. Rhinehart, and of the dispute over their authenticity is therefore plausible, as is her account of Hattie having devoured all the mythology she could find before her time at Harvard.

67. Fitz, *Silko: Writing Storyteller*, 211.

68. Regier, "Revolutionary Enunciatory Spaces," 144.

69. Silko, *Yellow Woman*, 144.

Bibliography

Ackerman, Hans-W., and Jeanine Gauthier. "The Ways and Nature of the Zombi." *Journal of American Folklore* 104 (1991): 466–93.

Acosta, Joseph de. *The Natural and Moral History of the Indies.* Repr. from the English edition, trans. Edward Grimston, 1604. Ed. Clement R. Markham. London: Hakluyt Society, 1880.

Aldred, Lisa. "Plastic Shamans and Astroturf Sun Dances." *American Indian Quarterly* 24, 3 (2000): 329–52.

Alexander, Hartley Burr. *The Religious Spirit of the American Indian: As Shown in the Development of His Religious Rites and Customs.* Chicago: Open Court, 1910.

———. *The World's Rim: Great Mysteries of the North American Indians.* Lincoln: University of Nebraska Press, 1953.

Alexie, Sherman. *Reservation Blues.* London: Minerva Press, 1996.

Anderson, Paul Allen. *Deep River: Music and Memory in Harlem Renaissance Thought.* Durham, N.C.: Duke University Press, 2001.

Andrews, William L. *The Literary Career of Charles W. Chesnutt.* Baton Rouge: Louisiana State University Press, 1980.

Anonymous. "Concerning Negro Sorcery in the United States." *Journal of American Folklore* 3, 11 (1890): 281–87.

Anonymous. "Is Everybody Superstitious?" *Harper's Weekly,* October 21, 1893: 1012–17.

Apess, William. *A Son of the Forest and Other Writings.* Ed. Barry O'Connell. Amherst: University of Massachusetts Press, 1997.

Arnold, Ellen L., ed. *Conversations with Leslie Marmon Silko.* Jackson: University Press of Mississippi, 2000.

———. "Listening to the Spirits: An Interview with Leslie Silko." *Studies in American Literatures* 10, 3 (1998): 1–33.

Atkins, John. *A Voyage to Guinea, Brazil, and the West Indies in His Majesty's Ships the Swallow and the Weymouth.* London, 1735.

Austin, Mary. *The American Rhythm: Studies and Reexpressions of Amerindian Songs.* 1930. Repr., New York: Cooper Square Publishers, 1970.

———. "The Path on the Rainbow." 1918. Repr. in *Literature of the American Indians: Views and Interpretations,* ed. Abraham Chapman. New York: New American Library, 1975.

Baer, Florence E. *Sources and Analogues of the Uncle Remus Tales.* FFC, no. 228. Helsinki: Suomalainene Tiedeakatemia, 1980.

Baker, Houston A., Jr. *Afro-American Poetics: Revisions of Harlem and the Black Aesthetic.* Madison: University of Wisconsin Press, 1988.

————. *Workings of the Spirit: The Poetics of Afro-American Women's Writing.* Chicago: University of Chicago Press, 1991.

Baker, Lee D. *From Savage to Negro: Anthropology and the Construction of Race, 1896–1954.* Berkeley and Los Angeles: University of California Press, 1998.

Bal, Mieke. "Telling Objects: A Narrative Perspective on Collecting." In *The Cultures of Collecting,* ed. John Elsner and Roger Cardinal. London: Reaktion Books, 1994.

Baraka, Amiri. *Black Music.* New York: Apollo, 1968.

Barkan, Elazar, and Ronald Bush, eds. *Prehistories of the Future: The Primitivist Project and the Culture of Modernism.* Stanford, Calif.: Stanford University Press, 1995.

Barrows, John H. *The World's Parliament of Religions.* Chicago: Parliament, 1893.

Bataille, Georges, et al. *Encyclopaedia Acephalica.* London: Atlas Press, 1995.

Baudin, P. *Fetichism and Fetich Worshippers.* Trans. M. McMahon. New York: Benziger Press, 1885.

Baudrillard, Jean. *For a Critique of the Political Economy of the Sign.* St. Louis: Telos Press, 1981.

Beard, James Melville. *K.K.K. Sketches, Humorous and Didactic.* Philadelphia: Claxton, Remsen and Haffelfinger, 1877.

Bechet, Sidney. *Treat It Gentle: An Autobiography.* 1960. New York: Da Capo Press, 1978.

Belgrad, Daniel. *The Culture of Spontaneity: Improvisation and the Arts in Postwar America.* Chicago: University of Chicago Press, 1998.

Bell, Michael Edward. "Pattern, Structure, and Logic in Afro-American Hoodoo Performance." Ph.D. thesis, Indiana University, 1980.

Benes, Peter, ed. *Wonders of the Invisible World: 1600–1900.* Boston: Boston University, 1995.

Benjamin, Walter. *One Way Street and Other Writings.* Trans. Edmund Jephcott and Kingsley Shorter. London: Verso, 1979.

Bennett, Hal Zina. *Zuni Fetishes: Using American Objects for Meditation, Reflection and Insight.* New York: Harper Collins, 1993.

Bennett, Lerone. *The Negro Mood.* Chicago: Johnson, 1964.

Bentley, William. *The Diary of William Bentley.* 1902. Gloucester, Mass.: Peter Smith, 1962.

Berger, Maurice. *Fred Wilson: Objects and Installations 1979–2000.* Baltimore: Center for Art and Visual Culture, University of Maryland, 2001.

Berns, Marla C. *Dear Robert, I'll See You at the Crossroads: A Project by Renée Stout.* Seattle: University of Washington Press, 1995.

Berry, Bertice. *The Haunting of Hip Hop.* New York: Broadway Books, 2001.

Berry, Jason. *The Spirit of Black Hawk: A Mystery of Africans and Indians.* Jackson: University of Mississippi Press, 1995.

Bickley, R. Bruce, Jr., ed. *Critical Essays on Joel Chandler Harris.* Boston: G. K. Hall, 1981.

Bier, Lisa. *American Indian and African American People, Communities and Interactions: An Annotated Bibliography.* Westport, Conn.: Praeger, 2004.

Black, Mary B. "Ojibwa Power Belief System." In *The Anthropology of Power: Ethnographic Studies for Asia, Oceania, and the New World,* ed. Raymond D. Fogelson and Richard N. Adams. New York: Academic Press, 1977.

Blu, Karen I. *The Lumbee Problem: The Making of an American Indian People.* New York: New York University Press, 1980.

Borden, Pamela, ed. *Go Gater and Muddy the Water: Writings by Zora Neale Hurston from the Federal Writers' Project.* New York: Norton, 1999.

Bosman, William. *A New and Accurate Description of the Coast of Guinea.* London, 1705.

Brandon, William. *The Magic World: American Indian Songs and Poems.* New York: William Morrow, 1971.

Branson, Oscar T. *Fetishes and Carvings of the Southwest*. Santa Fe, N. Mex.: Treasure Chest Publications, 1976.

Breen, Timothy Hall. "The Conflict in *The Golden Bough*: Frazer's Two Images of Man." *South Atlantic Quarterly* 66, 2 (1967).

Breslaw, Elaine G. *Tituba, Reluctant Witch of Salem: Devilish Indians and Puritan Fantasies*. New York: New York University Press, 1996.

Brinton, Daniel G. *Religions of Primitive Peoples*. New York: Putnams, 1899.

Brown, David H. "Conjure/Doctors: An Exploration of a Black Discourse in America, Antebellum to 1940." *Folklore Forum* 23, 1–2 (1990): 3–46.

Brown, Joseph Epes. *The Spiritual Legacy of the American Indian*. New York: Crossroads, 1987.

Burnham, Clara Louise. *Sweet Clover: A Romance of the White City*. Boston: Houghton Mifflin, 1894.

Burton, Frederick. *American Primitive Music, with Especial Attention to the Songs of the Ojibways*. New York: Maffat, Yard, 1909.

Burton, Rainelle. *The Root Worker*. New York: Penguin, 2001.

Butler, Jon. *Awash in a Sea of Faith: Christianizing the American People*. Cambridge, Mass.: Harvard University Press, 1990.

Campbell, Mary Schmidt. *Tradition and Conflict: Images of a Turbulent Decade, 1963–1973*. New York: Studio Museum in Harlem, 1985.

Carby, Hazel V. "The Quicksands of Representation: Rethinking Black Cultural Politics." In *Reading Black, Reading Feminist: A Critical Anthology*, ed. Henry Louis Gates, Jr. New York: Meridian, 1990.

———. *Race Men*. Cambridge, Mass.: Harvard University Press, 1998.

Carpenter, Cari. "Detecting Indianness: Gertrude Bonnin's Investigation of Native American Identity." *Wicazo Sa Review* (Spring 2005): 139–59.

Carpenter, Carole H. "Arthur Huff Fauset, Campaigner for Social Justice: A Symphony of Diversity." In *African-American Pioneers in Anthropology*, ed. Ira E. Harrison and Faye W. Harrison. Urbana: University of Illinois Press, 1999.

Carpenter, Jane H., with Betye Saar. *Betye Saar*. San Francisco: Pomegranate, 2003.

Carr, Brian, and Tova Cooper. "Zora Neale Hurston and Modernism at the Critical Limit." *Modern Fiction Studies* 48, 2 (2002): 285–313.

Casid, Jill H. " 'His Master's Obi': Machine Magic, Colonial Violence, and Transculturation." In *The Visual Culture Reader*, ed. Nicholas Mirzoff. London: Routledge, 1998.

Castronovo, Russ. "The Antislavery Unconscious: Mesmerism, Vodun and 'Equality.' " *Mississippi Quarterly* 53, 1 (1999): 41–56.

Charleston, Steven. "From Medicine Man to Marx: The Coming Shift in Native Theology." In *Native American Religious Identity: Unforgotten Gods*, ed. Jace Weaver. Mary Knoll, N.Y.: Orbis Books, 1998.

———. "The Old Testament of Native America." In *Native and Christian: Indigenous Voices on Religious Identity in the United States and Canada*, ed. James Treat. New York: Routledge, 1996.

Chatelain, Heli. "African Fetishism." *Journal of American Folklore* 7 (1894): 303–4.

Chesnutt, Charles W. *The Colonel's Dream*. 1905. Upper Saddle River, N.J.: Gregg Press, 1968.

———. *The Conjure Woman and Other Conjure Tales*. Ed. Richard H. Brodhead. Durham N.C.: Duke University Press, 1994.

———. "Post Bellum, Pre-Harlem." *Crisis* 40 (June 1931): 19–34.

———. "Superstitions and Folklore of the South." *Modern Culture* 13 (1901): 231–35. Repr. in *Charles W. Chesnutt: Essays and Speeches*, ed. Joseph R. McElrath, Jr., Robert C. Leitz, and Jesse C. Crisler. Stanford, Calif.: Stanford University Press, 1999.

Cheyfitz, Eric, ed. *The Columbia History of Native American Literature in the US since 1945.* New York: Columbia University Press, 2006.

Chireau, Yvonne P. *Black Magic: Religion and the African American Conjuring Tradition.* Berkeley and Los Angeles: University of California Press, 2003.

Christy, David. *A Lecture on African Civilization, Including a Brief Outline of the Social and Moral Condition of Africa and the Relation of American Slaves to African Civilisation.* Cincinnati: J. A. and U. P. James, 1850.

Clements, William M., ed. *Native American Folklore in Nineteenth Century Periodicals.* Athens, Ohio: Swallow Press, 1986.

Clifford, James. "Ethnographic Surrealism." In *The Predicament of Culture: Twentieth-century Ethnography, Literature and Art.* Cambridge, Mass.: Harvard University Press, 1988.

Cochran, Robert. "Black Father: The Subversive Achievement of Joel Chandler Harris." *African American Review* 38, 1 (2004): 21–34.

Comaroff, Jean, and John Comaroff. "Alien-Nation: Zombies, Immigrants, and Millennial Capitalism." *South Atlantic Quarterly* 101, 4 (2002): 779–805.

Comte, August. *The Positive Philosophy.* Trans. and condensed by Harriet Martineau. New York: Calvin Blanchard, 1855.

Cone, James H. *Spirituals and the Blues.* New York: Orbis Books, 1991.

Coombs, Annie E. *Reinventing Africa: Museums, Material Culture and Popular Imagination in Late Victorian and Edwardian England.* New Haven, Conn.: Yale University Press, 1994.

Corbey, Raymond. "Ethnographic Showcases, 1780–1930." *Cultural Anthropology* 8, 3 (1993): 338–69.

Cordova, Viola F. "The European Concept of *Usen*: An American Aboriginal Text." In *Native American Religious Identity: Unforgotten Gods*, ed. Jace Weaver. Mary Knoll, N.Y.: Orbis Books, 1998.

Corn, Wanda M. "Marsden Hartley's Native Amerika." In *Marsden Hartley*, ed. Elizabeth Mankin Kornhauser. New Haven, Conn.: Yale University Press, 2002.

Cortez, Jayne. *Jazz Fan Looks Back.* Brooklyn, N.Y.: Hanging Loose Press, 2002.

Cruz, Jon. *Culture on the Margins: The Black Spiritual and the Rise of American Cultural Interpretation.* Princeton, N.J.: Princeton University Press, 1999.

Davis, Wade. *Passage of Darkness: The Ethnobiology of the Haitian Zombie.* Chapel Hill: University of North Carolina Press, 1988.

———. *The Serpent and the Rainbow.* London: Collins, 1986.

Dayan, Joan. *Haiti, History and the Gods.* Berkeley and Los Angeles: University of California Press, 1995.

De Brosses, Charles. *Du Culte des dieux fétiches, ou parallèle de l' ancienne religion de l'Égypte avec la religion actuelle de Nigritie.* Paris, 1760.

Deloria, Philip J. *Playing Indian.* New Haven, Conn.: Yale University Press, 1998.

Deloria, Vine, Jr. *For This Land: Writings on Religion in America.* Ed. James Treat. New York: Routledge, 1999.

DeMallie, Robert, and Douglas R. Parks, eds. *Sioux Indian Religion: Tradition and Innovation.* Norman: University of Oklahoma Press, 1987.

Deren, Maya. *Divine Horsemen: The Living Gods of Haiti.* London: Thames and Hudson, 1953.

Derrida, Jacques. *Spectres of Marx: The State of the Debt, the Work of Mourning and the New International.* New York: Routledge, 1994.

Dick, Bruce, and Amritjit Singh. *Conversations with Ishmael Reed.* Jackson: University Press of Mississippi, 1995.

Dilworth, Leah. *Imagining Indians in the Southwest: Persistent Visions of a Primitive Past.* Washington, D.C.: Smithsonian Institution Press, 1996.

Dollard, John. *Caste and Class in a Southern Town*. New York: Doubleday, 1937.

Donaldson, Laura E. "Making a Joyful Noise: William Apess and the Search for Post-colonial Method(ism)." In *Messy Beginnings: Postcoloniality and Early American Studies*, ed. Malini Johar Schueller and Edward Watts. New Brunswick, N.J.: Rutgers University Press, 2003.

————. "On Medicine Women and White Shame-ans: New Age Native Americanism and Commodity Fetishism as Pop Culture Feminism." *Signs: Journal of Women in Culture and Society* 24, 3 (1999): 677–96.

————. "Son of the Forest, Child of God: William Apess and the Scene of Postcolonial Nativity." In *Postcolonial America*, ed. Richard C. King. Urbana: University of Illinois Press, 2000.

Douglas, Aaron. Unpublished MS. March 18, 1923. Special Collections, Fisk University Library, Nashville, Tennessee.

Douglass, Frederick. *My Bondage and My Freedom*. 1855. New York: Dover, 1969.

————. *Narrative of the Life of Frederick Douglass, an American Slave*. 1845. New York: Dolphin Books, 1963.

Doy, Gen. *Black Visual Culture: Modernity and Postmodernity*. London: I. B. Tauris, 2000.

Driskell, David C., ed. *African American Visual Aesthetics: A Postmodernist View*. Washington, D.C.: Smithsonian Institution, 1995.

DuBois, William E. B. *The Quest for the Silver Fleece*. Chicago: A. C. McClurg, 1911.

————. "The Religion of the American Negro." *The New World: A Quarterly Review of Religion, Ethics and Theology* 9 (1900): 614–25.

————. *The Souls of Black Folk*. Ed. Henry Louis Gates, Jr., and Terri Hume Oliver. New York: Norton, 1999.

Duck, Leigh Ann. "'Rebirth of a Nation': Hurston in Haiti." *Journal of American Folklore* 117 (2004): 127–46.

Dunham, Katherine. *Island Possessed*. Chicago: University of Chicago Press, 1969.

Durham, Jimmie. *A Certain Lack of Coherence: Writings on Art and Cultural Politics*. London: Kala Press, 1993.

Durland, Steven. "'Call Me in '93': An Interview with James Luna." *High Performance* 14, 4 (1991): 34–39.

Dutton, Wendy. "The Problem of Invisibility: Voodoo and Zora Neale Hurston." *Frontiers: A Journal of Women's Studies* 13, 2 (1993): 131–52.

Eastman, Charles. "Sioux Mythology." In *International Folklore Congress of the World's Columbian Exposition*. Chicago: Charles H. Sergel, 1898.

Eastman, Charles Alexander (Ohiyesa). *The Soul of the Indian: An Interpretation*. 1911. Lincoln: University of Nebraska Press, 1980.

Ellen, Roy. "Fetishism." *Man* n.s., 23, 2 (1988): 213–35.

Elliot, Michael A. *The Culture Concept: Writing and Difference in the Age of Realism*. Minneapolis: University of Minnesota Press, 2002.

Ellis, A. B. "Evolution in Folklore: Some African Prototypes of the 'Uncle Remus' Stories." *Appleton's Popular Science Monthly* 48, 1 (1895): 93–104.

————. "The Indwelling Spirits of Men." *Popular Science Monthly* 36 (1890): 794–801.

Ellis, Juniper. "Enacting Culture: Zora Neale Hurston, Joel Chandler Harris, and Literary Ethnography." In *Multiculturalism: Roots and Realities*, ed. C. James Trotman. Bloomington: Indiana University Press, 2002.

Ellison, Ralph Waldo. *Collected Essays*. New York: Modern Library, 1995.

Elster, Jon, ed. *Karl Marx: A Reader*. Cambridge: Cambridge University Press, 1986.

Emmons, George T. *The Tlingit Indians*. Ed. Frederica de Laguna. Seattle: University of Washington Press, 1991.

Errington, Shelly. *The Death of Primitive Art and Other Tales of Progress*. Berkeley and Los Angeles: University of California Press, 1998.

Evans, Brad. *Before Cultures: The Ethnographic Imagination in American Literature, 1865–1920*. Chicago: University of Chicago Press, 2005.

Evans, E. P. "Recent Recrudescences of Superstition." *Appleton's Popular Science Monthly* 48, 1 (1895).

Fabian, Johannes. *Time and the Other: How Anthropology Makes Its Object*. New York: Columbia University Press, 1983.

Fenton, James. *Children in Exile: Poems 1968–1984*. New York: Vintage, 1984.

Fisher, Rudolph. *The Conjure-Man Dies: A Mystery Tale of Dark Harlem*. 1932. Ann Arbor: University of Michigan Press, 1992.

Fitz, Brewster E. *Silko: Writing Storyteller and Medicine Woman*. Norman: University of Oklahoma Press, 2004.

Fletcher, Alice C. "The Indian Messiah." *Journal of American Folklore* 4, 12 (1891): 57–60.

Flowers, Arthur. *Another Good Loving Blues*. London: Secker and Warburg, 1993.

———. *De Mojo Blues: De Quest of HighJohn de Conqueror*. New York: E. P. Dutton, 1985.

Floyd, Samuel A., Jr. *The Power of Black Music: Interpreting Its History from Africa to the United States*. New York: Oxford University Press, 1995.

Forbes, Jack D. *Black Africans and Native Americans: Color, Race and Caste in the Evolution of Red-Black Peoples*. Oxford: Basil Blackwell, 1988.

Ford, Douglas. "Sherman Alexie's Indigenous Blues." *Melus* 27, 3 (2002): 197–215.

Franko, Mark. "Aesthetic Agencies in Flux: Talley Beatty, Maya Deren, and the Modern Dance Tradition in *Study in Choreography for Camera*." In *Maya Deren and the American Avant-Garde*, ed. Bill Nichols. Berkeley and Los Angeles: University of California Press, 2001.

Frisbie, Charlotte J. *Navajo Medicine Bundles or Jish: Acquisition, Transmission, and Disposition in the Past and Present*. Albuquerque: University of New Mexico Press, 1987.

Fulbright, John. "Hopi and Zuni Prayer-sticks: Magic, Symbolic Texts, Barter or Self-Sacrifice?" *Religion* 22 (1992): 221–34.

Gardner, Daniel. *A New System of Indian Doctoring*. Windsor, Vt.: Statesman Office, 1839.

Gardner, Eric. "*The Complete Fortune Teller and Dream Book*: An Antebellum Text by Chloe Russel, a Woman of Colour." *New England Quarterly* 78, 2 (2005): 259–88.

Gates, Henry Louis, Jr., and K. A. Appiah, eds. *Zora Neale Hurston: Critical Perspectives Past and Present*. New York: Amistad, 1993.

Genovese, Eugene D. *Roll Jordan Roll: The World the Slaves Made*. New York: Vintage Books, 1976.

Gershenhorn, Jerry. *Melville J. Herskovits and the Racial Politics of Knowledge*. Lincoln: University of Nebraska Press, 2004.

Gillman, Susan. *Blood Talk: American Race Melodrama and the Culture of the Occult*. Chicago: University of Chicago Press, 2003.

———. "Pauline Hopkins and the Occult: African-American Revisions of Nineteenth-Century Science." *American Literary History* 8, 1 (1996): 57–82.

Gilroy, Paul. "Questions of a 'Soulful Style': Interview with Paul Gilroy." In *Soul: Black Power, Politics and Pleasures*, ed. Monique Guillory and Richard C. Green. New York: New York University Press, 1998.

Glave, E. J. *In Savage Africa*. New York: Russell and Son, 1892.

Gliozzi, Giuliano. "The Apostles in the New World: Monotheism and Idolatry between Revelation and Fetishism." *History and Anthropology* 3 (1987): 123–48.

Godelier, Maurice. *Perspectives in Marxist Anthropology*. Cambridge: Cambridge University Press, 1977.

Gomez, Michael A. *Exchanging Our Country Marks: The Transformation of African Identities in the Colonial and Antebellum South*. Chapel Hill: University of North Carolina Press, 1998.

Gonzalez, Ambrose E. *The Black Border: Gullah Stories of the Carolina Coast*. Columbia, S.C.: State Company, 1922.

Gordon, Avery F. *Ghostly Matters: Haunting and the Sociological Imagination*. Minneapolis: University of Minnesota Press. 1997.

Gordon, Deborah. "The Politics of Ethnographic Authority: Race and Writing in the Ethnography of Margaret Mead and Zora Neale Hurston." In *Modernist Anthropology: From Fieldwork to Text*, ed. Marc Manganaro. Princeton, N.J.: Princeton University Press, 1990.

Gorn, Elliot J. "Black Spirits: The Ghostlore of Afro-American Slaves." *American Quarterly* 36, 4 (1984): 549–65.

Gose, Peter. "Sacrifice and the Commodity Form in the Andes." *Man* n.s. 21, 2 (1986): 296–310.

Gover, Robert. "An Interview with Ishmael Reed." *Black American Literature Forum* 12 (1978): 12–19.

Griaule, Marcel. *Conversations with Ogotemmêli, an Introduction to Dogon Religious Studies*. London: Oxford University Press, 1965.

Gruesser, John Cullen. *Black on Black: Twentieth-Century African American Writing about Africa*. Lexington: University Press of Kentucky, 2000.

Guillory, Monique, and Richard C. Green, eds. *Soul: Black Power, Politics and Pleasures*. New York: New York University Press, 1998.

Gundaker, Grey. *Signs of Diaspora/Diaspora of Signs: Literacies, Creolization, and Vernacular Practice in African America*. New York: Oxford University Press, 1998.

Gussow, Adam. *Seems like Murder Here: Southern Violence and the Blues Tradition*. Chicago: University of Chicago Press, 2002.

Halbertal, Moshe, and Avishai Margalit. *Idolatry*. Cambridge, Mass.: Harvard University Press, 1992.

Hallowell, A. Irving. "Ojibwa Ontology, Behavior and World View." In *Culture and History: Essays in Honor of Paul Radin*, ed. Stanley Diamond. New York: Columbia University Press, 1960. Repr. in *Teachings from the American Earth: Indian Religion and Philosophy*, ed. Dennis Tedlock and Barbara Tedlock. New York: Liveright, 1975.

Hamilian, Leo, and James Vernon Hatch, eds. *Roots of African American Drama: An Anthology of Early Plays, 1858–1938*. Detroit: Wayne State University Press, 1972.

Hanegraaff, Wouter J. "The Emergence of the Academic Science of Magic: The Occult Philosophy in Tylor and Frazer." In *Religion in the Making: The Emergence of the Sciences of Religion*, ed. Arie L. Molendijk and Peter Pels. Leiden: Brill, 1998.

Hansen, Chadwick. "The Metamorphosis of Tituba, or Why American Intellectuals Can't Tell an Indian Witch from a Negro." *New England Quarterly* 47, 1 (1974): 3–12.

Harding, Rachel E. *A Refuge in Thunder: Candomblé and Alternative Spaces of Blackness*. Bloomington: Indiana University Press, 2000.

Harjo, Joy. "Interview with Joy Harjo." *Religion and Literature* 26, 1 (1994): 55–64.

Harris, Joel Chandler. *The Bishop and the Boogerman*. New York: Doubleday, Page, 1909.

———. *Free Joe and Other Georgian Sketches*. New York: P. F. Collier & Son, 1887.

———. *Nights with Uncle Remus: Myths and Legends of the Old Plantation.*1883. Ed. John T. Bickley and R. Bruce Bickley. New York: Penguin, 2003.

———. "Plantation Music." *The Critic* 3, 95 (1883): 505–6. Repr. in *The Negro and His Folklore in Nineteenth-Century Periodicals*, ed. Bruce Jackson. Austin: University of Texas Press, 1967.

———. *Uncle Remus, His Songs and Sayings: The Folklore of the Old Plantation.* New York: D. Appleton, 1881.

Harris, Juliette. "The Black-Indian Connection in Art: American Portraits, Soulscapes and Spirit Works." *International Review of African American Art* 17, 1 (2000): 2–40.

Harris, Michael D. "Resonance, Transformation and Rhyme: The Art of Renée Stout." In Wyatt MacGaffey and Michael D. Harris. *Astonishment and Power.* Washington, D.C.: Smithsonian Institution, 1993.

Harrison, Paul Carter, ed. *Totem Voices: Plays from the Black World Repertory.* New York: Grove Press, 1989.

Hartley, Marsden. *The Collected Poems of Marsden Hartley, 1904–1943.* Ed. Gail R. Scott. Santa Rosa, Calif.: Black Sparrow Press, 1987.

———. "Redman Ceremonials: An American Plea for American Esthetics. *Art and Archaeology* 9, 1 (1920): 7–14.

Hartman, Saidiya. *Scenes of Subjection: Terror, Slavery and Self-Making in Nineteenth-Century America.* New York: Oxford University Press, 1997.

Hegel, G. W. F. *The Philosophy of History.* 1837. Trans. J. Sibree. New York: Dover, 1956.

Helbling, Mark. "'My Soul Was with the Gods and My Body in the Village': Zora Neale Hurston, Franz Boas, Melville Herskovits, and Ruth Benedict." *Prospects* 22 (1997): 285–322.

Hemenway, Robert E. *Zora Neale Hurston: A Literary Biography.* Urbana: University of Illinois Press, 1977.

Hennepin, Louis. *A New Discovery of a Vast Country in America.* 1697. Ed. Reuben Thwaites. Chicago: McClurg, 1903.

Hertzberg, Hazel W. *The Search for an American Identity: Modern Pan-Indian Movements.* Syracuse, N.Y.: Syracuse University Press, 1971.

Hewitt, J. N. B. "Orenda and a Definition of Religion." *American Anthropologist* n.s., 4 (1902): 33–46.

Hewitt, M. J. "Betye Saar, an Interview." *International Review of African American Art* 10, 2 (2004).

Higginson, Thomas Wentworth. "Negro Spirituals." *Atlantic Monthly* 19 (1867): 685–94.

Hill-Tout, Charles. *The Origin of the Totemism of the Aborigines of British Columbia.* Transactions of the Royal Society of Canada. Ottawa: J Hill and Sons, 1901.

Hinsley, Curtis M. "Hopi Snakes, Zuni Corn: Early Ethnography in the American Southwest." In *Colonial Subjects: Essays on the Practical History of Anthropology*, ed. Peter Pels and Oscar Salemnik. Ann Arbor: University of Michigan Press, 1999.

———. "Zunis and Brahmans: Cultural Ambivalence in the Gilded Age." In *Romantic Motives: Essays on Anthropological Sensibility*, ed. George W. Stocking, Jr. Madison: University of Wisconsin Press, 1989.

Hittman, Michael. *Wovoka and the Ghost Dance.* Lincoln: University of Nebraska Press, 1990.

Hodge, Frederick W., ed. *Handbook of American Indians North of Mexico.* Washington, D.C.: Smithsonian Institution Bureau of American Ethnology, 1910. Bulletin 30.

Hodgen, Margaret T. *Early Anthropology in the Sixteenth and Seventeenth Centuries.* Philadelphia: University of Pennsylvania Press, 1964.

Hoefel, Roseanne. "'Different by Degree': Ella Cara Deloria, Zora Neale Hurston, and Franz Boas Contend with Race and Ethnicity." *American Indian Quarterly* 25, 2 (2001): 181–202.

Hoffman, W. J. "The Midewiwin Society of the Ojibwa." *Bureau of American Ethnology, Annual Report* 8. Washington, D.C.: Smithsonian Institution, 1885–86.

Holland, Sharon Patricia. *Raising the Dead: Readings of Death and (Black) Subjectivity.* Durham, N.C.: Duke University Press, 2000.

Holler, Clyde, ed. *The Black Elk Reader.* Syracuse, N.Y.: Syracuse University Press, 2000.

Holley, Marietta. *Samantha at the World's Fair, by Josiah Allen's Wife.* New York: Funk and Wagnall, 1893.

Hopkins, Pauline. *Contending Forces: A Romance Illustrative of Negro Life in North and South.* 1900. New York: Oxford University Press, 1988.

————. *Of One Blood.* Published in serial form from 1903. Repr., London: X Press, 1996.

Horne, Gerald. *Race Woman: The Lives of Shirley Graham Du Bois.* New York: New York University Press, 2000.

Hosmer, H. L. *The Octoroon.* New York: Follett, Foster, 1863.

Hoxay, Fredric W., ed. *Voyages of the "Columbia" to the Northwest Coast, 1787–1790 and 1790–1793.* Boston: Massachusetts Historical Society, 1941.

Hume, David. *The Natural History of Religion. In Dialogues and the Natural History of Religion,* ed. J. C. A. Gaskin. Oxford: Oxford University Press, 1993.

Hurston, Zora Neale. *Folklore, Memoirs, and Other Writings.* New York: Library of America, 1995.

————. "Hoodoo in America." *Journal of American Folklore* 44 (1931): 317–417.

————. *Jonah's Gourd Vine.* 1934. London: Virago Press, 1987.

————. *Moses, Man of the Mountain.* 1939. Urbana and Chicago: Illinois University Press, 1984.

Hyatt, Harry Middleton. *Hoodoo-Conjuration-Witchcraft-Rootwork: Beliefs Accepted by Many Negroes and White Persons, These Being Orally Recorded among Blacks and Whites.* Hannibal, Miss.: Western Publishing,1970–80.

Ingraham, Joseph Holt. *Lafitte, the Pirate of the Gulf.* London: J. S. Pratt, 1845.

Irek, Malgorzata. "From Berlin to Harlem: Felix von Luschan, Alain Locke and The New Negro." In *The Black Columbiad: Defining Moments in African American Literature and Culture,* ed. Werner Sollors and Maria Diedrich. Cambridge, Mass.: Harvard University Press, 1994.

Irr, Caren. "The Timeliness of *Almanac of the Dead,* or a Postmodern Rewriting of Radical Fiction." In *Leslie Marmon Silko: A Collection of Critical Essays,* ed. Louise K. Barnett and James L. Thorson. Albuquerque: University of New Mexico Press, 1999.

Isaacs, Hope L. "*Orenda* and the Concept of Power among the Tonawanda Seneca." In *The Anthropology of Power: Ethnographic Studies for Asia, Oceania, and the New World,* ed. Raymond D. Fogelson and Richard N. Adams. New York: Academic Press, 1977.

Jackson, Bruce. "Another Kind of Doctor: Conjure and Magic in Black American Folk Medicine." In *African-American Religion: Interpretive Essays in History and Culture,* ed. Timothy E. Fulop and Albert J. Raboteau. New York: Routledge, 1997.

Jackson, Bruce. *The Negro and His Folklore in Nineteenth-Century Periodicals.* Austin: University of Texas Press, 1967.

Johansen, Bruce Elliott, ed. *Encyclopedia of Native American Legal Tradition.* Westport, Conn.: Greenwood Press, 1998.

Johnson, F. Roy. *The Fabled Doctor Jim Jordan: A Story of Conjure.* Murfreesboro, N.C.: Johnson Publishing, 1963.

Johnson, James Weldon. *Along This Way: The Autobiography of James Weldon Johnson.* 1933. New York: Penguin, 1990.

————, ed. *The Book of American Negro Poetry.* Rev. ed. New York: Harcourt, Brace and World, 1959

Johnston, Devin. "Nathaniel Mackey and Lost Time: 'The Phantom Light of All Our Day.'" *Callaloo* 32, 2 (2000): 563–70.

Jonaitis, Aldon. "Creations of Mystics and Philosophers: The White Man's Perceptions of Northwest Coast Indian Art from the 1930s to the Present." *American Indian Culture and Research Journal* 5, 1 (1981): 1–45.

Jones, Charles C. *Antiquities of the Southern Indians, Particularly of the Georgian Tribes.* New York: D. Appleton, 1873

———. *Negro Myths from the Georgia Coast.* Boston: Houghton, Mifflin, 1882.

Kadlec, David. "Zora Neale Hurston and the Federal Folk." *Modernism/Modernity* 7, 3 (2000): 470–85.

Kaplan, Carla, ed. *Zora Neale Hurston: A Life in Letters.* New York: Doubleday, 2002.

Kassanoff, Jennie A. "'Fate Has Linked Us Together': Blood, Gender, and the Politics of Representation in Pauline Hopkins's *Of One Blood.*" In *The Unruly Voice: Rediscovering Pauline Elizabeth Hopkins,* ed. John C. Gruesser. Urbana: University of Illinois Press, 1996.

Katz, William Loren. *Black Indians: A Hidden Heritage.* New York: Atheneum, 1986.

Kerkering, John D. *The Poetics of Racial and National Identity in Nineteenth-Century American Literature.* Cambridge: Cambridge University Press, 2003.

Koritz, Amy. "Re/Moving Boundaries: From Dance History to Cultural Studies." In *Moving Words: Re-writing Dance,* ed. Gay Morris. London: Routledge, 1996.

Krause, Aurel. *The Tlingit Indians: Results of a Trip to the Northwest Coast of America and the Bering Straits.* 1885. Trans. Erna Gunther. Seattle: University of Washington Press, 1956.

Krips, Henry. *Fetish: An Erotics of Culture.* Ithaca, N.Y.: Cornell University Press, 1999.

Kruger, Steven F. "Fetishism, 1927, 1461, 1614." In *The Postcolonial Middle Ages,* ed. Jeffrey Jerome Cohen. New York: St. Martin's Press, 2000.

Kupperman, Karen O. *Indians and English: Facing off in Early America.* Ithaca, N.Y.: Cornell University Press, 2000.

Lafitau, Joseph François. *Customs of the American Indians Compared with the Customs of Primitive Times.* 1724. 2 vols. Trans. and ed. William Fenton and Elizabeth Moore. Toronto: Champlain Press, 1974.

Lang, Andrew. *Custom and Myth.* 1884. London: Longmans, Green, 1910.

Lange, Art, and Nathaniel Mackey, eds. *Moment's Notice: Jazz in Poetry and Prose* Minneapolis: Coffee House Press, 1993.

Le Clercq, Chrétien. *New Relation of Gaspesia, with the Customs and Religion of the Gaspesian Indians.* 1691. Trans. and ed. William F. Ganong. Toronto: Champlain Society, 1910. Repr., Westport, Conn., Greenwood Press, 1968.

Leighton, Patricia. "The White Peril and l'Art Nègre: Picasso, Primitivism and Anticolonialism." *Art Bulletin* 72, 4 (1990): 609–30.

Lemke, Sieglinde. *Primitivist Modernism: Black Culture and the Origins of Transatlantic Modernism.* Oxford: Oxford University Press, 1998.

Levin, Gail "American Art." In *"Primitivism" in 20th Century Art: Affinities of the Tribal and Modern,* ed. William Rubin. New York: Museum of Modern Art, 1984.

Levine, Lawrence W. *Black Culture and Black Consciousness: Afro-American Folk Thought from Slavery to Freedom.* Oxford: Oxford University Press, 1977.

Levi-Strauss, Claude. *Totemism.* Boston: Beacon, 1963.

Lewis, Ignatius. *The New Fortune Book of OBI or West Indian Astrologer. By the Jamaican Seer of Colour.* London, 1823.

Lippard, Lucy R. "Sapphire and Ruby in the Indigo Gardens." In *Secrets, Dialogues, Revelations: The Art of Betye and Alison Saar: Essays by Lucy R Lippard, Ishmael Reed and Judith Wilson,* ed. Elizabeth Shepherd. Los Angeles: Wight Art Gallery, University of California, 1990.

Lock, Graham. *Blutopia: Visions of the Future and Revisions of the Past in the Work of Sun Ra, Duke Ellington, and Anthony Braxton.* Durham, N.C.: Duke University Press, 1999.

Locke, Alain, ed. *The New Negro.* 1925. New York: Simon and Schuster, 1992.

Long, John. *Voyages and Travels of an Indian Interpreter and Trader.* 1791. Ed. Reuben Gold Thwaites. Cleveland: Arthur H. Clark, 1904.

Lott, Eric. *Love and Theft: Blackface Minstrelsy and the American Working Class.* Oxford: Oxford University Press, 1995.

Ludington, Townsend. *Marsden Hartley: The Biography of an American Artist.* Boston: Little, Brown, 1992.

Ludwig, Sami. "Dialogic Possession in Ishmael Reed's *Mumbo Jumbo*: Bakhtin, Voodoo, and the Materiality of Multicultural Discourse." In *The Black Columbiad: Defining Moments in African American Literature and Culture,* ed. Werner Sollors and Maria Diedrich. Cambridge, Mass.: Harvard University Press, 1994.

Lummis, Charles F. *The Land of Poco Tiempo.* London: Sampson Low, Marston. 1893.

MacGaffey, Wyatt. "African Objects and the Idea of the Fetish." *Res* 25 (1994): 123–31.

MacGaffey, Wyatt, and Michael D. Harris. *Astonishment and Power.* Washington, D.C.: Smithsonian Institution, 1993.

Mackey, Nathaniel. *Atet A.D.* San Francisco: City Lights, 2001
———. *Bedouin Hornbook.* Los Angeles: Sun and Moon Press, 1997.
———. "Cante Moro." In *Sound States: Innovative Poetics and Acoustical Technologies,* ed. Adalaide Morris. Chapel Hill: University of North Carolina Press, 1997.
———. *Discrepant Engagement: Dissonance, Cross-Culturality, and Experimental Writing.* Cambridge: Cambridge University Press, 1993.
———. *Eroding Witness.* Urbana: University of Illinois Press, 1985.
———. *Whatsaid Serif.* San Francisco: City Lights, 1998.

Malraux, André. *Picasso's Mask.* New York: Holt, Rinehart and Winston, 1976.

Manuel, Frank E. *The Eighteenth Century Confronts the Gods.* Cambridge, Mass.: Harvard University Press, 1959.

Marcus, Greil. *Mystery Train: Images of Rock 'n' Roll Music.* New York: Dutton, 1975.

Mark, Joan. *A Stranger in Her Native Land: Alice Fletcher and the American Indians.* Lincoln: University of Nebraska Press, 1988.

Marrant, John. *A Narrative of the Lord's Wonderful Dealings with John Marrant, a Black (Now Going to Preach the Gospel in Nova Scotia). Taken down from His Own Relation, Arranged, Corrected and Published by the Rev. Mr. Aldridge.* London, 1785.

Martin, Reginald. "An Interview with Ishmael Reed." *Review of Contemporary Fiction* 4, 2 (1984).

Masuzawa, Tomoko. "Troubles with Materiality: The Ghost of Fetishism in the Nineteenth Century." *Comparative Studies in Society and History* 42, 2 (2000): 242–67.

May, Katja. *African Americans and Native Americans in the Creek and Cherokee Nations, 1830s to 1920s: Collision and Collusion.* New York: Garland, 1996.

McBride, Bunny. *Molly Spotted Elk: A Penobscot in Paris.* Norman: University of Oklahoma Press, 1995.

McCall, George J. "Symbiosis: The Case of Hoodoo and the Numbers Racket." In *Mother Wit from the Laughing Barrel: Readings in the Interpretation of Afro-American Folklore,* ed. Alan Dundes. Jackson: University Press of Mississippi, 1990.

McCann, Sean, and Michael Szalay. "Do You Believe in Magic? Literary Thinking and the New Left." *Yale Journal of Criticism* 18, 2 (2005): 435–68.

McElrath, Joseph R., Robert C. Leitz, and Jesse C. Crisler, eds. *Charles W. Chesnutt: Essays and Speeches.* Stanford, Calif.: Stanford University Press, 1999.

McFeeley, Eliza. *Zuni and the American Imagination.* New York: Hill and Wang, 2001.

McLennan, J. F. "The Worship of Animals and Plants." *Fortnightly Review* 12 (1869): 407–27; 13 (1870): 194–216.

McGaa, Ed (Eagle Man). *Mother Earth Spirituality: Native American Paths to Healing Ourselves and Our World.* New York: Harper Collins, 1990.

McNeil, B. C. "Review of *Mules and Men*." *Journal of Negro History* 21, 2 (1936): 223–25.

McPherson, Dennis H., and J. Douglas Rabb. "Transformative Philosophy and Indigenous Thought: A Comparison of Lakota and Ojibwa World Views." *Papers of the Algonquian Conference* 29 (1997): 202–10.

McWillie, Judith, et al. *Another Face of the Diamond: Pathways through the Black Atlantic South*. Atlanta: New Visions Gallery of Contemporary Art, 1989.

Medicine, Bea. "Ella Cara Deloria." In *Women Anthropologists: A Biographical Dictionary*, ed. Ute Gacs, Aisha Khan, Jerrie McIntyre, and Ruth Weinberg. New York: Greenwood Press, 1988.

Mercer, Kobena. *Welcome to the Jungle: New Positions in Black Cultural Studies*. New York: Routledge, 1994.

Meyer, Leroy N., and Tony Ramirez. "'Wakinyan Hotan': The Inscrutability of Lakota/Dakota Metaphysics." In *From Our Eyes: Learning from Indigenous Peoples*, ed. Sylvia O'Meara and Douglas West. Toronto: Gramond Press, 1996.

Mikell, Gwendolyn. ""Feminism and Black Culture in the Ethnography of Zora Neale Hurston." In *African-American Pioneers in Anthropology*, ed. Ira E. Harrison and Faye W. Harrison. Urbana: University of Illinois Press, 1999.

——. "When Horses Talk: Reflections on Zora Neale Hurston's Haitian Anthropology." *Phylon* 43 (1982): 218–30.

Miller, Christopher L. *Blank Darkness: Africanist Discourse in French*. Chicago: University of Chicago Press, 1985.

Mitchell, Joseph. *The Missionary Pioneer, or A Brief Memoir of the Life, Labours and Death of John Stewart (Man of Colour) Founder, under God of the Mission among the Wyandotts at Upper Sandusky, Ohio*. New York: J. C. Totten, 1827.

Mitchell, W. J. T. "Romanticism and the Life of Things: Fossils, Totems and Things." *Critical Inquiry* 28 (2001): 167–84

Mooney, James. *The Ghost-Dance Religion and Wounded Knee*. 1896. Abridged ed. Chicago: University of Chicago Press, 1965.

——. *Myths of the Cherokees*. Nineteenth Annual Report of the Bureau of American Ethnology, 1897–1898. Part 1. Washington, D.C.: Washington Printing Office, 1900.

Moore, David L. "Return of the Buffalo: Cultural Representation as Cultural Property." In *Native American Representations: First Encounters, Distorted Images and Literary Appropriations*, ed. Gretchen M. Bataille. Lincoln: University of Nebraska Press, 2001.

Moore, Rachel O. *Savage Theory: Cinema as Modern Magic*. Durham, N.C.: Duke University Press, 2000.

Morgan, Philip D. *Slave Counterpoint: Black Culture in the Eighteenth-Century Chesapeake and Low Country*. Chapel Hill: University of North Carolina Press, 1998.

Morrison, Kenneth M. "Montagnais Missionization in Early New France: The Syncretic Imperative." *American Indian Culture and Research Journal* 10, 3 (1986): 1–23.

Moses L. G. *The Indian Man: A Biography of James Mooney*. Urbana: University of Illinois Press, 1984.

Moses, Wilson Jeremiah. *Afrotopia: The Roots of African American Popular History*. Cambridge: Cambridge University Press, 1998.

Motz, Marilyn. "The Practice of Belief." *Journal of American Folklore* 111 (1998): 339–55.

Mullen, Harryette. "African Signs and Spirit Writing." *Callalloo* 19, 3 (1996): 670–89.

Mullen, Patrick B. "Belief and the American Folk." *Journal of American Folklore* 113 (2000): 119–43.

Mulvey, Laura. "Some Thoughts on Theories of Fetishism in the Context of Contemporary Culture." *October* 65 (1993): 3–20.

Murphy, Jeanette Robinson. "The Survival of African Music in America." *Popular Sci-*

ence Monthly 55 (1899): 660–72. Repr. in *The Negro and His Folklore in Nineteenth-century Periodicals*, ed. Bruce Jackson. Austin: University of Texas Press, 1967.

Murray, David. "Cultural Sovereignty and the Hauntology of American Identity." In *Mirror Writing: (Re-)Constructions of Native American Identity*, ed.Thomas Claviez and Maria Moss. Glienicke: Galdsa-Wilch Verlag, 2000.

———. *Indian Giving: Economies of Power in Early Indian-White Encounters*. Amherst: University of Massachusetts Press, 2000

———. "The Red and the Black: Autobiography and the Creation of Mixed Blood Identity." In *Writing and Race*, ed. Tim Youngs. London: Pluto Press, 1995.

Nadell, Martha Jane. *Enter the New Negroes: Images of Race in American Culture*. Cambridge, Mass.: Harvard University Press, 2004.

Nassau, Robert Hamill. *Fetichism in West Africa: Forty Years' Observation of Native Customs and Superstitions*. New York: Charles Scribner's Sons, 1904.

Neal, Larry. *Hoodoo Hollerin' Bebop Ghosts*. Washington, D.C.: Howard University Press, 1974.

Newell, William Wells. "On the Field and Work of a Journal of American Folk-Lore." *Journal of American Folklore* 1, 1 (1888): 3–7.

———. "Review of *Negro Myths of the Georgia Coast*." *Journal of American Folklore* 1, 2 (1988): 169–70.

———. "Second Annual Meeting of the American Folklore Society." *Journal of American Folklore* 4 (1891): 1–12.

Nielsen, Aldon Lynn. *Black Chant: Languages of African American Modernism*. Cambridge: Cambridge University Press, 1997.

Niezen, Ronald. *Spirit Wars: Native North American Religions in the Age of Nation Building*. Berkeley and Los Angeles: University of California Press, 2000.

Owen, Mary Alicia. "Among the Voodoos. In *International Folklore Congress of 1891*, ed. Joseph Jacobs and Alfred Nutt (1892).

———. *The Daughter of Alouette*. London: Methuen, 1902.

———. *Folklore of the Musquakie Indians of North America and Catalogue of Musquakie Beadwork and Other Objects in the Collection of the Folk-Lore Society*. London: David Nutt, 1904.

———. *Old Rabbit, the Voodoo and other Sorcerers: Voodoo Tales as Told among the Negroes of the Southwest*. New York: Putnam's Sons, 1893.

———. "Voodooism." In *International Folklore Congress of 1891* (1892).

Pagels, Elaine. *The Gnostic Gospels*. New York: Random House, 1979.

Palmer, Robert. *Deep Blues: A Musical and Cultural History of the Mississippi Delta*. New York: Penguin, 1981.

P[ark], S. M. "Voodooism in Tennessee." *Atlantic Monthly* 64 (1889): 376–80.

Patterson, Michelle Wick. "'Real' Indian Songs: The Society of American Indians and the Use of Native American Culture as a Means of Reform." *American Indian Quarterly* 26, 1 (2002): 44–66.

Peabody, Charles. "Notes on Negro Music." *Journal of American Folklore* 16 (1903): 148–52.

Pels, Peter. "Occult Truths: Race, Conjecture, and Theosophy in Victorian Anthropology." In *Excluded Ancestors, Inventible Traditions: Essays Toward a More Inclusive History of Anthropology*, ed. Richard Handler. Madison: University of Wisconsin Press, 2000.

———. "The Spirit of Matter: On Fetish, Rarity, Fact and Fancy." In *Border Fetishisms: Material Objects in Unstable Places*, ed. Patricia Spyer. New York: Routledge, 1998.

Phillpotts, Eden. *The Golden Fetich*. New York: Dodd, Mead, 1903.

———. "The Obi Man." *Harper's Weekly*, July 1, 1893: 617–18.

Piersen, William D. "Black Arts and Black Magic: Yankee Accommodations to African

Religion." In *Wonders of the Invisible World: 1600–1900*, ed. Peter Benes. Boston: Annual Proceedings of the Dublin Seminar for New England Life, 1995.

————. *Black Legacies: America's Hidden Heritage*. Amherst: University of Massachusetts
Press, 1993.

————. *Black Yankees: The Development of an Afro-American Subculture in Eighteenth-Century
New England*. Amherst: University of Massachusetts Press, 1988.

Pietz, William. "Death of the Deodand: Accursed Objects and the Money Value of
Human Life." *Res* 27 (1993): 97–108.

————. "Fetish." In *Critical Terms for Art History*, ed. Robert S. Nelson and Richard
Schiff. Chicago: University of Chicago Press, 1996.

————. "Fetishism and Materialism: The Limit of Theory in Marx." In *Fetishism as
Cultural Discourse*, ed. Emily Apter and William Pietz. Ithaca, N.Y.: Cornell University Press, 1993.

————. "The Fetish of Civilization: Sacrificial Blood and Monetary Debt." In *Colonial
Subjects: Essays on the Practical History of Anthropology*, ed. Peter Pels and Oscar
Salemink. Ann Arbor: University of Michigan Press, 1999.

————. "The Problem of the Fetish." Parts 1, 2, and 3. *Res* 9 (1985): 5–17; 13 (1987):
23–45; and 16 (1988): 105–23.

Pokagan, Simon. "Indian Superstitions and Legends." *The Forum* 35 (1898): 618–29.

Pollard, Edward E. *Black Diamonds Gathered in the Darkey Homes of the South*. New York:
Pudney and Russell, 1860.

Pomedi, Michael M. *Ethnophilosophical and Ethnolinguistic Perspectives on the Huron Indian
Soul*. Lewiston, N.Y.: E. Mellen Press, 1991.

Porter, Kenneth W. *The Black Seminoles: History of a Freedom-Seeking People*. Gainesville:
University Press of Florida, 1996.

Porterfield, Amanda. "American Indian Spirituality as a Countercultural Movement."
In *Religion in Native North America*, ed. Christopher Vecsey. Moscow: University of
Idaho Press, 1990.

Powell, Richard J. *The Blues Aesthetic: Black Culture and Modernism*. Washington, D.C.:
Washington Project for the Arts, 1989.

Powers, William K. "The Supernatural." In *Native American Religions: North America. Selections from "The Encyclopedia of Religion,"* ed. Lawrence E. Sullivan. New York: Macmillan, 1989.

Pratt, Scott L. "Wounded Knee and the Prospect of Pluralism." *Journal of Speculative
Philosophy* 19, 2 (2005): 150–66.

Puckett, Newbell Niles. *Folk Beliefs of the Southern Negro*. Chapel Hill: University of North
Carolina Press, 1926.

Raboteau, Albert J. *Slave Religion: The "Invisible Institution" in the Antebellum South*. Oxford:
Oxford University Press, 1978.

Radano, Ronald M. "Denoting Difference: The Writing of the Slave Spirituals." *Critical Inquiry* 22 (1996): 506–44.

————. "Soul Texts and the Blackness of Folk." *Modernism/Modernity* 2, 1 (1995):
71–95.

Ragin, Hugh. *An Afternoon in Harlem*. Montreal: Justin Time, 1998.

Randolph, A. Philip. "The Human Hand Threat." In *Mother Wit from the Laughing Barrel: Readings in the Interpretation of Afro-American Folklore*, ed. Alan Dundes. Jackson: University Press of Mississippi, 1990.

Randolph, Paschal Beverley. *The Wonderful Story of Ravalette*. New York: Sinclair Tousey,
1863.

Rawick, George P., ed. *The American Slave: A Composite Autobiography*. Englewood Cliffs,
N.J.: Greenwood Press, 1972.

Reed, Ishmael. *Conjure: Selected Poems, 1963–1970*. Amherst: University of Massachusetts Press, 1972.

———. *Mumbo Jumbo*. London: Allison and Busby, 1988.

———. "Saar Dust: An interview with Betye Saar." In *Secrets, Dialogues, Revelations: The Art of Betye and Alison Saar: Essays by Lucy R. Lippard, Ishmael Reed and Judith Wilson*, ed. Elizabeth Shepherd. Los Angeles: Wight Art Gallery, University of California, 1990.

———. *Shrovetide in Old New Orleans*. New York: Doubleday, 1978.

Regier, Ami. "Material Points of Self and Other: Fetish Discourses and Leslie Marmon Silko's Evolving Conception of Cross-Cultural Narrative." In *Leslie Marmon Silko: A Collection of Critical Essays*, ed. K. Barnett and James L. Thorson. Albuquerque: University of New Mexico Press, 1999.

———. "Revolutionary Enunciatory Spaces: Ghost Dancing, Transatlantic Travel, and Modernist Arson." *Modern Fiction Studies* 51, 1 (2005): 134–57.

Repplier, Agnes. "On the Benefits of Superstition." *Atlantic Monthly* 58, 346 (1886): 176–86.

Rice, Julian. *Before the Great Spirit: The Many Faces of Sioux Spirituality*. Albuquerque: University of New Mexico, 1998.

Richards, Dona. "The Implications of African-American Spirituality." In *African Culture: The Rhythms of Unity*, ed. Molefi Kete Asante and Kariamu Welsh Asante. Trenton, N.J.: Africa World Press, 1990.

Richards, John W. "African-American Folklore in a Discourse of Folkness." *New York Folklore* 18 (1962): 73–89.

Richmond, Cora. *Ouina's Canoe and Christmas Offering, Filled with Flowers for the Darlings of the Earth, Given through her Medium, "Water Lily" (Mrs. Cora V. L. Richmond)*. Ottumwa, Iowa: D. M. and N. P. Foz, 1882.

Roach, Joseph. *Cities of the Dead: Circum-Atlantic Performance*. New York: Columbia University Press, 1996.

Root, Deborah. *Cannibal Culture: Art, Appropriation and the Commodification of Difference*. Boulder, Colo.: Westview Press, 1996.

Rubin, William. "Accumulation: Power and Display in African Sculpture." *Artforum* 13 (May 1975): 35–47.

Rucker, Walter C. *The River Flows On: Black Resistance, Culture, and Identity Formation in Early America*. Baton Rouge: Louisiana State University Press, 2006.

Russell, Chloe. *Complete Fortune Teller and Dream Book by Chloe Russell, a Woman of Colour of the State of Massachusetts, Commonly Termed the Old Witch or Black Interpreter*. Boston, 1821.

Rydell, Robert W. *All the World's a Fair: Visions of Empire at American International Expositions*. Chicago: University of Chicago Press, 1984.

Sagard, Gabriel. *The Long Journey to the Country of the Hurons*. 1632. Toronto: Champlain Society, 1939.

Salisbury, Neal. *Manitou and Providence: Indians, Europeans and the Making of New England, 1500–1643*. New York: Oxford University Press, 1982.

Saxon, Lyle, Edward Dreyer, and Robert Tallant, eds. *Gumbo Ya-Ya: A Collection of Louisiana Folktales*. Boston: Houghton Mifflin, 1945.

Schenck, Theresa M. "The Algonquian Totem and Totemism: A Distortion of the Linguistic Field." *Papers of the Algonquian Conference* 28 (1996): 341–53.

Schmidt, Francis. "Polytheisms: Degeneration or Progress?" *History and Anthropology* 3 (1987): 9–60.

Schrader, Robert Fay. *The Indian Arts and Crafts Board: An Aspect of New Deal Indian Policy*. Albuquerque: University of New Mexico Press, 1983.

Schrager, Cynthia. "Pauline Hopkins and William James: The New Psychology and the

Politics of Race." In *The Unruly Voice: Discovering Pauline Elizabeth Hopkins*, ed. John Cullen Gruesser. Urbana: University of Illinois Press, 1996.

Schroeder, Patricia R. "Rootwork: Arthur Flowers, Zora Neale Hurston, and the 'Literary Hoodoo' Tradition." *African American Review* 36, 2 (2002): 263–72.

Seager, Richard Hughes, ed. *The Dawn of Religious Pluralism: Voices from the World's Parliament of Religions, 1893*. LaSalle, Ill.: Open Court, 1993.

Seitz, William C. *The Art of Assemblage*. New York: Museum of Modern Art, 1961.

Shapiro, Warren. "Claude Levi-Strauss Meets Alexander Goldenweiser: Boasian Anthropology and the Study of Totemism." *American Anthropologist* 93 (1991): 599–610.

Silko, Leslie Marmon. *Almanac of the Dead*. New York: Penguin, 1992.

———. "Bingo Big." *Nation* 260 (June 12, 1995): 856–60.

———. *Gardens in the Dunes*. New York: Simon and Schuster, 1999.

———. *Yellow Woman and a Beauty of the Spirit: Essays on Native American Life Today*. New York: Simon and Schuster, 1996.

Simpkins, Cuthbert O. *Coltrane: A Biography*. Perth Amboy, N.J.: Herndon House, 1975.

Smith, Theophus H. *Conjuring Culture: Biblical Formations of Black America*. New York: Oxford University Press, 1994.

Sobel, Mechal. *The World They Made Together: Black and White Values in Eighteeenth-Century Virginia*. Princeton, N.J.: Princeton University Press, 1987.

Sollors, Werner. "Benjamin Franklin's Celestial Telegraph, or Indian Blessings to Gaslit American Drawing Rooms." *American Quarterly* 35, 5 (1983): 459–80.

Steckley, John. "Brebeuf's Presentation of Catholicism in the Huron Language: A Descriptive Overview." *University of Ottawa Quarterly* 48, 1–2 (1978): 93–115.

Steiger, Brad. *Totems: The Transformative Power of Your Personal Animal Totem*. New York: Harper Collins, 1997.

Steinmetz, Paul B. "The New Missiology and Black Elk's Individuation." In *The Black Elk Reader*, ed. Clyde Holler. Syracuse, N.Y.: Syracuse University Press, 2000.

Stocking, George W., Jr. "Animism in Theory and Practice: E. B. Tylor's Unpublished 'Notes on "Spiritualism"'" *Man* 6 (1971): 88–104.

———. *Victorian Anthropology*. New York: Free Press, 1987.

Stowe, David W., Jr. *How Sweet the Sound: Music in the Spiritual Lives of Americans*. Cambridge, Mass.: Harvard University Press, 2004.

Sullivan, Moira. "Maya Deren's Ethnographic Representation of Ritual and Myth in Haiti." In *Maya Deren and the American Avant-Garde*, ed. Bill Nichols. Berkeley and Los Angeles: University of California Press, 2001.

Sundquist, Eric J. *The Hammers of Creation: Folk Culture in Modern African-American Fiction*. Athens: University of Georgia Press, 1992.

———. *To Wake the Nations: Race in the Making of American Literature*. Cambridge, Mass.: Harvard University Press, 1993.

Surin, Kenneth. "Transform the World, Change Life: Michael Taussig's Poetics of Destruction and Revelation." *South Atlantic Quarterly* 92, 2 (1993): 261–94.

Tallant, Robert. *Voodoo in New Orleans*. Gretna, La.: Pelican, 1998.

Taussig, Michael T. *The Devil and Commodity Fetishism in South America*. Chapel Hill: University of North Carolina Press, 1980.

———. *The Nervous System*. New York: Routledge, 1992

———. *Shamanism, Colonialism, and the White Man: A Study in Terror and Healing*. Chicago: University of Chicago Press, 1987.

Taylor, Bron. "Earthen Spirituality, or Cultural Genocide? Radical Environmentalism's Appropriation of Native American Spirituality." *Religion* 27 (1997): 183–215.

Tedlock, Barbara, ed. *Dreaming: Anthropological and Psychological Interpretations*. Cambridge: Cambridge University Press, 1987.

Terry, Richard R. *Voodooism in Music and Other Essays.* London: Burns Oates and Washbourne, 1934.

Thompson, Robert Farris. *Flash of the Spirit: African and Afro-American Art and Philosophy.* New York: Random House, 1984.

————. *The Four Moments of the Sun: Kongo Art in Two Worlds.* Washington, D.C.: National Gallery of Art, 1981.

Thwaites, Reuben Gold, ed. and trans. *The Jesuit Relations and Allied Documents: Travels and Explorations of the Jesuit Missionaries in New France, 1610–1791.* Cleveland: Burrows Brothers, 1896–1901.

Tooker, Elisabeth. *An Ethnography of the Huron Indians, 1615–1649.* Syracuse, N.J.: Syracuse University Press, 1991.

Toomer, Jean. *Cane.* 1923. New York: Norton, 1988.

Torgovnick, Mariana. *Gone Primitive: Savage Intellects, Modern Lives.* Chicago: Chicago University Press, 1990.

Trefzer, Annette. "Possessing the Self: Caribbean Identities in Zora Neale Hurston's *Tell My Horse*." *African American Review* 34, 2 (2000): 292–312.

Troyer, Carlos. *Indian Music Lecture: The Zuni Indians and Their Music.* Philadelphia: Theo. Presser, 1913.

Tucker, Lindsey. "Recovering the Conjure Woman: Texts and Contexts in Gloria Naylor's *Mama Day*." *African American Review* 28, 2 (1994): 173–88.

Tucker, Vera Smith. "Purloined Identity: The Racial Identity of Tituba of Salem Village." *Journal of Black Studies* 30, 4 (2000): 624–34.

Tylor, Edward Burnet. *Primitive Culture: Researches into the Development of Mythology, Philosophy, Religion, Language, Art and Custom.* 2 vols. 1871. New York: Henry Holt, 1889.

Van Beek, Walter E. A. "Dogon Re-Studied: A Field Evaluation of the Work of Marcel Griaule." *Current Anthropology* 32, 2 (1991): 139–67.

Vecsey, Christopher. "American Indian Environmental Religions." In *American Indian Environments: Ecological Issues in Native American History*, ed.Christopher Vecsey and Robert W. Venables. Syracuse, N.Y.: Syracuse University Press, 1980.

Vest, Jay Hansford C. "From Bobtail to Brer Rabbit." *American Indian Quarterly* 24, 1 (2000): 19–43.

Vizenor, Gerald. *Fugitive Poses: Native American Indian Scenes of Absence and Presence.* Lincoln: University of Nebraska Press, 1998.

Wald, Elijah. *Escaping the Delta: Robert Johnson and the Invention of the Blues.* New York: Harper Collins, 2004.

Walker, Benjamin B. *The Indian Practice of Medicine, Being a Treatise Divested of Professional Terms, on the Nature, Causes, Symptoms and Treatment.* Louisville, Ky.: John C. Noble, 1847.

Wardlaw, Alvia J. and Robert V. Rozelle, eds. *Black Art—Ancestral Legacy: The African Impulse in African-American Art.* Dallas: Dallas Museum of Art, 1989.

Warren, William Whipple. *History of the Ojibwa Nation.* Minneapolis: Ross and Haines, 1957.

Weeden, Howard. *Bandanna Ballads.* New York: Doubleday & McClure, 1899.

Werner, Craig Hansen. *Playing the Changes: From Afro-Modernism to the Jazz Impulse.* Urbana: University of Illinois Press, 1994.

Weyler, Karen. "Race, Redemption, and Captivity in the Narratives of Briton Hammon and John Marrant." In *Genius in Bondage: Literature of the Early Black Atlantic*, ed. Vincent Carretta and Philip Gould. Lexington: University Press of Kentucky, 2001.

White, Bruce M. "Encounters with Spirits: Ojibwa and Dakota Theories about the French and Their Merchandise." *Ethnohistory* 41, 3 (1995): 369–405.

White, Nathan Francis. *Voices from Spirit-land.* New York: Partridge and Brittan, 1854.

White, William S. *The African Preacher: An Authentic Narrative.* Philadelphia: Presbyterian Board of Publications, 1843.

Whitten, Norman E., Jr. "Contemporary Patterns of Malign Occultism among Negroes in North Carolina." *Journal of American Folklore* 75 (1962): 311–25.

Whittle, Kay. *Native American Fetish Carvings of the Southwest.* Altglen, Pa.: Schiffer, 1998.

Williams, Roger. *A Key into the Language of America, or an Help to the Language of the Natives in That Part of America called New England.* Ed. John J. Teunissen and Evelyn J. Hinz. 1643. Detroit, Mich.: Wayne State University Press, 1973.

Willis, William S. "Franz Boas and the Study of Black Folklore." In *The New Ethnicity: Perspectives from Ethnology,* ed. John Bennett. St. Paul, Minn.: West Publishing, 1975.

Wilson, Charles Reagan. "Shamans and Charlatans: The Popularization of Native American Religion in Magazines, 1865–1900." *The Indian Historian* 12, 3 (1979): 6–13.

Wilson, Olly. "The Heterogeneous Sound Ideal in African-American Music." In *Signifyin(g), Sanctifyin', and Slam Dunking: A Reader in African American Expressive Culture,* ed. Gena Dagel Caponi. Amherst: University of Massachusetts Press, 1999.

Wolfe, Patrick. *Settler Colonialism and the Transformation of Anthropology: The Politics and Poetics of an Ethnographic Event.* London: Cassell, 1999.

Writers Program. *Drums and Shadows: Survival Studies among the Georgia Coastal Negroes.* Savannah Unit, Georgia Writers' Project. 1940. Repr., Westport, Conn.: Greenwood Press, 1973.

Ziolkowski, Eric J. *A Museum of Faiths: Histories and Legacies of the 1893 World's Parliament of Religions.* Atlanta: Scholars Press, 1993.

Zitkala Ša. *American Indian Stories.* 1921. Lincoln: University of Nebraska Press, 1985.

———. *Dreams and Thunder: Stories, Poems, and The Sun Dance Opera.* Ed. P. Jane Hafen. Lincoln: University of Nebraska Press, 2001.

———. "The School Days of an Indian Girl." *Atlantic Monthly* 85 (1900): 185–94

———. "Why I Am Not a Pagan." *Atlantic Monthly* 90 (1902): 801–3.

Zumwalt, Rosemary Levy. *American Folklore Scholarship: A Dialogue of Dissent.* Bloomington: Indiana University Press, 1988.

Index

Acosta, Joseph de, 13–14, 155 n.61
African Americans, 5, 31–38, 43, 77, 80–85,
    158 n.95; artists, 7–8, 80–82 (*see also* Saar,
    Betye; Stout, Renée); beliefs of, 1–4 (*see also*
    conjure; fetishism; hoodoo; magic;
    voodoo); and folklore, 33, 43, 47–50, 84,
    144–45; folklore collections, 50–59;
    identity, 85–86; and superstition, 4, 48–50,
    57, 63–64, 163 n.36; writers, 7–8, 59–70,
    80
African American Spiritual churches, 90
Africans, 11–12, 20–21, 173 n.52; art of, 80,
    104–10; cultural survivals of, 68, 82–88,
    116, 174 n.57; Dogon people, 124–25;
    fetishes of, 106, 109; masks of, 73–74, 103
Alexie, Sherman, *Reservation Blues*, 127–29,
    132, 141
American Folklore Society, 144–45
American Indian peoples, 74–80; Algonquian,
    23–24, 151 n.23, 154 n.53; Cherokee, 165
    n.62; of Georgia, 164 n.58; Haida, 154
    n.53; Hopi, 157 n.87; Huron, 25–26;
    Iroquois, 24, 31, 161 n.13; Lakota (Sioux),
    31, 158 n.92; Lumbee, 87; Mardi Gras, 90;
    Mi'kmaq, 25–27, 156 n.74; Mohawk, 28;
    Montagnais, 25–26; Narragansett, 24–25;
    of the Northwest coast, 23, 170 n.12;
    Ojibwa (Chippewa), 21–23, 29, 156 n.83;
    Potawatomi, 44; of the Southwest, 170
    n.12; Zuni, 29–30, 130, 157 n.87. *See also*
    British Columbia Indians
American Indians: artists, 7–8, 78–80, 130;
    beliefs of, 1–4, 44–45, 134–35; and
    Christianity, 5, 150 n.13; folklore of,
    47–48; and identity, 128–29, 132; and

monotheism, 157 n.92; and museum
    collections, 74–76; poetry of, 78; preachers,
    5; rhythm of, 77; songs of, 77–78, 129; and
    spirituality, 41–42, 129, 130–35, 154 n.56,
    158 n.92; spokespeople, 86; terminology
    used, 149 n.1; writers, 7–8, 44–47, 78–80,
    87. *See also* animism; fetishism; manitou;
    totemism
Anderson, Mother Leafy, 90
Andrews, William, 68–69
animism, 17–19, 23, 30, 154 n.56
anthropology, 7, 17–19, 31, 72, 83–84, 86–89,
    182 n.85; "salvage ethnography," 170 n.12
Apess, William, 5
appropriations, 103, 130–35, 184 n.13; New
    Age, 129, 131; in Silko, 139–40
art: African American, 7–8, 80–82;
    assemblage, 33–34, 72, 102, 104–10; and
    ceremony, 102, 103, 109–10; and conjure,
    102, 107–8, 110–12; and magic, 73–74,
    106–10, 114; and modernism, 71–76; and
    religion, 107–9
assimilation policies, 43–44
Atkins, John, 12
Austin, Mary, *The American Rhythm*, 76–77
Australian aborigines, 22

Baker, Houston, 102, 112–14, 115; *Afro-
    American Poetics: Revisions of Harlem and the
    Black Aesthetic*, 114; criticism of, 179 n.47;
    Workings of the Spirit, 113
Baker, Josephine, 74
Baker, Lee, 84
Baraga, Bishop, *Dictionary of the Otchipwe
    Language*, 29

Baraka, Amiri, 115–16
Baudin, Rev. P., *Fetichism and Fetich Worshippers*, 20–21
Beard, James Melville, *K.K.K. Sketches, Humorous and Didactic*, 49–50
Bell, Michael Edward, 105, 107–8; "Pattern, Structure, and Logic in Afro-American Hoodoo Performance," 33–34
Benjamin, Walter, 71–72
Bennett, Hal Zina, *Zuni Fetishes: Using American Objects for Meditation, Reflection and Insight*, 130–31
Bennett, Lerone, 35
Berns, Marla, 111
Berry, Jason, 90
Black Arts movement, 116
Black Elk, 31
Black Hawk, 90
Black, Mary, 29
Black World Repertory, *Totem Voices*, 131–32
blues music, 35, 116, 127–29, 168 n.101, 180 n.61; and conjure, 111–12. *See also* Alexie, Sherman
Blues Revival, 127
Boas, Franz, 31, 83–84, 86–87, 88
body, the, 35–36, 66, 69
Bosman, William, 11–12
Brandon, William, 78, 141
Brebeuf, Jean de, 26
Brinton, Daniel, *Religions of Primitive Peoples*, 23
British Columbia Indians, 154 n.53
Brodhead, Richard, 64, 65, 67
Brown, David, 34, 35
buffalo, return of, 78, 141
Burnham, Clara Louise, *Sweet Clover: A Romance of the White City*, 43
Butler, Jon, 3

capitalism, 137–38, 152 n.38, 182 n.83
Carby, Hazel, 86
Carpenter, Jane, 106
Carr, Brian, 92–93
Castronovo, Russ, 41
ceremony, and art, 102, 103, 109–10
Charleston, Steve, 133
Chase-Riboud, Barbara, 105
Chatelain, Heli, 21
Chesnutt, Charles, 64–70; *The Colonel's Dream*, 69; *The Conjure Woman*, 64–69; —, "The Goophered Grapevine," 68; —, "The Marked Tree," 67–68; —, "Po' Sandy," 65;

"Dave's Neckliss," 67, 68; "Dumb Witness," 69; "Trobe's Tribulations" in *Southern Workman*, 68
Chireau, Yvonne, 35
Christy, David, *A Lecture on African Civilization, Including a Brief Outline of the Social and Moral Condition of Africa and the Relation of American Slaves to African Civilization*, 32
cinema, 71–72
Clifford, James, 72, 73, 170 n.11
collections: of African American materials, 74; of American Indian materials, 74–76; of conjure objects, 87, 170 n.12; of folklore, 50–59; museum, 72–76, 170 n.12, 172 n.38. *See also* Hurston, Zora Neale
Coltrane, John, 123, 183 n.97
commodification, of spirituality, 102, 130–35, 184 n.13
Comte, August, 15
conjure, 9, 33–36, 52–53, 56–59, 63–70, 118, 159 n.107, 160 n.108; and art, 102, 107–8, 110–12; bag contents, 166 n.63; and Christianity, 168 n.100; collecting of objects, 87, 170 n.12; exoticism of, 172 n.40; and music, 111–12, 116–17; and slave resistance, 36–38; and women, 179 n.47. *See also* Hurston, Zora Neale
Cooper, Tova, 92–93
Cordova, Viola, 134
Cornell, Joseph, 105
Covarrubias, Miguel, photographs in Hurston's *Mules and Men*, 97
Cruz, Jon, 47–48, 84
Cullen, Countee, "Heritage," 80
cultural survivals, 68, 82–88, 101, 116, 174 n.57
Cunard, Nancy, *Negro*, 89
Cushing, Frank Hamilton, 29–30, 104, 157 n.84; *Zuni Fetiches*, 30

Darwin, Charles, 19
Davis, Wade, 97
Dayan, Joan, 97–98
de Brosses, Charles, *Du Culte des dieux fétiches, ou parallèle de l'ancienne religion de l'Égypte avec la religion actualle de Nigritie*, 10, 11–16, 17, 23
Deloria, Ella Cara, 86, 87
Deloria, Philip, 131
Deloria, Vine, 131
Dilworth, Leah, 75, 77
disease, 40–41

Donaldson, Laura, 26, 150 n.13, 184 n.13
"double vision," 34, 95
Douglas, Aaron, 80
Douglass, Frederick, autobiography, 36–37
Driskell, David, 105
DuBois, W. E. B., 84; *The Quest of the Silver Fleece*, 60; *The Souls of Black Folk*, 59–62; —, "The Coming of John," 60–62; —, "Of the Faith of the Fathers," 59–60
Dunham, Katherine, 93–94
Durham, Jimmie, 103; "American Indian Culture: Traditionalism and Spiritualism in a Revolutionary Struggle," 134; and the FBI, 185 n.22; and Marxism, 133–34
Durkheim, Emile, *The Elementary Forms of Religious Life*, 22
Dutton, Wendy, 94

Eastman, Charles: and pluralism, 172 n.36; "Sioux Mythology," 44; *The Soul of the Indian*, 79
Eisenstein, Sergei, 71
Eliot, T. S., 71
Ellington, Duke, "Black, Brown and Beige," 83
Elliott, Michael, 143–44
Ellis, Juniper, 52
Ellison, Ralph, 126; *Invisible Man*, 67
Epes Brown, Joseph, 31
Epstein, Jean, 72
"Eternal Life Spiritualist Church," 90
"ethnographic surrealism," 170 n.11
ethnography, 72, 86–89, 182 n.85; "salvage," 170 n.12
Evans, Brad, 45

Fabian, Johannes, 74
Fauset, Arthur Huff: "American Negro Folk Literature," 173 n.53; *Black Gods of the Metropolis*, 85; in *The New Negro*, 85
Feest, Christian, 72
fetishes, 73–74, 118, 130; African, 106, 109; Zuni, 29–30, 130
fetishism, 4, 6–7, 9–23, 30, 138; commodity, 19, 130, 136–38; pure, 13, 15; in Silko, 136–38
Fitz, Brewster, 147
Fletcher, Alice, 43–44, 78; "The Indian Messiah," 144–45
Flowers, Arthur, *Another Good Loving Blues*, 112
folklore, 43–47; African American, 47–50, 84;

American Indian, 47–48; collections of, 50–59
folklore studies, 47–59, 162 n.26
folk practices, 33
Foster, Hal, 103
Frazer, James G., 6, 39, 45, 152 n.33
Freud, Sigmund, 19–20; *Totem and Taboo*, 22

Gates, Henry Louis, 115, 178 n.12
Genovese, Eugene, 36
Ghost Dance religion, 78–79, 142–48, 186 n.50; and Mooney, 143–45; in Silko, 138–39, 141–45
Gillman, Susan, 41
glossolalia (speaking in tongues), 147
Gnosticism, 146–47, 187 n.66
Gordon, Avery, 55
Gorn, Elliott, 50
gospel music, 116, 180 n.61. *See also* spirituals
Gothic, the, 55–56
Graham, Martha, 77
Graham, Shirley: *The Hairy Ape*, 83; *In Dahomey*, 81; *The Star of Ethiopia*, 81; *Tom Tom*, 81–83
Green, Al, 122
Griaule, Marcel, 125
Gundaker, Grey, 34

Haiti, 93–96
Halbertal, Moshe, 12–13
Harding, Rachel, 36
Harlem Renaissance, 80–83, 88, 112, 116–18
Harper, Michael, 125
Harris, Joel Chandler, 50–56, 165 n.62, 173 n.53; *The Bishop and the Boogerman*, 53–55; "Free Joe and the Rest of the World," 55; *Nights with Uncle Remus: Myths and Legends of the Old Plantation*, 51–53; *Told by Uncle Remus*, 53; *Uncle Remus, His Songs and Sayings: The Folklore of the Old Plantation*, 51
Harris, Michael D., 109, 110
Harris, Wilson, 119–20
Hartley, Marsden, 75–77; "The Festival of the Corn," 75; in *Poetry*, 76
Hartman, Saadiya, 119–20
haunting, 55–56, 182 n.85
Hawkins, Coleman, 114–15
Hegel, Georg Wilhelm Friedrich, 17
Helms, Mary, 72–73
Hemenway, Robert, 92, 99
Hennepin, Louis, 24, 28–29

Herskovits, Melville, 84–85, 86, 87; in *The New Negro*, 85
Hewitt, J. N. B., 31
Hewitt, M. J., 107
Higginson, Thomas Wentworth, song collecting, 52
Holley, Marietta, *Samantha at the World's Fair*, 43, 161 n.13
hoodoo, 9, 33–36, 89–92, 112, 116, 178 n.25
Hopkins, Pauline: *Contending Forces*, 63; *Of One Blood*, 62–63
Hosmer, H. L., *The Octoroon*, 32
Howe, Julia, 43
Hume, David, *Natural History of Religion*, 12
Hurston, Zora Neale, 7, 85–101, 107, 173 n.57; and anthropology, 86–89; book illustrations, 96–97; "The Eatonville Anthology" in *The Messenger*, 89; and Haiti, 93–96, 175 n.94; "High John de Conquer," 100–101; initiation into hoodoo, 91–92, 96–97; *Jonah's Gourd Vine*, 101; in the *Journal of American Folklore*, 89, 90, 92; *Moses, Man of the Mountain*, 98; *Mules and Men*, 86–93, 113; in *Negro*, 89, 90–91; *Tell My Horse*, 89, 93–98, 99, 101, 114; *Voodoo Gods: An Inquiry into Native Myths and Magic in Jamaica and Haiti* (English edition of *Tell My Horse*), 94
Hyatt, Harry Middleton, 33

identity: African American, 85–86; American Indian, 128–29, 132; racial, 175 n.94
idolatry, 10, 12–14, 18, 29, 164 n.58; Christian discourse on, 13–14
Ingraham, Joseph Holt, *Lafitte, the Pirate of the Gulf*, 4, 61
International Folklore Congress, 44, 58
"Is Everybody Superstitious?" 47

Jackson, Mahalia, 116
jazz, 77, 83, 117–18, 123, 181 n.71, 183 nn. 97, 104
Johnson, James Weldon, 62, 117; *Autobiography of an Ex-Colored Man*, 46
Johnson, Robert, 111, 127–29
Jones, Charles Colcock, *Negro Myths from the Georgia Coast*, 56–57
Jones, Lois Mailou, *Les Fétiches*, 80
Journal of American Folklore, 45, 84, 89; and William Wells Newell, 48
Journal of Negro History, 3, 93

Kasanoff, Jennie, 63
Kerkering, John, 40–41
Kirk, Rahsaan Roland, 123
Knox, William, 3–4
Krips, Henry, 13
Ku Klux Klan, 49–50

Lafitau, Father Joseph-François, *Mœurs des sauvages ameriquains, comparés aux mœures des premiers temps*, 16–17, 27–28
Laveau, Marie, 110–11, 174 n.73
Le Clercq, Chrétien, 16; *New Relation of Gaspesia*, 26–28
LeJeune, Paul, 25
Leland, Charles, 58, 59
Levy-Bruhl, Lucien, 71
Lewis, Norman, *American Totem*, 132
Lindsay, Vachel, 116
Lippard, Lucy, 110
Locke, Alain, *The New Negro*, 81, 85, 118
Long, John, 21–22
Lorca, Federico García, 125–26
loss, 119–21
Lott, Eric, 48
Lummis, Charles, 30
Luna, James: *The Artifact Piece*, 109; *The End of the Frail*, 109; and ritual, 109–10
lynchings, 122, 168 nn. 101, 106

MacGaffey, Wyatt, 104, 106; in *Astonishment and Power*, 108
Mackey, Nathaniel, 102, 118–26, 135, 177 n.121; *Bedouin Hornbook*, 121; *Eroding Witness*, 125; *From a Broken Bottle Traces of Perfume Still Emanate*, 118–20; "Grisgris Dancer," 120; "Ohnedaruth's Day Begun," 123; "Song of the Andoumboulou," 123–24
magic, 4, 18–19, 39–40, 64, 88, 160 n.108; and art, 73–74, 106–10, 114; and music, 114–26; and religion, 1, 6–8, 39–40, 89–91, 99–100, 102; sympathetic, 40, 68, 71, 89, 152 n.33
manitou, 9, 16–17, 22, 23–26, 28–29
Manuel, Frank, 12
Margalit, Avishai, 12–13
Marx, Karl, 19, 118, 137–38
Marxism, 133–34, 182 n.83
materiality, 20–21, 35–36, 159 n.107; and spirituality, 1, 9–11, 13, 133–34, 182 n.83
McGaa, Ed Eagle Man, *Mother Earth*

Spirituality: Native American Paths to Healing Ourselves and Our World, 132

McLennan, J. F., 22

mesmerism, 40, 41

Mikell, Gwendolyn, 94

Mills, Florence, 74

minstrel shows, 48–49

miscegenation, 54, 63, 69

mixed races, 2–3, 57–58, 64, 174 n.57

Modernism, 7, 80; and art, 71–76; and primitivism, 71–78, 103

Monroe, Harriet, *Poetry*, 76

Mooney, James, 78, 79, 143–45, 165 n.62; as the conjurer, 187 n.55

Moore, David, 141

museum collections, 72–76, 170 n.12

Museum of Modern Art (MOMA), *"Primitivism" in 20th Century Art: Affinity of the Tribal and the Modern*, 103

music, 81, 114, 121, 180 n.61, 181 n.73; African American, 80–83; blues music, 35, 116, 128–29, 168 n.101, 180 n.61 (*see also* Alexie, Sherman); and conjure, 116–17; and dance, 77, 117; gospel, 116, 180 n.61; jazz, 77, 83, 117–18, 123, 181 n.71, 183 nn. 97, 104; and magic, 114–26; rhythm, 77, 177 n.121; and slavery, 119–21; songs, 52, 77, 78, 80, 129, 163 n.47; soul, 180 n.58; spirituals, 35–36, 60, 62–63, 83, 92, 100, 124

Nadell, Martha Jane, 97

Native American Church, 79

Neal, Larry, 116

Neihardt, John, 31

New Age, 7–8, 130–33, 147, 148; and American Indian spirituality, 154 n.56; appropriations by, 129, 131; and consumerism, 184 n.13; in Silko, 139–40

Newell, William Wells, 56–57; *Journal of American Folklore*, 48

New Negro, 80–83; writers, 84

occult, the, 40–41, 63, 64. *See also* spiritualism

O'Neill, Eugene: *Emperor Jones*, 83; *The Hairy Ape*, 83

orality, 143, 159 n.102

Owen, Mary Alicia: "Among the Voodoos," 175 n.81; lectures, 58; *Old Rabbit, the Voodoo and the Sorcerers*, 57–58

Page, Thomas Nelson, 65

Peabody, Charles, 61

Pels, Peter, 18, 40

periodicals, 45–48. See also *Journal of American Folklore*; *Journal of Negro History*

peyote, 79

"phantom limb," 119, 182 n.83

Phillpotts, Eden, "The Obi Man," 47

Picasso, Pablo: and African masks, 73–74, 103; *Les Desmoiselles d'Avignon*, 73, 103, 177 n.5

Piersen, William, 50

Pietz, William, 10–11, 13

Pitt Rivers Museum (Oxford), 169 n.6

Pointer, Jonathan, 5

Pokagan, Simon, 44–45; "Indian Superstitions and Legends," 44

Pollard, Edward E., *Black Diamonds Gathered in the Darkey Homes of the South*, 50–51

Pollock, Jackson, *Totem* 1 and 2, 132

possession by a spirit, 40–41, 94–98, 175 n.94

"primitive," the, 2, 6–7, 10

"primitive religions," 4, 9–10

primitivism, 7, 71–78, 103

Primitivism: High and Low, 103

"Primitivism" in 20th Century Art: Affinity of the Tribal and the Modern, 103

Prosser, Gabriel, 37–38

Raboteau, Albert, 84

race, 40–43, 114, 150 n.12; hierarchies of, 1, 6, 9–10, 42, 45, 62; mixing of, 2–3, 57–58, 64, 174 n.57

Radano, Ronald, 62, 115

Randolph, Paschal Beverley, *The Wonderful Story of Ravalette*, 42

Rasles, Sébastien, 23–26

Reed, Ishmael, 102, 107–8; as the conjurer, 181 n.65; *Mumbo Jumbo*, 116–18

Regier, Ami, 136–37, 142–43, 147

Reiss, Winold, 80

religions, 3, 11–17, 20–21; and art, 107–9; Christianity, 3, 5, 13–14, 26–28, 133, 150 n.13, 168 n.100; and folklore, 43; hierarchies of, 1, 9–10, 162 n.29; and magic, 1, 6–8, 39–40, 89–91, 99–100, 102; missionaries, 3, 4, 25–29, 32, 133; monotheism, 12, 17, 20, 155 n.61, 157 n.92; "primitive," 4, 9–10; and science, 6, 39–40; syncretism of, 142–47, 159 n.107

revitalization movements, 79, 184 n.13; Ghost

Dance religion, 78–79, 138–39, 141–48, 186 n.50
rhythm, 77, 177 n.121
Rogers, J. A., 118
Romanticism, 78, 134–35
rootwork, 33, 36–37, 46–47, 180 n.47
Rubin, William, 104
Rucker, Walter, 37–38
Russell, Chloe, *Complete Fortune Teller and Dream Book*, 69–70

Saar, Alison, *Conkerin' John*, 110
Saar, Betye, 102, 105–8, 110; *Africa*, 106; *Fragments of Fate*, 107; *Mojotech*, 107; *Nine Mojo Secrets*, 106–7; *Redbone and Black: Crossings of 2001*, 108; *Sanctified*, 107; *Spirit Catcher*, 105–6
Sacred Circles, 103
Sagard, Gabriel, 25–26
Schmidt Campbell, Mary, 106
science, and religion, 6, 39–40
Seabrook, Charles, *The Magic Island*, 93
Seals, Mother Catherine, 91
Seitz, William, *The Art of Assemblage*, 104
Senghor, Léopold, "The Totem," 131
Silko, Leslie, 128, 130, 135–48; *Almanac of the Dead*, 135–41, 148; *Ceremony*, 135; *Gardens in the Dunes*, 141–48
slavery, 35–36, 66, 168 n.101; and conjure, 36–38; experience of, 68; and music, 119–21; resistance to, 36–38; and voodoo, 98–100
Smith, Theophus, *Conjuring Culture*, 35
Sobel, Mechal, 33
Society for the Propagation of the Gospel, 3
Society of American Indians, 79
songs, 80, 163 n.47; American Indian, 77–78, 129; collecting of, 52
soul music, 180 n.58
soul, the, 114
spirit rapping, 41
spiritualism, 19, 20–21, 40; child-spirits, 152 n.37. *See also* occult, the
spirituality, 7–8, 9–11, 77–78, 101; American Indian, 41–42, 129, 130–35, 154 n.56, 158 n.92; commodification of, 102, 130–35, 184 n.13; and materiality, 1, 9–11, 13, 133–34, 182 n.83
spirituals, 35–36, 60, 83, 100, 124; commodification of, 92; essentialist use of, 62–63

"spirit-work," 112–13, 114
Spotted Elk, Molly, 74, 170 n.13
Steckley, John, 26
Stewart, John, 5
storytelling, 50–52, 113–14, 173 n.53
Stout, Renée, 102, 105, 108–9, 110–12; in *Astonishment and Power*, 108; *Dear Robert, I'll See You at the Crossroads*, 111; *Fetish 1*, 109; *Fetish 2*, 109; *Headstone for Marie Leveau*, 110
sublime, the, 134–35
Sundquist, Eric, 101
superstition, 6–7, 40–42, 44–50, 162 n.32; African American, 4, 48–50, 57, 63–64, 163 n.36; white, 44–45, 47, 50
syncretism: of native spirituality, 26, 129; in postcolonial terms, 186 n.48; of religions, 90–91, 142–47, 159 n.107

Taussig, Michael, 137–38; *Shamanism, Colonialism and the Wild Man*, 138
technology, 138
Tituba, 165 n.61
Toomer, Jean, *Cane*, 114
totemism, 9, 21–23, 131–32
totems, 9, 154 n.53; family, 153 n.48
Totems (self-help publication), 131
Turner, Nat, 37–38
Twain, Mark, *Huckleberry Finn*, 55
Tylor, Edward, *Primitive Culture*, 17–19

"vanishing American," 75, 161 n.13
vernacular signs, 34
Vesey, Denmark, 37–38
voodoo, 40–41, 81–83, 92–93, 95–101, 116–17, 179 n.39; founding god of, 166 n.70; and slavery, 98–100
"Voodooism in Tennessee," 57

Wagner, Richard, 61
Walker, Alice, 85
Warren, William Whipple, *History of the Ojibwa Nation*, 22
Weber, Max, 75
Weston, Jesse L., 71
white Americans, 1–3, 7; spirit rapping, 40, 44; spiritualism, 41, 44; and superstition, 44–45, 47, 50
White, Bruce, 25
White, Nathan Francis: "American Freedom," 41; *Voices from Spirit-land*, 41
Whorf, B. L., 134

Williams, Roger, 24–25

Willis, William S., 84

Wilson, Fred, 103–4; *The Other Museum*, 103–4; *Picasso/Whose Rules*, 103; *Spoils*, 104

Wilson, Olly, 124

World's Columbian Exposition 1893, 42–44

World's Parliament of Religions 1893, 43–44

Young, Al, "Body and Soul," 114–15

Zitkala Ša: *American Indian Stories*, "The Great Spirit," 46; on rootwork, 46–47; *The Sun Dance Opera*, 79; "Why I Am a Pagan," 46

zombies, 97–98

Acknowledgments

This book has its roots in ideas developed during a Research Fellowship at the Shelby Cullom Davis Center at Princeton University, 2000–2001. I'm grateful to Tony Grafton and Ken Mills for their hospitality and encouragement and for providing an unfailingly stimulating and supportive intellectual environment. Further research was carried out in 2003 at the Huntington Library, aided by a Mayers research fellowship and a British Academy research grant, and at the Library Company of Philadelphia and the Pennsylvania Historical Society, with the help of a Barra Foundation International Fellowship. I want to thank all the staff of these institutions, and Jim Green of the Library Company in particular, for their expert help and patience.

Essential though these forays into such fine research libraries are, the intellectual support and friendship of colleagues in the School of American and Canadian Studies at Nottingham (as well as regular sabbatical support from the school) have, as always, been indispensable. And without my wife Gill's presence, and warm tolerance of all the time spent on it, this book, like so much else in my life, would be neither possible nor meaningful.

Some sections of the book have been published in earlier versions as "Object Lessons: Fetishism and the Hierarchies of Race and Religion," in *Conversion: Old Worlds and New*, ed. Ken Mills and Anthony Grafton (University of Rochester Press, 2003), and "Representation and Cultural Sovereignty: Some Case Studies," in *Native American Representations: First Encounters, Distorted Images and Literary Appropriations*, ed. Gretchen Bataille (University of Nebraska Press, 2001).